The Better Business Bureau A TO Z Buying Guide

Published with the
Council of Better Business Bureaus, Inc.
Produced by The Benjamin Company, Inc.
Distributed by Henry Holt and Company, Inc.
Written by Virginia Schomp

AN OWL BOOK

HENRY HOLT AND COMPANY
New York

A **BENJAMIN** BOOK

Consumers cannot always find accurate information on which to base intelligent decisions in today's marketplace.

This comprehensive buying guide provides a wealth of knowledge on products and services from A to Z, including cost-cutting tips, shopping checklists, service and maintenance information, and sources of more information.

I believe consumers will find this guide truly valuable and I commend the Council of Better Business Bureaus for this helpful document and for continuing its dedication to consumer education.

Bonnie Guiton

Special Adviser to the President
for Consumer Affairs

Preface

Today, as consumers face new and complex challenges in the marketplace concerning food and nutrition labeling, health care issues, and environmentally safe products, it is more important than ever before that there be a single reference source offering the "basics" on how to buy goods and services.

The *Better Business Bureau A to Z Buying Guide*, based on extensive resources used by the Council and augmented by decades of BBB experience, provides consumers with the essential information needed to make wise, economical purchasing decisions on hundreds of products and services.

Refer to this handy guidebook before making purchases—large or small. A knowledgeable buying decision supported by thorough research and expert opinion leads to greater customer satisfaction, benefiting consumers and businesses alike.

JAMES H. MCILHENNY, President
Council of Better Business Bureaus, Inc.

Acknowledgments

The Council of Better Business Bureaus and the publishers wish to express sincere gratitude to all the agencies, businesses, and associations that provided information and assistance in the compiling of this guidebook:

ADT Company, Inc.
Air Conditioning Contractors of America
Air-Conditioning & Refrigeration Institute
American Association of Homes for the Aging
American Association of Retired Persons
American Automotive Leasing Association
American Cemetery Association
American Council for an Energy-Efficient Economy
American Council of Life Insurance
The American Dietetic Association
American Heart Association
American Homeowners Foundation
American Home Sewing Association, Inc.
American Institute of Certified Public Accountants
American Movers Conference
American Watchmakers Institute
Association of Home Appliance Manufacturers
Automotive Information Council
Bankcard Holders of America
The Better Sleep Council
Bicycle Institute of America
Board of Governors of the Federal Reserve System
The Brookings Institution
Car Care Council
The Carpet and Rug Institute
Cemetery Consumer Service Council
Consumer Credit Institute of The American Financial Services Association
Consumer Federation of America
Consumer Product Safety Commission
Consumer's Research, Inc.
Consumers Union
Contact Lens Society of America
Continental Association of Funeral and Memorial Societies, Inc.

Cookware Manufacturers Association
The Cosmetic, Toiletry and Fragrance Association
Direct Marketing Association, Inc.
Electronic Industries Association
Environmental Protection Agency
Federal Trade Commission
Floor Covering Installation Board
Food and Drug Administration
The Furniture Information Council of The American Furniture Manufacturers Association
The General Electric Company
Hanley-Wood, Inc.
Health Insurance Association of America
Insulation Contractors Association of America
Insurance Information Institute, Inc.
IntelliChoice, Inc.
Internal Revenue Service
International Board of Standards and Practices for Certified Financial Planners, Inc.
International Fabricare Institute
International Racquet and Sports Association
Jewelers of America, Inc.
The Lawn Institute
Massachusetts Audubon Society
Metropolitan Life Insurance Company
Montgomery County (MD) Office of Consumer Affairs
Morris County (NJ) Office of Consumer Affairs
National Association of Computer Dealers
National Association of Consumer Agency Administrators
National Association for the Education of Young Children
National Association of Enrolled Agents
National Association of Home Builders Remodelors Council™
National Association of Insurance Commissioners

The National Association of Personal Financial Advisors
National Association of Realtors®
National Association of the Remodeling Industry
National Burglar and Fire Alarm Association, Inc.
National Fire Protection Association
National Foundation for Consumer Credit, Inc.
National Institute on Aging-Gerontology Research Center
National Insurance Consumer Organization
National Moving and Storage Association
National Pest Control Association, Inc.
National Safety Council
New York State Public Health Department Bureau of Radiology Protection
North American Securities Administrators Association
Nursing Home Advisory & Research Council, Inc.
Office of the Special Adviser to the President for Consumer Affairs
The President's Council on Physical Fitness and Sports
Professional AudioVideo Retailers Association
Professional Lawn Care Association of America
Publications International, Ltd.
Sears, Roebuck, and Co.
Telecommunications Research & Action Center
Toy Manufacturers of America, Inc.
U.S. Bureau of Labor Statistics
U.S. Department of Agriculture
U.S. Department of Energy
U.S. Department of Health and Human Services
U.S. Department of Housing and Urban Development
U.S. Department of Justice
U.S. Office of Consumer Affairs
U.S. Postal Service

Introduction

ABOUT THE BBB

Shopping wisely for a product or service involves careful and prudent decision making. Whether you are thinking about buying a major household appliance or searching for professional services, you need to ask yourself a number of questions. What are my options? How can I get the best value for my dollars? What data must I have to make an informed buying decision? Where should I make my purchase? How much will it cost? Is the seller reputable? How can I be sure? What recourse do I have if I am dissatisfied?

In the 1990s, consumers seeking answers to these important concerns face additional challenges. Work, family, and other responsibilities seem to take up more and more of our free time, the variety of available products and services multiply, and technical terms and advertisements for goods and services appear less understandable to even the wisest shopper. That's why today, more than ever, consumers need the practical, "down-to-earth" buying information, advice, and assistance offered by the Better Business Bureau system.

Founded in 1912 by a group of business executives who banded together to fight dishonesty in advertising, the Better Business Bureau (BBB) network today consists of 200 local BBB offices throughout the United States and Canada, all working in cooperation with the Council of Better Business Bureaus (CBBB), headquartered in Arlington, Virginia. The Council, a nonprofit membership organization of ethical businesses, promotes truth and fairness in the marketplace and protects consumers through voluntary self-regulation and monitoring activities.

Services offered by Better Business Bureaus include:

- Providing you with information about a specific company, including a reliability report, before you do business with it.
- Helping you resolve a complaint against a business, including, in many areas, the final step of binding arbitration. (See "The Next Step," *If You Have A Complaint*, pages 363–65.)
- Providing information on charitable organizations before you make a contribution.
- Providing consumer education on products and services, including books, pamphlets, and other publications, to help you make informed buying decisions.

In addition, Better Business Bureaus:

- Monitor advertising and selling practices
- Alert consumers to bad business and advertising practices
- Disseminate consumer information through newspapers, radio, television, and printed literature
- Provide speakers for schools, civic groups, and business organizations

Of interest to most consumers, however, is the direct role the Better Business Bureau can play in their lives. In 1989, the BBB system responded to 10.5 million consumer inquiries and complaints, with the majority of consumer contacts—8 million—taking the form of prepurchase inquiries.

Bureaus maintain extensive files on business firms and organizations in their service areas. A call to your local BBB can help you obtain basic facts such as how long a firm has been in business, whether or not consumers have reported problems in dealing with the company, and the manner in which those problems were resolved. You should be aware, however, that Bureaus *do not* appraise or compare the quality of specific product models, *do not* provide legal advice or recommendations, and *do not* endorse any product, service, or company.

The Council of Better Business Bureaus, through its operating divisions, also conducts a variety of public interest programs. Supported through the membership of private business, CBBB is not a government agency. However, it does maintain a liaison with various state and federal departments and regulatory agencies, promoting an understanding of voluntary self-regulation while offering an efficient and speedy alternative for solving marketplace problems without the need for complicated, expensive, time-consuming legal procedures.

Council divisions and programs include the following:

The **National Advertising Division** (NAD) and the **National Advertising Review Board** (NARB) work to ensure truth and accuracy in national advertising, through a process of complaint investigation and resolution. Since 1971, NAD has resolved more than 2,800 complaints against national advertisers.

The **Children's Advertising Review Unit (CARU),** a department of NAD, establishes self-regulatory guidelines that promote truth, accuracy, and sensitivity in advertising directed to children under the age of 12.

The **Law and Standards Division** works in cooperation with trade associations, regulatory agencies, and industry representatives in developing voluntary standards for the advertising and selling of goods and services. The division also investigates and reports on industry trade practices.

The **Alternative Dispute Resolution Division (ADR)** promotes the use of third-party mediation and arbitration for settling disputes between consumers and businesses. In 1989, BBB CARE$_{sm}$, a unique ADR program, was established to expand the scope of dispute resolution services available to the business community. That same year, the ten-year-old **BBB AUTO LINE** program, the nation's largest program for resolving disputes between consumers and manufacturers, served domestic and foreign automotive manufacturers in more than 116,383 consumer satisfaction cases.

The **Philanthropic Advisory Service (PAS)** develops standards for charitable solicitations and promotes their use by soliciting organizations. Each year, PAS collects and evaluates information on hundreds of national charities and produces reports and other donor information materials for businesses and the interested public.

The **Public Affairs Division** reaches millions of consumers annually through its public service announcements and consumer-oriented programs broadcast by major radio networks and stations nationwide. The division also publishes monthly "Tips For Consumers" columns, which are carried by leading newspapers and magazines throughout the United States, and disseminates news releases warning consumers and businesses of questionable practices and fraudulent schemes.

The **Publications Division** distributes to the public more than two million *Tips On* . . . consumer information and business advisory booklets each year, covering a wide variety of products and services. The division also publishes authoritative reference information for advertising practitioners and professionals as well as books advising consumers and businesses on how to protect their money and operations from schemes, scams, and frauds.

The programs and services of the Better Business Bureau system and the Council are intended to guide you toward informed buying decisions by providing you with the know-how for making wise choices. That is the message of the Better Business Bureaus and of this book as well. Based on numerous resources, including leading trade association experts and 78 years of BBB experience, *The Better Business Bureau A to Z Buying Guide* is designed to give you the basic information you need to make prudent purchasing decisions.

Whether you are shopping for a humidifier or a house, looking for a tax preparer or a lawyer, having your car repaired or home insulation installed, or planning any other purchase, major or minor, take advantage of the services offered by the Better Business Bureau system. Remember, investigating before you invest makes it less likely that you will spend your well-earned dollars unwisely and more likely that you will be a successful and satisfied consumer.

Note: The price ranges quoted in this book are based on studies of currently advertised retail prices; actual market prices will vary according to dealer, model, market conditions, and geographical region.

Air Cleaners

In any home, there are many potential sources of indoor air pollution. Smoking; cleaning products and pesticides; unvented or malfunctioning stoves, furnaces, and space heaters; building materials; furnishings; outside air pollution; and a number of other sources may contribute to the problem. The health consequences of indoor air pollution range from immediate symptoms such as eye, nose, and throat irritation to more serious effects which may show up many years later, including emphysema and other respiratory diseases, heart disease, and cancer.

Do air cleaners offer an effective solution to the problem of indoor air pollution? According to the U.S. Environmental Protection Agency (EPA) and the U.S. Consumer Product Safety Commission (CPSC), the answer depends on the type and strength of the pollutant source and the type and model of air cleaner.

HOW AIR CLEANERS WORK

There are many styles and sizes of air cleaners (also known as air purifiers) on the market, ranging from relatively inexpensive tabletop models to sophisticated and expensive whole-house systems.

A **whole-house system** is connected to the central forced-air heating system in your home. As air is drawn through the heating system, it passes through a filter that traps particles of dust and dirt. There are three types of air filters:

- **Standard filters**, the least efficient and least expensive variety, are designed to catch only the larger and more visible particles. According to the Air-Conditioning & Refrigeration Institute, a manufacturers' trade association, their efficiency is about 3 to 5 percent.

- **Media filters** are more effective than standard filters but also more expensive. This type of filter is about 25 to 35 percent effective at removing very small particles such as pollen, dust, cooking grease, and some tobacco and cooking smoke.

- **Electronic air cleaners**, the most efficient and costly of all air filters, use an electrical charge to attract and retain microscopic pollutant particles. They can remove up to 95 percent of the dirt, dust, and smoke that circulate through the air in a home.

A whole-house air cleaning system usually must be installed by a heating and air-conditioning contractor. Homeowner maintenance involves checking, cleaning, and/or replacing filters according to the schedule recommended by the manufacturer and contractor.

Tabletop models, or **room air cleaners**, are generally much less efficient than whole-house systems. They work in one of three ways:

- **Filter-only models** consist of a flat or pleated filter and a fan that draws air through the filter. The type of filter varies. *HEPA (high-efficiency particulate-arresting) filters*, which are made of densely packed glass fibers, and *electret filters*, which use an electrical charge to attract and trap particles, are among the most effective.

- **Negative-ion generators** propel electrons into the air, where they give air molecules a negative charge; the charged molecules attract particles of smoke and dust, which then settle out of the air. Most units have a fan and a filter to hold the particles, which otherwise would settle on walls, drapes, and tabletops.

- **Electrostatic precipitators** electrically charge airborne particles as air is drawn into the unit, then attract and trap them on magnetic plates.

AN EFFECTIVE SOLUTION?

According to the EPA and CPSC, some air cleaners are highly effective at removing particles from the air, while others, including most tabletop models, are much less efficient. No type of air cleaner has been proven effective at reducing gaseous pollutants, such as radon, carbon monoxide, and formaldehyde gas.

If your goal is simply to remove airborne dust and tobacco smoke, you may find an air cleaner helpful. The more effective models do a good job of removing dust, pollen, and smoke; the smell associated with smoke is more difficult to remove, however, since odors are basically gases rather than particles.

How well a particular model of air cleaner works depends on how efficiently it collects pollutants from indoor air and how much air it draws through the cleaning or filtering element. The efficiency of a whole-house system is expressed in terms of its percentage efficiency rate; see page 4 for general ratings. The performance of a room air cleaner is generally rated in terms of its **CADR**, or Clean Air Delivery Rate.

The CADR standard was developed in 1985 by the Association of Home Appliance Manufacturers (AHAM) to allow for an accurate appraisal of an air cleaner's effectiveness and for comparisons among different models. To apply the standard, AHAM measures each model's effectiveness in removing smoke, dust, and pollen, and assigns CADRs to indicate the number of cubic feet of air cleaned per minute of each type of particle. The higher the CADR, the less time it takes to cleanse the air. The chart on page 6* shows the time it takes at five representative CADR

*Source: Association of Home Appliance Manufacturers.

levels for a room air cleaner to rid the air of 90 percent of smoke, dust, and pollen particles in a draft-free 10 × 12-foot room. (The first line shows the time required for natural air exchange to remove particles when no air cleaner is operating.)

CADR	Smoke	Dust	Pollen
0	128 minutes	110 minutes	22 minutes
20	61 minutes	56 minutes	18 minutes
40	40 minutes	38 minutes	16 minutes
80	24 minutes	23 minutes	12 minutes
160	13 minutes	13 minutes	9 minutes
320	7 minutes	7 minutes	5 minutes

CHOOSING A UNIT

A whole-house system is generally the most effective *and* most expensive type of air cleaner you can buy. Your heating and air-conditioning contractor or dealer can recommend the unit best suited for your house and your family's particular needs. (Also see "Choosing a Contractor," *Air Conditioners*, pages 14–15.) The most reliable point of comparison among various whole-house systems is their Atmospheric Dust Spot Efficiency; for further details on this measure of efficiency as well as the air cleaner certification program of the Air-Conditioning & Refrigeration Institute (ARI), you may want to contact ARI at 1501 Wilson Boulevard, Suite 600, Arlington, VA 22209.

If you are considering the purchase of a room air cleaner, you will find that prices range from about $80 for small tabletop units to $600–plus for large console models. The point of comparison to consider among various units is their CADR rating. Some models carry AHAM certification seals showing ratings.* For those that don't, you might try looking in the February 1989 issue of *Consumer Reports* magazine;** the article uses tests similar to the standard developed by AHAM to assign CADR numbers to 26 console and tabletop models.

Other facts to consider when selecting a room air cleaner include the unit's weight and portability; its noise level when operating; and the cost and ease of replacement of filters as well as how often they must be changed.

Also remember these facts:

1. The strength of a pollutant source is an important factor in determining the effectiveness of an air cleaner. Tabletop air cleaners in particular

---

*For a complete listing of all currently certified room air cleaner models with their CADR data, send a stamped, self-addressed envelope to: Association of Home Appliance Manufacturers, Room Air Cleaner Certification Program, 20 North Wacker Drive, Chicago, IL 60606.

**Consumers Union, Mount Vernon, NY.

may not remove satisfactory amounts of pollutants from strong nearby sources.

2. The larger the room, the longer a particular unit will take to cleanse the air. By the same token, a less efficient (and possibly less expensive) model may be adequate for cleansing a small enclosed space.

3. The long-term performance of any air cleaner depends upon maintaining it according to the manufacturer's directions.

4. According to the EPA and CPSC, the most effective methods for improving the air quality in your home include eliminating individual sources of pollution and improving ventilation by opening windows and doors, using exhaust fans, and/or installing heat recovery ventilators (also known as air-to-air heat exchangers). These devices, which can be installed in windows or as part of a central air system, increase ventilation by drawing outside air into the home and conserve energy by recovering the heat from air that is exhausted to the outdoors. Heat recovery ventilators are most easily installed in central air systems in new homes or during extensive remodeling; window units can be installed in existing homes.

The EPA/CPSC booklet *The Inside Story: A Guide to Indoor Air Quality* (publication #460V) provides detailed information on steps you can take to control specific sources of indoor air pollution. To order, send 50¢ to: R. Woods, Consumer Information Center-K, P.O. Box 100, Pueblo, CO 81002. The free U.S. Department of Energy fact sheet *Air-to-Air Heat Exchangers* provides information on heat recovery ventilators. To order, write: Renewable Energy Information, P.O. Box 8900, Silver Spring, MD 20907.

Air Conditioners

Strictly defined, air-conditioning involves far more than just cooling air. The process of *conditioning* air for maximum indoor comfort includes controlling its cleanliness, moisture level, and temperature simultaneously. Air can be conditioned by a room air conditioner or a central air-conditioning system, or by a heat pump, which operates very much like a conventional air-conditioning system but also provides heat. In this chapter, we'll refer to air-conditioning as most people think of it: the cooling of air for comfort inside homes and buildings.

An air-conditioning unit cools air by extracting the heat from indoor air and transferring it outside. A chemical refrigerant absorbs excess indoor heat through an evaporator coil; a compressor pumps the refrigerant through a closed system of piping to an outside condenser coil, where a fan blows outside air over the hot coil, transferring heat from the refrigerant to the air outdoors.

ROOM AIR CONDITIONER OR CENTRAL AIR?

Air-conditioning equipment ranges from small, window-size units to central systems. **Room air conditioners** are household appliances; in some cases, they can be moved from home to home and from room to room within a home. Average prices range from about $300 to $450. Window units are relatively easy to install and maintain, and they provide a reliable system for cooling and dehumidifying smaller spaces. However, the use of most room air conditioners requires the sacrifice of the use and view of a window, and to some people the noise they generate can be annoying.

A **central air-conditioning system** cools, filters, and dehumidifies the air in an entire house. Once installed, a central system is an integral part of the home. Central air is quiet, it can filter out dust and pollen (an important consideration for allergy sufferers), and its installation can add value to a home. But a central air-conditioning system is also very expensive to buy and install, so its purchase should be given the same careful consideration that the homeowner gives to any other major investment.

The question of whether a central system or a battery of room air conditioners is the better option for you can only be answered after an evaluation of the pros and cons of each system and an examination of your own individual circumstances. These might include the size of the area to be cooled in your home, how well your home is insulated, the temperatures you want to maintain, the size of your family, and whether every room needs cooling. As a general rule of thumb, central air-conditioning is the most cost-effective choice if more than three rooms require conditioning. But to accurately compare costs, you'll need to estimate the expense of purchase, installation, operation, and maintenance of each system; a reliable air-conditioning contractor can help you make this comparison (see "Choosing a Contractor", pages 14–15).

COOLING CAPACITY AND UNIT EFFICIENCY

Whether you are in the market for a central air-conditioning system or a room air conditioner, the two most important factors to consider are the unit's cooling capacity and its efficiency. **Cooling capacity**—the amount of heat a unit can remove from an enclosed space—is measured in British thermal units per hour (BTU/hr). The higher the BTU/hr rating, the greater the unit's cooling capacity.

Choosing a unit with the right cooling capacity—that is, a unit correctly sized for your house—is critical. If the unit is too small, it won't deliver enough cold air. On the other hand, an oversized unit can actually cool the area too quickly; its thermostat will shut off before it's had a chance to dehumidify the air, and the excess moisture that remains will give the air a cold, clammy feeling.

The cooling capacity required depends on a number of factors, including the size of the area to be cooled, number and location of windows, and amount of insulation. A reliable air-conditioning contractor or dealer can help you determine your needs. Or, if you are purchasing a room air conditioner, you can make the calculations yourself by using the "Cooling Load Estimate Form" on pages 10–11. (Additional copies of the form are available through the Association of Home Appliance Manufacturers; send 35¢ with your request to: AHAM, 20 North Wacker Drive, Chicago, IL 60606. Many dealers also make the form available on their premises as a reference.)

The **efficiency** of an air-conditioning unit is unrelated to its cooling capacity. While Unit A and Unit B both may be able to maintain constant, comfortable temperature and humidity levels in a given space, Unit A, the more efficient model, will use less energy in the process and thus cost less to operate than the less efficient Unit B. Although the initial cost of the more efficient model will probably be higher, lower operating costs over the life of the unit can compensate for the higher purchase price. (Also see "Energy Costs," *Appliances*, pages 26–28.)

The efficiency of room air conditioners is expressed as the EER (Energy Efficiency Ratio). With a central air-conditioning system, the number to look for is the SEER (Seasonal Energy Efficiency Ratio). *The higher the EER or SEER, the more energy-efficient the unit.*

Instructions for using Cooling Load Estimate Form
for Room Air Conditioners

(FROM AHAM STANDARD RAC-1)

A. This cooling load estimate form is suitable for estimating the cooling load for comfort air-conditioning installations which do not require specific conditions of inside temperature and humidity.

B. The form is based on an outside design temperature of 95°F dry bulb and 75°F wet bulb. It can be used for areas in the continental United States having other outside design temperatures by applying a correction factor for the particular locality as determined from the map.

C. The form includes "day" factors for calculating cooling loads in rooms where daytime comfort is desired (such as living rooms, offices, etc.), as well as "night" factors for calculating cooling loads in rooms where only nighttime comfort is desired (such as bedrooms). "Night" factors should be used only for those applications where comfort air-conditioning is desired during the period from sunset to sunrise.

D. The numbers of the following paragraphs refer to the correspondingly numbered item on the form:

1. Multiply the square feet of window area for each exposure by the applicable factor. The window area is the area of the wall opening in which the window is installed. For windows shaded by inside shades or venetian blinds, use the factor for "Inside Shades." For windows shaded by outside awnings or by both outside awnings and inside shades (or venetian blinds), use the factor for "Outside Awnings." "Single Glass" includes all types of single-thickness windows, and "Double Glass" includes sealed air-space types, storm windows, and glass block. Transfer only one number, representing the largest cooling load, to the right hand column.

2. Multiply the total square feet of *all* windows in the room by the applicable factor.

3a. Multiply the total length (linear feet) of all walls exposed to the outside by the applicable factor. Doors should be considered as being part of the wall. Outside walls facing due north should be calculated separately from outside walls facing other directions. Walls which are permanently shaded by adjacent structures should be considered as being "North Exposure." Do not consider trees and shrubbery as providing permanent shading. An uninsulated frame wall or a masonry wall 8 inches or less in thickness is considered "Light Construction." An insulated frame wall or a masonry wall over 8 inches in thickness is considered "Heavy Construction."

3b. Multiply the total length (linear feet) of all inside walls between the space to be conditioned and any unconditioned spaces by the given factor. Do not include inside walls which separate other air-conditioned rooms.

4. Multiply the total square feet of roof or ceiling area by the factor given for the type of construction most nearly describing the particular application. (Use one line only.)

5. Multiply the total square feet of floor area by the factor given. Disregard this item if the floor is directly on the ground or over a basement.

6. Multiply the total width (linear feet) of any doors or arches which are continually open to an unconditioned space by the applicable factor.

NOTE — Where the width of the doors or arches is more than 5 feet, the actual load may exceed the calculated value. In such cases, both adjoining rooms should be considered as a single large room, and the room air conditioner unit or units should be selected according to a calculation made on this new basis.

7. Total the loads estimated for the foregoing 6 items.

8. Multiply the sub-total obtained in Item 7 by the proper correction factor, selected from the map, for the particular locality.

9. Multiply the number of people who normally occupy the space to be air conditioned by the factor given. Use a minimum of 2 people.

10. Determine the total number of watts for lights and electrical equipment, except the air conditioner itself, that will be *in use* when the room air conditioning is operating. Multiply the total wattage by the factor given.

11. Add the loads estimated in the foregoing items 8 through 10 to obtain the total estimated design cooling load in BTU/hr.

E. For best results, a room air conditioning unit or units with a cooling capacity rating (determined per AHAM RAC-1) close to the estimated load should be selected. In general, a greatly oversized unit which would operate intermittently will be much less satisfactory than one which is slightly undersized and which would operate more nearly continuously.

F. Intermittent loads such as kitchen and laundry equipment are not included in this form.

Cooling Load Estimate Form for Room Air Conditioners*

Heat Gain From	Quantity	FACTORS				BTU/hr (Quantity × Factor)
		Night	Day			
1. WINDOWS, heat gain from direct radiation of the sun. (Total all windows for each exposure, but transfer only one number, representing the largest cooling load, to the right hand column.)			No Shades	Inside Shades	Outside Awnings	(Area × Factor)
Northeast	____ sq ft	0	60	25	20	_____
East	____ sq ft	0	80	40	25	_____
Southeast	____ sq ft	0	75	30	20	_____ Use
South	____ sq ft	0	75	35	20	_____ only
Southwest	____ sq ft	0	110	45	30	_____ the
West	____ sq ft	0	150	65	45	_____ largest
Northwest	____ sq ft	0	120	50	35	_____ load
North	____ sq ft	0	0	0	0	_____
			These factors are for single glass only. For glass block, multiply the above factors by 0.5; for double glass or storm windows, multiply the above factors by 0.8.			_____
2. WINDOWS, heat gain by conduction (Total for **all** windows)						
Single glass	____ sq ft	14	← 14 →			_____
Double glass or glass block	____ sq ft	7	← 7 →			_____
3. WALLS (based on linear feet of wall)			Light Construction		Heavy Construction	
a. Outside walls North exposure	____ ft	20	30		20	_____
Other than North exposure	____ ft	20	60		30	_____
b. Inside walls (between conditioned and unconditioned spaces only)	____ ft	30	← 30 →			_____
4. ROOF OR CEILING (Use one only.)						
a. Roof, uninsulated	____ sq ft	5	← 19 →			_____
b. Roof, with 1 inch or more insulation	____ sq ft	3	← 8 →			_____
c. Ceiling, with occupied space above	____ sq ft	3	← 3 →			_____
d. Ceiling, insulated, with attic space above	____ sq ft	4	← 5 →			_____
e. Ceiling, uninsulated, with attic above	____ sq ft	7	← 12 →			_____
5. FLOOR (Disregard if floor is directly on ground or over basement)	____ sq ft	3	← 3 →			_____
6. DOORS AND ARCHES CONTINUOUSLY OPEN TO UNCONDITIONED SPACE (linear feet of width)	____ ft	200	← 300 →			_____
7. SUB-TOTAL	XXXX	XXX	← XXX →			_____
8. GEOGRAPHICAL LOCATION MAP FACTOR			(Item 7) × _____ Factor From Map			_____
9. NUMBER OF PEOPLE	____	600	← 600 →			_____
10. LIGHTS AND ELECTRICAL EQUIPMENT IN USE	____ watts	3	← 3 →			_____
11. TOTAL COOLING LOAD [BTU/hr to be used for selection of room air conditioner(s)]	XXX	XX	← XXX →			_____

*Published and distributed by the Association of Home Appliance Manufacturers.
For more precise determination of heat load, consult *ASHRAE Handbook of Fundamentals*.

Under federal law, every room air conditioner sold today is required to carry an Energy Guide label showing the model's cooling capacity, its EER, and how it compares in efficiency with other models of similar cooling capacity. The label includes a cost grid to help you estimate the unit's annual operating cost based on your local electric rate and the number of hours per year that you'll use the air conditioner.*The minimum EER rating acceptable under federal standards varies according to the type or "class" of room air conditioner; the absolute minimum for any unit manufactured after January 1, 1990, is 8.0.

Courtesy of the Association of Home Appliance Manufacturers.

To determine the efficiency of a central air-conditioning system, you'll need to ask the contractor for the SEER of the equipment recommended. Beginning in 1992, a minimum SEER of 10.0 will be required for all split-system air conditioners; for single-package systems,** the federal minimum will be 9.7, effective in 1993. Additionally, all central systems manufactured after June 1989 are required to carry a label specifying the SEER; that information is also in your owner's manual.

ROOM AIR CONDITIONERS

According to the Association of Home Appliance Manufacturers, there are three types of room air conditioners available:

- **Window models.** Used in ordinary, double-hung windows up to 40 inches wide. The unit is simply installed in the opened window.
- **Special-application models.** Used in narrow, vertical windows. Installation usually requires the removal of a windowpane. These include *casement-only models,* used in crank-out casement windows, and *slider/casement models,* used in casement windows that either slide on horizontal tracks or crank open.

---

*Contact your local electric utility for information on your area's *cooling load hours* (the estimated number of hours you'll use the unit annually) as well as local electricity rates.

**See page 14 for an explanation of split-systems and single-package systems.

- **Through-the-wall models.** Installed in an outside wall. These units consist of a sleeve, which is installed in an exterior wall, and a cooling system designed for installation in the sleeve.

Once you've determined the cooling capacity and type of room air conditioner you require, you're ready to shop. Besides the EER of various models, other factors you'll need to weigh before making a selection include such performance and design features as ease of controlling airflow, accessibility of the filter, number of fan speeds, compatibility of styling with room decor, and noise level.

Take the time to compare the features *and* prices of a number of available models. Ask friends and neighbors about the units they have used: how long they've been in operation and how they've performed. Visit your library and check through consumer magazines for information on model performance and price ranges. Deal with a retailer you can rely on, and check the reputation of the retailer with the Better Business Bureau. Make the warranty part of your buying decision; read it carefully and compare the terms of warranties offered with different brands and models.

Installation and Maintenance

Window-model and special-application air conditioners usually can be installed with a minimum of time and effort, but *be sure to carefully follow the manufacturer's instructions.* Through-the-wall models generally require installation by a heating and air-conditioning contractor.

Before installing any air conditioner, check its electrical requirements. Inadequate wiring wastes power, reduces efficiency, may damage the unit, and *can be dangerous.* If you are uncertain about the electrical wiring in your house, *have it checked by an electrician, public utility, or other qualified source* before the unit is installed.

Maintenance of a room air conditioner is simple but essential if the unit is to perform reliably. Follow the recommendations in your owner's manual and these tips:

- Check the filter every two weeks; vacuum, wash, or replace it as necessary.
- Never remove the filter to get more air.
- If unusual sounds or odors develop, if smoke is detected, or if the fan or cooling action stops, turn off the unit and have it serviced.

CENTRAL AIR-CONDITIONING SYSTEMS

Central systems are composed of one or more basic air-conditioning units plus a mechanism for distributing conditioned air throughout the living space. There are many types of central systems, but most are a variation of the **split-system** or **single-package system**. Most single-family homes have a split-system, which places one of its heat exchangers (including the compressor) outdoors and the other (including the evaporator or cooling coil) indoors. A single-package system combines both heat exchangers in the same unit, which is usually located outdoors.

A **total comfort system** is more elaborate than a basic central air-conditioning system. The additional components can include a central electronic air cleaner, a central humidifier, and zone controls allowing different temperature settings for different rooms.

The most important factor involved in the installation of a central air-conditioning system to an existing home is the presence or absence of ductwork in the house. If the home is heated by steam or hot water in radiators, there are usually no air ducts in place. In such a case, installation requires extensive (and expensive) remodeling in which it's usually necessary to open and refinish walls in order to install the ductwork. But if the home has central forced-air heating, including a central blower and ducts, installation is comparatively simple. The air-conditioning unit and controls are added, and cool air is routed through the existing heating ducts; however, some alteration or addition of ducts may still be necessary.

Choosing a Contractor

Since a central air-conditioning system must be custom-tailored for each individual home, it is vital that you hire a contractor who is reliable and competent. Following these guidelines can help:

1. Ask friends and neighbors for recommendations; the newspaper classifieds and the yellow pages of your phone book are additional sources to check.

2. Once you have the names of a few prospects, ask the contractors for references and check them. Contact your local Better Business Bureau for a reliability report on each prospect.

3. Ask at least three contractors to inspect your house and give you a *written* cost estimate. The estimate should include: the total cost of equipment and labor; a calculation of the cooling capacity needed; a full description of the system, its size, and its SEER; and a description of any additional work required for installation of ducts, registers, and electrical wiring.

4. Check with your electric utility to be sure electrical service to your home is adequate to handle the added load of the air-conditioning system. If it is not, additional wiring and increased electrical power input will be required. In most areas, a contractor must be, or must

use, a licensed electrician for this work, and must also obtain a permit for the installation of the system.

5. Your utility company also can help you evaluate the energy efficiency of your home by performing a whole-house energy audit. (There may be a fee for this service.) Drafts and poor insulation can add significantly to the operating cost of an air-conditioning system. An energy audit will give you detailed recommendations on the estimated cost and anticipated savings of additional insulation, caulking, or weather stripping.

6. Compare the contractors' estimates, and be sure to look at more than just costs. Compare the size of the equipment each contractor plans to use (noted in BTU/hr); if size varies significantly, something is wrong, and you should ask the contractors to explain how they arrived at their cooling capacity estimates.

7. Compare warranties. Most contractors offer a one-year warranty on the installation, and manufacturers usually warrant air-conditioning equipment for one year, with a four-year extension on the compressor. Many contractors also provide at least one free "callback" after installation to check the system. Also check out service contracts, available through many contractors, which provide for periodic maintenance of equipment and repairs as needed. These can be a good investment. But before you buy a service contract, make sure it spells out what parts and services are covered. And because service contracts vary significantly in coverage, it pays to compare coverage under contracts offered by several different companies.

Service and Maintenance

Proper care of your central air-conditioning system can prolong its life, improve its efficiency and your comfort, and cut costs. A routine yearly checkup—performed *before* the peak cooling season—by the contractor who installed the system or by a service technician is the key. In addition, follow these tips from the Air Conditioning & Refrigeration Institute (ARI):

☐ Check disposable filters every two months (once a month during peak use) and replace when necessary. Clean permanent filters as directed by the manufacturer. Never operate the system without filters in place.

☐ Make the cleaning of duct outlets and registers part of your regular housecleaning routine.

☐ Occasionally clean ducts by removing a few registers and inspecting the ducts from the inside with a flashlight (be sure to look at return air ducts). Call a contractor or service technician if the insides of ducts need cleaning.

15

☐ If an air-conditioning system stops working properly, call your air-conditioning contractor right away and have the problem checked out.

COST-CUTTING TIPS

Following these basic rules can help you cut the costs of keeping cool, whether you choose room air conditioners or a central air-conditioning system:

* Shop for your air conditioner in the off-season—late winter or early spring.
* Follow the tips on maintenance provided by your owner's manual and your contractor, and on pages 13 and 15.
* Close air gaps by caulking, weather-stripping, and insulating.
* Close drapes and blinds on windows facing the sun.
* If possible, install room air conditioners in a shaded window—but avoid areas where outside dust, odors, or pollen will be drawn into the unit.
* Set the thermostat at the highest comfortable setting and leave it there—constantly turning the thermostat up and down can waste considerable amounts of energy.
* Don't run residential air-conditioning when the outside air temperature falls below 60°F.
* Whenever possible, schedule heat-producing work (cooking, washing clothes) for cooler early morning and evening hours.
* Use an exhaust fan when cooking to remove excess heat and moisture.
* Keep windows and doors closed when the cooling system is on.
* Keep any outside units free of leaves, shrubbery, and grass to prevent obstruction of the airflow.
* During "brownouts"—heat-wave shortages of electrical power—raising your thermostat a few degrees can help save electricity. But don't turn off your central air-conditioning system. It can take several hours, and increased amounts of electricity, to cool off a house after the heat and humidity have risen while the system is shut off. If power is temporarily cut off *completely*, however, you should turn off the thermostat to avoid contributing to a sudden surge of demand when service is restored.

Answering Machines

[Also see *Telephones—Conventional, Cordless, and Cellular*, pages 323–32.]

Nearly one-third of all American households have an answering machine, according to the Electronic Industries Association, and owners use their machines more than any other household electronic product. It's easy to understand the fast-growing appeal of these small devices. Answering machines are always there to take a call when you can't, and for many owners they also provide a handy means for screening out less-favored callers. Further, while today's answering machines are smaller, sleeker, easier to use, and more versatile than the models of just a half-dozen years ago, prices have remained relatively unchanged. A particular model's price is largely a reflection of its "talent," with the simple machines starting at about $50 and more versatile, feature-laden models retailing for $200 or more. Let your needs and your budget guide your choice. The following catalog of features and terminology common to today's answering machines can help you explore the terrain and define your needs before you shop.

ANSWERING MACHINE FACTS AND FEATURES

Cassette vs. digital. Technology now gives you a choice between cassette-based and digital answering machines; here are some facts that may help you make that decision.

☐ **Cassette models.** All earlier-model answering machines and most of today's models store both your outgoing message and incoming calls on audiocassette tapes. *Two-cassette* models use separate tapes for greeting and incoming messages; these may either be standard-size cassette tapes or matchbook-sized microcassettes. Two-cassette models using standard cassettes are typically the largest and bulkiest style of answering machine. *One-cassette* answering machines generally are smaller than the two-cassette models; however, they can be somewhat more awkward to use. Since both outgoing and incoming messages are stored on the same tape, the machine must first play your greeting and then fast-forward through any previously stored messages to find a blank spot on which to record the current message. Your caller must wait until the machine is ready to record and is usually limited to a message of one minute.

☐ **Digital machines** use computer chips to store either your greeting alone *(digital/cassette models)* or both greeting and incoming message *(all-digital models)*. Digital answering machines are relatively new on the market; they offer several advantages over cassette models along with a few major drawbacks. On the plus side, digital machines are smaller, more convenient to use, and more reliable. As for negatives, they cost more than similarly equipped cassette-based machines, voice quality is inferior, and their memory capacity is smaller, limiting the length of your greeting and, on all-digital models, the number and length of incoming messages as well.

VOX. Some answering machines are designed to record incoming messages for a given period, typically 30 or 60 seconds, and then switch off and reset in the record mode. Most newer machines are equipped with VOX, a voice-activated system which keeps recording as long as the caller speaks. Some VOX-equipped models still give you the option of limiting call length, to keep a particularly verbose caller from using up the tape or to avoid the possibility of the machine mistaking static on the phone line for speech and continuing to record after the caller has hung up.

Playback. Some answering machines require you to rewind the tape before listening to recorded messages; with others, playback is accomplished at the touch of a single button. After playback, the machine may automatically rewind to the beginning of the tape so that new messages will be recorded over the old, or it may record at the end of previously stored messages unless you choose to rewind. Neither system is inherently superior to the other; your choice is a matter of personal preference.

You may also want to consider these additional playback conveniences, available on various models in all price ranges:

• The machine stops playback at the end of the most recent batch of recorded messages rather than continuing to play to the end of the tape.

• It allows you to rewind to a chosen spot within the tape to review a particular message, rather than requiring you to rewind to the beginning.

• It lets you skip from the beginning of one message to the beginning of the next in order to quickly locate the message you want.

Remote access. This feature, available on most mid- to higher-priced answering machines, allows you to listen to stored messages when you are away from home. With a **beeper remote**, you phone home and, while your greeting plays, signal the machine with a special tone generated by a small electronic device; the machine then plays back the accumulated messages. **Beeperless remotes** are more convenient to use; you signal the machine by pressing one or more numbers on a tone-phone keypad.

Depending on the model, that sequence of keys may be preset at the factory or you may be able to select and program your own code. Keep in mind that with a beeperless remote, you must use a tone phone to access your messages; a beeper model allows use of either a tone or pulse phone. Additional features you might want to look for on remote-capable answering machines include:

- **Toll-saver**, which saves you the expense of phoning an "empty" machine; the answering machine will ring longer if there are no messages, giving you time to hang up before a connection is made.
- **Remote recording**, which lets you change your outgoing greeting by phone.
- **Remote on**, which lets you turn on the answering machine by phone.
- **Announcement breakthrough**, which allows you to break in on your greeting to signal the machine rather than having to listen to the whole greeting before accessing your messages.
- **Automatic reset**, which automatically sets the machine back to the record mode after the last message has been played. Without this feature, you must remember to play an additional signal or code to reset.

Call counting. The least sophisticated answering machines let you know that you have a recorded message by means of a solid or blinking light. Some models also use a lighted signal to tell you how many calls have been recorded—the code for three calls, for example, might be three flashes in rapid sequence, then a pause. The most helpful call counters use a digital numerical display to tell you how many messages have been received.

Built-in phone. Integrated phone/answering machines can save space and money; these all-in-one units often cost less than buying a comparably featured phone and answering machine individually. When evaluating a telephone/answering machine, consider the features of each component separately, using the catalog of features provided in this chapter and on pages 324–27 of *Telephones—Conventional, Cordless, and Cellular.*

Plus these extras. You may want to look for one or more of the following convenience features:

- **Call screening**, which lets you listen to incoming calls as they are recorded.
- **Auto disconnect**, which automatically turns off and resets the machine if you pick up the phone receiver while a message is being recorded.
- **Voice time/date stamp** which automatically records the time and day each message was received.
- **Personal memo**, which lets you record and store personal messages for other family members.

- **Color-coded message storage,** which uses different colors to point out recorded "hang-ups," incoming messages, and memos.

- **Timer message transfer,** which lets you program the machine to phone you at another number at a specified time so that you can review recorded messages.

- **Two-way recording,** with which you can record ongoing conversations; some machines alert the caller with a periodic beep.

SHOPPING FOR ANSWERS

As you shop for an answering machine that offers a competitive price on the features that suit your intended use, keep the following tips in mind:

1. Check out an unfamiliar retailer through a call to the local Better Business Bureau.

2. Look for a machine with logically arranged, easy-to-use controls and a clearly written instruction manual.

3. Try out the machine in the store, if possible. Listen to the sound quality of recorded messages, and consider the convenience of performing various functions. For example, how easy is it to record and review your outgoing message, to set the machine to record incoming calls, to listen to recorded incoming messages, and to review messages by remote? Also be sure to ask whether there are any limitations on the length of your outgoing message or on incoming calls.

4. Compare warranties and return policies before making your decision.

Apartments

For confirmed city dwellers, young people taking their first flight from the parental nest, parents presiding over that suddenly empty nest, and others who prefer or require a relative absence of responsibility and long-term financial commitment in housing, apartment living is the best and often the only choice. In some communities, finding a suitable apartment can be a simple matter of scanning the classified ads, touring the available rentals, selecting the one that offers the most for your dollars, and bargaining with the landlord over the terms of the lease. In many areas, however, affordable apartments are so scarce that you'll feel lucky if you manage to find virtually *anything* in your price range. In that case, a quick peek at the rooms and the lease before you sign are likely to be the only precautions you take.

Regardless of the state of the housing market in your area, it is important to observe some basic precautions before renting an apartment—even if your prudence means that you lose a rental or two to other, more eager seekers. At stake are the comfort and safety of your home, as well as your rights as a tenant. To protect those interests, you must be prepared to (1) know what you want and can afford, (2) methodically examine prospective apartments, and (3) carefully read the lease before signing.

THE SEARCH

Before you start looking for an apartment, spend some time thinking about your needs. Is renting really the right choice for you? If so, what features do you require in an apartment and how much rent can you afford to pay each month? For tips on making those decisions, see "To Buy or Not to Buy," "Defining Your Dream," and "What Can You Afford?" on pages 189–92 of the *Home Buying* chapter.

There are three common approaches to apartment-hunting: scanning the classified ad sections of the newspapers that serve the areas you like; consulting an apartment rental agency or real estate broker; and searching entirely on your own. The rule for the classified ad approach is "The earlier, the better." Particularly in areas where reasonably priced apartments are scarce, the rental you see advertised in Sunday morning's classifieds may well be taken by Sunday afternoon.

Apartment ads may be placed by landlords or by brokers; you can also contact a broker on your own to ask about available rentals. Finding an apartment through a broker can save you time and effort *if* you follow some guidelines.

1. Be specific and firm about the type of apartment and neighborhood you are willing to consider.
2. Get as much information as you can over the phone before spending time looking at an apartment.
3. Take your business elsewhere if a broker persists in showing you apartments that are far below your standards or advertises "dream" apartments that you are told are "unavailable" for one reason or another.

Remember, too, that if you locate an apartment through a rental agency, you'll have to pay a broker's fee, which may be equal to one month's rent or a fixed percentage of the first year's rent. However it is calculated, that fee can make a substantial dent in your checkbook, usually at a time when you also have to pay the landlord a security deposit and the first one or two months' rent.

If time and distance allow, conducting your own independent search can be an effective and inexpensive alternative or adjunct to the classified ad and agency routes. Let friends know you are looking; they may be able to tell you when an apartment becomes available in the building where they live before the landlord puts it on the market. Explore the neighborhoods you like. Look for "apartment for rent" signs, and talk with doormen and building superintendents about anticipated vacancies.

APARTMENT HUNTER'S CHECKLIST

Bringing along a written list of questions and considerations when examining an apartment can help you save time and avoid overlooking important details. Certain qualities will have particular importance to you. You may prefer a very quiet building, well-lighted rooms, or play space outside, for example. Put your "must-haves" at the top of the list, and also include these items:

The Building

☐ Is the *lobby or entrance hall* clean and well lighted? _____
☐ Is there a *doorman* on duty? _____ What hours? _____
☐ If there is no doorman, is there a *speaker system*? _____ Are the outside doors kept securely locked? _____
☐ Are *hallways, stairways, and elevators* clean, well lighted, and secure? _____ Are there clearly marked *fire alarms and fire exits*? _____
☐ Is there a *resident superintendent*? _____ If not, how do you arrange for emergency service? _____

☐ Are *refuse facilities* neat and accessible? _____
☐ What is the condition of any *additional facilities?* Laundry room? _____ Recreation areas? _____ Parking lot or garage? _____ Others? _____

The Apartment

☐ Is the *door* well secured, with lock, chain, viewer? _____
☐ Do the *heating and/or air-conditioning* systems seem to work well? _____ Is there adequate *cross-ventilation?* _____
☐ Are *walls, floors, and ceilings* clean and in good condition? _____ Is *soundproofing* adequate? _____
☐ Are *windows* in good condition and easily opened and closed? _____ Are *screens* provided? _____
☐ Do *kitchen appliances* look reasonably clean? _____ In good condition? _____
☐ Do *bathroom fixtures* look reasonably clean? _____ In good condition? _____
☐ Any signs of *insects or rodents?* _____
☐ Are there enough *electrical outlets*, with adequate voltage, for your needs? _____
☐ Is *closet space* adequate? _____ Any other storage space? _____
☐ How is the *noise level* from outdoors? _____ From apartments above, below, and around you? _____
☐ Other problems or pluses? _____

The Terms

☐ What is the *rent per month?* _____
☐ Are there *extra charges* for parking space, utilities, etc.? _____
☐ Is a *security deposit* required? _____
☐ What is the *duration* of the lease? _____

THE LEASE

The lease—the contract under which you rent your apartment—should protect you as well as it protects the landlord. Like all other contracts, it should be read carefully and understood thoroughly before you sign. Reading, unfortunately, is not always followed by understanding, thanks to the legal terminology used in many standard lease forms. If time and the landlord permit, you may want to have the lease examined by your lawyer or by someone else familiar with real estate law. Local tenants' associations, your state office of the attorney general, or your city, county, or state housing authorities might also be able to provide information on provisions that are and are not permissible in a lease.

As a practical matter, however, you may well find yourself in a situation where delay in signing the lease can mean losing the apartment you want. In such a case, insist on being given at least enough time to read the lease carefully, ask about any terms you do not understand, and ask to have any objectionable clauses changed or deleted. Make sure the document specifies the following:

- The amount of rent and security deposit, and whether utility charges are included in the rent.

  The security deposit, which is usually one or two months' rent, protects the landlord against your damaging the apartment or failing to make a rent payment. It should be returned to you when you move, minus any bona fide charges for damage, cleanup, etc. Many states have passed legislation restricting the maximum size of the security deposit and limiting the amount of time the landlord can retain your deposit once you have moved out. In some states, the deposit must be placed in an escrow account, where it will gain interest payable to the renter.

- The term of the lease, and conditions under which your rent can be increased during that term.

- All appliances, fixtures, and furnishings that come with the apartment, and who is responsible for their repair.

- All building services, such as the hours of the doorman.

- All oral promises made by the landlord or rental agent.

Also watch for these clauses:

- Does the lease state how many persons may occupy the apartment? If so, does the figure allow for any anticipated growth in your household?

- Does it give you permission to sublet if you want to move before the lease is up or if you plan on being away for a lengthy period?

- Are pets prohibited? Are there any restrictions on activities such as playing TV sets or stereos at certain hours or storing personal items in specified areas?

If the landlord agrees to change a clause you object to, make sure it is crossed out and/or revised on all copies of the lease, with the change initialed by both you and the landlord.

It's a good idea to take photos of the entire apartment when you move in *and* out, to document conditions and forestall future problems in recovering your security deposit. If disputes should arise over maintenance or other matters, put your requests to the landlord in writing. Those records can help prove your case if you need to take your complaints to the local housing authorities or to court.

Appliances

Major home appliances represent an important investment in both dollars and convenience. Before buying any new appliance, it pays to:

1. **Define your needs.** Will you use the appliance often enough to make it a reasonable, practical purchase? What are your personal cooking, storage, and/or serving styles and preferences? Consider personal preferences and lifestyle as well as the present and future size of your family when making your choice.

2. **Know your space limitations.** Will the appliance fit in the available space, with adequate clearance for ventilation and servicing? How will you get it in the house—can it be taken up or down stairs, and will it fit through doors and hallways? Do you have adequate space to store small appliances where they will be readily accessible?

3. **Research the available models.** This book includes purchasing tips on a number of specific appliances; see the table of contents for topics covered. The consumer product-rating publications available at your library or newsstand can also provide buying advice, along with brand and model comparisons.

4. **Look into convenience features and quality of construction.** Appliances with features that eliminate certain chores—such as self-cleaning ovens and frost-free refrigerators—may pay back in time saved what they cost in dollars spent. But remember that appliances with special features generally cost more both to purchase and to operate.

5. **Consider energy costs.** (See pages 26–28.)

6. **Shop for a dealer** as carefully as you shop for the brand and model of appliance. Compare prices and reputation for reliability. Deal with a retailer you know and trust, or check with the local Better Business Bureau for a complaint report. Find out exactly what is included in the purchase price—an exceptionally low price may be no bargain if the dealer adds on hefty charges for delivery and installation.

7. **Compare warranties.** Insist on seeing warranties before you buy, and compare terms. Find out whether warranty protection is "full" or "limited," what any limitations or exclusions are, and how long coverage lasts. Is warranty service provided in your home or at a service center? If you must return the appliance for service, who pays for pickup, delivery, and/or shipping?

ENERGY COSTS

When you buy an appliance, you not only pay the sales price; you also commit yourself to paying the costs of running the unit over its lifetime. The cost of operating a small appliance, such as a coffee maker, toaster, or vacuum cleaner, does not contribute significantly to your electric bill, since small appliances generally are used for only short periods of time. However, energy costs relating to the operation of major appliances can really add up. For example, according to the American Council for an Energy-Efficient Economy (ACEEE), a nonprofit organization committed to the adoption of energy-conserving technologies and practices, the cost of running a refrigerator for 15 to 20 years is typically *three times* as high as the original purchase price.

Buying an energy-efficient appliance may cost more initially, but the higher purchase price usually is more than made up by reduced operating costs over the lifetime of the unit. The following tips from the ACEEE can help you shop for the most economical and energy-efficient appliances.

Energy Guide Labels

Required by federal law on all new refrigerators, refrigerator/freezers, freezers, water heaters, washing machines, dishwashers, and room air conditioners, Energy Guide Labels provide a simple means for comparing the costs of operating those appliances.

The sample Energy Guide Label on page 27 shows:

1. The appliance's yearly energy cost in dollars, based on an estimate of hours of use per year and a varying standard energy price. (For room air conditioners, the large number is not dollars but the unit's EER—see "Cooling Capacity and Unit Efficiency," *Air Conditioners*, pages 9–12.)

2. How the appliance compares in energy efficiency with other models of comparable size and type on the market.

3. A cost table that allows you to estimate the appliance's yearly operating cost, based on your local electric or gas rates. (Contact your local utility or check your latest utility bills to see how much you pay per kilowatt-hour (kwh) of electricity or therms of natural gas.)

Often, finding the best buy in an appliance is a simple matter of comparing the figures in Energy Guide Labels and choosing the most efficient model. Sometimes, though, the choice is not so clear. For example, you may be looking for a room air conditioner that will only be used a few nights each year in your part of the country. In that case, will lower operating costs offset the higher price of the more efficient model? Following is a formula for computing the **lifecycle costs** of various appliances—the total of their purchase price plus their estimated lifetime

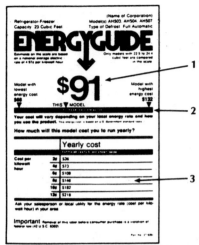

Courtesy of the American Council for an Energy-Efficient Economy.

energy costs. When comparing models with similar features, the best and most accurate way to tell which is the best buy is by comparing lifecycle costs.

Computing Lifecycle Costs*

To compute lifecycle cost, you will need to know:

1. The appliance's **purchase cost** (obtained from the dealer)
2. The **cost of energy** (obtained from your local utility)
3. The **yearly energy cost** to operate the appliance (obtained from the Energy Guide Label)
4. The **estimated lifetime** of the appliance in years (see table on page 28)
5. A **discount factor**—a number that adjusts for inflation and for the fact that a dollar spent today does not have the same value as a dollar spent in the future, since today's dollar could be invested and earn interest over time (see table on page 28)

This information can be plugged into the following formula:

$$\text{LIFECYCLE COST} = \text{PURCHASE PRICE} + \left(\text{ANNUAL ENERGY COST} \times \text{ESTIMATED LIFETIME} \times \text{DISCOUNT FACTOR} \right)$$

*Source: American Council for an Energy-Efficient Economy.

CHARACTERISTICS OF APPLIANCES FOR LIFECYCLE COST COMPARISONS

Appliance	Average Lifetime (in years)	Discount Factor*
Water heater (electric)	13	0.83
Water heater (gas)	13	0.83
Refrigerator/freezer	20	0.76
Freezer	20	0.76
Air conditioner (central)	12	0.84
Air conditioner (room)	15	0.81
Range/oven	18	0.78
Washing machine	13	0.83
Clothes dryer	18	0.78
Dishwasher	12	0.84

*Based on a real discount rate of 5 percent and an energy price escalation rate of 2 percent per year above inflation.

Saving Energy and Money with Home Appliances, published by the ACEEE and the Massachusetts Audubon Society, contains a worksheet for computing lifecycle costs, plus further information on buying energy-efficient appliances, including tips on shopping for energy-conserving features on appliances not required to carry Energy Guide Labels. The ACEEE also publishes The Most Energy-Efficient Appliances, a booklet listing the top-rated appliances by type and size. To order, send $2.00 for each booklet to: The American Council for an Energy-Efficient Economy, 1001 Connecticut Avenue, N.W., Suite 535, Washington, DC 20036.

You may be offered a **service contract** when you purchase a new appliance. Service contracts, or extended warranties, are optional agreements you can purchase to extend the coverage on an appliance beyond the manufacturer's warranty period. Terms vary widely. Before buying a service contract, it's wise to consider a number of factors, including:

• What the contract costs, what it covers, and its term

• How likely the appliance is to need repairs during the term of the service contract and how much those repairs might cost

• Whether the contract duplicates any part of the warranty's coverage

• Who would provide service under the contract—the dealer who sold you the appliance or an independent repair shop

• Whether there are any additional costs, such as a deductible or mandatory servicing visits

• Whether you can purchase the service contract at a later date

For further information on what to look for in a service contract, send for the free pamphlet Facts for Consumers: Service Contracts from the Federal Trade Commission, Public Reference Branch, Sixth and Pennsylvania Avenues, Room 130, Washington, DC 20580.

Audio and Video Equipment

The buying tips and precautions that follow apply to the purchase of nearly any consumer electronics product. For detailed information on the features, operation, and selection of specific types of audio and video equipment, see *Camcorders*, pages 65–68; *Cassette Decks*, pages 76–78; *Compact Disc Players*, pages 90–94; *Stereo Systems*, pages 308–13; *Television Sets*, pages 333–36; and *Videocassette Recorders*, pages 344–47.

SHOPPER'S CHECKLIST

1. When shopping for consumer electronics, it is important to deal with a knowledgeable, reliable retailer who can guide you through the maze of multiplying features and technical terms and help you find the model that best suits your needs and budget. Ask friends and colleagues for recommendations on dealers who have given them satisfactory service, and contact the local Better Business Bureau for a reliability report. Ask whether the store is an authorized dealer for the brand you are considering; if in doubt, call the manufacturer to confirm the names of authorized dealers. You may also want to look for membership in the Professional AudioVideo Retailers Association (PARA), an organization that promotes professionalism and business ethics within the audiovideo industry, and/or the National Association of Retail Dealers of America (NARDA), an association of retailers and distributors of household appliances and consumer electronics.

2. Selecting the "right" equipment is a matter of balancing the performance and features you want with a price you can afford. Listen to, look at, and compare a number of different models. Be sure to look not only for a high-quality picture or sound but also for easy-to-use controls and clear, readable displays. And remember that discounting is common in audio and video products; you can expect to pay as much as 25 percent below list price for most brands.

3. Ask to look at the instruction manual and warranty before you buy. Make certain that the manual is written in understandable English and that the warranty details exactly what is covered and what you must do to obtain service.

4. Ask about the store's return policy, and find out whether there is any charge if you decide to return the merchandise.

5. Avoid purchasing "gray goods." These products, which are commonly sold through mail-order catalogs or "deep-discount" retailers, are

foreign goods imported through unauthorized channels. Gray goods often come at a bargain price, but they may not operate on standard 110-volt U.S. current or may not have UL (Underwriters Laboratory) safety approval. They also generally do not carry a valid manufacturer's warranty, and the instruction manual may not be written in English.

6. A number of publications are available at your library or newsstand which can give you details on the performance and reliability of particular models. Helpful periodicals include *Consumer Reports,** *Stereo Review,*** *Audio,**** *Video,***** and *Video Review.******

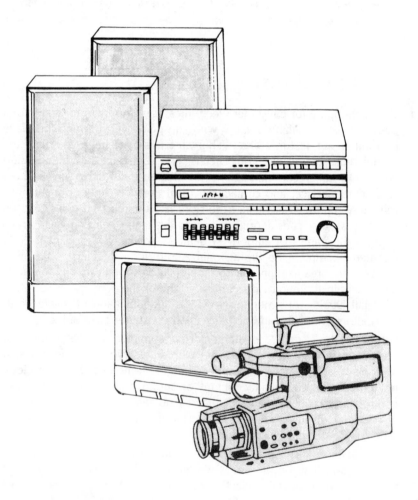

*Consumers Union, Mount Vernon, NY.
**Diamondis Communications, Inc., New York, NY.
***Audio Publishing, New York, NY.
****Reese Communications, Inc., New York, NY.
*****Viare Publishing Corp., New York, NY.

Automobiles

BUYING A NEW CAR

Your new car may well be the second most expensive single purchase you ever make, topped only by your investment in a home. Yet many people—carried away by "new car fever" or the patter of a persuasive salesperson—may make a less careful and considered decision about buying a new car than they might about buying a new VCR. All too often, those hasty decisions mean the buyer spends too much money on a car that turns out to be too expensive to operate and maintain or that is otherwise unsuited to his or her needs.

There is a better way to shop for a new car. The following step-by-step guide is designed to help you get the best deal possible on a reliable car that meets your driving needs and preferences as well as your budget.

Step #1: Get the Facts

Before you step into a dealer's showroom, you need to do some homework. Your primers are the consumer and automotive magazines and paperback books that introduce and evaluate new cars; look for them at your local library or bookstore. Literature about new cars is also available in dealer showrooms and at auto shows, which are held around the country usually in late winter and early spring. In the publications you gather, you'll find information on car prices, ease and efficiency of operation, safety features, available equipment and options, and fuel economy.

The first decision you need to make concerns your individual needs and preferences. Do you want a large, intermediate, compact, or subcompact car? Two doors or four? A sedan, a station wagon, a van? For each of these different styles, consider relative costs, including the initial purchase price as well as anticipated operating and repair bills; comfort; maneuverability; safety; and suitability for your lifestyle, your driving habits, and the size of your family.

Once you've determined what type of vehicle fits your needs, you're ready to narrow your choice to several models of that type within your price range. You'll find that the average cost of subcompacts ranges all the way from $7,500 to $10,500, compacts from $10,500 to $15,000, midsize and large cars from $14,000 to $17,000, and sports or luxury vehicles from $25,000 to over $45,000.* Don't forget to keep an eye on estimated operating and maintenance costs, too.

*Statistics from *The Complete Car Cost Guide*, ©1989 IntelliChoice, Inc., San Jose, CA.

Finally, you'll need to make some choices regarding optional equipment. Consider how much an option will cost, the benefit you'll receive from it, and how it might affect the resale value of the car. Compare the price of single options and special option packages, which usually combine several popular options, such as power steering and automatic transmission, with "extras" such as cruise control and remote-control outside mirrors. The option package is a good deal if its total price is no more than the cost of the major options you want. But if buying the total package means you'll pay extra for options you don't need, you're better off buying options individually.

Step #2: Shop for a Dealer

When you buy a car, you're buying service, too. Ask friends and coworkers about the dealerships from which they have bought cars or where they have their cars serviced. Contact the local Better Business Bureau for a reliability report on each dealer you are considering. Visit several dealers and look for a clean, pleasant sales floor and a neat, orderly service area.

Step #3: Get Ready to Bargain

Most dealers, particularly those selling domestic cars, are willing to negotiate on the size of their profit margin—the difference between what the car cost them and what you pay for it. But how do you estimate the size of the dealer's profit and thus how much room there may be to bargain?

The **sticker price** shown on the new car's window represents the manufacturer's estimate of the car's fair market value, with the dealer's markup built in. But in order to negotiate, you need another critical piece of information: the **dealer's cost.** That figure is included on a document you'll rarely see—the dealer's invoice. You can also find dealer's costs in some auto and consumer magazines and in book-length guides to new car prices.

It's a good idea to prepare a worksheet before you shop, listing the dealer's costs and suggested retail prices for the particular models and options that interest you. Armed with that worksheet, bargain *up* from the dealer's costs. According to Consumers Union*, you should be able to negotiate a selling price that is about $200 to $500 over dealer's costs for a new domestic car. You'll find less bargaining room with cars in high demand—for these, you may have to pay full sticker price. You may still

*Consumer Reports Books How to Buy a New Car, ©1988, Consumers Union, Mount Vernon, NY.

be able to save, however, by making sure you're not buying options you don't need or want.

Shop several dealers for the best price; one good method is to start your search farther from home and work your way in. By the time you visit your nearest dealer, you'll have a collection of figures to bargain with. Most dealers will match any reasonable offer.

Also keep these tips in mind when you comparison-shop:

1. Don't be rushed into a snap decision by "limited-time offers" or other sales tactics.

2. If the salesperson questions the accuracy of the figures on your worksheet, ask to be shown the dealer's invoice in order to confirm the dealer's costs.

3. You may save a few dollars—and get exactly the color and options you want—by ordering a car from inventory rather than buying one on the dealer's lot. (This isn't always possible, though, with high-demand autos.) You'll usually wait a month or two for delivery of a domestic car.

4. If the dealer offers a rebate on your purchase, factor that into your overall price. But don't let the incentive dissuade you from comparison-shopping; some of the rebate's cost to the dealer may be added back into your bill.

5. Negotiate the price of the new car without a trade-in, then bargain over the value of your old car. The monthly *N.A.D.A. Official Used Car Guide**, available through your library, bank, or insurance agent, provides figures on the average trade-in value of most cars. (Of course, your old car's condition also affects its value.)

Step #4: Take a Drive

Take the car for a test drive long enough to give you an adequate feel for the following characteristics:

☐ **Comfort.** Check headroom, legroom, seat support, and ease of entering and exiting.

☐ **View.** Look for good all-around visibility.

☐ **Controls.** Are switches, controls, and instruments easy to reach and operate?

☐ **Performance.** Observe the smoothness and noise level of the ride. How does the engine perform when you turn on the air conditioner, accelerate, or climb a hill?

☐ **Handling.** Try parallel parking, sharp turns, and sudden braking (within safe driving limits, of course).

*National Automobile Dealers Used Car Guide Co., McLean, VA.

☐ **Fit and finish.** The appearance of paint, seams, and moldings can be a good indicator of overall quality.

Step #5: Shop for Credit

If you have the resources, paying cash for a new car can be the least expensive purchasing option. If you need or prefer to finance your purchase through an installment loan, it's wise to settle on a price for the car *before* discussing financing with the dealer.

Dealers sometimes offer very low financing rates as sales incentives for specific models. Often, however, those savings carry their own price tag. The dealer may not be willing to negotiate on the price of cars for which special financing rates are available or may offer the deal only on specific cars in stock, with costly options you don't want or need. Further, along with low rates the dealer may require a relatively large down payment or offer relatively short loan terms, which translate into prohibitively high monthly payments, or very long terms, which mean high finance charges.

Keep any limitations and restrictions on the low-financing offer in mind as you compare the dealer's rates against those available from conventional lenders, such as banks, savings and loans, credit unions, and other financial institutions. You may find that you have more flexibility in arranging the amount of down payment and the length of the repayment period with a conventional loan. New car loan terms are commonly 36 to 48 months. The longer the term, the more interest you pay; however, selecting a longer term can also bring monthly payments down to a level you can comfortably afford.

For tips on comparison-shopping for an installment loan, see "Closed-End Credit: Shopping for a Loan," *Credit and Installment Buying*, pages 130–33.

Step #6: Accepting Delivery

Before you sign on the dotted line, read the sales contract carefully and be certain every aspect of the deal you negotiated is accurately spelled out. Check the math on all figures, and make sure the order is signed by a dealership officer or manager—the salesperson's signature alone may not be binding.

When you take delivery of your new car, follow this inspection checklist from the Automotive Information Council, a nonprofit membership group that provides information about the automotive industry, before signing any final papers:

1. Take delivery in daylight; any flaws or damage will be easier to spot.

Warranties and Service Contracts

New car warranties vary widely in coverage. They may extend from one year or 12,000 miles to six years or 60,000 miles. There may be a deductible—an amount you have to pay for repairs before warranty coverage kicks in. And most warranties are limited in varying degrees, which means that particular components are not covered or are covered for a shorter period.

Ask the dealer about the details of the warranty on cars you are considering, and get the warranty offer in writing. Warranties must specify which parts of the car are covered, for how long, by whom (the dealer or the manufacturer), and what you are required to do to keep the warranty in force and to obtain service. When comparing warranties, remember that the reliability of the car (a factor you may be able to predict with the help of data from auto and consumer magazines) is just as important as the quality of warranty coverage.

Some new car dealers offer an extension on the warranty in the form of an **extended service contract** through the manufacturer, the dealer, or an outside firm. The warranty is included in the price of the car; a service contract costs extra. Before buying an extended service contract, read it carefully and consider the following questions:

- What is the difference between the coverage under the warranty and under the service contract? Service contracts usually duplicate warranty coverage during the first year or two—if you decide to buy one, it may be wise to purchase the contract *not* when you buy your car but a year or two later.

- What repairs are covered? Extended service contracts often have numerous limitations and exclusions that may significantly lessen their value.

- What is the cost? Are there additional fees and deductibles?

- How long does the contract last, and what is the cancellation and refund policy?

2. Inspect the body, paint, and trim for flaws. Check door, hood, and trunk alignment. Check the interior to make sure upholstery and trim fit properly.

3. Double-check your invoice against the window sticker. Is everything you paid for included?

4. Review the owner's manual with the salesperson, and make sure other drivers in the family read it later.

5. Ask the salesperson to demonstrate the function of each knob and button. Ask about settings for complicated electronic options.

Auto Brokers

If you can't face the prospect of trekking from dealer to dealer in search of the best new car bargain, an auto broker may offer an attractive alternative. A broker acts as middleman between you and the dealers, locating the car you want and the dealer willing to sell it at the lowest price. Some "full-service" brokers may also arrange financing, sell your old car, or perform just about any related service. There may be no charge for a broker's services, or you may be required to pay a fee as high as several hundred dollars.

Because they buy in volume, auto brokers may be able to negotiate a lower price than you could obtain on your own. But before using a broker, observe these precautions:

- Ask how long the company has been in business. If the broker offers to buy the car from the dealer and then sell it to you, make sure the broker has a state dealership license.
- Ask for references from several recent customers, and check them.
- Ask the local Better Business Bureau for a complaint report.

6. If you discover a problem, make an appointment to have it corrected as soon as possible.

BUYING A USED CAR

Each year, according to the Federal Trade Commission (FTC), Americans spend about $85 billion to buy more than 17 million used cars. They choose a used car for its indisputable advantages: low price (about $8,000 less on average than a new car), slower depreciation, and greater flexibility in cost and availability. Of course, along with these advantages, there are certain risks: A used car may have major mechanical or structural problems, replacement parts may be hard to find, the seller may misrepresent the car's mileage or condition, and warranty coverage may not be available.

The smart shopper's challenge is to make the most of a used car's advantages and minimize its risks.

Preshopping Homework

Before launching your search for a good deal in a used car, spend some time considering many of the same questions that would apply to a new car purchase: how you'll use the vehicle; how long you plan to keep it; the size, style, and appearance you need or prefer; and your budget for the purchase as well as for operating and maintenance/repair costs.

What style auto suits your driving needs and budget—two-door, four-door, sedan, station wagon, compact? Ask friends about their experiences and satisfaction with their older cars—would they buy the car again? Check auto and consumer magazines and books for information on the reliability records of various models. The annual *Consumer Reports Books Guide to Used Cars** can be particularly helpful in pointing out potential repair problems and trouble spots. The monthly *Consumer Guide® Used Cars Rating Guide*** also gives photos of each auto and price ranges keyed to the condition of the car. In addition, the National Highway Traffic Safety Administration (NHTSA) operates a toll-free hotline (800–424–9393) through which you can find out if a particular vehicle has ever been recalled for safety defects.

To help you investigate and compare prices, several publications are available which give approximate dealer and consumer prices for many models. Your library, bookstore, bank, or insurance agent should have a copy of the monthly *N.A.D.A. Official Used Car Guide****, monthly *Kelley Blue Book*****, or quarterly *Old Car/Truck Red Book******. Also check your local newspaper's ads for an overview of current used car prices in your area. Comparing prices of similar makes and models can give you an idea of which seller offers the best deals.

There are a number of sources to consider when looking for a used car:

- **New car dealers** often sell the best of the cars they acquire through trade-in deals. Those cars may cost more than used cars available from other sellers, but they are more likely to have undergone necessary repairs in the dealer's service department. They're also likely to come with a limited warranty from the dealer.

- **Used car dealers** generally sell vehicles that have seen a bit more use and abuse than those on the new car dealer's lot. You'll pay less, but the car is less likely to have received needed repairs. Used car dealers also may offer limited warranties.

- Some **car rental agencies** sell used rental cars; these are generally 9 to 12 months old and have been driven less than 25,000 miles. The company usually can provide the car's maintenance and repair records, and may offer a limited warranty. But mileage on rental cars is often relatively high on a per-year basis, and the cars may suffer from the wear and tear that comes from use by a variety of drivers.

- **Bank and loan companies** sometimes sell repossessed cars to pay off defaulted loans. Quality varies from car to car. But since the vehicle is being sold not because the owner wanted to dispose of it but to

*Consumers Union, Mount Vernon, NY.
**Publications International, Ltd., Lincolnwood, IL.
***National Automobile Dealers Used Car Guide Co., McLean, VA.
****Kelley Blue Book, Irvine, CA.
*****Maclean Hunter Market Reports, Inc., Chicago, IL.

The FTC "Buyers Guide"

Under the FTC's Used Car Rule, all sellers of used cars (except private owners) are required to place a large sticker called a "Buyers Guide" in the window of their used cars, light-duty vans, and light-duty trucks. The Buyers Guide tells you whether the vehicle comes with a warranty and, if so, which systems are covered, how long coverage applies, and what percentage of repair costs the dealer will pay.

The Buyers Guide also alerts you when a car is being sold with implied warranties only or with no warranty at all ("as is"). About half of all used cars sold by dealers come with no warranty. The dealer has no further responsibility for a car sold "as is" once the sale is complete and you drive off the lot.

Under most state laws, if the car does not come with a written warranty but is also not sold "as is," it is covered by an **implied warranty.** Depending on your state's particular laws, the implied warranty may guarantee that the car will run or that it will live up to the seller's assurance that it is fit for a particular purpose, such as pulling a trailer. Your state consumer protection office can provide more information about the specifics of implied warranty coverage.

recover the amount due on a loan, it's possible to get a good price on a good car.

- **Private owners** usually sell their cars through newspaper ads. It can be time-consuming to comb a sea of clunkers in search of a pearl, and warranty and repair services are not available. On the other hand, you may find a well-maintained car selling for less money than you would pay a dealer.

If you buy a used car from a private owner, ask for the car's maintenance and repair records and, if the seller is the first owner, for records of the original purchase. Also check the title to make sure the person selling the car is the rightful owner.

If you are considering buying from a dealer, check out the dealer's reputation and reliability first. Ask for the names and numbers of several previous customers and contact them to find out how they were treated *after* the sale and whether the car was as reliable as the dealer represented it to be. Also call the local Better Business Bureau for a complaint report.

Checking It Out

When you are judging the quality of a used car, try to inspect the car in daylight and in good weather. Bring a friend along, if possible, to help you make a thorough appraisal.

It's impractical to expect perfection in a secondhand car. Be willing to compromise on minor problems that you can correct yourself, but at the same time don't let yourself be talked out of focusing on more serious defects. Also be alert: Some sellers are adept at masking problems, and a steam-cleaned engine and gleaming new paint job are no indication of the quality of the machinery beneath. Finally, it is essential to take the car on a road test before committing yourself to a purchase. If you are not allowed to test-drive the car, *don't buy it.* Take your friend along when you make the road test; if the dealer insists on accompanying you, do the driving yourself and ask the seller to sit in the back.

Following is a checklist of items to look for **and** look out for when evaluating a used car.

On-the-Lot Checklist

☐ **Body.** Look for rust, particularly at the bottom of fenders, around lights and bumpers, on splash panels, under doors, in the wheel wells, and under trunk carpeting. Small blisters may indicate future rust sites. Check for paint that doesn't quite match, gritty surfaces, and paint overspray on chrome—all possible signs of a new paint job masking body problems. Look for cracks, heat-discolored areas, and loose bumpers—warning signs of a past accident.

A welded seam may mean that the car is actually a body shop's "rebuilt" creation from salvaged parts. Look for welded seams in the trunk and on the floor; bumps under the paint around the windshield or rear window or between doors may indicate a rough welded seam beneath the paint.

☐ **Tires.** New tires on a car with less than 25,000 miles may indicate that the odometer has been turned back. Uneven wear on the front tires usually indicates either bad alignment or front suspension damage. Don't forget to check the condition of the spare tire.

☐ **Battery.** Look on the sticker for the guarantee date. A battery generally needs to be replaced after 25,000 miles.

☐ **Doors, windows, trunk lid.** Look for close fit and ease of opening and closing. A door that fits unevenly may indicate that the car was involved in a collision.

☐ **Window glass and lights.** Look for hairline cracks and tiny holes.

☐ **Tailpipe.** Black, gummy soot in the tailpipe can mean worn rings or bad valves—and expensive repairs.

☐ **Shock absorbers.** Lean hard on a corner of the car and release; if the car keeps rocking up and down, the shocks may need replacing.

☐ **Fluids.** Oil that is whitish or has white bubbles can be a sign of major mechanical problems. Also check the radiator fluid; it shouldn't look rusty. With the engine idling, check the transmission fluid; it shouldn't smell rancid or look dark brown. Check for leaks and stains under the car, on the underside of the engine, and around hoses and valve covers.

☐ **Lights and mechanical parts.** Make sure all headlights, taillights, brake lights, backup lights, and directional signals work properly. Try out the radio, heater, air conditioner, and windshield wipers.

☐ **Interior.** Check the upholstery for major wear and tear; don't forget to look under floor mats and seat covers. Check the adjustability of seats, and make sure seat belts work. Check the steering wheel; unlocked, with the engine off, it should have no more than two inches of play.

Lots of wear on the driver's seat of a car with low mileage may indicate tampering with the odometer. So may heavy wear on the brake and accelerator pedals. A musty smell could mean that the car was damaged in a flood or that rain leaks in.

Road Test Checklist

☐ The car should start easily and without excessive noise. Once the car has warmed up, listen for engine noise as you drive; unusual sounds may be signs of major trouble.

☐ Drive over rough road surfaces; watch for unusual vibrations, noises, or odors.

☐ Make several stops and starts, at varying but safe rates of speed, on a clear, level road surface. The car should accelerate without hesitation and should brake without grabbing, vibrating, or pulling to one side. When you step firmly on the brake pedal, it should feel firm, not spongy.

☐ Have your friend look at the exhaust while you let the car decelerate from 45 mph to about 15 mph, then step hard on the gas. Blue smoke may mean worn rings or valves; white smoke may indicate a cracked block.

☐ Try turning at various speeds. Too much sway or stiffness can mean bad shocks and/or front end problems. Turn the wheel all the way from one side to the other; power steering should feel smooth, with little or no squealing.

☐ Check the wheels for "dog-tracking"—have your friend stand behind the car as you slowly drive away; if the back wheels head slightly to one side, the car has major frame problems.

☐ Look for these signs of odometer tampering: white lines between the numbers, two or more numbers that don't line up, vibration of the $1/_{10}$ mile number while the car is moving.

Finally, take the car you are considering buying to a reliable repair shop or auto diagnostic center, and have the mechanic give it a once-over. You'll have to pay for this service, but the $30 or $50 you invest up front may save you many more dollars down the road. Ask for a written estimate of the costs to repair any problems the mechanic finds, and use that estimate as a bargaining chip when you make your offer.

Signing the Contract

Take your time and read both sides of all pages of any contract before you sign. Make sure that all the blanks have been filled in, that all the salesperson's verbal promises are included, and that the type of warranty that comes with the car is spelled out. If you are required to make a deposit, ask whether it is refundable and under what circumstances, and make sure that information is also included in the contract.

Most state laws require dealers in used cars to provide the buyer with a signed statement verifying the mileage at the time of sale. If you have questions about odometer fraud, or if you've already bought a car and have proof that the odometer was tampered with, call the NHTSA's hotline: 800–424–9393.

TO BUY OR TO LEASE?

In the wake of the 1986 Tax Reform Act, which phases out the tax deductions for interest on car payments, many consumers are turning for the first time to leasing rather than buying their new cars. When you lease a car, it remains the property of the leasing company, or "lessor." You make monthly payments for the use of the car over a specified period of time, and at the end of the lease, the car may be returned to the lessor.

Auto Equity Promotions

If you run into trouble maintaining your regular payments on a car you have bought or leased, you may be tempted to respond to an ad that promises to help by assuming your payments. Auto equity promoters operate by taking possession of a car and continuing payments for the owner or lessee after selling or subleasing the car to a third party.

There are better ways to solve your credit problems. In several states, it is illegal to assume a sales contract or to sublease without the written permission of the lienholder or leasing company. Further, if the auto equity promoter fails to keep up the payments, your car may be repossessed; your credit rating would be damaged and you would still owe any balance due on the car.

If you are having credit problems, see "Dealing with Debt," *Credit and Installment Buying*, pages 136-37. And steer clear of promoters who offer a "quick fix" for car payment problems.

Monthly payments are generally lower for leases than for auto loans, and often no down payment is required. Those lower payments and initial costs appeal to consumers who find that they can lease a more upscale car than they could afford to buy. And since most cars quickly decline in value (as opposed to investments such as a home which generally increase in value), a financial rule of thumb—"Own an appreciating asset, lease a depreciating asset"—seems to apply.

Of course, leasing has its less favorable aspects as well. Over the long run, the total cost of an auto lease may be roughly equal to or even slightly greater than the cost of a loan, and your payments buy neither equity nor ownership—at the end of the lease, you do not own the car. Further, you may be required to pay unexpected end-of-lease costs and penalties. Finally, it can be difficult to understand lease agreements and to compare offers from various companies to make sure you are getting the best deal.

Which option—leasing or buying—is right for you? Following is a checklist of considerations and an explanation of costs that can help you make that choice. And if you decide in favor of leasing, the shopping tips on pages 44–45 can help you negotiate the most favorable terms.

You Should Consider Leasing If:	You Should Consider Buying If:
You trade in your car every two or three years	You plan to keep your car four or more years
You do not have the cash assets for a down payment on an auto loan	You drive more than 15,000 miles per year (see page 46)
You cannot (or prefer not to) borrow money	You want to establish a credit rating
	You plan to move during the lease term (see page 45)

If you use your car for business purposes, certain tax benefits may apply whether you lease or buy. You may want to discuss leasing with your accountant or tax adviser if taxes will play a major role in your decision.

The Costs of Leasing

There are two types of lease agreements: the closed-end lease (sometimes called a "net" or "walkaway" lease) and the open-end lease (sometimes called a "finance" lease).

Under a **closed-end lease**, your responsibilities end when you return the car to the leasing company at the end of the lease term. With an **open-end lease**, you have additional obligations: If the appraised value of the car when you return it is less than the amount that was estimated in the original agreement (its "estimated residual value"), you may have to pay all or part of the difference. Under the federal Consumer Leasing Act, that **end-of-lease payment** is limited in most cases to an amount no greater than three times the average monthly payment. Some open-end contracts also give you the right to a refund if the car is appraised or sold for *more* than its estimated residual value.

Open-end leases are most commonly offered to businesses. However, if you are faced with a choice, keep in mind that with an open-end lease, monthly payments are usually lower but there is an added risk of a higher *total* cost.

Your dealer, leasing company, and bank or other lender can help you calculate the total cost for either a closed-end or an open-end lease and compare it with the costs of purchasing a car on credit. On the purchasing side of the column, be sure to factor in all the costs of ownership, including the down payment on an auto loan, the lender's finance charge, and additional expenses such as insurance, maintenance, repairs, taxes, licensing, etc. Also take into account the amount you might realize on the eventual resale of the car you own. To help you fill in the leasing side of the column and make a complete and accurate comparison, following is a look at the various costs involved in leasing.

Initial costs

- **Prepayment of the first monthly payment and possibly the last.**
- **Capitalized cost reduction.** Like a down payment on a car purchase, this reduces your monthly payments. Capitalized cost reduction is generally optional, and the amount you pay is usually up to you.
- **Sales tax, title, registration, and license fees.** Depending on the terms of the agreement you negotiate, the lessor may absorb some or all of these fees. They are sometimes added into the monthly payments.
- **Insurance.** Some lessors provide insurance; if not, you must buy it on your own.

Continuing costs

- **Periodic payments.** The lessor determines the price of the car, then subtracts its estimated residual value (see above). Profit is added in, and the total is divided into equal monthly installments.
- **Repairs and maintenance.** You may be entirely responsible for these costs, or the lessor may assume all or part of them, often in exchange for an additional monthly fee. In most cases, the vehicle manufacturer provides a warranty, and the leasing company may offer its own warranty. Many lessors also offer extended service plans. (For a discussion of warranties and extended service plans, see page 35.)

Final costs

- **Excess mileage charge.** With a closed-end lease, the contract commonly specifies a mileage allowance or limitation. If you exceed the mileage limit, you usually have to pay a penalty. In open-end leases, any excess mileage normally is reflected in the final appraised value of the car.
- **Excess wear charge.** You are responsible for any damage beyond normal wear and tear.
- **Disposition charge.** Some lessors require you to pay the costs of preparing the returned vehicle for sale.
- **Default penalties.** Varying costs and penalties will be imposed if you default on your lease obligations.
- **End-of-lease payment.** Applies only to open-end leases; see page 43.

Shopping for an Auto Lease

The programs and financial arrangements offered by different leasing companies can vary as much as car models themselves. Keep the following checklist in mind as you analyze and compare deals:

1. Remember that it is just as important to negotiate a good price on a leased car as on a car you purchase. (See pages 32–33 for bargaining tips.)
2. Get estimates from at least three different leasing companies and compare both the total price and terms of each lease. Ask friends for recommendations on leasing companies they have used, and contact the local BBB for a reliability report on each company.
3. Since your monthly payments are based in part on the car's estimated value at the end of the lease term, you can save money by selecting a car that does not decrease in value quickly. The annual *Complete Car Cost Guide** is one good source that provides anticipated resale values for hundreds of current makes and models.
4. If the leasing company offers insurance, shop around and compare estimates for the same coverage from several insurance companies. (Also see "Auto Insurance," pages 48–52.)
5. To be sure you are comparing apples to apples, ask the following questions and compare the totals of *all* costs in the deals offered by various leasing companies. Remember that many of the charges discussed here are negotiable—most lenders will drop or absorb at least some extraneous fees.
   - How much is the initial payment and what does it cover? How much is the monthly payment and what additional fees does it

*IntelliChoice, Inc., San Jose, CA.

include? What is the total amount of all lease payments, including initial costs?

- Is insurance coverage available? If so, what coverage at what cost? If not, what private coverage is needed to satisfy lease requirements?
- Who is responsible for repairs and maintenance? What, if any, warranty coverage applies? Does the warranty extend through the term of the lease? If an extended service contract is offered, what does it cover and what does it cost?
- With an open-end lease, what would be the maximum charge you would have to pay if the vehicle were worth less at the end of the lease than the estimated residual value specified in the contract?
- What are the mileage limitations and excess mileage charges? What is the default charge? The disposition charge?
- What costs would be involved if you moved to another city, state, or country during the lease term? (Some leasing companies will increase the monthly payments or convert the lease to a loan if you move.)
- What are the penalties and costs if you end the lease early? (Some leasing companies charge **prepayment penalties** ranging all the way from $100 to $2,000–plus. Also ask the lessor to calculate the **early-termination cost** at the end of each year of the contract; the early-termination cost is the difference between the amount you would still owe on the contract at the time the lease was broken and the car's then-estimated value.)
- Is a stolen or wrecked car considered an early termination of the lease? (If so, your insurance would cover the car's current value but you would still be liable for penalties and the early-termination cost.)
- Are there any financial advantages in extending or renewing the lease? Do you have the option of purchasing the vehicle at the end of the lease? If so, what would be the purchase price or the formula used to calculate that price?

The Lease Agreement

The lease is an important legal document that defines your rights and liabilities in connection with using and paying for the vehicle. Before you sign the contract, make sure you understand and accept all terms and conditions. Be particularly aware of the following:

- Leases are usually written for a term of five years. But for many people, one of the attractions of leasing is driving a new car every two or three years. Also, a longer lease term can mean higher maintenance costs for an aging car. *Don't accept a lease for a term longer than you plan to drive the car*—penalties and charges for early termination of a lease can be substantial.

- Make sure the mileage allowance in your lease fits your driving patterns. Leases commonly stipulate a 15,000 to 18,000 per year mileage limit, with excess mileage charges of generally 8¢ to 12¢ per mile. Making slightly higher monthly payments for a higher mileage allowance is almost always less expensive than paying excess mileage penalties.
- Make sure the contract is very specific about what constitutes "normal wear and tear" on the vehicle, and about repair and maintenance requirements.

Renting a Car

The National Association of Attorneys General guidelines governing rental car advertising make it somewhat easier to shop for the best rental car rates today than it might have been just a few years ago. Under these guidelines, companies are required to include *all* charges and penalty fees in the rates they advertise. But unless you know what to expect at the rental counter, you may still find yourself paying more than you need to. Here are some tips that can help end some of the confusion—and save you money in the process:

1. Do your comparison-shopping ahead of time by calling several rental car companies to ask about prices and terms.
2. If you are flying to your destination and then renting a car, you may pay less for renting from a company inside the terminal than one outside the airport property.
3. If you are planning a long trip, ask for an unlimited-free-mileage plan. Otherwise, you may end up paying a high per-mile fee for exceeding a set mileage limit.
4. Advertised specials often offer appealing rates, but they generally apply only to a particular car, time, and place. To "lock in" a special rate, reserve a car in advance by phone, and get a reservation number and the phone agent's name. With some companies, making an advance reservation can itself qualify you for a discount rate.
5. Fees and penalty charges vary from company to company. Ask for and compare each company's policy regarding the following:
   - **Additional drivers** (registration of a second driver).
   - **Young drivers** (some companies charge drivers under age 25 an additional $5 or $10 a day).
   - **Refueling** (refilling the gas tank if you return the car with less than a full tank).
   - **Late returns** (returning the car later than the time you agreed).

- **One-way rentals** (If you return the car at a location other than the original rental site, you'll usually pay a drop-off charge. Generally, the more miles between sites, the higher the charge.)

6. A handful of states require rental car companies to absorb the costs of insuring their vehicles; everywhere else, when you rent a car, you'll be offered insurance. The most common option offered is the collision damage waiver (CDW), which is technically not insurance but absolves you of financial responsibility if the car is damaged in an accident. Without this coverage, you might be liable for up to the full market value of a totaled car. But the CDW is expensive, often costing about $10 a day. Do you need rental car insurance? Keep these facts in mind:

- If you use your credit card to pay for the rental, the card issuer may provide coverage; check your credit card agreement before renting a car.

- Also check your personal auto insurance policy. About 60 percent of policies already cover rentals—but check with your insurance agent to make sure your coverage is sufficient, especially if the rental car company holds drivers liable for theft and vandalism as well as accidents. Remember that your personal policy usually won't cover you if you're renting the car on a business trip. And be aware that if you are compelled to put through a claim on a rental car with your insurance company, you'll probably have to pay for damages out of your own pocket while your insurer is processing the claim, and it's possible that your auto insurance rates may rise.

- You may also be offered these additional forms of insurance when you rent a car:

  Extended liability options increase your liability coverage for accidental injuries, often up to $1 million, and provide uninsured and underinsured motorist coverage. **Personal accident coverage** provides life and medical insurance for the driver and passengers. **Personal effects insurance** covers the personal items in the car.

  Again, these forms of insurance may simply duplicate coverage you already own, through your auto, homeowners, or health policies. Before renting a car, check with your insurance agent to see what your personal policies cover and whether you need additional insurance. If you are a frequent renter, you may want to consider revising your personal insurance to fully cover you when you rent a car.

AUTO INSURANCE

As the costs of health care and car repairs continue to rise, so does the price tag on auto insurance. Knowing how much of which type of coverage you really need can help you cut the cost of insuring your car.

There are six basic areas of auto insurance coverage:

Bodily injury liability pays for your legal defense and for claims for which you are legally liable if you or anyone else driving your car injures or kills someone. You and your family are also covered when driving someone else's car with permission.

Property damage liability pays the costs of legal defense and claims if your car damages someone else's property. Coverage also applies when you or a family member is driving someone else's car.

Medical payments insurance pays medical and funeral expenses resulting from accidental injuries to you and any passengers in your car, regardless of fault. Coverage also applies if you or a family member is injured by a car while walking or riding in another car.

Uninsured motorist coverage pays for bodily injury to you or a family member caused by an uninsured motorist or a hit-and-run driver. A companion coverage, **underinsured motorist coverage**, pays your medical bills when they exceed the amount covered under another insured driver's bodily injury liability limits.

Collision insurance pays for damage to your car resulting from any type of collision or from turning over.

Comprehensive insurance pays the costs when your car is stolen or damaged by fire, flood, vandalism, or another specified peril.

How Much Coverage Do You Need?

The legal minimum for required auto insurance varies from state to state. Your insurance agent or your state Department of Insurance can explain the specific requirements that affect you. The following general guidelines can help you decide how much of which types of coverage you need within the limits prescribed by law.

Liability coverage

Bodily injury and property damage liability coverage are usually sold together and stated in three figures. For example, a policy with 100/300/50 liability coverage would pay a maximum of $100,000 to any one person you injured in a single auto accident, $300,000 for the total bodily injury when more than one person was involved in the accident, and $50,000 per accident for all property damage claims. Thus, if four people were injured in one accident, the policy would pay each person damages no greater than $100,000, with the total of all payments not to

No-Fault Insurance

The intent of no-fault insurance is to eliminate expensive and time-consuming lawsuits that determine which of the parties involved in an accident was at fault and thus which party's insurance company must pay damages. In states with a no-fault law, policyholders look to their *own* insurance company for reimbursement of financial losses, regardless of who was at fault. However, no-fault laws vary considerably from state to state in the amount and type of benefits insurers must pay and in the conditions that allow for lawsuits. Check with your insurance agent or state Department of Insurance to determine whether your state has a no-fault law, how it works, and how its provisions affect your insurance needs.

exceed $300,000. Many companies also will write a "single limit" policy, which pays one total amount that is allocated as needed in a specific accident. For example, $300,000 of single-limit coverage could pay $300,000 in personal injury and property damage to one injured person.

Most states have financial responsibility laws under which a person involved in an automobile accident may be required to furnish proof of financial responsibility, usually in the form of automobile liability insurance or, in some areas, another approved form of security. Because health care costs, auto repair bills, and the amounts in verdicts awarded by juries are high and rising, most insurance experts recommend that you buy *more* liability coverage than your state's law requires. A minimum of 100/300/50 is often suggested. People with large assets to protect should consider buying even more coverage through an "umbrella" policy, which can provide as much as $1 million or more in liability coverage, often at surprisingly affordable rates.

Medical payments coverage
States without no-fault laws usually do not require medical payments coverage, and if you and your family are adequately protected by a health insurance policy, you may not need it. Some insurance experts, however, recommend buying a small amount of additional coverage to protect nonfamily passengers in your car.

In states that *do* have no-fault insurance laws, auto owners are required to buy personal injury protection (PIP), which offers a comprehensive package of medical benefits, covering such expenses as wages lost by an injured person and some funeral expenses. Some states allow policyholders to save on their PIP premium by "coordinating" benefits with their health insurance plan, making the health policy the primary provider of medical payments.

Uninsured motorist coverage

Your state may not require you to carry uninsured motorist coverage, but most experts agree that it is an important part of an auto insurance package. As premiums continue to rise, more people decide to drive without insurance; it's up to you to purchase the personal injury protection that they should have. Also consider adding underinsured motorist coverage, which in many policies will bring the other insured party's coverage up to the limits of your own policy, as long as that does not exceed $100,000/$300,000 of bodily injury liability. The combined cost of both forms of coverage usually only comes to a small portion of your total premium.

Collision and comprehensive insurance

If you are still paying off the cost of your car, the lender will probably require you to carry collision and comprehensive insurance. But if you own an older car with little cash value, the costs of these two forms of coverage may be more than they are worth. The amount the insurance company would pay in a claim related to damage or theft of your car is limited to its resale value (or "book" value) minus the deductible. With an older car, that payment might not be sufficient to cover the costs of repair or replacement—and the premiums you pay for those reduced benefits might still account for as much as 40 percent of your total auto insurance premium.

In deciding whether to buy collision and comprehensive coverage, consider the age and value of your car and how much risk you are willing and able to assume. Some experts recommend dropping collision once your car has lost one-third of its original value. Some suggest dropping comprehensive at the same time, while others recommend retaining comprehensive, since it provides broader coverage, including protection against theft, at a lower cost. All agree, however, that if you retain one or both forms of coverage, there is still one good way to cut your premiums: Collision and comprehensive insurance are usually sold with a deductible, which often ranges from $100 to $1,000 for collision and $50 to $500 for comprehensive. Selecting a high deductible—and absorbing modest repair bills yourself—can mean considerable savings.

It Pays to Shop Around

Auto insurers determine the rate you will pay by considering your age, sex, marital status, and driving record, and the same characteristics of other covered family members. They also look at the record of claims in the geographical area where your car is usually kept, whether the car is primarily used for business, commuting, or pleasure, and the damage and theft records on cars of the same make and model.

The insurance rates of companies doing business in your state are reviewed and approved by a state regulatory agency. Even so, there are often surprising differences in the rates charged by various insurers. In some cities, the cost of the same coverage for the same individual varies by more than 100 percent! Wherever you live, shopping around may save you hundreds of dollars.

It's a good idea to ask for a quote from at least four different insurance companies. Make sure you are comparing quotes for the same kind of policy, with the same limits and deductibles. And as you compare rates, keep the following tips in mind:

1. Compare service, too. Ask how long it takes the company to settle a typical claim and how claims are processed. Are you required to obtain one or several estimates for repairs or does the insurer have its own claims service center? Does the company settle undisputed parts of a claim without waiting for resolution of contested portions? Under what circumstances could your rates be increased or your coverage canceled? (Also see "Your Insurance Provider," *Insurance*, pages 236–37.)

2. Ask about the availability of discounts, which may include but not be limited to the following cases:

   □ Multipolicy holders—persons who insure two or more cars with the same company

   □ Drivers with good driving records, or those who carpool or use their car very infrequently

   □ Young drivers who pass approved driver-education courses, who maintain good grades in school, or who are resident students at a college more than 100 miles from home

   □ Cars equipped with air bags, automatic seat belts, or antitheft devices

   □ Nondrinkers or nonsmokers

3. The type of car you own can have a major effect on the premiums you pay—insurers consider the high-powered sports car a far greater risk than the family station wagon. Although most people overlook the added expense in pursuit of their "dream" car, it can be a wise precaution to ask your insurance agent what collision and comprehensive coverage would cost on the car you want to buy.

Filing a Claim

Here's what to do if you are involved in an auto accident or if your car is damaged or stolen:

> If you have a poor driving record or have not been driving long enough to establish a good record, you may be considered a "high risk" and have difficulty buying insurance through regular channels. In such a case, you may be referred to a state-run insurance pool, known as an "assigned risk" pool, where the cost of insurance is higher. In some states, "substandard" or "nonstandard" insurance companies will also cover high-risk drivers, but they often charge even higher rates than the assigned risk plan. However you obtain high-risk coverage, you generally can requalify for regular insurance after maintaining a spotless driving record for a period of time.

1. First, call for medical help if anyone is injured. In a serious accident, call the police and do not leave the scene until they arrive. Note the reporting officer's name and badge number, and ask how to obtain a copy of the official accident report.
2. Get the other driver's name, address, phone number, driver's license number, insurance company name, and policy number. Also get the names and phone numbers of any witnesses. Write down the date and location of the accident, weather conditions, traffic signs or signals, and anything else you feel is relevant. If a camera is available, photograph the scene.
3. Phone your own insurance company as soon as possible, regardless of who was at fault.
4. Keep a record of any expenses you incur as a result of the accident; check your policy and ask your agent if they are reimbursable.
5. If you cannot find a reliable shop willing to repair your car for the price your insurance company has agreed to pay, notify the company and ask for a higher settlement. Do not accept an inadequate amount or sign away your rights to additional claims.
6. Keep a complete file of all paperwork relating to the claim.
7. Be aware that if you have collision insurance and the other driver was at fault according to a police report, you may be entitled to a refund of your deductible, as long as your own insurance company pays for your repairs and then is able to collect from the other driver's insurer.

CAR REPAIRS

Getting your car fixed can be a tricky business. While most mechanics are able and honest, car repair foul-ups and rip-offs are all too common. How can you be certain you will be dealt with fairly and competently? Fortunately, even if you know little or nothing about cars, there are some steps you can take to be reasonably sure of good service.

Finding a Repair Shop

Repair sources include the following:

New car dealers. Costs tend to be high, and it can take weeks to schedule an appointment. But mechanics are generally well trained and know your specific make and model thoroughly.

Specialty shops and franchised dealers. The focus is on a specific system, such as mufflers or transmissions. Prices are generally fair and service fast and convenient, but mechanics may not know much more about your car than the system that is their particular specialty.

Chain stores. Large retailers sometimes have auto service departments, where service is usually fast and convenient but, like that of specialty shops, limited.

Independent garages and service stations. Prices can be competitive, a variety of services is usually available, and customer satisfaction on average tends to be relatively high. It can also be easier to develop a one-on-one relationship with a mechanic. But parts and possibly labor may come with no warranty.

Diagnostic centers. Advanced monitoring equipment is used to diagnose complex problems or simply to perform periodic checkups. Some diagnostic centers are completely independent, while others are connected with a repair shop.

Whatever type of facility you choose to use for car repairs, the following tips can help you find an honest, skilled mechanic:

1. Ask friends and coworkers where they take their cars. Your auto insurance agent and auto parts store may also be able to recommend reliable local shops.

2. Visit several prospects—look for a busy facility with a clean, organized work area and mechanics whose attitude is professional and who are willing to listen.

3. Find out about the credentials of the mechanics employed by the repair shop. Mechanics certified through the National Institute for Automotive Service Excellence (NIASE),* for example, have been tested for competence in one or more of eight categories of repair. Look for a notice of ASE certification on the plaques on the shop's walls or the patches on mechanics' clothing. Or ask whether the shop employs certified mechanics and in what repair areas they are certified.

4. In many states, the American Automobile Association (AAA) approves specific repair shops. Strict standards regarding equipment, mechanic qualifications, and customer satisfaction are used to determine whether

*For a free list of repair facilities that employ ASE-certified mechanics, send a stamped, self-addressed envelope to: ASE, 13505 Dulles Technology Drive, Herndon, VA 22071.

a facility qualifies for AAA approval. The AAA also investigates and arbitrates complaints regarding approved shops.

5. Call your local Better Business Bureau for reliability and complaint reports on the service shops you are considering.

At the Shop

Follow these tips and precautions when you take your car in for repairs:

1. Write down your name, daytime phone number, and a specific, thorough description of your car's symptoms, and give that information to the service manager or mechanic. *Don't request a specific repair*—let the shop do the diagnosis. If a repair order is filled out, read it over before signing it and make sure it completely and accurately describes your car's problem.

2. Whenever possible, discuss your service needs with the mechanic who will be doing the work rather than with a service writer or other middleman. If your car's symptoms are difficult to describe, request that the mechanic take a test drive with you.

3. Ask for a specific cost estimate of the repairs. If you are told that the car must be examined first, ask the mechanic to give you an estimate of the cost of the inspection and then phone you with estimated repair costs before work is done. Make certain the repair order specifies that no repairs or replacements are to be made without your authorization.

4. If you disagree with the mechanic's diagnosis or think an estimate is too high, remember that as long as the car is operating, you can always take it down the street to another garage. You'll pay for the second opinion, but you may save yourself the expense of unnecessary or overpriced repairs.

5. When you pick up your car, ask the service manager or mechanic to explain all work done. Don't hesitate to question anything you don't understand. Ask to see old parts that were replaced, and ask the mechanic to point out any major new parts that were installed. If unauthorized work was performed on your car or if you are charged substantially more than the original estimate, *complain*.

6. Get and keep a copy of your repair bill, which should itemize all parts by description, number, and cost, and show the cost of labor for each repair. If any of the work was covered by a warranty, make sure those charges are deducted from your bill.

7. Ask for a written guarantee or warranty of labor and replacement parts. A written warranty should clearly state what it covers and for how long, any exclusions or conditions, what your responsibilities are for operation and maintenance to keep coverage in effect, how to obtain repair work under the warranty, and service provisions if the car fails out of town.

8. Ask for a test drive before paying for repairs. If problems remain, take the car back and request satisfaction.

Protect Yourself

These final tips can help minimize both the costs of car repairs and the possibility of getting taken when you take your car in for service:

1. Familiarize yourself with your owner's manual and warranty. By following the manufacturer's recommendations for periodic inspection and maintenance, you can improve your car's performance, increase its fuel efficiency, and extend its life. The manual may contain advice that can help you solve some common problems yourself. And the manual and warranty will tell you how to follow the manufacturer's requirements to keep the warranty in effect for the full term, and whether specific repairs are covered.

2. Keep a notebook or other record of car service, with copies of repair orders, as a ready reference. If you do some maintenance yourself, note the date and the car's mileage and keep receipts for oil, parts, etc. These records will remind you and your mechanic when maintenance is due. They can also be a valuable aid if there is ever a question of whether the car has been maintained in accordance with warranty requirements.

3. Be suspicious of ads offering specific repair services at a very low price. Some unethical shops advertise unrealistically low prices that do not cover additional parts and labor needed to do an adequate repair job; others may lure customers with low prices, then try to sell expensive, possibly unnecessary, repairs.

4. Before starting out on a long road trip, make sure your car is in good working condition. If you need emergency road service, follow the tips above and these additional precautions:

   • If possible, check a phone directory and have your car towed to a local dealer. If you belong to an auto club, it may be able to provide recommendations of reliable local service shops.

   • If you are towed to a shop about which you know nothing, call the local Better Business Bureau for a complaint report before authorizing work.

- If you are suspicious of the shop's diagnosis or estimate, it may be worthwhile paying to have your car towed elsewhere for a second opinion.
- If your car is under warranty, ask the shop for a statement indicating the circumstances and necessity for repairs, an itemized repair order, and, if possible, the return of defective parts in the boxes that held the new ones. Present all these items to your dealer as soon as possible to back up your request for reimbursement of repair costs.

BBB AUTO LINE

In 1988, the Better Business Bureau system assisted more than 155,000 consumers with automobile-related complaints through the BBB AUTO LINE. This nationwide program provides mediation and arbitration services to help consumers and auto manufacturers settle complaints out of court. For information and assistance, contact your local BBB.

Bicycles

In 1988, an estimated 88 million people—one out of every three in the U.S.—rode a bicycle for recreation, exercise, transportation, or competition. If you're thinking of joining their ranks, you'll soon discover that the wide variety of bikes on the market today can make it difficult to know where to begin. But if you plan and shop wisely, you'll find the bike that's right for you.

BIKE BASICS

Bicycles have come a long way in the past few years. Each of the four basic types of bicycles described below is suited to a different application; your riding needs and preferences will determine your choice.

Mountain or all-terrain bikes (ATBs) increase in popularity every year, outselling traditional "10-speeds" in some parts of the country. Their straight (as opposed to downturned or "drop") handlebars let riders sit upright, a wide gearing range makes them easier to ride up hills, and their rugged construction can take a good deal of use and abuse. Most mountain bikes can accept load-carrying racks—one reason they're so popular with commuters. Mountain bikes are ideal for riding on off-road trails or packed-dirt roads and for relatively short trips on pavement; their fat tires and the upright sitting position make them less comfortable on longer road rides.

Sport bikes (also called **recreational, road, touring,** or **sport/touring** bikes) are popular for commuting, recreation, fitness, and group cycling. Equipped with drop handlebars and narrow tires, this bike will remind you of the old 10-speed that gathered dust in your basement—although today it's more likely to have 12, 15, or 18 speeds. Sport bikes are relatively comfortable, light, and easy to handle; they're a good choice for most road-riding needs.

City bikes are a cross between sport and mountain bikes. They're a little less nimble than the former and not as well designed for hilly terrain as the latter, but they handle well on most city streets.

Racing bikes are designed for speed, efficiency, and quick handling. With drop handlebars and ultralight, narrow tires, racing bikes are light and responsive; they can also be less comfortable and more fragile than other styles. This is the choice for cyclists who are relatively fit and who like hard, fast riding on the open road.

BUYING THE BIKE

Once you have an idea of which bicycle style suits your needs, how do you choose the bike that will give you the best value for your dollar? A good beginning is to shop around for a dealer even before you start to look at bikes.

Unless you are an expert in the nuts and bolts of bicycle equipment, fit, and service, your selection of a dealer can be even more important than the type or brand of bike you buy. The right dealer will carry a selection of bicycles, equipment, and accessories, and will have a knowledgeable staff that can direct you toward the bike that's most appropriate for your needs and budget, make sure the bike fits you properly and is assembled and adjusted correctly, and provide quality service and maintenance.

To find a good dealer, ask friends where they shop or look at the ads in local sports publications. Visit a couple of different shops and observe how they handle customers. Check the reputation of dealers with cyclists and with your local Better Business Bureau.

There is little difference in the technical quality of bikes in the same price category, according to the Bicycle Institute of America (BIA). Roughly, those categories break down as follows: **Under $300**—A variety of bikes for children or infrequent riders; **$300 to $500**—A good selection of mountain and sport bikes, plus a few racing bikes, for serious recreational cyclists; **$500 to $800**—Lighter, more responsive, more durable bikes for long-distance, competitive, or fitness cyclists; **$800–plus**—"Pro" bikes with top-of-the-line (and costly) components and materials.

Your best bet, once you've narrowed your selection to a particular style and to a few bikes in that style that meet your budget, is simply to take each for a short test drive. Look for the bike that feels most comfortable and manageable.

Finally, one of the most important qualities to consider when selecting a bike is proper fit. Some aspects of fit can be adjusted (seat height, saddle tilt, etc.), while others are an inherent part of the bike's design (such as the length of the top tube, the horizontal bar that runs from the seat to the handlebars). An important element of fit is frame size—you can judge that yourself, says the BIA, by straddling the top tube. When you stand with your feet flat on the ground, there should be one inch (three or four for a mountain bike) between the top tube and your crotch. Again, a good dealer can help you find a bike with the proper fit and can make any necessary adjustments.

EQUIPMENT AND ACCESSORIES

The dealer has assembled and adjusted your bike, but before you take it home there are a few basic accessories you'll need. The first and most critical is a helmet. Each year nearly 70,000 cyclists suffer serious head injuries; three out of four of those injuries could be prevented by helmets. Modern bike helmets are lighter, cooler, and more stylish than they were just a few years ago; costs run from about $40 to $80. Try on a few helmets to find the best fit, and buy one that carries the sticker of either the Snell Memorial Foundation or the American National Standards Institute (ANSI), which indicates that the helmet has met or exceeded strict testing standards.

Other accessories to consider: a frame pump, a patch kit for flat tires, a rack and panniers (bags), toe clips and straps, a water bottle, and cycling gloves.

SHOPPING AND CARE TIPS

1. When buying a bike for a child, fit is particularly important. A bike that's too big will be hard to mount and dismount, hard to control, and *unsafe*. Ask your retailer for guidance in buying the right bike, and be sure to buy your child a helmet, too.

2. If you plan to take your child along on your own bicycle excursions, check with your dealer to make sure the bike you are planning to buy is suitable for a child seat. The seat should be securely attached over the rear wheel of your bike and should have guards to protect a child's feet from getting tangled in the wheel, a high back for support, and a sturdy shoulder harness.

3. Just as you shop for a bike and a dealer, you should also shop for a warranty. Read it carefully before you make a purchase, and don't accept a dealer's verbal interpretation—the written warranty is the final word. Some dealers offer additional warranty services, such as a free 30-day tune-up.

4. A few minutes of simple maintenance often can prevent major mechanical problems. Follow these tips:

   • Keep your bike indoors to prevent rust and corrosion. Wipe away dust and grease periodically.

   • Inspect your tires for cuts and loss of pressure before each ride. Keep them inflated to their recommended pressure.

   • Lubricate your bike's chain every 300 miles or so (more frequently if you ride off-road or in the rain).

   • Check the tightness of bolts and nuts every few weeks.

Burglar Alarm Systems

[Also see *Fire Protection*, pages 156–65.]

In 1987, according to the U.S. Department of Justice, more than 4 million American homes were burglarized and there were 5.6 million attempted or successful unlawful residential entries. Taking nearly any reasonable precautionary step to safeguard your home, such as installing secure locks and fasteners on windows and doors, can lower your odds of becoming a victim. But for real peace of mind, you may be considering the installation of a home security system. According to the National Burglar and Fire Alarm Association, a trade organization representing the alarm industry, case studies indicate that most burglars are scared off by the presence of an alarm system and police studies show that electronically secured homes are five to six times less likely to be burglarized than unprotected homes.

KNOW YOUR OPTIONS

Residential alarms range all the way from $15 magnetic devices that can detect when a door or window is opened to $1,000-plus professionally installed alarm systems that can detect an emergency, set off an alarm, phone for help, and perform a variety of other functions. There are three basic types of alarms: stand-alone alarms, wireless alarm systems, and hard-wired alarm systems.

Stand-alone alarms are inexpensive (from about $15 to $100, depending on type and model) and can be self-installed. These self-contained devices include:

- *Battery-operated magnetic contact sensors* that attach to a door, window, or skylight and sound a local alarm when that entrance is opened
- *Ultrasonic or infrared sensors* that plug into a wall outlet and sound off when motion is detected in the room.

Wireless alarm systems are also relatively inexpensive (from about $150 to $600) and can be purchased at many hardware stores and home centers and installed by the homeowner. They have three main components: sensors, a control unit, and an alert mechanism.

There are a number of different types of sensors, including, for example, the magnetic contacts and ultrasonic or infrared sensors described above, but all sensors fall into one of two general categories. *Perimeter sensors* use various means to detect when windows or doors are opened or when window glass is broken; *inside sensors* detect motion inside the home through microwave, ultrasonic, or infrared technology. There are also *combination sensors*, which combine both technologies.

The *control unit* interprets the signals it receives from the sensors and, when necessary, activates the alert mechanism. That *alert mechanism* may be a loud siren or bell, flashing strobe lights, and/or an automatic telephone dialer that can dial one or more prearranged numbers, such as the police department or an answering service, and play a recorded message or coded signal. Or, for a monthly fee of about $20 to $30, you can choose to have your alarm system tied into a special alarm-monitoring service, or "central station," in which case the alert mechanism will send a signal to the station through your regular telephone line or a special line leased from the phone company. Upon receiving your system's signal, the service typically will verify the alarm and then notify police or fire officials.

The alarm system's entry or *access panel*, which is mounted near the front door or another commonly used entry, usually is a push-button pad; you enter your code number to turn the system on and off. A delay mechanism gives you time (usually 30 to 60 seconds) to enter and exit the house without setting off the alarm.

In general, the more features a system has, the more it costs—you'll usually pay more, for example, for a system with more sensors or for one with outdoor as well as indoor sirens. A number of sophisticated features are available as standard equipment with some of the more expensive units or can be purchased as options to expand less costly basic systems. These include safeguards and conveniences such as a "panic button," often placed by the nightstand or front door, which lets you manually activate the alert mechanism; a medical-alert button for calling an ambulance; smoke detectors that sound a fire alarm and contact the monitoring service or fire department (also see *Fire Protection*, pages 156–65); a remote-control device to let you operate the system from your car; and even a device that allows you to turn lights and appliances on and off by phone.

Hard-wired alarm systems have the same basic components and generally the same features and options as wireless systems. However, while a wireless system uses battery-powered transmitters to connect all components to the control unit, a hard-wired system makes those connections by wires. A professionally designed hard-wired system can cost from about $1,000 to $3,000 when installed in an existing home; installing the same system in a house while it is being built can cut costs. Installation of a professionally designed system usually must be performed by a professional contractor, since it involves drilling and snaking wires through the walls, floors, and ceiling. Most alarm companies that design hard-wired systems will provide the equipment suited to your home and your security needs, install the system in accordance with local building and electrical codes, service the system, and arrange for central station monitoring.

CHOOSING A SYSTEM

When deciding which type of alarm system suits your needs, carefully evaluate both your security requirements and your budget. You might begin by calling your local police department; many police departments have crime prevention units which can help homeowners assess their needs and can recommend specific security measures.

An effective basic system to protect your home while you are away might include door alarms on outside doors, a motion sensor in a key area such as the main inside stairway, an indoor horn, and a central station connection. If you live in a high-crime neighborhood or an isolated area, are often away from home most of the day or evening or for long periods, or keep valuable items in the house, you might be wise to consider investing in a complete security system. The most effective system includes both perimeter and inside sensors tied to a central station. For maximum protection, install both indoor and outdoor sirens and/or lights. The lights and sound indoors are intended to keep or get the burglar *out*; the outdoor alarm and lights serve to alert the neighborhood and direct police or security personnel to your home.

Remember that a siren or bell is of limited use if there is no one around to hear it. If you decide not to invest in hooking up your system to a central station, an automatic telephone dialer can be a useful option, particularly if you live in a remote area or a neighborhood in which most homes are empty from nine to five.

Also keep these tips and recommendations in mind when shopping for a residential alarm:

- There is no such thing as a completely burglar-proof system. However, a good alarm system can help deter most burglars and afford you peace of mind in the process.

- Check local ordinances before buying a system. Some areas require permits for alarm installation, and some require that alarms automatically shut off after several minutes. (Look for a model that will reset itself after shutting off.)

- Also check with your local police department before buying a system for its automatic telephone-dialing capabilities. Because of staff shortages, many police departments, particularly those in large cities, will not accept such calls. Your alternatives: signing up with a central station, programming your automatic dialer to phone a series of other numbers where you or a family member or neighbor might be reached, or installing sirens alone.

- Consider talking with your insurance agent before purchasing an alarm system to find out how much of a discount on your homeowners insurance premiums the installation of various systems would provide. According to the National Burglar and Fire Alarm Association, discounts for a professionally installed system may range from about 2 to 30 percent, depending on the sophistication and reliability of the system.

- Be sure to compare the *total* price of various alarm systems, including the cost of installation and all the features and options you require.
- Keep the special needs of family members in mind when you shop. For homes with children or with adults who are ill, disabled, or bedridden, an emergency button that manually activates the alarm and calls for assistance can be a valuable option. If you have pets, inside motion detectors could set off frequent false alarms; outdoor and window/door sensors might be a better choice.
- If the system includes an automatic dialer, consider including a local alarm that will sound if the phone line is cut or disturbed, and look for a dialer that will bypass incoming calls, so a burglar cannot circumvent the system by keeping the phone line busy.
- Make sure all equipment carries the seal of a recognized testing laboratory, such as Underwriters Laboratory (UL) or Factory Mutual Research Corporation.
- Wireless alarm systems can offer the same advantages as hard-wired systems but at a significantly lower cost. Also, they are portable; you can take the system with you if you move. However, since they are powered by batteries, wireless systems are somewhat more vulnerable to failure. Also, most store-bought wireless systems do not give you the option of tying into a central monitoring service.
- If you install a hard-wired system, investing in a battery backup, which would keep the system operating during a power outage, is a wise precaution.
- If you are considering the purchase of an ultrasonic or infrared stand-alone alarm, remember that these devices are designed to monitor only small areas, such as an apartment. And keep in mind that stand-alone alarms which sound a siren *inside* your home offer little protection unless you or a close neighbor are on the scene.
- For a copy of the National Burglar and Fire Alarm Association (NBFAA) booklet *Considerations When Looking For a Home Burglar Alarm System*, send $1.00 and a self-addressed, stamped, legal-size envelope to: NBFAA, 7101 Wisconsin Avenue, Suite 1390, Bethesda, MD 20814–4805.

INSTALLATION

Most wireless alarm systems are relatively easy to install, and the manufacturer usually provides a telephone "help line" in case you run into trouble. Be sure to check into your area's building codes before beginning work to make sure you are in compliance with local ordinances.

If you decide to invest in a hard-wired system, follow these tips and precautions when choosing an installer:

1. Contact the local Better Business Bureau and state consumer protection office for the complaint records of companies you are considering. In 1988, U.S. Better Business Bureaus answered more than 44,000 requests for information on alarm system dealers.

2. You may want to look for an alarm company that is UL-listed, indicating that the installer has passed rigorous tests of competence. UL will also provide references of listed companies in your area. Look in your phone directory or contact the organization's headquarters at 333 Pfingsten Road, Northbrook, IL 60062. For the names of National Burglar and Fire Alarm Association (NBFAA) member companies in your area, contact: NBFAA, 7101 Wisconsin Avenue, Suite 1390, Bethesda, MD 20814–4805.

3. Ask the companies for references and contact previous customers to check on their level of satisfaction with the system and with the follow-up service they received.

4. Ask for written estimates from at least three alarm companies, and compare the total cost of all services and options. Estimates should be based on a careful and detailed survey of your home. Make sure the bids specify the type of equipment to be used, the points of protection, the installation charge, the monthly service charge, if applicable, and the maintenance schedule. Some companies provide a free maintenance check once a year, while others charge for this service. If the alarm will be tied into a central monitoring station, find out whether the police or the service's own security staff are alerted when an alarm sounds, and ask what the anticipated response time would be to an alert from your system.

5. Compare warranties. Ninety days of coverage is standard, but some companies back their work for one year.

6. Never pay the full fee before installation; withhold at least 50 percent until the system has been installed and tested to ensure that all components are operating properly.

7. Carefully review the contract, which should include all the information detailed in the estimate, and make sure you understand all contract terms before signing. Remember that federal law allows you a 72-hour "cooling-off" period in which you are entitled to change your mind and cancel a contract signed in your home.

8. Some alarm companies offer leasing; the company retains ownership of the equipment and you pay an installation charge plus a monthly rental fee; you'll also pay a separate monitoring fee if you choose to hook up the system to a central station. Leasing can be a cost-effective option if you plan to move within a few years, but if you stay put, leasing is usually more expensive in the long run.

Camcorders

[Also see *Audio and Video Equipment*, pages 29–30; *Videocassette Recorders*, pages 344–47.]

Just five years after the introduction of camcorders to the U.S. market in 1985, these small, portable home video cameras/recorders have found their way into about 10 percent of American homes, according to the Electronic Industries Association. And with sales clicking along at the rate of about 2.5 million units a year, it looks as if the niche carved in American culture by these electronic marvels will only deepen and widen in the 1990s. Camcorders are used to chronicle important family events—weddings, graduations, Baby's first steps—create personal travelogues of vacations and family outings, compile video inventories of household possessions, and serve as training aids for golfers, tennis players, and other sports enthusiasts. With the connection of a few cables to a TV set, they can even serve as a substitute for the videocassette recorder, enabling owners to view prerecorded tapes or their own video creations on TV.

The size and price of camcorders have decreased each year since their introduction, while the number of available features has multiplied. Following is an overview of the equipment available on the market today. Knowing your options before you shop can help you zoom in on the camcorder with the features best suited to your intended use and a price that matches your budget.

FOCUS ON FEATURES

Format. Like their cousin the videocassette recorder, camcorders come in several different formats, none of which are compatible; that is, a tape recorded in a VHS camcorder cannot be played in an 8mm VCR.

☐ **VHS** is currently the most popular format in both camcorders and VCRs. Weighing in at about eight or nine pounds, VHS camcorders are the largest and heaviest of the available styles and are designed to rest on the shoulder during filming. They use standard one-hour, one-hour-40-minute, or two-hour tape cassettes.

☐ **VHS–C** (compact VHS) cameras are smaller and, at about three pounds, lighter than the typical VHS unit. They use a smaller 20-minute cassette, which can be played back on a VHS videocassette recorder with the use of a special adapter.

☐ **S–VHS (Super–VHS)**, available in both VHS and VHS–C model camcorders, offers markedly improved picture quality along with stereo recording. You will need an S-VHS videocassette recorder, however, as well as a high-quality TV set equipped with a special S-VHS (Y/C) connector to see and hear the difference.

☐ **The typical 8mm (eight-millimeter)** camcorder is as small and light as a VHS-C model but offers longer recording time on a two-hour tape cassette. That matchbook-sized 8mm cassette cannot be dropped into your VCR for playback unless you also own an 8mm VCR, but it can be viewed by hooking up the camcorder directly to any model TV.

☐ **Hi-band 8mm (or Hi8)**, the latest of the camcorder formats, offers the same high-quality picture and stereo capability as S-VHS plus the longer playing time of the 8mm format.

When deciding which kind of camcorder to buy, you'll want to consider performance, convenience, and cost.

For most viewers, the differences in picture quality between VHS and 8mm cameras are so minor as to be nearly imperceptible; 8mm, however, may have a slight edge in the quality of sound recorded.

As for convenience, the standard VHS cameras are considerably bulkier and heavier than VHS-C and 8mm models. Remember, though, that much of the weight of the heavier cameras rests on your shoulder. Even at two or three pounds, the smaller units can feel heavy and become hard to hold steady after resting in the palm of your hand a few minutes. Also remember to consider convenience of playback. You'll need to make some TV connections to play 8mm tapes unless you also own an 8mm VCR. VHS and VHS-C cassettes, on the other hand, can be played either in the more common VHS-format home equipment or in a camcorder hooked up to a TV set.

Finally, while costs may range from about $600 to $1,200 for VHS, VHS-C, and 8mm cameras, they can run as high as $1,700 to $2,000 or more for S-VHS and Hi-band 8mm models. Both the S-VHS and Hi-band formats also require special, more expensive tape cassettes, although they can record with regular cassettes in the unenhanced VHS or 8mm mode.

Autofocus. A standard feature on nearly all camcorders, autofocus adjusts the lens to ensure a clear focus on your subject. The electronics of autofocus can be "confused" by certain filming conditions—for example, if you attempt to shoot a very small or very distant object; a scene with both near and far elements, such as a subject behind a mesh fence; or a nonreflective object such as a black curtain. Also, moving the camera too quickly from subject to subject can cause uneven shifts in focus. Some camcorders let you compensate for these challenges to the capabilities of autofocus by switching to a *manual focus* mode or temporarily altering the *focusing zone*, the size of the area in which focusing occurs.

Autoexposure. Another nearly universal feature, autoexposure allows the camcorder to choose the proper lens aperture, or opening, and shutter speed for a given scene and lighting situation. Like autofocus, autoexposure may not work well in every situation; in some models, a display in the electronic viewfinder tells you when conditions are unfavorable for automatic exposure setting. Some models then give you the option of compensating either by means of a *backlight* switch, which adjusts for strong light behind the subject, or by temporarily switching to manual exposure.

Automatic white balance. Available on virtually all models, automatic white balance permits the camera to deliver realistic colors by adjusting for the differences between natural and artificial light. In certain unusual situations, such as the filming of a scene composed almost entirely of one color, this feature may not function perfectly. Some models allow you to compensate through various manual controls.

Electronic viewfinder. This small black-and-white TV screen in the eyepiece shows you what you are filming so that you can accurately judge and adjust framing, lighting, and focus. Many models also display various items of information in the viewfinder—that you are in the record mode, for example, or that the camcorder is running out of tape or battery power. Another feature common in electronic viewfinders is "record review," which allows one-touch review of the last few seconds of tape recorded.

Be wary of low-priced camcorders without an electronic viewfinder; these models, often equipped with an optical viewfinder or viewing window like that on a regular camera, usually have no playback capability—to view tapes you must use a separate VCR. You may want to look for a camcorder with an *adjustable viewfinder,* which can be swung about to allow use with either eye, tilted to permit viewing when you set up the camera on a table or tripod, and/or focused to compensate for nearsightedness or farsightedness.

Zoom lens. Most camcorders are equipped with a zoom lens, which lets you close in on your subject without moving the camera. The best zoom lenses are motorized so that they work at the touch of a button. The customary 6-to-1, or 6X, zoom takes you 6 times closer to your subject. The higher the ratio, the greater the span between one end of the zoom range and the other; that is, a 2.5-to-1 ratio gives you limited telephoto ability while a 12-to-1 lens packs considerable zoom power.

Low-light performance. Nearly all camcorders will deliver a good, clear picture in outdoor light or in a well-lighted room. Differences between models begin to show up when the lights dim; the poorer-quality cameras may then show a blurred, grainy scene. A model's *"lux" number* is intended to indicate how well the camera films in low light. The lower the number (from 40 to 1), the better. A *CCD (charged-coupled device) image sensor*, available on some models, can improve picture quality in low-light situations.

Microphones. Most camcorders have a microphone mounted on the camera body, which picks up nearly any sound your ear can hear. A *directional microphone* gives precedence to sounds directly in front of the camera, allowing for a slight reduction in background noise. S-VHS and Hi-band 8mm models have two separate microphones to allow stereo recording.

Plus these extras. You may also want to look for one or more of the following extra performance and convenience features and accessories:

- A **flying erase head** allows "seamless" editing—one filmed scene smoothly follows another without gaps or blips in between.

- A **high-speed shutter** allows filming of fast action without blur.

- A **fade control** lets you gradually darken one scene and fade in the next.

- **Freeze-frame** or **still-frame** lets you freeze the action on the screen and play back clear, single shots, much like the "freeze-action" control on a VCR.

- A **character generator** or **keyboard** lets you "stamp" the date and time on your picture. Some models also allow you to create your own combinations of figures and letters to impose a video title on the screen.

- An **electronic gyroscope** helps eliminate jiggling of the picture on a model with a long zoom lens.

- **Time-lapse recording**, used in conjunction with a tripod, allows you to film the hatching of an egg or the opening of a flower.

- **Special-effects animation** lets you produce fancy creations such as an animated cartoon composed of single-frame pictures shot separately and then shown in fast sequence.

- **Dubbing** lets you superimpose a new sound track on a scene previously filmed.

- **Index search** simplifies the process of locating a particular segment on a recorded tape.

- A **separate lighting unit** can be mounted on top of the camera body to provide extra clarity in low-light situations.

- A **wireless microphone** eliminates background noise from your recording, for the most professional filming; the speaker's voice is transmitted to a receiver plugged into the camera.

- A **tripod** can allow you to set up the camera and forget it—for candid shots at a party, for example. It's also useful for lengthy filming of any scene.

- A **remote-control device** allows you to operate your camcorder from the couch when you hook it up to the TV set in place of a VCR.

- A **carrying case** protects the camcorder when it's not in use and may let you conveniently carry some accessories as well.

Carpets and Rugs

Carpet can absorb sound, reduce heating and air-conditioning costs, and add beauty, color, and comfort to a home. Yet there is such a wide variety of available fibers, styles, colors, and prices that knowing which carpet is right for your rooms is no simple matter. To make a wise selection, you need to know enough about carpet to be able to understand labels, ask the right questions, and compare products.

READING CARPET LABELS

Most carpet samples have two labels, one identifying the fiber and its manufacturer and the other carrying the carpet manufacturer's name and warranty. Although there may seem to be a great number of different carpet fibers, nearly every fiber name that you will find in the carpet showroom is simply a brand name representing one of the five basic or "generic" types of carpet pile fibers: nylon, olefin, polyester, acrylic, and wool.

The chart on page 70 lists the five basic carpet fibers and the most common brand names within those generic categories. If, as you shop, you come across a trade name not included in this chart, simply ask the salesperson to identify the type of fiber that the name represents.

Each of the five generic carpet fibers has different characteristics; your choice should be based on a consideration of your intended use, personal preferences, and budget.

Nylon makes up about 80 percent of all carpets sold in the U.S. It is resistant to static, mildew, soil, and water-soluble stains, holds up well to wear, and comes in a wide range of colors and prices. *Advanced generation nylons* cost more than regular nylon but have an improved, built-in ability to conceal and resist most soils and stains.

Olefin (polypropylene) carpet yarns, used most commonly in indoor-outdoor carpet, are strong, wear-resistant, easily cleaned, and naturally resistant to static, moisture, and mildew. Olefin carpets have either a smooth or nubby surface, with a felt-like, rather than plush, texture. Less expensive than nylon, olefin is notably colorfast but comes in a limited range of colors.

Polyester carpet yarns are noted for their color clarity and soft "hand" (feel). They are resistant to water-soluble stains, easily cleaned, and relatively inexpensive. However, they are not as durable as nylon and are not resistant to oily stains.

Branded Fiber Chart*

NYLON

[1]Anso®
[1]Anso® IV
[1]Anso® IV with Halofresh™
[5]Antron®
[5]Antron® III
[5]Antron® Plus
[2]Enkalon®
[2]Enkalon® with built-in
  Scotchgard®
[8]Wear-Dated® Ultron®
[8]Wear-Dated® Ultron® with
  locked-in Scotchgard®
[4]Zeftron™

OLEFIN

[6]Herculon®
[6]Herculon® IV
[6]Herculon® Nouvelle
[3]Marquesa® Lana

POLYESTER

[7]Pentron®
[7]Trevira®

ACRYLIC

[8]Acrilan®
[4]Zefran®

[1]Allied Fibers & Plastics
[2]American Enka Company
[3]Amoco Fabrics Company
[4]Badische Corporation

[5]E. I. DuPont de Nemours & Company
[6]Hercules, Inc.
[7]Hoechst Fibers Industries
[8]Monsanto Fibers & Intermediates Company

*Source: The Carpet and Rug Institute.

Acrylic fibers offer the look and feel of wool at a much lower cost. Carpets made from acrylic fibers are resistant to static, mildew, and water-soluble (but not oily) stains. Acrylic is not as wear-resistant as nylon.

Wool, the only natural fiber used in carpet, is soft, luxurious, and extremely durable. Carpets made of wool are available in a wide range of colors and textures. However, they are a good deal more expensive than carpets made of manmade fibers, and wool is less resistant to moisture and mildew as well as harder to clean than nylon.

CONSTRUCTION AND TEXTURE

Most carpet today is "tufted"; that is, made by a process in which hundreds of tufts, or stitch-like placements of yarn, are embedded in a backing material.

In **loop pile carpets**, the yarn on the face of the carpet forms a loop, with both ends anchored in the carpet back. With **level loop pile**, the loops are of equal height, making a smooth and level surface; the texture varies with the height of the loop. With **multilevel loop pile**, the loops are of two or three different heights; this carpet style also may be called "sculptured" or "carved."

Loop pile carpets come in a variety of colors and patterns and generally resist wear well.

Cut pile carpet is formed when the top of the carpet yarn loop is cut, leaving two individual yarn tufts. Different styles within this texture category are created by variations in the amount of "twist" applied to the yarn, the size and luster of the yarn, and the type of heat-setting. Styles include:

- **Velvets and plushes**, which are made from yarns with very little twist. The surface appearance is smooth, level, and elegant.
- **Saxonies**, which use yarns that are twisted together and heat-set to lock in the twist. Each tuft end in a saxony carpet is distinguishable in the surface, creating a subtle pattern which is quite different from and somewhat less formal than the velvets, in which all tuft ends blend together.
- **Frieze** (pronounced "free-zay") carpets, which are made from tightly twisted yarns that bend in different directions. The dense, low-pile surface has a nubby texture and is extremely durable.

Cut pile carpets (except for frieze carpets) generally do not resist wear quite as well as loop pile carpets. They also are susceptible to "shading"—an apparent variation in color tone that results when the pile in one area of the carpet is pushed in a slightly different direction than the pile in adjacent areas. Foot tracks are more noticeable in cut pile carpets than in other textures.

Cut and loop pile carpet is a combination of cut and loop yarns; the contrast creates a variety of interesting sculptured effects.

BEFORE YOU SHOP

In order to get the best carpet buy for your money, you will need to take some time to define your requirements and your budget. Here are some questions you should be able to answer before you step into a carpet showroom:

1. **How much carpet do you need?** Carefully measure your room(s), including closets, hallways, and offsets, with a steel tape measure, and take these measurements with you when you shop. To get a rough idea of the square yardage you will need, you can also make these calculations: Multiply the width of the room by its length to get the number of square feet; next, divide the number of square feet by nine to get the number of square yards. Remember, though, that there is almost always unavoidable waste in the installation of carpet, so the actual square yardage required will be somewhat greater than the room's dimensions.

2. **What are the traffic patterns and usage of the room you are carpeting?** Is it used primarily for play, entertaining, or sleep? Are food and beverages brought into the room? How many children use the room and how often? Do you have pets? Is there an outside entrance? How important is elegance relative to easy maintenance and cleanup?

   Answering these questions can help you identify the high-traffic, heavy-wear floors in your home—stairs, halls, family rooms, etc.—which require the most durable, high-quality carpet fibers and construction. Entrance and eating areas also call for carpet with good soil and stain resistance. Choosing a lightweight, medium-grade carpet for rooms that get less use, such as your bedroom, can allow you to devote more of your budget to the heavy-traffic floors. Inexpensive, less wear-resistant carpets may be adequate for areas that require little use, such as a guest room.

3. **Will the carpet need to coordinate with upholstery fabrics, draperies, etc.?** If so, bring fabric and/or paint samples with you when you shop so there is no question of color match. Place carpet samples on the floor to judge color, and compare color under both natural and artificial light. Take carpet samples home with you before making your final choice so that you can view the colors in their final settings. (Also see "Choosing Color," page 74.)

4. **How much can you afford to spend?** Carpet may cost anywhere from $5 to $100 or more per square yard. Keep in mind that, as with any long-term investment, the true cost of carpet is a reflection of its length of satisfactory service; a carpet that lasts 10 years can be a better buy than a less expensive carpet that lasts only 2 or 3 years. When deciding on a budget, remember to add in the costs of padding and installation, as well as any finance charges if you are planning to buy on time.

5. **What are your future plans?** Are you settling into a home or are you likely to be transferred soon? High-quality wall-to-wall carpet can be a good investment *if* you stay to enjoy it. However, if you are living in an apartment or plan to move in a year or two, economy-grade carpet or room-size or area rugs might be a better buy.

CHOOSING A RETAILER

One of your first shopping decisions is the selection of a reputable retailer who has the knowledge and experience to answer your questions and help you choose the carpet best suited to your intended use and your budget.

You might begin by asking friends and neighbors where they have received satisfactory service. Look for a carpet dealer who is well known and well established in your community, and be sure to contact the local Better Business Bureau for a complaint report. As you shop, you will compare prices, of course, but you should also give careful consideration to the retailer's reputation and service. Search until you find a store with a knowledgeable staff who will give your questions the attention they deserve, and remember that a reliable retailer will have an interest in keeping you satisfied, in standing behind the installation, and in helping you with any maintenance questions.

QUALITY CHECKLIST

The quality of carpet is a reflection of its performance—how well it maintains its original appearance under normal use and maintenance. The key determinants of a carpet's performance are the inherent characteristics of its fiber and construction. As you shop, keep in mind the fiber and construction characteristics noted earlier. When communicating your needs and preferences to the retailer, be as specific and accurate as possible in describing the end use for which the carpet is intended. Also keep an eye out for the following quality features:

☐ **Density**, the amount of face yarn in the carpet, is one of the most important quality considerations. As a general rule, the denser the carpet, the better its quality. When comparing carpet samples of the same fiber type, bend the carpet and note how close the individual tufts are to one another and how much of the backing is exposed. Also press on the pile with one finger to see how easy it is to penetrate to the backing.

☐ **Twist**, the winding of the yarn around itself, is put into the yarn prior to carpet manufacture. One way to judge the quality of the twist of cut pile samples is to look closely at the cut ends of the individual yarns. In a high-quality carpet, they will be neat, tight, and well defined.

☐ **Heat-setting** locks the twist into yarns, enabling them to hold their twist through use and cleaning. When buying cut pile carpet, read the label or ask the salesperson whether the yarn has been heat-set.

☐ **Pile height and weight** affect appearance and cost. As weight and height increase, the luxurious appearance and the cost of carpet increase as well. However, when carpet with a high pile and low density or weight is used in high-traffic areas, it can develop "corn rowing"—a process that occurs as some of the tufts are crushed underfoot and others are held erect by pressure from the crushed tufts. In general, a medium-height or short, dense pile is a better choice than a high-pile carpet for high-traffic areas.

Choosing Color

Carpet color is an integral part of your room's decorating scheme. When choosing color, keep these tips in mind:

• Dark colors can make a large room seem more intimate; so can large patterns or sculptured carpets.

• Light colors can expand a small room; so can carpet that is the same shade as or a lighter shade than the walls.

• Dark colors hide dark soil but show light-colored soil, lint, and dust.

• Light colors conceal lint and dust but show darker soil.

• Patterned designs are better than solid colors for disguising spots and stains.

CARPET SHOPPER'S CHECKLIST

Finally, keep these recommendations and precautions in mind when you shop for carpet and rugs:

1. When comparing prices, make sure you are comparing the same quantities. Don't be misled by ads offering low prices on carpet by the square *foot*; wall-to-wall carpet is commonly sold by the square yard.

2. A carpet pad protects the carpet's backing, absorbs the crushing and grinding of footsteps, minimizes shifting, and serves as a sound and heat insulator. Most commonly available are rubber and urethane foam pads; rubber pads provide a firmer feeling underfoot but urethane is somewhat less expensive and gives soft but uniform support. Make sure the pad you buy is at least one-half inch thick.

3. If you plan to move within the next few years or if you want to show off your wood, tile, or other hard-surface floor, an area rug can be a better choice than wall-to-wall carpet. Rugs have these added advantages: There are no installation costs, and you can turn them periodically to distribute wear and increase their life. Quality characteristics are basically the same for rugs as for carpets.

4. Be sure to ask if the price being quoted for your new carpet includes pad and installation. Does the installation price include the moving of furniture and removal of the old carpet and pad? Are there any additional charges, such as for installing carpet on steps, handling heavy furniture, or delivering carpet outside the retailer's immediate service area?

5. Before signing a carpet installation contract, review it carefully. Make sure it includes the carpet's manufacturer, style name, fiber content,

and color name; a full description of the padding; the number of square yards to be installed; the price per square yard; and the total purchase price, including any installation and finance charges. Also make sure you receive a *written* warranty that specifies exactly what is covered and what the warrantor will do if a problem develops.

6. It has been reported that chemical vapors emitted by some new carpets occasionally may cause eye and throat irritation, nausea, or other health problems. To reduce your exposure, ask the dealer to air out the carpet before delivery, keep your windows and doors open during installation, and keep air-conditioning turned on for 48 hours afterward.

7. Save carpet and rug labels; they may prove valuable if a problem develops that the dealer cannot or will not solve.

8. Follow these recommendations from the Carpet and Rug Institute, a trade association of carpet and rug manufacturers, to prolong the beauty and life of your carpets and rugs:

- Protect carpets and rugs from direct sunlight.

- Use furniture glides or cups under the legs of heavy pieces of furniture and, if possible, move furniture a few inches each week.

- Do not pull out loose snags or pills that appear above the surface of the carpet; instead, snip them with scissors to the length of the other tufts.

- Reverse area rugs every 6 to 12 months to distribute wear.

- Thoroughly vacuum at least once a week to remove loose, gritty soil, which can cut carpet fibers. (Also see *Vacuum Cleaners*, pages 341–43.)

- Take care of accidents or spills as soon as they occur. Liquids should be blotted with clean white towels, paper towels, or tissues; semisolids may be gently scraped up with a rounded spoon or dull knife.

- Before using a carpet cleaning product or spot removal solution, pretest it on an inconspicuous area of the carpet or rug. Use a minimum amount of cleaning solution to avoid wetting the backing, and speed drying by blotting with white tissues, turning up the heat, and/or using fans.

- The Carpet and Rug Institute publishes several guides to carpet maintenance, including *Carpet and Rug Care Guide*, *Spot and Stain Removal Guide*, and *Chemical Spots and Stains on Carpets and Rugs*. Send $1.00 for each booklet and a stamped, self-addressed envelope to: Accounting Department, The Carpet and Rug Institute, Box 2048, Dalton, GA 30722–2048.

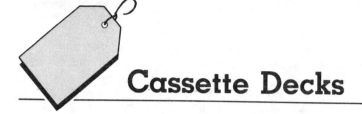

Cassette Decks

[Also see *Audio and Video Equipment*, pages 29–30; *Compact Disc Players*, pages 90–94; *Stereo Systems*, pages 308–13.]

The cassette tape deck, often a standard component in a home stereo system, is one of the most popular audio units. It is the only audio component that lets you not only play a commercial recording but also create your own recordings for playback at home, in your car, or in a portable cassette player. Those musical creations might include concerts taped from your FM radio, copies of entire record albums or compact discs, or collections of your favorite selections from a number of albums or CDs.

Cassette decks range in price from about $100 to $2,000 or more. If your musical requirements are not too exacting, a deck at the lower end of that range may suit your needs. With a somewhat more generous budget, you'll find that, thanks to continuing technological refinements, most models in the $300 to $500 range offer both excellent performance and a number of handy operating features once found only on the more expensive units. Following is a look at the terminology you will encounter as you shop for a cassette deck, along with tips on the relative virtues and shortcomings of various features.

☐ **Single vs. dual decks**. "Dual," "double," or "dubbing" decks can hold two cassettes at once, allowing you to make copies of prerecorded tapes or of your own creations. According to most sources, overall sound quality is better with single than dual decks, particularly at the lower end of the price scale. On the other hand, if you plan to copy cassettes, a dual deck can be a convenient alternative to purchasing a second single deck.

☐ **Frequency response.** Frequency response is a measure of how smoothly and uniformly a cassette deck handles all the frequencies within the audio range. This is largely a function of how well the electrical characteristics of the deck dovetail with the magnetic properties of the tape. (Also see "Tips on Tapes," page 77.) Until recently, most decks had a frequency response upper limit of 15,000 or 18,000 Hertz (Hz); frequency response can now be as high as 20,000 Hz on better machines, lending subtle improvements to the quality of the higher musical tones.

☐ **Noise reduction circuits.** Most cassette decks are equipped with one of three systems for reducing background noise, hiss, and distortion: Dolby B, Dolby C, or dbx. Dolby B produces the least noise reduction of the three systems. Dolby C offers expanded noise reduction and

Tips on Tapes

The quality of the tape you play is as integral a part of sound accuracy as is the performance of the tape player. Tapes commonly come in varying lengths, from 40 to 120 minutes of recording time, and in three different types; the type you buy should depend on your intended use.

Type I ("normal") tapes are the least expensive variety and are best suited for recording tasks that do not require a high degree of sound quality: recording speech, for example, or taping a record for playback in the car.

Type II ("high bias") tapes are somewhat more expensive than Type I tapes and are better equipped for more demanding jobs such as recording an FM broadcast or record for playback in a portable "boom box," or recording a compact disc for use in your car's cassette player.

Type IV ("metal") tapes are designed for the most demanding recording tasks, when sound quality matters the most: taping CDs for home playback, for example.

also greatly improves the dynamic range—the span between the softest and loudest notes the tape can retain—in the upper (treble) frequencies. The dbx system offers a high degree of noise reduction and even greater improvements in dynamic range; however, a tape recorded with dbx encoding is not suitable for playback on cassettte decks lacking dbx circuitry, which include most car players.

☐ **Dolby HX Pro.** This system allows the deck to sense and adjust to very loud musical passages during recording, thus preventing volume "overload" and consequent sound distortion. HX Pro-equipped decks are particularly well suited for copying compact discs onto tape.

☐ **Recording level indicator.** Recording with the volume too high can cause tape "overload"—sound distortion in the loudest passages. The recording level (VU) meter shows you the strength of the signal throughout recording and allows you to adjust volume as needed. Meters differ from model to model. Bar graph, LED meters are particularly easy to read and allow constant, precise monitoring; the more segments on the meter, the more exact your monitoring can be.

☐ **Adjustable bias control.** This feature allows you to manually fine-tune the bias—the inaudible signal generated by the deck to meet the requirements of the type of tape being used and thus reduce distortion. *Automatic bias control* does the fine-tuning for you, for optimum audio accuracy.

☐ **Three tape heads.** Some cassette decks have only two audio heads (the metal structures that transfer the electrical signal to the tape), one for erasing and one for recording. Three-head models have a third separate head for playback. This allows you to monitor a recording as it is being made and adjust volume or bias as needed.

☐ **Auto-reverse.** Auto-reverse allows the deck to automatically change direction when it reaches the end of a tape, reversing to play or record on the other side. This convenience, however, usually comes at the price of reduced overall sound quality.

☐ **Tape counter.** The counter, which may be either a mechanical display or an electronic digital display, tells you how long the machine has been recording or playing so that you can find a particular spot on the tape quickly or calculate how much space is left for recording. Some models have a handy "time remaining" feature which makes the calculations for you.

☐ **Tape type selection.** With manual tape type selection, you must remember to set a switch that tells the deck what type of tape you are recording on. With automatic selection, the deck "reads" holes in the cassette case and reaches its own conclusions.

☐ **Multiplex filter (MPX).** The multiplex filter removes certain inaudible tones present in FM broadcasts which may interfere with tape recording. The filter must be switched off when recording from other musical sources or sound quality will diminish slightly.

☐ **Other features.** You might also be interested in these convenience features:

  • **Continuous record**, found in some dual decks, lets you automatically record a long selection on two consecutive tapes.

  • **Automatic timing** lets you connect the deck to a household timer to start recording or playback at a set time.

  • A **record mute control** lets you insert silent gaps between the musical selections you record.

  • **Cue and review** allows you to fast-forward while listening to a speeded-up version of the tape, to quickly locate a particular spot.

  • **Tape scan** lets you listen to the first few seconds of each selection on a tape—another aid to speedy location of a particular tune.

  • **Music search** allows you to program the recorder to automatically locate a particular song by counting the silent gaps between selections.

  • A **headphone jack** is found on most cassette decks; look for a model with headphone volume control.

  • A **remote-control jack** lets you connect your deck to an audio component with remote control operation.

  • A **microphone jack** allows you to record live music.

☐ Be sure to follow the manufacturer's recommendations for routine maintenance; in most cases, this simply involves an occasional cleaning and demagnetizing to retain sound quality.

Child Care Services

In 1988, according to the U.S. Bureau of Labor Statistics, 56 percent of all American mothers with children under the age of six were employed. Clearly, the demand for child care services today is at an all-time high. If you are a single, working parent or if both you and your spouse have jobs outside the home, you may well be facing one of the most important decisions of your life—that of choosing the person or center that will care for your child when you cannot be at home.

The following compilation of advice from child care experts can help you select a child care program that will be right for both you and your child. Outlined below is a step-by-step approach to selecting child care that can help make your search easier. And on pages 81–84 you will find a checklist of qualities to look for and questions to ask as you size up child care prospects.

HOW TO FIND A GOOD EARLY CHILDHOOD PROGRAM

1. **Start your search early.** Depending on the number of child care facilities in your area and the nature of the demand, waiting lists at the most popular centers in your area may be as long as a year. Checking with other local parents about their experiences in locating child care can give you an idea of how early you will need to begin your search. In any case, allow a minimum of six months to thoroughly investigate all options.

2. **Decide which child care option is right for you.**

    A family day care home—usually a mother who cares for children in her home, often along with her own children—can offer an infant or young toddler the kind of constant, individual attention that children need at this early age. A home care setting can be a relatively inexpensive alternative to a day care center. However, most states do not require family day care homes to be licensed, and in those states that do, licensing requirements generally are neither strict nor vigorously enforced.

    Another option you might consider, particularly if you have several small children, is to hire a **caregiver to come to your home or a live-in caregiver**. If you frequently work late or travel, having a caregiver on the scene can be a welcome convenience. This option also offers the advantage of care that continues even when your child has a cold or other minor illness. However, this can be one of the most expensive forms of child care.

Day care centers typically restrict their services to children who are at least two years old, although some also take infants. Beginning at about age three, children can derive great benefit from learning in a social setting and from the stimulation of being with their peers. Day care centers must be registered or licensed by the state.

Nursery schools and preschools both provide care and give children a head start on their education. Many of these programs, however, are only available a few hours a day or a couple of days a week, so making additional child care arrangements may be necessary.

Before- and/or after-school care for school-age children may be one of the services offered by a family day care home or day care center, or may be available through your child's school.

3. **Contact as many resources as possible** as you put together your list of prospective child care providers. Talk with other parents. Check with local churches, synagogues, clubs, and/or civic organizations. Contact the early childhood department of a local college. Contact local public school officials or the board of education; a number of school districts offer some form of child care or allow community groups to use their facilities. Your state licensing agency or a local child care resource and referral agency may be able to refer you to programs in your community, and your city, county, or state department of human services may be able to provide a list of licensed facilities. Your phone directory and the classified ads in your local newspaper can point you to local child care centers and to mothers who care for children in their home.

   You may also want to contact the National Association for the Education of Young Children (NAEYC), the professional organization for early childhood educators. This organization may be able to help you locate a referral service in your area or a child care center accredited by the National Academy of Early Childhood Programs, an NAEYC division. NAEYC also publishes a helpful brochure, *How to Choose a Good Early Childhood Program*. To order, send 50¢ and a stamped, self-addressed envelope to: National Association for the Education of Young Children, 1834 Connecticut Avenue, N.W., Washington, DC 20009.

4. **Make appointments to visit the child care providers on your list.** Plan to spend at least an hour in each facility. Once you have narrowed down your choice to a few prospects, you may want to visit each several times, at different times of the day, or arrange to spend an entire day. During your visits, talk with the director and caregivers, ask questions, and look for the quality indicators detailed on pages 81–84.

5. **Keep your own needs in mind but be flexible, too.** Affordability and convenient hours and location are important, of course, but the bottom-line consideration is the quality of care. You may be able to compromise a little on cost or hours, but it is critical not to overlook

deficiencies in service, even when your need for affordable child care is urgent.

6. **Ask for references and check them.** Ask the center or caregiver you are considering for the names of at least three other parents whose children attend, and call those parents to ask about their experiences and their opinion regarding the level of care.

7. **Once you have selected a child care facility**, arrange for your child to visit for a couple of hours before it is time to spend an entire day. Make sure the center always knows where to reach you if necessary and where to reach a backup person if you are unavailable.

8. **Be sure to check into the availability of child care-related employee benefits.** For example, some employers support programs in the community, for which employees are given preference; others offer Dependent Care Assistance Plans, also known as salary reduction plans, which let you save on the income taxes you would pay on the portion of your paycheck that covers child care expenses.

CHILD CARE CHECKLIST

Following are qualities to look for and questions to ask when evaluating a child care service:

Facilities and Equipment

☐ Is the center licensed? Does it carry appropriate liability insurance in case of accident or injury?

☐ Is the physical space clean, bright, and inviting? Is there sufficient space indoors and a fenced-in play area outdoors? NAEYC recommends that you look for at least 35 square feet of usable playroom floor space indoors and 75 square feet outdoors per child.

☐ Are the rooms well ventilated and comfortable in both warm and cold weather?

☐ Is space well organized, with separate places to play, eat, and sleep? Is there space for children to play in groups and alone? Is there a place for each child's personal belongings?

☐ Is there enough play equipment? Are toys easy for children to find, reach, and put away? Are there a variety of toys appropriate to the children's various age groups?

☐ Do you feel welcome and comfortable in the environment?

Safety

☐ Are toys safe for all age groups? Are toys and play equipment kept clean and in good repair? Is there cushioning material beneath all climbing structures, slides, and swings?

☐ Are potentially harmful substances, such as medicines and cleaning products, kept in a locked cabinet out of children's reach? Are electrical outlets covered? Are electrical cords safely secured and not frayed?

☐ Are there sufficient working smoke detectors and fire extinguishers? Are exits clearly marked? Is there an emergency exit plan?

☐ Are outdoor play areas secure and free of debris? Is there always an adult present outdoors to supervise children?

☐ Are sanitary procedures followed? Are toilet areas kept clean? Do caregivers wash hands after changing diapers or assisting children in the toilet, and before preparing or serving food? Are children's hands washed after toileting and before eating?

☐ Is a well-stocked first-aid kit readily available? Is there always a staff member present who is trained in first-aid procedures, including CPR? Are emergency phone numbers clearly posted? Is the staff qualified to meet any special health needs, such as administering allergy pills or shots, insulin shots, etc.?

☐ Are current medical records and emergency information kept on file for each child?

☐ Are parents promptly notified regarding illness and accidents?

☐ Are security procedures followed regarding authorization to pick up children?

Staff

☐ What is the child-to-staff ratio and the size of the group? Appropriate ratios and group sizes vary according to the age of the children, and may also be determined by state licensing requirements. The NAEYC recommends these limits:

- For infants, no more than 8 children, with two or more adults
- For two- and three-year-olds, no more than 16 children, with two or more adults
- For four- and five-year-olds, no more than 20 children, with two or more adults

☐ In a family day care home with one mother as caregiver, are there no more than two infants, or five toddlers or older children, including the mother's own children?

☐ What is the staff turnover rate? How long have caregivers been at the center?

☐ Have caregivers had training in child care and development? Do they participate in continuing training workshops or seminars? In an informal setting such as a family day care home, have the mothers demonstrated an interest in learning about children by participating in local child development seminars or reading books about early childhood learning and growth?

☐ Are caregivers friendly and responsive to children's needs? Do they listen to and communicate with the children? Do they both play with children and let them play by themselves, as appropriate? Do they have realistic goals for children? Do they give explanations rather than orders? How do they handle arguments between children? What do they do when a child comes to them with a problem?

☐ What kind of discipline is used? Is the center willing to discuss disciplinary methods with you? Do caregivers use constructive discipline to try to guide children into proper behavior rather than harsh criticism or punishment?

☐ If your child is an infant, observe how caregivers relate to the other infants in the home or center. Do they talk with them and hold them during bottle feedings? Are feeding and nap times tailored to each child's individual schedule?

☐ Do the children seem happy and involved, and do they relate easily with the staff?

☐ Do caregivers encourage your involvement? Will they provide regular reports on your child's activities and progress? Are you encouraged to visit anytime?

Activities

☐ Is there a clear, predictable program that provides children with time for structured learning, indoor and outdoor play, and quiet times? Is there a good balance between structured and free activities? Will the center provide you with a weekly schedule of activities?

☐ Are alternative activities and space provided for children who do not want to participate in group activities?

☐ Are activities interesting and appropriate to the different age groups? Are there picture books, puzzles, and construction sets, as well as art and music activities and supplies? Are materials available that allow hands-on, creative, and imaginative play? Are there plants, animals, or other natural science objects for children to care for and observe?

☐ Is there a program of field trips so children can learn about other people and places?

☐ Are transitions between activities smooth?

☐ Are children encouraged to learn self-help skills, such as dressing, toileting, and eating, as they are ready?

☐ Where do children nap and for how long? Is there an individual mat, crib, or cot for each child? Are alternative, quiet activities available to children who do not want to nap?

☐ How and when are meals served? Are meals and snacks nutritious and appealing? Will the center provide you with a weekly menu of meals and snacks?

☐ If your child has special needs, such as special learning services or handicap facilities, is the center able to meet those needs?

Costs and Hours

☐ What is the basic fee, and what is and is not included? What is the payment schedule?

☐ What are the center's hours and holiday schedule? What is the policy regarding children's illnesses?

☐ In a family day care home, is a substitute caregiver available during the regular caregiver's illness or vacations?

EVALUATING YOUR CHOICE

Your job doesn't end once you have selected the program that best meets your child's needs and your schedule and budget. As your child attends the facility, be alert to his or her reactions. Does your child look forward to going to the center or absolutely dread it? What does he or she say about daily activities at the center? It may take a month or two for a child to adjust to a new environment. Sometimes, however, a negative reaction can be a sign that something is wrong. Be particularly alert to sudden changes in behavior, such as unaccustomed depression, fearfulness, or withdrawal. Also keep in touch with the situation by periodically asking caregivers or the center's director how your child is doing. Get to know the staff and develop a good working relationship with them. Visit from time to time—with an occasional surprise visit—to continue your observations and evaluations.

A good early childhood program can enrich a child's life, providing opportunities for social interaction, intellectual stimulation, and emotional growth. Keep looking until you find the program that will keep your child comfortable, safe, and happy. The rewards of your persistence will come in the benefits your child receives and in your own peace of mind.

Clothes Dryers

[For information and advice on selecting a retailer, saving on energy costs, and appliance service and service contracts, see *Appliances*, pages 25–28.]

Because the basic design of the clothes dryer is so uncomplicated, just about any model you buy will do an acceptable job of drying the laundry. Some dryers, however, will handle the job more efficiently than others, and some have added convenience features that can help make your washday a shade easier.

STYLES AND SIZES

From the outside, most brands and models of clothes dryers look pretty much alike. All dryers are front-loading and are styled to match their companion washers. All have a rotating drum to hold the laundry; drying is accomplished by hot air that is forced through the drum.

The standard dryer is 27 to 29 inches wide; prices range from about $200 to $500. Compact "apartment-size" dryers, from 24 to 27 inches wide, are available for smaller spaces. These can be installed beside a compact washer, stacked on a special rack, hung on a wall, or purchased as a one-piece unit with the washer. Some compact dryers are portable so that they can be rolled away for storage. A good compact washer/dryer pair may cost from about $600 to $1,000.

Dryers must be installed in an area that permits proper venting, with ductwork arranged in the shortest, straightest path to the outdoors. Compact 120–volt dryers can be used without venting, if necessary, as long as the dryer is not used in an enclosed space.

FACTS AND FEATURES

Capacity. Dryers generally are available in compact, standard, and large-capacity models, but one manufacturer's "large" may be another's "super capacity." A more accurate point of comparison is the load capacity that each unit is designed to handle. A large-capacity dryer usually can accommodate 18 to 20 pounds of wet laundry, a standard model from 14 to 16 pounds, and a compact model 13 pounds or less.

Controls. Clothes dryers may use one or more of three different types of drying systems: time setting, thermostat sensing, and/or moisture sensing.

Gas or Electric?

Your choice between a gas or electric clothes dryer will be largely determined by the fuel/power availability in your home and your local utility rates. In general, electric dryers cost less to purchase but more to operate, because of the higher cost of electricity.

For maximum efficiency, an electric dryer should have a minimum rating of 4400 watts. You'll usually need a 208– or 240–volt outlet; some models operate on 120 volts, but these take twice as long to dry a load of clothes as the 240–volt models. All compact dryers are electric and operate on either 120 or 240 volts.

Gas dryers require a professionally installed direct gas line and should have a rating of at least 20,000 BTU/hour for top performance. They also require a 120–volt outlet or an electrical supply of 240, 208, or 120 volts to power such features as the motor, light, and ignition.

Time setting controls, the least expensive option, simply let you set the length of time that clothes will be dried at a preset temperature. **Thermostat sensing** or **automatic drying** models use a thermostat and timer combination to regulate drying time; the thermostat monitors the temperature of the air leaving the drum and cycles heat on and off as needed until the timer completes its cycle. **Moisture sensing** or **electronic controls**, available on the more expensive models, use moisture sensors inside the drum to sense temperature and moisture level, and turn the dryer off as soon as clothes are dry.

Both thermostat sensing and moisture sensing controls are more efficient than timed drying, and models equipped with these drying systems usually also give you the option of drying clothes for a preset time or to a preset degree of dryness. Moisture sensors are the most accurate and efficient of the three drying systems and are generally the most expensive as well, adding about $30 to $60 to the price of the dryer.* However, because moisture sensors are better at gauging when clothes are dry, they can reduce overdrying of fabrics and cut energy consumption by about 10 to 15 percent.**

Cycles. Clothes dryer cycles typically include "regular," "permanent-press," and "knits" or "delicates." These cycles adjust the temperature level at which clothes are dried so that it corresponds to the needs of various fabrics. Many dryers also have an "air-dry" or "fluff" setting for blowing unheated air through delicate articles. And some models have an "extra care" or "press care" feature, which minimizes wrinkling by

*Source: *Consumer Reports*, October 1989, Consumers Union, Mount Vernon, NY.
**Source: American Council for an Energy-Efficient Economy.

continuing to tumble clothes, without heat, for a period of time after the drying cycle ends; a periodic signal reminds you to unload the dryer.

Extra features. Other performance and convenience features you may find in clothes dryers include: a low-heat "touch-up" cycle for removing wrinkles from dry clothing; a "cool-down" cycle, which tumbles clothes in cooler air during the last 5 or 10 minutes of operation, cutting energy use and reducing wrinkles; stationary drying racks, which can be inserted on the door or inside the drum for drying items such as sneakers or sweaters without tumbling; an end-of-cycle signal (some models let you adjust the volume of the signal or turn it off completely); a lint signal, which sounds when the filter needs cleaning; electronic touch-pad controls, which give you precise control over times and temperatures but can be expensive to purchase and service; an interior drum light; an extra-wide door for easier loading and unloading; and a fabric softener dispenser.

☑ CLOTHES DRYER CHECKLIST

Following is a checklist of factors you may want to consider when selecting a clothes dryer:

- ☐ Is the dryer's energy source—gas or electric—the right choice given the available utility connections and your utility rates?
- ☐ Will your available space accommodate the dryer and allow proper venting?
- ☐ Is the dryer's capacity adequate for your needs?
- ☐ Does it have either thermostat sensing (automatic) or moisture sensing (electronic) controls?
- ☐ Does it have at least three cycle settings ("regular," "permanent-press," and "air-dry")?
- ☐ Does it have an "extra care" or extended tumbling period for minimizing wrinkles?
- ☐ Does it have any extra performance or convenience features you might want, such as a "touch-up" cycle, a "cool-down" cycle, stationary drying racks, an end-of-cycle signal, an interior light, etc.?
- ☐ Are controls convenient and easy to operate?
- ☐ Is the filter easy to see, reach, and clean?

Clothing

If your closet is full of clothes you never wear, you're not alone. Nearly everyone has spent money on a fashionable item that quickly went out of style or on clothing that for one reason or another was simply the wrong choice. Following is a list of shopping "do's and don'ts" that can help you build an attractive, versatile wardrobe and avoid clothes-buying disasters.

Do:	Don't:
• Invest the bulk of your clothing budget in classic items that will serve you for years.	• Buy something just because it's in fashion—it may not be the right choice for your looks or your wardrobe, and it's likely to go out of style quickly.
• Choose the best quality you can afford for the items you will wear most. (See "Quality Checklist," page 89.)	• Buy piecemeal. Instead, plan for a cohesive, well-put-together wardrobe.
• Comparison-shop at home, using catalogs and newspaper ads.	• Select a clothing store on the basis of price alone. Look for a convenient location (in case you need to make returns), a helpful sales staff, a good reputation (check with your local Better Business Bureau if in doubt), and a generous refund and exchange policy.
• Take advantage of end-of-season sales to add to next year's wardrobe.	
• Build your wardrobe around one basic color group, such as navy and gray or maroon and black. Select major clothing items in those colors, and save bright complementary hues for shirts, blouses, and accessories.	• Buy clothes that are too tight, with the intention of losing a few pounds.
• Check care labels before you buy, and make maintenance costs part of your buying decision.	• Use last season's measurements when ordering from a catalog. To be sure the item you order will fit properly, check your dimensions again.
• Ask about refund and exchange policies before making your purchase.	• Buy an item—no matter how "perfect"—that doesn't go with anything else in your wardrobe.
• Save clothing tags and sales receipts until you have worn and cleaned the item.	• Buy something that's not quite right, just because the price is good. If you don't feel comfort-
• Give preschoolers a chance to learn shopping skills by letting	

them share in the selection of their own clothes.

- Accept the fact that a few expensive mistakes are inevitable when teenagers shop for clothes. They will learn to shop and spend more wisely if allowed to make their own choices within a set budget.
- Follow manufacturer's instructions for garment care.

able in a garment, chances are you'll never wear it.

- Overspend on one-occasion-only outfits. Try to select clothes that you'll be able to wear again.

Quality Checklist

Clothing that is carefully made looks better, fits better, and lasts longer. You can expect to pay more for quality construction—but at the same time, it's a mistake to assume that all expensive clothing is well made. When shopping for clothes, look for the following quality features. (You may also want to review the clothes-shopping tips and precautions in *Drycleaning*, page 142.)

- ☐ Comfortable, correct fit
- ☐ Small, even stitches
- ☐ Smooth, unpuckered seams; seams at least one-half inch wide and finished to prevent raveling
- ☐ Adequate hem for the type of garment; finished to prevent raveling
- ☐ Reinforced buttonholes; buttons neither too large nor too small
- ☐ Well-fitted lining, tailored to be long enough and wide enough for the garment
- ☐ Secure attachment and balanced placement of shoulder pads
- ☐ Pattern matches well at seams, armholes, and collar
- ☐ Double stitching on clothing intended for heavy wear

Compact Disc Players

[Also see *Audio and Video Equipment*, pages 29–30; *Stereo Systems*, pages 308–13.]

If it's been a while since you last visited a record store, you may be in for a surprise the next time you decide to buy an LP. In many record outlets, those bins full of cellophane-covered album jackets have been nearly or completely replaced by row on row of rectangular cardboard boxes holding one of the biggest revolutions ever to happen to high-fidelity sound—the compact disc.

Introduced to the U.S. consumer market in 1983, the compact disc (CD) is smaller than the traditional 33⅓ rpm record album (full-length recordings come on five-inch discs, "singles" on three-inch CDs), has a longer playing time (about 75 minutes of sound recorded all on one side), and may cost about 25 to 40 percent more. It also uses an entirely different technology to store music.

ANALOG VS. DIGITAL RECORDING

A vinyl LP record contains one long, continuous groove; music is stored in the form of variations in the depth and frequency of minute cuts or wiggles in the groove. Because these wiggles are comparable or *analogous* to the sound wave patterns that they represent, this music storage system is known as **analog recording**. A compact disc, on the other hand, is created through the **digital recording** system. Just beneath the surface of the tough, durable, plastic compact disc are millions of microscopic pits holding musical information that has been *digitally encoded*, or converted into binary numbers (ones and zeros).

While music is reproduced from an LP record by means of a needle, or stylus, that is tracked through the groove, the information stored on a compact disc is "read" by a laser beam in the CD player. Internal circuitry in the player recognizes variations in the laser beam light reflected by the disc and converts those variations into electrical signals. The electrical signals are amplified and converted into analog signals, which can then be played as music by your stereo system.

The process of playing an LP subjects the recording to wear; little by little the needle wears away the subtle undulations in the groove that correspond to the music you hear. Record albums also scratch and break easily. Compact discs, on the other hand, last indefinitely with reasonable care. Nothing but light touches the CD as it is played, so there is no wear. The tough surface of the disc makes it inherently resistant to scratches and damage, and if minor scratches do occur, they generally do not affect playing performance. Further, with a sophisticated CD player, the disc offers flexible "cueing"—the ability to program the order of play of the different musical selections on the CD.

The most important difference between a CD and an LP as far as most listeners are concerned, however, only becomes apparent when the disc is played. With a compact disc, there is virtually no audible sound distortion, none of the "wow and flutter" that can be caused by variations in stereo turntable speed, none of the LP's pops, crackles, and clicks, and no background noise or hiss. And the wider dynamic range of the CD, which allows greater contrast between the loudest and softest passages, delivers a sound that comes close to duplicating live music.

Of course, to enjoy the advantage of CD sound, you need to have a CD player. The many variations in convenience and operating features, the technical language used to promote those features, and the wide range of prices among CD players can make it difficult to decide which brand and model to buy. The following look at terms and options can help you make an informed choice.

CD PLAYER FEATURES AND OPTIONS

All CD players use the same basic technology, and for some listeners, the quality of the sound produced by a $100 player may be indistinguishable from that of a $2,000 model. For music lovers with highly discriminating tastes and equally elevated budgets, there are top-of-the-line models with technological refinements that provide subtle sound enhancement. Such "fine-tuning" features include 18– or 20–bit digital-to-analog converters, separate digital and analog power supplies, 3 vs. 1 laser, and suspended subchassis, among other tongue twisters. The improvements offered by these high-priced refinements generally are difficult or impossible for the average consumer to detect. For that reason, this chapter will concentrate instead on the more readily apparent differences in operating and convenience features offered by various models.

1. **Programmability.** Each separate musical selection or movement in a compact disc recording is assigned a *track number*, which is noted on the disc. All CD players allow you either to play a single disc nonstop or to call up a particular track number and begin play at that point. Many models also let you program a number of other functions related to the order of play. In general, the more sophisticated the player's programming abilities, the greater its cost.

Some moderately priced CD players can be programmed to play specific tracks on a single disc, as long as the tracks you select are in ascending order. More expensive models may allow you to program the player to jump from one disc to another and back again for a continuous selection of from 9 to 50 tracks, depending on model. Other programming functions include:

- **Index play**, which lets you select the playing of specific melodic themes within a musical piece, if the manufacturer has inserted index numbers at those points
- A **shuffle** feature, which allows the player to jump from one track to another in random sequence
- **Playing time access**, which lets you program the machine to begin playing at a given point of time within a given track
- **Repeat play**, which tells the machine to keep playing a particular disc or particular tracks within a disc
- **Program memory**, which "remembers" the tracks you prefer on a disc and will repeat your selections the next time you insert that disc

The length of time it takes the player to find a programmed track varies somewhat from model to model, so you may want to compare track-locating speed as you shop. Also keep in mind that programmability is a feature that can seem very attractive in the store but less practical once you bring the CD player home. When deciding which programming features are worth their added cost, it is wise to consider how often you are likely to use the feature as well as how easy the machine is to program.

2. **Multidisc play.** Most CD players can handle only one disc at a time, but a player with a *changer* can play a number of discs—usually from 5 to 10—automatically. A changer can be a welcome convenience if you enjoy an evening of uninterrupted music, but the cost of this convenience usually adds about $100 to $200 to the price of the player.

Changers come in two styles: cartridges and carousels. The boxlike cartridges generally hold more discs and take up less room than the rotating carousels. The carousels, however, are easier to load and unload, particularly if you want to play just one disc. Some models have a handy extra feature: both a cartridge *and* a separate drawer for easy insertion of a single CD.

3. **Remote control.** The number of functions that you can perform with a remote-control device varies from model to model. If you are looking for a player with a remote, compare the capabilities of various models; one useful feature to look for is remote volume control.

4. **Fast search.** Most CD players will move forward or back from one track to the next. Some have an added feature that allows you to "fast-forward" through a track while listening to a periodic sampling of the musical content; the sound will be choppy, but it won't be the

COMPACT DISC PLAYERS

high-pitched "chipmunk" sound you hear when fast-forwarding an audiotape.

5. **Headphone jack.** Nearly any pair of stereo headphones can be plugged into a CD player equipped with a headphone jack, but the quality of the headphones will affect the quality of the sound you hear. Ask the salesperson for advice in selecting headphones to use with your new player and try out several models, looking for both sound fidelity and comfort. Also make certain the CD player you select has a headphone volume control.

6. **Three-inch disc compatibility.** Most CD players will accept the smaller CD "singles"; some require an adapter to accommodate three-inch discs.

7. **Filters.** All CD players have either an analog or a digital filter; the purpose of the filter is to suppress distortions that might occur when the digital signal is converted into analog form. Analog filters eliminate unwanted frequencies after the signal has been converted, while digital filtering occurs before the conversion process. According to some audio enthusiasts, digital filtering produces better tonal quality, but the average listener is not likely to detect any difference.

8. **Oversampling.** Oversampling allows the CD player to scan each portion of the disc 2, 4, 8, or even 16 times to smooth out audio distortion. However, since audible distortion is rare in CD players, the improvement in sound quality offered by multiple oversampling is questionable.

9. **Three-beam laser system.** This feature uses lenses and prisms to split the laser beam into three parts. The claimed advantage is that a three-beam system improves the way the laser beam "tracks," or follows the path of the microscopic pits beneath the surface of the disc.

10. **Portable players.** Portable CD players, which are not much larger than the CDs themselves, are designed to be carried over the shoulder or to fit into a home or car audio system. Portables may offer fewer features at a somewhat higher cost than comparable tabletop models.

CD PLAYER CHECKLIST

Keep these tips and precautions in mind as you shop for and use your CD player:

• Nearly any model you select will deliver high-quality sound. For most listeners, the only noticeable difference between the lowest- and highest-priced CD players is the convenience features available on the more costly models. When deciding which of the many available features are important to you and thus worth their extra cost, consider your personal listening habits. If you enjoy an evening of uninterrupted background music, for example, a changer model may be worth the added expense. However, if you usually play a single record from beginning to end, you probably don't need to pay extra for a changer or for elaborate programming features. By the same token, whether you need a model with remote control—and whether that should be a basic remote with "play," "stop," and "pause" buttons or a more elaborate remote with, for example, "fast search" or "repeat" controls—depends on your personal music-listening habits.

- A CD player can be connected to nearly any existing stereo system. However, if you own an older system with a low-power receiver or amplifier or low-efficiency loudspeakers, you may find that the greater dynamic range of compact discs can cause sound distortion or even damage your stereo, particularly at higher volumes. In general, the larger your listening room and the louder you prefer your music, the more powerful receiver and the more efficient speakers you will need. A knowledgeable salesperson should be able to tell you whether your present stereo system will accommodate your new CD player and how to modify your system, if necessary.

- The quality of the compact disc itself will affect the quality of the music you hear. Not all CDs are mastered carefully enough to better the performance of the vinyl LP; classical music in particular may sound constricted and lacking in resonance. Further, recordings originally made using analog technology and later transferred to a compact disc may have an audible background hiss not found in original digital recordings. Look for the recording history on the disc cover: "ADD" or "AAD" indicate that the CD was originally an analog recording, "DDD" means that it is an original digital recording, and "DAD" reveals that the original digital recording was converted to analog at some point during the recording process. You may want to ask to listen to the recording on a CD player in the store before making your purchase; also be sure to ask about refund and exchange policies.

- Compact discs are far more durable than LP records, but they do require a reasonable amount of care. Handle discs by their edges, and wipe off lint and fingerprint smudges with a dry, lint-free cloth; wipe radially, from the center of the disc out, rather than in a circle. Store discs in their plastic containers, or "jewel boxes," and avoid sliding them on rough surfaces. While slight scratches are overlooked by a CD player, deep scratches can cause the player to skip or repeat.

Computers

Shopping for a personal computer can seem an overwhelming assignment. An incredible array of products beckons from newspaper ads, mail order catalogs, and retail shelves, all chattering away in a bewildering language of ROMs, RAMs, CPUs, and other inscrutable acronyms. Nevertheless, millions of American consumers have taken the plunge. According to the Electronic Industries Association, a manufacturers' trade group, 23 percent of American households own a personal computer. If you are considering joining this growing pool of the "computer literate," some preshopping planning and research are on the menu. Defining how you will use your PC, understanding the technical terms and computer industry jargon you will encounter, and developing a total budget for your home computer system can help you make careful and cost-effective buying decisions.

TYPES OF COMPUTERS

There are two basic categories of personal computers: desktop and laptop.

Desktop computers sit on a desk or table top; equipped with keyboard, monitor, disk drives, and perhaps a printer or modem, they can take up a good deal of space. Desktop computers generally run a wide variety of software and may cost anywhere from under $100 to $3,000 or more.

Laptop computers generally weigh only about 10 or 12 pounds and operate on batteries; many also can be plugged into standard household current. With prices averaging several hundred dollars higher than those of comparably equipped desktop models, laptops offer portability at a price. A laptop computer may be a good choice for the businessperson who travels or the college student who wants to cart the machine between home and school. Besides the higher price tag, however, drawbacks often include a smaller screen and less convenient keyboard.

A newcomer to the portable PC category, the *notebook computer*, is even smaller and more convenient to transport than the laptop, weighing in at anywhere from 1½ to 6 pounds. These slim machines typically cannot match the features and performance of the conventional laptops; prices nevertheless remain in the relatively upscale neighborhood of $2,000 to $3,000.

Special shopping considerations for portable computers may be found throughout the following discussion of computer components. Remember to compare the operating time of various models. All battery packs for laptop and notebook computers are rechargeable; look for a model with at least three hours of use between chargings.

COMPUTER COMPONENTS

A computer system is made up of five basic elements: the central processing unit, its memory, a data and program storage source, an input device, and an output device. Following is an overview of these basic components plus the most popular *peripherals*, or add-on devices which can be purchased to extend the computer's power and versatility.

CPU. The central processing unit, or CPU, also known as the microprocessor, is the computer's "brain." Located on one *chip*, or miniature silicon wafer, the CPU processes virtually all the information in the computer, regulating the flow of data among the computer's parts and between the computer and any peripherals. Once a program is loaded into the computer's memory, the CPU is able to act on directions received through an input device such as a joystick or keyboard. When its work is done, the CPU sends data to an output device, which may be a disk drive, video monitor or screen, printer, or modem.

Memory. There are two categories of computer memory: ROM (read only memory) and RAM (random access memory). ROM contains the basic "intelligence" placed in the computer by its manufacturer; in most cases, ROM is permanent and unchangeable. RAM is of greater importance to you as a computer buyer and user, since the amount of RAM determines how much information a computer can store and process and thus whether it has the capacity to fit the programs you plan to use. RAM changes constantly as information is added, and loses its contents when the system's power is turned off.

Memory generally is measured in **bytes, kilobytes**, and **megabytes**. One byte equals the memory capacity needed to store one character (one letter, number, symbol, or space). One kilobyte equals 1,000 bytes; thus one kilobyte (1K) of memory could store a document of approximately 1,000 (actually 1,024) characters. One megabyte equals 1,024 kilobytes.

When you load a program into the computer, the program itself takes up a certain amount of memory. A simple calculator program might only require 1K of memory, a typical computer game about 16K or more, and a complex word processing program perhaps 32K or more; the software box or instructions indicate the size in kilobytes of the program. The memory capacity left over once a program is loaded determines the amount of space available for storing the data you create. Thus, if your computer has 48K of RAM and you load a 32K word processing program, you will have 16K of RAM left, or only enough room to store 16,000 characters—about 11 double-spaced typed pages.

According to the National Association of Computer Dealers, personal computer memory ranges all the way from 32 kilobytes to 16 megabytes. As a general rule, the greater the memory capacity, the higher the computer's price. A computer with 256K should be adequate for most applications; 512K or 640K will give you greater flexibility for trying out more complex, business-oriented programs. If you are buying your first computer with the intent of exploring its uses or trying out simple games or educational programs, you might choose to invest in an inexpensive "starter" model with limited memory, and add memory later in the form of do-it-yourself plug-in expansion cards or modules. Keep in mind, though, that each model of computer has a limit on its memory potential. If you think you will need greater capacity in the future, make sure your computer is designed to "grow" to hold the programs you may want to buy.

Data and program storage. The most common medium for storing the programs you load into your computer and the data you generate is the *diskette*, or floppy disk. Diskettes come in two sizes: 5¼ inch and 3½ inch. Both sizes consist of a circular disk coated with magnetic particles; 5¼–inch disks are enclosed in a protective jacket, while 3½–inch disks are protected by a somewhat more sturdy hard plastic case with a sliding metal door. There are also several different diskette storage formats, including *single-density*, *double-density*, and *quad-density*; double-density disks hold twice as much data as single-density and quad-density hold more data than either. Disks also may be *single-sided* or *double-sided*; double-sided disks store data on both sides, again doubling the storage capacity. To further complicate matters, there are *hard-sectored* and *soft-sectored* disks; the computer locates data differently on each. When you buy software, the box or jacket will indicate the model of computer for which the diskette is designed. When you buy blank diskettes, however, you'll need to know exactly which size and type of disk your computer requires. If uncertain, ask the computer dealer for guidance in buying the right diskettes for your specific model.

If you need to store large amounts of information, you may want to invest in a **hard disk**. Hard disks typically can store from about 10 to 30 megabytes (10 million to 30 million bytes) as compared to the 360–kilobyte (360,000–byte) capacity of a double-sided, double-density floppy disk.* That greater capacity can allow you to load all of your programs and data onto one hard disk, eliminating the need to store separate floppies. Hard disks also increase the speed at which programs run and at which software is loaded into memory. A hard disk may cost from $300 to a few thousand dollars, depending mostly on capacity, and it may be purchased either as a built-in component or as an add-on device.

*Source: National Association of Computer Dealers.

To transfer data back and forth between your floppy disk or hard disk and your computer's memory, you'll need a **disk drive.** A hard disk drive is permanently closed; you cannot remove the disk from the machine. For this reason, even if you own a hard disk and a hard disk drive, you will still need to use floppy disks to load new programs and other data into the hard disk and to make *backup disks* (extra copies of the information stored on a disk, which are made as a precaution should the data on the original disk become damaged).

Some computers come equipped with one or two built-in floppy disk drives; with other models, you must buy the disk drive separately. On a system with only floppy disk drives, it is usually a good idea to have two drives; this makes it easier to copy disks and to run programs contained on more than one disk.

Input devices. The CPU receives data and instructions either from the disk drive or from an input device such as a game controller, a graphics device, or a keyboard.

- **Game controllers** may include low-cost *game paddles,* which let you control the movement on the screen in two directions; *joysticks,* which are more expensive but allow quicker, finer control; or *trackballs,* which let you move objects around on the screen by spinning a ball. Game controllers are usually sold as add-on components. Before purchasing one of these devices, make sure it is designed to work both with your specific model of computer and with the software you plan to use.

- **Graphics devices** are used to create computer pictures. *Digitizers* and *light pens* are small penlike devices; the digitizer is used on the desktop while the light pen draws directly on the screen. A *mouse* is a small device which, when rolled on a desktop or pad, moves the *cursor* (an on-screen position indicator such as a square, rectangle, or arrow) allowing you to access various functions—to select from a *menu* listing the choices you have in the program, for example. A *plotter* is a device that makes an on-screen copy of a picture you have created on paper. Again, make certain your computer software can accommodate a particular graphics device before you buy, and be aware that to use the device, you may also need to invest in a special software package.

- The **keyboard** is the input device most commonly used with personal computers. With a keyboard, you can type documents, input the information required by computer programs, and/or write your own programs. Most computer keyboards look and feel much like a typewriter keyboard, although the layout of the keys differs somewhat from model to model. Be sure to test the feel and ease of use of a keyboard before you buy. You also may want to look for convenience features such as a second, separate keypad for numbers, which can be handy if you will be using the computer to input numerical data, and/or programmable function keys, which enable you to type a frequently used phrase or command with the touch of a single designated key.

The keyboards on laptop computers are usually more compact than those on desktop models. When shopping for a laptop, look for a keyboard that is at least 11 inches wide for comfortable use. Also be sure to compare the "click" of the keys if quiet operation is important—if, for example, you will be using the computer to take notes in the library.

Displays. The display, or screen, may be built into the computer or may be purchased separately. Following is a look at the relative merits of the three commonly used types of personal computer displays:

• **TV set.** The least expensive method of displaying computer information is to attach the computer to your home TV set. To accomplish this, you will need an *RF modulator,* a small box that converts the computer's video signal into a TV channel signal. An RF modulator is built into some computer models and with others must be purchased separately. The computer image displayed on a TV screen tends to be fuzzy, which can be a problem if you type and read documents for extended periods. The other drawback of this type of display is that the TV set is limited in the number of *columns,* or characters per line, that it can display, usually to about 40 characters, as compared to the 80–character width (including margins) of the standard business letter. If you are planning to use your computer mainly for entertainment and your budget is limited, using your TV set as a display can be a good way to get started. Before buying the computer, however, make sure you will be satisfied with this type of display by asking to see a demonstration of the complete computer system with all components connected, including the RF modulator and a standard TV set.

• **Video monitor.** A video monitor looks much like a TV set without channels. Designed to be directly connected to a computer, video monitors offer a sharper image than a TV hookup, plus the advantage of a screen dedicated to computer use—using the computer won't tie up the family's TV set.

To increase legibility, many video monitors display enlarged characters on the screen; this usually limits the maximum number of columns that can be displayed to about 30 or 40, making it difficult to visualize a standard printed page. An optional plug-in circuit board may be purchased to reduce the size of the characters and increase the display to 80 columns, but those reduced characters can be difficult to read on an ordinary monitor. A *high-resolution monitor* offers a solution—it allows easy viewing of small characters and can be a worthwhile investment if you plan to use your computer as a word processor. A monitor's degree of resolution is measured in *pixels,* or dots; the more pixels, the more detailed and realistic the computer image. Resolution may range from about 64,000 for a low-resolution monitor to 480,000 for a very high-resolution monitor, although there is no industrywide standard.

Video monitors may deliver either a *monochrome* or *color* display. If you plan to use your computer for entertainment, education, or color-graphics work, the ability to reproduce color via either a color monitor or a color TV set can be essential. However, high-resolution color monitors, also known as *RGB monitors*, are expensive—prices can reach as high as $2,000 or more, as compared to the $100 to $200 price tag on most standard monochrome monitors. For word processing or similar applications, a monochrome screen may serve you just as well, at a lower price. Black-and-white monochrome screens are available, but a green or amber display is generally considered less eye-fatiguing; an antiglare screen can also minimize eye strain.

Monitors range in size from 5 to 19 diagonal inches; for comfortable viewing, look for a screen of at least 12 inches. You also may see screen size described in numbers such as "24 × 80," meaning that the screen will display 24 lines, each 80 columns wide.

Before buying a monitor, be sure to ask for an in-store demonstration. With a monochrome model, look for bright, sharp characters and sharp contrast between characters and background; with a color monitor, keep an eye out for the sharpness of text or graphics and the vividness of colors.

Operating Systems

Without an operating system, a computer is merely a collection of high-tech components. The operating system is the set of *software programs* that allow your computer, applications programs (see page 106), disk drives, and peripherals to "talk" with one other. It may be built into the computer's permanent memory, written on the same disk as an applications program, or purchased on a separate disk. When stored on a disk, it is called a disk operating system, or DOS.

A variety of operating systems are in use with personal computers today, each differing in the basic commands required for use and in speed of operation. However, the most important consideration as you shop for a computer is whether the software you want to use is written to work with the specific operating system of the model you are thinking of buying. Some software is written to run on only one model of computer, while other programs—especially those using the popular MS–DOS, or "IBM–compatible," operating system—are designed to work with several different models. Again, the box or jacket containing the software will indicate the models of computers with which it is compatible. If a particular program is not written for your computer's operating system, you may well be able to find a similar program that is compatible with your DOS.

- **Liquid crystal displays.** The liquid crystal display, or LCD, commonly used in calculators and watches is also the standard on laptop and notebook computers. *Reflective LCD screens* can be difficult to read in poor light; *backlighted super twist LCD screens* are a good deal more readable, although even this variety cannot produce as sharp a picture as a video monitor and can be difficult to view at an angle.

  All LCD screens are monochrome, but many portable computers give you the option of hooking up a color monitor in place of the LCD screen when you want to run programs requiring color.

COMPUTER PERIPHERALS

Printers. Unless you use your computer solely for games or educational programs, there will be times when you will want to print out the information entered and processed in its memory. Four types of printers are commonly available for use with personal computers: dot matrix, letter-quality, ink-jet, and laser. Prices range all the way from about $200 to $800 for a full-featured dot-matrix model to $3,000 or more for a well-equipped laser printer.

- **Dot-matrix printers,** the most popular choice for home use, form type by means of tiny wires that punch a ribbon to create a *matrix*, or pattern of dots, for each letter. The jagged-looking "computer type" thus created can be fine for personal use and correspondence but may not be suitable for business letters and documents. Some dot-matrix printers allow you to reduce printing speed in order to create characters that look more like those of an electric typewriter. When used with the appropriate software, some also are capable of printing graphics. Prices vary according to printing speed, the number of dots in the matrix (5 × 7 for crude type, 9 × 12 for excellent print quality), and other features.

- **Letter-quality printers** commonly use the *daisy wheel* familiar to many office computer users. Daisy-wheel print is typewriter quality; however, this type of printer is relatively slow and noisy. Prices are somewhat

*Letter created by
dot matrix printer*

*Daisy wheel
(commonly used in letter-quality printers)*

higher than those of dot-matrix printers and vary according to printing speed and other features.

- **Ink-jet printers** operate much like dot-matrix models, with the characters formed by tiny dot patterns. However, while the standard dot-matrix printer uses a ribbon, an ink-jet printer uses ink contained in a replaceable cartridge. Ink-jet printers are fast and quiet, but they require the use of special, more costly tinted paper.

- **Laser printers** work very much like photocopying machines, using light to transfer an image onto a printing drum and toner to set it on paper. They are fast and very quiet, and they produce type and graphics that come close to typesetting quality.

As you shop for a computer printer, keep in mind that the range of choices for printers is much smaller than for computers, and that not all printers can work with all computers. That potential incompatibility is due mainly to the fact that there are two different types of connections, or *interfaces*, between printer and computer: serial and parallel. If your printer and computer have incompatible interfaces, you may be able to solve the problem by adding a plug-in printer interface card or expansion module, at a cost of about $100. Another potential area of incompatibility exists between the printer and your software. When you buy software, look on the box or jacket for a listing of the printer brands the program can support. And to be certain of avoiding problems, insist on a demonstration in the store, with the printer connected to the computer model you own or plan to buy, running the software you require.

A good way to evaluate printers is to print out a page of type from each model, and compare the following features:

- **Type quality.** Besides judging the legibility and quality of characters, keep in mind that, when used with the appropriate software, many printers are capable of producing not only letters, numbers, and punctuation but also print "enhancements" such as boldface, italics, or underlining. Some more deluxe printers go a step further, with built-in software that allows the creation of a number of special graphic symbols.

- **Speed.** How long does it take each printer to do its job? Printer speed is measured in characters per second (cps); however, when comparing speed remember that cps does not take into account the length of time each printer takes to return the carriage and advance the paper.

- **Operating noise level.** Letter-quality printers are the noisiest; for quieter operation, you may choose to purchase an optional acoustical enclosure.

- **Paper width and columns.** If you plan to print letters, you'll need a printer capable of producing 80 or more columns, or characters per line, and accepting paper at least 8½ inches wide. For accounting or financial planning applications, you may prefer a super-wide 132–column printer.

- **Paper handling.** There are three basic methods for feeding paper into the printer's roller. *Friction feed*, the lowest-cost option, works like a standard typewriter, with paper simply pulled over the roller sheet by sheet. *Pin feed* uses pins that stick through holes on both sides of 9½–inch-wide continuous form paper. *Tractor feed* operates like the pin feed method but can be adjusted for a variety of paper widths.

Modems. A modem is a box or card that connects your computer to a telephone line, opening the door to the outside world. With a modem, you might exchange "electronic mail" with other computer users, dial into hundreds of different free computer "bulletin boards" across the country, transmit data from your home to your office or your office to your clients, pay your bills by transferring funds from your bank account to your creditors' accounts, or use your computer to link up to information services that give you access to the latest news, stock market reports, or airline schedules. Modem costs may start as low as $90, with price increasing along with quality of construction, baud rate (see below), and other features.

There are two basic types of modems: external and internal. An **external modem** plugs into your computer via a cable and is usually enclosed in a sealed box containing a telephone jack for direct connection to the phone line. Alternatively, some of the least expensive external modems may feature an *acoustic coupler*—the telephone receiver is placed into two cups in the transmitting device and the computer is linked to the telephone lines by sound waves. Room noise sometimes can cause an acoustic coupler to send or receive incorrect characters. An **internal modem** may either be built into the computer or installed in the form of a computer card inserted into the computer's chassis. Costs are generally somewhat lower for internal than external modems, and there are no cable connections to make.

When shopping for a modem, consider these features:

- **Baud rate.** This is a measure of how fast the modem can send and receive data over the phone lines. The two most common baud rates are 300 and 1200—roughly 30 and 120 characters per second respectively—although faster speeds, such as 2400 and 9600 baud, are increasing in popularity. In general, the higher the baud rate, the more costly the modem. However, if you send a good deal of information over the phone lines, the savings on long-distance phone charges can make a modem with a higher baud rate a better buy over the long run.

- **Communications software.** To make your modem work, you'll need a telecommunications software package. Some modems come equipped with their own telecommunications program; purchased separately, such a program may cost $50 to $200 or more. The better programs feature *auto-dial* and *auto-answer*, which allow the computer to automatically dial and receive incoming calls.

- **Full- and half-duplex.** To ensure compatibility with the modems of other computer users, your modem should perform in both the full-duplex mode (both parties can transmit data simultaneously) and half-duplex (the parties take turns transmitting).

Other peripherals. Other popular add-on devices designed to enhance the computer's power and usefulness include:

- **Speech synthesizers**, which convert computer data into words, sounds, or music. Some computer models may require an external speaker to make a speech synthesizer work.
- **Music devices**, which include a variety of plug-in boards and other devices that enable you to compose music on the computer and play it through built-in speakers or your home stereo system. Some computer models have built-in music capabilities.
- **Home controllers**, in the form of plug-in modules or circuit boards, which allow you to program electrical devices in your home—to automatically turn on a light or other device at a specific time, for example.

A SYSTEM FOR SHOPPING

The preceding introduction to computer components, features, and terminology has given you an idea of the factors you'll need to consider as you plan and shop for a computer. Now here's a step-by-step approach to shopping for the particular system that will suit your needs, interests, and budget.

Step #1: Define Your Needs

The computer is a multifunctional tool, with home uses that include word processing, home management, education, and entertainment. Your family might use a home computer system to create mailing lists of friends or business associates and to print out envelopes or labels; to type letters or homework assignments; to draw up a budget and keep track of spending and investments; to play electronic games designed to teach spelling, math, or problem solving; or simply to have fun with videogames.

Defining why you want a computer and what uses it will perform in your household can help you avoid costly mistakes. For example, if you are mainly interested in playing games, whether for entertainment or education, a relatively inexpensive computer or perhaps even a videogame system that plugs into your TV set may serve you well. If you are buying a PC as a teaching aid for a student, you'll need to consider compatibility with the school's equipment; that can be as simple as a call to the school, college, or university to find out what hardware and software they use and whether they recommend a specific machine. If you plan to use your computer to create a newsletter, compile a mailing list, or prepare your tax returns, you'll need to determine both what software is available to perform those functions and what kind of computer is required to run the software you like. (Also see "Consider Software First," pages 106–108.)

It is important to remember that as technology marches on, the costly computer system you assemble today may be nearly obsolete in a decade. Buy with your *near-future* needs in mind—make sure the computer you are planning to buy will run the software you want now and may want in the next few years, but avoid buying a machine designed to take your child from cradle to college. Also be sure to consider the varying needs of family members. You may even decide that buying *two* PCs—an inexpensive model for running games and a more sophisticated machine for home business use—will prevent conflict and help you realize more from your total investment.

Step #2: Research the Field

Before plunging into computer territory, take the time to study the terrain; the more data you gather before you shop, the more likely you are to chart a steady course. Following are a few tips on potential sources of information and guidance:

- Talk to friends and business associates who own personal computers; these contacts can be a good source of advice on the convenience and usefulness of various models, the service and reliability of dealers, and pitfalls to avoid as you shop.
- Visit your local library, newsstand, or bookstore for copies of magazines and books covering personal computers. You'll find that a number of excellent nontechnical publications are available, some offering a complete introduction to the basics of computer or software purchase and use, others providing evaluations and price guidelines for new or used computers and for software. Remember that things change quickly in the computer field; it's best to look for information published within the past year.
- Watch the newspapers for announcements of computer shows in your area. A large computer show can give you an opportunity for hands-on experience on a wide variety of systems.
- Test your motivation and learn the basics through an introductory course to computers offered by a local school or computer dealer.

Step #3: Select a Dealer

Personal computers and software are available through a variety of sources, including computer stores, department stores and other general-merchandise retail outlets, and mail-order catalogs.

There are both advantages and drawbacks to buying computer goods by mail. Mail order companies may charge substantially lower prices than retail outlets, with discounts averaging 30 to 40 percent for hardware purchases and more than 50 percent on software.* They also typically offer a wide selection of merchandise and convenient comparison shopping and location of a dealer with a specific product in stock. These indisputable advantages are often offset, however, by several major drawbacks: the lack of pre- and post-shopping advice and technical support, the possibility of damage during shipping, and less convenient resolution of problems involving damaged or defective merchandise.

If you are a computer "expert," the advantages of mail order shopping may outweigh the disadvantages. For the less experienced computer user, a local retail establishment may be a better choice. Whatever your decision, use the same care in choosing your computer dealer as you do in selecting the computer itself. Ask friends and colleagues for recommendations of dealers who have given them satisfactory service; look for a courteous, knowledgeable sales staff, whether you make inquiries by phone or in person; ask about and compare return, exchange, and repair policies; check out the company's reliability record with a phone call to your local Better Business Bureau; and follow the shopping tips and precautions outlined on pages 108–110 and, if you buy by mail, in *Mail Order and Telephone Shopping*, pages 260–63.

Step #4: Establish a Budget

Assembling a complete computer system can end up costing far more than you originally anticipate. To help keep costs under control, make up a total budget before you shop, estimating the price for the computer, display, disk drive(s), peripherals such as a printer or modem, and supplies such as blank diskettes and printer paper and ribbons. Prices for each of these elements will vary widely depending on the model, the dealer, the state of competition in your geographic area, and other factors. You may want to consult newspaper and magazine ads, mail order catalogs, and computer or software buying guides as you draw up your estimated budget.

Step #5: Consider Software First

Applications software is a computer program designed to let you use your computer for a specific purpose—to play a game, assemble a mailing list, or calculate your taxes, for example. Before you begin to narrow your choices among different computer models, you'll need to decide what you want to do with your computer and what software is available to

*Source: *Consumer Guide® Computer Discount Shopping Guide*, ©1988 Publications International, Ltd., Lincolnwood, IL.

Used Computers and Computer Brokerages

If you crave a state-of-the-art computer system but can't afford the prevailing price, you may want to consider buying a used computer. Prices are often substantially lower for used computers than for the same models purchased new. And in 1989, according to the National Association of Computer Dealers, over $1.8 billion of used PCs were sold through a new and growing service industry: computer brokerages. These businesses neither own nor stock equipment; rather they match up potential sellers and buyers of used computer goods. To use a computer brokerage, you might either consult its magazine or newspaper ads or its printed listings of equipment and prices, or phone the brokerage directly with a specific model and budget in mind. When your offer on a particular product is accepted by the seller, you send in a check which is deposited by the brokerage in an escrow account. The computer is then shipped to you at the seller's expense; you have 48 hours following receipt to test the equipment before the check is released to the seller, with the exchange holding on to its commission, usually 10 percent of the selling price.

If you are thinking of buying a used computer—whether through a computer brokerage or from an individual seller who may have placed an ad in a newspaper or computer magazine—keep these tips and precautions in mind:

- Shop around at computer stores to decide on the equipment you want and to investigate current prices for new merchandise before beginning your search for a used version of that equipment.
- Make sure the computer or peripheral components you buy have a serial number on the back or bottom.
- Ask for the original boxes and instruction manuals.
- Before you buy, make sure the support and advice you may need are available, whether through a friend or colleague, a computer user group, a school, or some other source.
- Remember that used computers usually do not come with a warranty. If buying through a brokerage, it can be a wise precaution to have the equipment inspected by a computer repair technician during the escrow period. If buying directly from an individual seller, thoroughly test out all components and peripherals before agreeing to the purchase, and run the software you plan to use to make sure your programs are compatible with the computer.

perform those tasks. To help you make your selection, you might talk with friends and colleagues who own PCs, ask computer dealers for demonstrations of the particular programs that interest you, and read computer magazines for reviews of different programs. Once you've zeroed in on the particular software that best serves your needs, you'll be ready to shop for compatible computer equipment.

Keep an eye out for these features as you evaluate and compare software packages:

1. **Performance.** Does the program do everything you want it to do? How quickly does it perform its functions? Remember that performance will also vary with the capabilities of the computer running the software—that's why it's important to try out software on the complete system you plan to buy.

2. **Ease of use.** Look through the instruction manual and try out the program before you make your purchase. How easy is it to perform the functions you'll most commonly use? Is the program *menu driven*—that is, does it feature on-screen lists of the choices you have, to make it easy to perform functions without having to remember the specific command for each? Does it allow you to bypass the menu and type in commands once you become more experienced? Does it have *help screens*, self-explanatory instructions built into the program so you do not have to refer to the manual each time you have a question? Remember that the more complicated programs may take longer to master, and make sure the learning requirements of a particular program match your level of motivation.

3. **Support.** Where can you go if you have questions? Will the dealer provide answers? Does the software publisher provide a toll-free help-line number?

4. **Warranty.** What happens if there is a flaw in the diskette? Is a backup copy provided in case problems develop? Can you return a defective diskette for free or low-cost replacement?

5. **Price.** You may well find yourself spending more over the long run for all the software you want than for the hardware. According to the Electronic Industries Association, software is typically priced at $10 to $50 per program, with some personal business programs costing as much as several hundred dollars. Keep in mind, though, that a wide variety of *public domain*, or noncopyrighted, software is available at low cost through some individual programmers, computer user groups, schools, and software dealers. Check with your computer manufacturer or a local school or user group for details on sources and prices.

Step #6: Compare Computer Models

In order to make a wise selection, you'll need to spend a good deal of time both with dealers and alone with computer equipment as you evaluate and select the elements of your computer system. Shopping considerations related to memory, disk drives, input devices, screens, and peripherals are found on pages 96–104. Here are some additional factors to consider:

1. **Compatibility.** Before you begin testing computers, you should already know which software is available for a given model. It is important to try out the software you plan to buy by running the program with the completely assembled computer system.

2. **Ease of use.** Is the instruction manual, or *documentation*, provided with the computer clearly written and easy to understand? If not, are other useful instruction books or "tutorial" disks available for the particular computer model? How easy is it to make the computer do what you want it to do? Don't rely on a salesperson's presentation alone in making this evaluation. Bring along a task you want to perform with your computer, such as compiling a mailing list, and try entering the information—you'll quickly learn whether you can live with a particular system.

3. **Support.** Where can you go to get questions answered? Is there a toll-free manufacturer's help line? Are there magazines or local user groups that specialize in the particular computer? Does the retailer sponsor free or low-cost training programs?

Speaking in Computerese

If you want to write your own computer programs, you will need to learn a new language. The most popular computer languages include the following:

- **BASIC** is the most widely used computer language. Depending on the model of computer, it may be permanently stored in ROM (see page 96) or, less conveniently, you may have to load it in from a diskette each time you want to write or run a program.

- **Logo**, available with a number of PCs, is easy for children to learn and can be used to create computer drawings.

- **Pascal, C,** and **assembler** are languages for expert programmers. Programs written in Pascal or C may run on a variety of computers, but each computer has its own unique assembler.

- **Prolog** allows the creation of "artificial intelligence" programs, which can imitate some of the ways in which people think.

Also available are software packages called **program generators**, which ask you a series of questions and use your answers to produce a finished program, enabling even fledgling computer users to create relatively sophisticated programs.

4. Repairs. How and where can you get the computer and/or its accessories repaired? How long do repairs typically take?

5. Warranty. Does the warranty cover parts, labor, or both? Is it full or limited? If limited, exactly what does it cover? How do you obtain service while the product is under warranty, and who pays any shipping costs? If the retailer offers a *service contract*, or extended warranty, ask the same questions about that coverage, and also make certain the retailer is authorized by the manufacturer to provide service. Remember that a warranty is free, but an extended warranty is a contract sold by the retailer; its coverage should begin only when the manufacturer's warranty ends.

6. Price. Whether you buy in a retail establishment or by mail, ask for a firm quote on the equipment you are considering and make sure you know exactly what the price covers. Buying a complete system package may save you money, but be sure to evaluate the quality of each element of the package individually, and be aware that some manufacturers or retailers may advertise a "bargain" price for a computer "system" without all the components needed for operation. Also remember that companies offering the lowest prices often do not provide the same level of service as their higher-priced competitors. Make sure the price includes all the technical support and assistance you may require. Finally, when comparing the prices offered by mail order companies, be sure to factor in shipping, handling, and insurance charges; sales tax; surcharges for credit care use; and any "membership" or "service" fee.

COMPUTER CARE

Your computer system represents a major investment. To keep it in top working order, follow these recommendations from the Electronic Industries Association:

1. Connect the computer to correctly wired three-wire electrical outlets, as recommended by the manufacturer. You may also want to buy a *surge protector*, a device that is plugged into the computer to avoid damage caused by sudden increases or decreases in electrical power.
2. Static discharge can damage computer circuits and disks. Install the computer in an uncarpeted room, or use an antistatic mat or antistatic spray on carpeting.
3. Keep a static-free dustcover over keyboard, printer, and disk drives when not in use.
4. Clean your disk drives according to the schedule recommended by the manufacturer, using a head-cleaning kit, available at most retail outlets that sell computers.

5. Wipe your keyboard occasionally with a clean, lint-free cloth, sprayed with antistatic cleaning fluid if necessary.

6. Protect computer and diskettes from heat, direct sunlight, liquids, humidity, dust, and cigarette smoke. Make sure air can circulate freely around the computer and peripherals.

7. Avoid bending diskettes, attaching notes to them, touching their magnetic surface, putting a new label on top of an old one, covering jacket holes or openings with a label, and forcing diskettes into the disk drive. Keep disks away from magnetic fields such as those generated by stereo or TV speakers and some paper holders, and use only a felt-tip marker to write on labels.

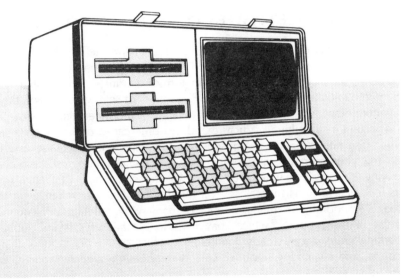

Courtesy of Electronic Industries Association.

Condos and Co-ops

Condominiums and cooperatives are often less expensive than single-family detached homes and offer many of the advantages of home ownership minus some of the responsibilities. There are some drawbacks, however, to condo and co-op ownership, as well as precautions to take when considering a purchase. Following is a rundown of advantages and disadvantages plus a checklist of special considerations for the prospective owner.

THE DIFFERENCE BETWEEN CONDOS AND CO-OPS

Condominiums come in many settings, from towering city high rises to townhouse complexes in landscaped surroundings. They can be located in newly constructed buildings or in former apartment houses that have been rehabilitated and modernized. Regardless of setting, when you buy a condominium, you are assuming ownership of the inner living space of a single unit in a multiunit structure and, in some cases, of the lot on which your unit sits. You are responsible for financing your purchase and for paying your mortgage and property taxes. You are also responsible for paying a monthly maintenance fee or assessment, which can range from as low as $50 to as high as several hundred dollars. In exchange for this fee, a condominium management company will maintain the common areas of the property, which may include the hallways, stairs, lobbies, parking areas, access roads, landscaping, club rooms, playground, tennis courts, and swimming pool, as well as the heating, air-conditioning, and electrical systems.

Ownership of the common areas is shared by all of the condo owners as a group, and the rules governing the use and maintenance of common property are set by a homeowners' or community association. As a condo owner, you are automatically a member of the association and have a voice in the operation and maintenance of the property. At the same time, you are bound by the association's rules. *Inside* your own unit, you are free to paint, build, and decorate as you please. *Outside*, there may be restrictions on your adding a porch awning, installing a roof antenna, or setting up a barbecue grill. There also may be regulations prohibiting small children or pets or giving the association the right of prior approval of potential lessors or buyers of your unit.

Like a condominium, a *cooperative* is a form of shared ownership. When you buy a co-op, however, you do not receive legal title to your unit and the shared property. Instead, you own shares in a corporation that holds the title to the entire property, and you receive a "proprietary lease" giving you the right to occupy one of the units and to use the common areas.

Another key difference between condos and co-ops involves the financing of the purchase. With a condo, you arrange for your own financing and pay your own mortgage; with a co-op, the purchase of the entire property by the co-op corporation is financed by a single "blanket" mortgage. Along with ownership, you agree to assume your share of the mortgage and property tax payments and to pay the monthly maintenance fee.

As a co-op shareholder, you have a vote in corporation matters regarding the management and maintenance of the property and you must abide by the rules of the owners' association.

ADVANTAGES AND DISADVANTAGES

There are significant differences between owning a traditional single-family detached home and condo or co-op ownership. Before making a major financial commitment, you will want to carefully consider the pros and cons of all your options. The checklist below can help. You also may want to review the discussions on buying vs. renting and defining your housing needs on pages 189–91 of Home Buying.

Advantages	Disadvantages
• Freedom from responsibilities for maintenance	• Monthly maintenance fee, which may rise periodically
• Often less expensive than a single-family home	• Less privacy and more restrictions on property use than with a single-family home
• Can be good investment if you are able to rent or sell your unit	• Possible restrictions affecting rental, sublease, or resale
• May have recreational amenities such as tennis courts, swimming pool, etc.	• Fee for upkeep of recreational facilities whether you use them or not
	• With a co-op, no outright home ownership or independent mortgaging

BEFORE YOU BUY

Most of the considerations and precautions that apply to the search for and purchase of a single-family home also apply to the purchase of a condo or co-op. For tips on setting a home buying budget, enlisting the services of a real estate agent, evaluating homes and neighborhoods, signing a contract, obtaining financing, closing a deal, and buying homeowners insurance, see pages 191–205 of *Home Buying*. Also observe these special precautions related to investment in a condo or co-op:

1. **Thoroughly investigate the reliability and reputation of the developer.** Talk to local real estate brokers, bankers, and the local Better Business Bureau. Is the developer reputable and well financed? Are there any outstanding liens or legal actions against the developer or the owners' association? Also talk to building residents or, if the building is brand-new or under construction, to owners of units in other buildings owned by the developer.

2. **Ask for and thoroughly read the following documents before signing a purchase agreement, and ask your lawyer to review them as well:**
   - The **declaration or offering statement**, which should contain a detailed description of the unit and the entire complex. When buying a condominium, also check the declaration to make certain the condo association carries sufficient liability insurance coverage for the entire development as well as adequate insurance on the building and common areas and grounds against fire and other perils. You may want to ask your attorney or insurance agent for advice in making this determination.
   - The **engineer's report**, which will indicate the condition of the building and whether the plumbing, wiring, or other structural elements need repair or replacement. If you are buying a unit in an older building, remember that you and the other owners will have to bear the cost of restoration of poorly maintained or outmoded components.
   - The **bylaws and house rules**, which detail the restrictions applying to your use of the property. Make sure you can live with these rules and regulations.
   - The **current operating budget**, which shows the income, expenses, and cash reserves of the association. Make sure the budget allows sufficient reserves for emergency repairs such as installation of a new roof or an overhaul of the air-conditioning or electrical system, particularly if you are buying a unit in an older building. If reserves are inadequate, you may be hit with large extra assessments to cover major repair bills. Check to be sure that some portion of the regularly monthly assessments goes toward emergency cash reserves.
   - The **management agreement**, which details the amount of your assessment, the schedule on which it must be paid, and the services it includes.

3. **Inspect the condition of the unit and the neighborhood as carefully as you would examine any prospective new home.** If you are buying a

new unit, you may want to hire an independent inspector familiar with multifamily construction. Also ask about the turnover rate of ownership; high turnover can be a warning sign of bad management. You may want to ask how many of the units were bought as rental properties; transients are less likely than permanent residents to be concerned about property upkeep, and there is less sense of belonging to a community in a high-rental neighborhood.

4. **Ask for a clear explanation of the role of the developer.** If the developer retains ownership and control over some common areas such as the land, parking facilities, or swimming pool, you may be forced to pay additional fees for use of those facilities or even for living on the site.

5. **When buying a new and/or incomplete unit, observe these additional precautions:**

   • Carefully read the description of planned construction. Does the developer have sufficient capital to finish the entire project? Where are additional buildings to be built in relation to your unit? Will there be sufficient parking space? Will soundproofing in shared walls be adequate? Are there guarantees, such as separate funds in an escrow account, to ensure the completion of swimming pools, tennis courts, or other planned recreational facilities? Make sure the plans for those amenities are specifically written into the contract and that facilities will be large enough to serve all anticipated residents.

   • Make sure the contract specifies that your down payment is to be placed in an escrow account where it will earn interest until the development is completed, and that it will be returned to you if a specified number of units cannot be sold by a particular date.

   • Ask whether warranties are available to protect against defects in construction. Also ask whether these warranties are backed by insurance.

Contact Lenses

Contact lenses are more comfortable, more convenient, and more versatile today than they were just a few years ago. There are hard lenses and soft, disposables and extended wear lenses, bifocals and astigmatism lenses, even lenses to turn brown eyes blue. With the variety of contact lenses and cleaning systems now on the market, you may be confused as to which products are right for you. The following look at the advantages and disadvantages of each lens type can help you make your choice. And whatever lens you choose, the tips and precautions on page 119 can help ensure enjoyable use of your purchase for years to come.

PROS AND CONS

In general, contact lenses are more expensive than eyeglasses, and they're not for everyone. If you have unsteady hands or dry eyes, are frequently exposed to airborne dust or vapors, or are unwilling to take the time and effort to follow meticulous cleaning practices, glasses can be the better choice. On the other hand, contact lenses do offer a number of advantages. They give better peripheral vision than glasses, eliminate the inconvenience of slipping spectacles or fogged-up lenses, and improve your vision without altering your looks.

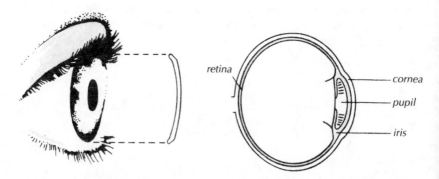

Contact lenses float on the veil of tears that covers the cornea, the clear tissue covering the iris and pupil. The cornea must receive oxygen directly from the air since it has no blood supply.

HARD LENSES

[The "original" lens; made of rigid plastic; oxygen cannot penetrate the lens but reaches the cornea when you blink; average initial cost between $100 and $200, average annual cost of care $60 to $100.]

Advantages	Disadvantages
Can be customized to conform precisely to the eye's needs, allowing excellent correction of most vision problems	Can be uncomfortable because oxygen cannot penetrate and because of relatively small size
The least expensive lens to buy and maintain	Hard to adapt to; if you stop using the lenses for several days, you must go through adaptation period again
Easy to care for	Usually cannot be worn longer than 8 to 14 hours without discomfort
Durable; can last 5 to 10 years or longer	More likely than soft lenses to occasionally pop out from the eye

RIGID GAS-PERMEABLE LENSES

[Made of rigid plastics designed to allow oxygen to pass through to the eye; average initial cost $200 to $350, average annual cost of care $60 to $100.]

Advantages	Disadvantages
The same high optical quality as hard lenses	Require more adaptation than soft lenses
More comfortable than hard lenses (although not as comfortable as soft)	More likely than soft lenses to occasionally pop out from the eye
Easier to care for than soft lenses	Can warp
Relatively durable, may last two to four years	
Can help correct astigmatism	

SOFT LENSES

[Currently the most popular lens; made of flexible plastic, containing varying amounts of water, that allows oxygen to pass through; average initial cost $150 to $300, average annual cost of care $100 to $300.]

Advantages	Disadvantages
More comfortable than hard or gas-permeable lenses	Less sharp vision than with hard or gas-permeable lenses and fewer options available for correcting all vision problems
Little or no adaptation needed	
May be worn for longer daily period than hard or gas-permeable lenses	Costly and troublesome to care for
Rarely pop out from the eye	If poorly cared for, can increase risk of eye infections
	Fragile; may last only six months to a year

EXTENDED WEAR LENSES

[Available as soft or gas-permeable; designed to be worn from one week to one month; allow oxygen to pass through even while you are sleeping; average initial cost $250 to $400, average annual cost of care $70 to $150.]

Advantages	Disadvantages
Vision correction 24 hours a day	Increased risk of corneal ulcers and serious eye infections
Even more comfortable than daily wear soft lenses	
Durable; may last two to three years	

DISPOSABLE LENSES

[Made of flexible plastic; designed to be worn for one week and then replaced; average annual cost $500 to $700.]

Advantages	Disadvantages
Comfortable	Less sharp vision than with hard or gas-permeable lenses and less options available for correcting all vision problems
No cleaning required; reduced risk of contamination	
Little risk of eye infection if used properly	Some users try to save money by wearing lenses longer than recommended, increasing the risk of eye infection

TIPS FOR SHOPPING, FIT, AND CARE

1. To ensure comfort and good vision, contact lenses must be custom-fit for the eye. That requires two steps: an eye examination and a fitting. Eye exams may only be performed by ophthalmologists and optometrists; some states permit opticians to perform fittings.

2. Shop around before selecting an eye specialist. Ask these questions:

   • **What do you charge for the eye exam, fitting, lenses, lens care kit, follow-up visits, and replacement lenses?** Use caution in considering low-priced "package" deals; make sure the price covers all necessary services, including adequate follow-up visits. (Generally recommended are regular follow-ups for three months and semiannual checkups for the next two to four years.)

   • **What part of your fee is refundable if I'm unable to adapt to contact lenses?** Nearly 10 percent of people cannot adjust to contacts, so an adequate refund policy can be good insurance.

   • **Will you provide copies of my eyeglass and contact lens prescriptions?** Under the Federal Trade Commission's Eyeglasses Rule, you are entitled to receive a copy of your eyeglass prescription but not necessarily your contact lens fitting results. You'll need those results if you plan to comparison-shop for lenses.

   • **Are you experienced in fitting rigid lenses?** Rigid lenses must be custom-made for the eye, and precise fit is critical.

3. Proper cleaning of contact lenses is essential; follow your eye care practitioner's instructions meticulously. You may want to ask your practitioner for recommendations on the lowest-priced brands of cleaning solutions, but don't casually switch between products on your own. A new cleaner may contain ingredients that make it incompatible with your lenses or with previously used solutions.

4. Extended wear lenses should be removed for cleaning once a week, even if designed for up to 30 days of wear. Never wear them longer than your eye care practitioner advises.

5. Wearing your lenses for too long a period can deprive your eyes of needed oxygen, leading to pain, redness, tearing, blurred vision, and, if the problem is allowed to continue, possible permanent impairment of sight.

6. Other potentially serious problems associated with contact lens use include allergic reactions to the lens or cleaning solutions, infection or ulcer of the cornea, and warping of the shape of the cornea. If pain, itching, tearing, redness, increased sensitivity to light, or blurred vision develop, remove your lenses. If symptoms persist for more than a few hours, contact a doctor immediately.

Cookware

The first "pan" may well have been a hot, flat stone placed over a fire. Today's cooks have a somewhat broader array of choices. Cookware comes in a wide variety of materials and a perplexing range of prices. Here are some tips that may help you sort out the features and values in those gleaming rows of pots and pans.

MATERIALS AND FINISHES

The most important characteristic of cookware is how well it conducts heat from the heat source to the food. Quick, even heat distribution depends largely on the material used, and material also is the major determinant of durability, ease of care, and price. The most commonly used cookware materials are:

Aluminum: A good heat conductor; durable; moderately priced. Cookware made of thicker aluminum cooks more evenly and is more durable (as well as more expensive). Thickness or *gauge* is usually described by a number—the *smaller* the number, the thicker the aluminum. Drawbacks: Light-gauge stamped aluminum cookware can warp or dent; heavy cast aluminum may become pitted; aluminum tends to stain from contact with minerals in food and water (automatic dishwashing compounds the problem). Stains can be removed by boiling an acidic substance such as vinegar or lemon juice in the pan.

Stainless steel: A poor heat conductor by itself, but the problem is overcome in high-quality cookware with the addition of a layer of copper, aluminum, or carbon steel. Durable; easy to clean; more expensive than aluminum. High heat can cause a rainbow-like discoloration called "heat tint," and cooking some starchy foods can stain the inside of the pan (stainless steel cleaner will remove the stains).

Copper: An excellent heat conductor; expensive. The higher the gauge of the copper, the better the heat distribution. Because copper itself is toxic, copper pots and pans have a tin, stainless steel, or silver lining. If the lining wears off through damage or frequent use, allowing the copper to show through, the pan must be retinned before use. Copper tarnishes easily and polishing can be a chore.

Cast iron: Heavy; durable; moderately priced. Cast iron provides slow, even heat and holds the heat well. To prevent rust, pans should be seasoned before use as directed by the manufacturer, should not be scoured or washed with soap or strong detergents, and should be dried over low heat. Cast-iron cookware with a porcelain finish does not require special seasoning or cleaning but can be more expensive.

Glass, ceramic, and glass-ceramic: Check the labels—some pieces can be used on the rangetop while others are suitable only for the oven. These materials heat somewhat unevenly but hold heat well, so cookware may double as a serving dish. Sudden cooling can be harmful to glass cookware; glass-ceramic withstands sudden extreme changes of temperature. Surfaces can be easily scratched and food may stick; some glass and ceramic pots and pans come with nonstick interiors. Moderately priced.

Porcelain enamel: Porcelain coatings are applied as a decorative touch over stainless steel, aluminum, cast iron, and carbon steel. Porcelain provides a smooth, nonporous cooking surface and is easy to clean, but it can chip, and prolonged use over high heat can cause it to melt. The thickness and quality of porcelain coatings vary directly with cost.

Nonstick finishes: Nonstick cookware surfaces clean easily and quickly, and food cooks in less fat without sticking to the pan. However, finishes are vulnerable to scratching by sharp kitchen tools or abrasive cleaners, and high heat can cause discoloring.

Microwave cookware: Most common metal cookware cannot be used in the microwave oven, since metal reflects microwave energy. A wide variety of cookware specially designed for the microwave is available, and many of your old glass and ceramic containers may also be used. But glazes and coatings can make some utensils unsuitable—it's important to read the recommendations of the microwave oven manufacturer and the cookware manufacturer. You can also make this simple check: Place the item you are testing in the oven, alongside one cup of water in a glass measuring cup. Heat on high power one minute. If the dish remains cool, it is safe for use in the microwave. If it is slightly warm, it may be used for quick reheating but not for cooking. If it is hot, it absorbs too much microwave energy for safe and efficient reheating or cooking and should not be used.

COOKWARE SHOPPING TIPS

1. Look for pots and pans with snug-fitting covers, flat bottoms, and straight sides; they're the most efficient energy users.
2. Handles and knobs should be made of a sturdy, heat-resistant material, preferably with a flame or heat guard for cool handling. Also check to be sure they are securely attached and sturdy enough to support the weight of the filled pan. A well-designed handle is balanced with the weight of the pan to prevent tipping.
3. Weight is usually a good indicator of quality: Food cooked in lightweight pans tends to stick and burn readily. But consider the pan's intended use as well—a very large cast-iron pan, for example, may be too heavy for everyday cooking.
4. Keep an eye out for construction features that may affect ease of cleaning; interior seams, crevices, or rough edges can harbor food and bacteria.

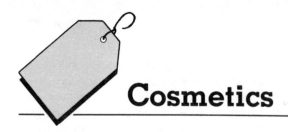

Cosmetics

According to the Cosmetic, Toiletry and Fragrance Association, American consumers spent about $16 billion in 1988 on cosmetics and other toiletry articles and preparations. There is persuasive evidence to suggest, however, that consumer purchases of cosmetics are on a downtrend. Increasingly, American women, faced with $16 lipsticks and tiny $100 jars of face cream, are buying less of their cosmetics at department stores and more at the local drugstore or supermarket. Price and convenience seem to be the key factors behind this trend, but there is another consideration as well. American consumers are becoming better informed in general, and women today are increasingly skeptical of ads claiming that a cream in a jar can perform miracles.

The advertising of cosmetics and fragrances has always been based largely on emotion and mystique—the dream that a certain perfume or skin lotion would change the buyer's life, imbuing her with the beauty and style of the perfect model in the ad. Gold-plated packaging, an "exclusive" brand name, and hints of "antiaging" properties all do their part, leading to cosmetics buying decisions that often are as emotion-based and ephemeral as the ads themselves. But to the informed cosmetics customer, value—the facts behind the claims—are growing in importance.

Discerning those facts can be a challenge. It's nearly impossible to evaluate a product on the basis of a classy package and persuasive, scientific-sounding performance claims. Following are some facts and buying tips that may help. First, you'll find a look at the meaning behind a few of the terms commonly used to promote skin care products and cosmetics, and then some tips for the smart, economical purchase and use of cosmetics and toiletries.

SKIN CARE TERMS

"Hypoallergenic." There are no federal or industrywide standards or criteria for a product to meet before its manufacturer can label it "hypoallergenic." In general, a hypoallergenic product usually does not include preservatives, fragrances, or other ingredients that have been shown to cause allergic reactions, and it usually has undergone extensive sensitivity testing. Thus, a hypoallergenic product may be *less likely* to cause an allergic reaction such as itching, redness, or swelling. However, since nearly all cosmetics companies perform extensive product tests— after all, no reputable firm wants to risk putting out a product that will cause widespread consumer dissatisfaction—the difference between regular and hypoallergenic cosmetics is minimal.

Keep in mind, too, that hypoallergenic does not mean that a product will not cause skin irritation, a topical reaction to chemicals in the product which usually results in redness or inflammation. Further, no product, hypoallergenic or not, can eliminate all risk of setting off an allergic response.

"Noncomedogenic." More common than allergic reactions to cosmetics are comedones—blackheads and whiteheads—caused by excess oil or grease. Again, there are no firm standards for labeling a product "noncomedogenic," and the testing criteria established by different cosmetics firms varies. However, most noncomedogenic products contain less oil and/or grease than regular products, so if you have oily or acne-prone skin, you may want to look for "noncomedogenic" or "water-based" on the label.

"pH-balanced." The pH is a measure of acidity or alkalinity in substances containing moisture. Normal, healthy skin has a mildly acidic pH; pH-balanced products are formulated with a corresponding pH level. The manufacturers' claim is that pH-balanced products are more compatible with, and thus gentler to, skin.

"For sensitive skin," "fragrance-free," "unscented," "dermatologist-tested," "allergy-tested," etc. These terms can mean whatever the manufacturer chooses. However, in general, products formulated "for sensitive skin" are pH-balanced and do not contain chemicals that have been shown to cause topical skin irritations. The claim for fragrance-free products is that they eliminate the possibility of allergic reactions to fragrances; however, some may contain masking fragrances, which are put in not to add a scent but to cover the negative scent of other ingredients.

COSMETICS SHOPPING TIPS

Good health is the basis for good looks. No amount of cosmetics can repair damage caused by poor nutrition, lack of sleep or exercise, or overexposure to sunlight. While new cosmetics-related products are beginning to trickle from the test tubes of pharmaceutical firms—products such as Retin-A, which has shown promise in repairing sun-damaged skin, and Rogaine, a chemical that may stimulate hair growth in some people with male-pattern baldness—it may be a long time before these prescription drugs find their way into the bottles and jars behind the cosmetics counter. Claims that a cosmetic can reverse or retard skin aging are false; in fact, the Food and Drug Administration has warned a number of cosmetics makers that their "antiaging" claims are unsubstantiated and unacceptable. Once you have rejected the myth behind such empty promises, observing a few simple guidelines can help you get the most value for your cosmetics dollar.

123

1. Many inexpensive or moderately priced products are available that offer the same variety and performance as the more expensive products. Let your judgment and your budget guide your choice.

2. Don't confuse cover-up with treatment. If you have a problem with acne, extremely dry or itchy skin, dandruff, scalp itching or dryness, etc., see your family doctor or dermatologist and follow the prescribed treatment.

3. If you have a history of allergic reactions to cosmetics, you may benefit from the fine differences in hypoallergenic and/or sensitive skin formulations.

4. If you have a problem concerning a cosmetics product, return it to the retailer or put your complaint in writing to the manufacturer. If your complaint concerns advertising, send a copy of your letter to your local Better Business Bureau. If you have experienced an allergic reaction or similar problem, a copy should also go to the Food and Drug Administration, 5600 Fishers Lane, Rockville, MD 20857.

COSMETICS AND SAFETY

The following tips on using and storing cosmetics can help you get the most benefit from these products and lessen the risk of contamination, allergic reactions, or other cosmetics-related injuries:

- Cosmetics are free of bacteria when you buy them, but once they have been opened, they provide a good medium in which the natural bacteria from your skin and your environment can grow. Date cosmetics when you buy them, and discard mascara after about six to eight months, other cosmetics after six months to a year. Also replace any cosmetics that change in odor, color, or consistency, regardless of their age.

- Wash your hands before applying cosmetics to reduce the amount of bacteria introduced into the product.

- Use mascara applicators with care. Severe infection can result from scratching the surface of the eye with a bacteria-laden applicator.

- Replace mascara and other eye cosmetics if you have had an eye infection; replace lipstick if it comes in contact with a cold sore.

- Keep cosmetics tightly covered and store them in a cool, dry place.

- Do not lend or borrow cosmetics.

- Remember that a product which you have used successfully for years can suddenly cause an allergic reaction. Discontinue the use of any product that causes irritation, and if your symptoms persist, see a doctor.

Credit and Installment Buying

In 1945, consumer credit outstanding in the United States amounted to less than $6 billion. As of 1971, it exceeded $135 billion. And by the end of 1988, consumers owed some $679 billion for personal loans, credit card accounts, department store accounts, automobile financing, and other credit purchases.

Credit is a convenience. It allows you to charge a meal on your credit card, pay for an appliance on the installment plan, or take out a loan to buy a house. With credit, you can make a purchase when you lack ready cash and enjoy your purchase while you're paying for it.

But the convenience of credit has strings attached. Credit is a service that you pay for. Money is a commodity, and in most cases, when you borrow it or delay payment for a purchase, you pay "rent." Interest is the rental fee charged for the use of money that belongs to a bank, retailer, or other lender. And the costs of credit can be substantial, even though the price of a single installment may seem easily affordable.

If you are thinking of applying for a loan or opening a credit card account, it pays to do some homework first. Understanding how the system works can help you figure out how much credit will cost you, whether you can afford it, and how to shop around for the best terms.

CREDIT TERMINOLOGY

There are two basic forms of credit:

- **Open-end credit** includes credit cards, department store "charge cards," and check overdraft accounts that let you write checks for more than your actual bank balance. In most cases, interest is charged if the purchase amount is not paid within a specified period of time (the *grace period*). The customer usually can choose how much of the monthly bill to pay at any one time. While a minimum payment amount is specified by the lender, paying only this amount ensures that the cardholder will be charged interest on any balance outstanding.

- **Closed-end credit** includes installment loans and purchases. A specific amount is borrowed (in installment purchases, the amount is the selling price of the merchandise) and is repaid in monthly installments over a specified period of time. Offered by banks, savings and loans, credit unions, finance companies, other financial institutions, and some dealers and retailers, this form of credit can be used to finance both small and major purchases, such as an appliance, an automobile, a house, or college tuition.

OPEN-END CREDIT: SHOPPING FOR A CREDIT CARD

The law requires all credit card solicitations and applications to contain certain basic information that can help you determine the costs of buying on credit and shop around for the best deal. The four key items to look for are: the annual percentage rate (APR), the method of calculating the finance charge, the grace period, and the annual fee.

The **finance charge** is the total dollar amount you pay to use credit. The **annual percentage rate** (APR) is the percentage cost of that credit on a yearly basis; bank cards' APRs can range from a low of about 13 percent to a high of 22 percent or more, with the average somewhere around 18 percent, or 1.5 percent a month. Some banks also offer variable-rate credit card accounts, in which the APR changes depending on a specified interest rate index, such as the prime rate or the market rates on short-term government securities. The finance charge you pay is determined by applying the APR to your *balance,* or the amount you owe.

Creditors use a number of different methods to calculate that balance. Some creditors subtract all payments made during the billing period before adding finance charges; this is known as the **adjusted balance method.** Others use the **previous balance method,** which gives you no credit for payments made during the billing period; in this case, the finance charge is applied to the balance at the end of the previous billing period. Under the **average daily balance method,** your balances for each day in the current billing period are added together and then divided by the number of days in the billing period.

As the chart below demonstrates, these three billing systems can result in a considerable variation in finance charges, even when the APR and the amount and pattern of purchases and payments remain the same.

	Adjusted Balance Method	Previous Balance Method	Average Daily Balance Method
Monthly Interest Rate	1.5%	1.5%	1.5%
Previous Balance	$400	$400	$400
Payment (on 15th day of billing period)	$300	$300	$300
Finance charge	$1.50 ($100 × 1.5%)	$6.00 ($400 × 1.5%)	$3.75 (average balance of $250 × 1.5%)

Another critical factor in determining the costs of credit is the **"free" or "grace" period**—the amount of time, if any, that the creditor gives you to pay your bills before finance charges begin. If there is *no* grace period, you begin to pay interest on the day your purchases are posted to your account. This means that even if you pay your bill in full and on time, you'll still be charged interest. Grace periods typically range from about 21 days to 30 days.

Annual fees are charged by many financial institutions for the privilege of carrying their card. These fees can range from $15 to $25 for standard cards or as high as $35 to $60 for "premium" cards that provide a higher line of credit. Some banks offer cards with no annual fee but a relatively high APR, and some have eliminated annual fees to attract and retain cardholders in the face of rising interest rates.

Other charges to consider when you shop for the best credit card deal include:

- The **minimum payment** required each billing period, calculated as a percentage of the outstanding balance
- The amount of any **late fee or penalty fee** charged for late payments or for exceeding your credit limit
- Any **transaction fees** charged for purchases

Which Card's for You?

How can you translate an evaluation of all these factors into the best credit card deal for you? The answer depends, in large part, on your own habits and preferences as a credit user.

- ☐ If you are an *"identification" user*—that is, you rarely charge purchases but rather use your credit card mainly as an ID for cashing checks, making hotel reservations, etc.—your best choice is a "major" or widely accepted card with a low annual fee.
- ☐ If you are among the 35 percent of credit card holders who charge purchases and usually pay their credit card bills in full each month, the APR isn't the most important consideration for you. Instead, the *"nonrevolving" credit user* should look for a low (or no) annual fee and a long grace period.
- ☐ If you are a *"revolving" credit user*—you use your card to purchase goods and services but frequently pay only a portion of the balance due each month—look for a low APR and a creditor that uses the adjusted balance or average daily balance method of calculating your balance. If you prefer to pay a lower monthly minimum, look for cards offering that feature. But remember that making low minimum payments means that it will take longer to pay off a given amount of credit and that you'll pay more interest in the process.

For both "nonrevolving" and "revolving" credit users, a "premium" card with its higher credit limit may be useful if the card will frequently be used for travel or large purchases. But keep in mind that you'll generally pay a higher annual fee for these "gold" cards. If you plan to make frequent charges, you may want to look for low (or no) transaction

> ## "You Can Qualify for A Major Credit Card—Regardless of Your Credit History!!!"
>
> Most credit cards are "unsecured"—that is, they allow you to use credit without having to put up any of your own assets as collateral. But for persons whose credit history prevents acceptance by a traditional credit card issuer, there is an alternative—a *secured* credit card account.
>
> Secured credit cards, often advertised with headlines like the one above, require you to place a deposit in a bank, savings and loan, or a company specializing in this type of offer. You are then granted a line of credit, with the credit limit based on a percentage of your deposit. These cards can be a useful means for rebuilding a damaged credit record. However, before applying for a secured card, you should get the answers to the following questions:
>
> - **What is the processing fee?** Processing fees for opening a secured credit card account may range as high as $50 to $100 and may not be refundable if your application is rejected.
>
> - **What are the additional fees or charges?** Ask for the same information that you would need to determine the costs of a traditional, unsecured credit card account. (See pages 126–27.)
>
> - **Where will the deposit be held?** Look for an established, recognized financial institution; if the institution is a savings and loan, ask whether it is FSLIC-insured.
>
> - **Will the account pay interest?** Most secured accounts pay interest on the unused portion of your deposit; be sure to ask about and compare rates.
>
> For further information on secured credit cards, you may want to contact Bankcard Holders of America, a nonprofit organization of credit issuers, at 560 Herndon Parkway, Suite 120, Herndon, VA 22070.

fees and low (or no) penalty fees for exceeding the credit limit. And, depending on personal preference, additional services offered by creditors may be a factor in your choice of credit cards. Such services include frequent-flyer points, travel or rental car insurance, purchase protection, check-writing privileges, cash availability through 24-hour automatic teller machines (ATMs), or any of a number of other extras.

Tips for Chargers

Being aware of the following facts and precautions can help you cut your credit costs and avoid credit card fraud:

- Avoid holding more cards than you need. Each card has a credit line, and the total could come to a sizable figure, thus reducing the amount of other credit available to you.

- New federal regulations require a credit card issuer to give you 30 days' notice before the card renewal date—this gives you time to cancel your more costly cards and look for a better deal elsewhere.

- With travel and entertainment cards, such as American Express and Diners Club, you must pay off your entire balance each month. Thus there are no interest charges—although there is an annual fee. These cards may offer additional credit services, such as credit for travel tickets. Before basing your choice of a card on the availability of such services, take the time to compare the full cost of credit, including annual fees and any other charges.

- Before selecting a card because of its extra service features (check-writing privileges or cash availability through ATMs, for example), consider whether you actually will need or use those services, and take into account any additional fees.

- It's also a good idea to compare the discount prices of merchandise available through some creditors' discount catalog programs with the prices a careful shopper might find in stores or retail catalogs.

- If you are considering choosing a variable-rate credit card, remember that unless the card issuer specifies a maximum interest rate, the rate can go as high as the interest rate ceiling specified by law in the state in which the creditor is located (and some states do not have *any* interest rate ceiling).

- Many charitable organizations are now offering credit cards to members, with a portion of the issuing bank's revenues from the card reverting to the charity. Before accepting such an offer, compare the credit terms offered with those of other card issuers and consider the alternative of simply making a donation to the cause.

- Follow these safeguards recommended by the Consumer Credit Institute of the American Financial Services Association to protect yourself from credit card fraud:

  1. Before signing a credit card bill, verify that the amounts and total are correctly shown in ink. After signing the bill, detach and destroy any carbons.

  2. When you receive a personalized credit card application in the mail and do not intend to apply for the card, tear up the application before discarding it.

  3. Don't write your credit card number on return cards or mailers that can easily be pulled open.

  4. Avoid giving your credit card number to a telephone solicitor. If you want to learn more about the product or service offered, ask the caller to mail you further information. Contact the merchant if you

"No-Bounce" Checking

Check overdraft accounts take the "bounce" out of your checking account by automatically covering any check you write that exceeds your account balance, up to a certain prearranged credit limit. That can be a convenience for people who tend to lose track of their balance—and pay the price in bounced-check charges. But as always, credit convenience does not come without its own price.

A check overdraft account covers your over-the-balance checks by transferring a sum of money from the credit line into your account. The minimum increment loaned to cover a $75 overdraft may be $100 at one bank, $500 at another; a few banks will advance only the amount needed to cover the loan.

Unlike a credit card account, check overdraft accounts generally allow no grace period; as soon as your check is posted to your account, you start paying interest on your borrowings. Interest rates are usually higher than the rate on installment loans. Repayment methods vary from bank to bank: You may be required to make minimum monthly payments using a special deposit slip, or you may be able to arrange to have funds automatically deducted from your checking account each month.

If you are thinking of applying for a check overdraft account, compare the APR charged by various lenders and ask about any service fees. Also determine the minimum advance that the bank will loan. There's no sense paying interest on a $500 advance when you've had the use of only a small fraction of that amount.

place a phone order using your credit card and do not receive the merchandise within a reasonable period. If a charge for unordered or undelivered goods appears on your credit card statement, notify the card issuer, in writing, right away.

5. Keep a record in a secure place of all your credit card account numbers and expiration dates, the name used on the card, and the phone number to call if a card is lost or stolen. If a card is missing, call the card issuer immediately.

6. You are responsible for up to $50 of unauthorized charges made on a stolen credit card before you notify the card issuer that the card is missing. When considering the purchase of credit card insurance, take into account that legal limit on your liability.

CLOSED-END CREDIT: SHOPPING FOR A LOAN

If you are in the market for a large loan for a major purchase, shopping around for the best value can save you hundreds—perhaps thousands—of dollars.

The federal Truth in Lending Act requires all lenders to provide prospective borrowers with two critical items of information that can help you compare terms: the **annual percentage rate** (APR) and the **finance charge.**

Just as with your credit card accounts, the APR is the interest rate you pay for credit on a yearly basis. The finance charge is the total dollar amount that the loan will cost you, including interest charges and sometimes other costs such as service charges, processing fees, some credit-related insurance premiums, or appraisal fees.

Even when you are aware of the terms a creditor is offering, it's easy to underestimate the difference in dollars that various terms can make. Suppose you are buying a $7,500 car. You put $1,500 down and need to borrow $6,000. Compare the three credit arrangements in the table below.

	APR	Length of Loan	Monthly Payment	Total Finance Charge	Total Cost
Creditor A	14%	3 years	$205.07	$1,382.52	$7,382.52
Creditor B	14%	4 years	$163.96	$1,870.08	$7,870.08
Creditor C	15%	4 years	$166.98	$2,015.04	$8,015.04

The lowest-cost loan is available from Creditor A. If lower monthly payments are important to you, Creditor B gives you the best deal—but by paying off the loan over a longer period of time, you add about $488 to your finance charge. If that four-year loan were only available from Creditor C, the APR of 15 percent would add approximately $145 to your finance charge.

Not long ago, finding the best loan deal was just that simple: a matter of carefully comparing the APRs and finance charges of the fixed-rate loans offered by various lending institutions. Today, adjustable-rate loans, in which the interest rate varies based on a formula related to some measure of prevailing interest rates, have made it necessary to carefully compare lending institutions when shopping for a mortgage, home equity loan, or auto loan.

With an adjustable-rate loan, the *starting rate*—the APR you'll pay for the first year of the loan—may be lower than the rate for a fixed-rate loan offered by the same lender. But if interest rates rise, the APR will also rise, by a set number of percentage points (the *margin*), as spelled out in the loan agreement.

No one, of course, can predict whether interest rates will rise, fall, or remain the same. So how do you choose between a fixed-rate and an adjustable-rate loan? First, it's critical to consider how high the adjustable rate might go. All adjustable-rate mortgages and home equity loans have a **lifetime cap**—a ceiling on how high the interest rate can climb. Federal law does not require caps, however, on adjustable-rate auto loans.

If the APR were to climb to its legal limit, could you still afford the monthly payments? Consider, too, whether there is enough of a difference between the APR of the fixed-rate loan and the starting rate of the adjustable-rate loan to justify your giving up the security of fixed monthly payments.

In the final analysis, only you can determine the degree of risk with which you feel comfortable. You may also want to ask your tax adviser or accountant for advice on the relative advantages and disadvantages of fixed-rate and adjustable-rate loans.

For a discussion of specific considerations related to financing of home and car purchases, see "Financing Your Purchase," *Home Buying*, pages 196–97, and "Step #5: Shop for Credit," *Automobiles*, page 34.

Shopping for an Installment Loan

The following guidelines from the Consumer Credit Institute and the Federal Trade Commission (FTC) can help prospective borrowers shop around for an installment loan that offers the best rates and terms:

1. First establish the amount of the purchase that you can finance with ready cash and the amount you must borrow.
2. If you've used a particular lending institution satisfactorily in the past, begin your credit shopping there.
3. Talk to a loan officer and ask what the APR and finance charge would be for the loan amount you are contemplating.
4. Ask what the monthly payments would be on the loan over a specified period of time. If the lending institution offers an adjustable-rate loan, ask what the payments would be if the rate increased to the maximum, or its lifetime cap. Also ask whether there is any annual cap, or limit on how much the rate can increase in any one year.
5. Other questions to ask and terms to compare regarding adjustable-rate loans include: How often does the rate change? Can the loan be converted to a fixed-rate loan at some future time? (This can be an advantage if interest rates skyrocket, although extra fees are often involved and the fixed rate you receive may be somewhat higher than what you might be able to find elsewhere at the time you convert.)
6. Take a careful look at your personal financial situation—your income, expenses, and debts—to determine whether you can afford to make the monthly payments without putting too much stress on your budget. (For tips on calculating your monthly net income and expenses, see "What Can You Afford?" *Home Buying*, pages 191–92.)
7. Check the ads in the business section of your local newspaper to compare rates offered by other lending institutions. You might also ask friends and business associates for recommendations on lenders. Once

you've identified several prospects, visit each lender's office to ask about loan rates and terms.

8. Any special needs you might have—for example, a fast turnaround on your loan application—should be investigated. Ask about the lender's policy on prepayment; some lenders will allow you to pay off your loan ahead of time or make larger payments, while others impose penalties for prepayment. Also check the fees or penalties for late payments, bad checks, and defaulting on the loan.

9. Compare the rates and terms of the lending institutions you have interviewed. Once you've identified the lender with the best offer, take a careful look at the loan contract you receive and make sure you understand and agree with all items before signing. The agreement may include a paragraph on credit insurance, which pays off the debt in full if death or major illness occurs before the final payment is made. Credit insurance is really term life insurance (see page 221) with rates that do not vary by age and with no evidence of insurability required. This can mean relatively high rates, particularly for young people. Credit insurance is optional; you cannot be denied a loan if you decide not to buy it.

Home Equity Loans

In the wake of the 1986 federal Tax Reform Act, many lending institutions are aggressively marketing home equity loans. While the act gradually

Buying on Time

Before signing a retail finance or credit contract, make sure it includes all of the following: exactly what you are buying; the purchase price; any other charges, such as installation fees or shipping costs; any down payment or trade-in allowances; total amount due; the number, amount, and due dates of all payments; the APR; the total finance charge; all verbal promises made by the salesperson.

Also ask about the company's policy on prepayment. Is there a penalty? Will any of the interest charges be refunded? Inquire, too, about the policy on missed payments. Is there any delinquency charge? Will the balance fall due? Will the item automatically be repossessed? Finally, consider whether you are willing and able to make the monthly payments out of your regular income, and how far your credit is already extended. Remember that credit costs money. While time payment plans allow you to get what you need or want when you don't have the cash to pay the entire cost, you usually pay more for merchandise when you buy it on time.

phases out deductions for nonmortgage consumer interest, it generally preserves deductions for interest on mortgage-related loans.

Most home equity loans are second mortgages that use your home's equity (its current market value minus any amount owed on it) as collateral for the loan. You can usually borrow up to 70 to 80 percent of your home's equity, through either a closed-end loan (a fixed sum which is repaid in monthly installments) or a home equity line of credit which can be accessed as needed, by check or credit card. With a home equity credit line, you pay interest only on the amount of credit used, not on the total amount available.

Both fixed-rate and adjustable-rate home equity loans and credit lines are available. In either case, interest rates tend to be significantly lower than the rates on credit cards and unsecured (no-collateral) personal loans. On the other hand, the lifetime caps (maximum rates) on adjustable-rate home equity loans tend to be a good deal higher than those on adjustable-rate mortgages. And unlike mortgages, equity loans rarely have a specified *annual* interest rate cap. Because your home serves as collateral for a home equity loan, this type of loan should be chosen only after a careful look at terms, costs, and potential problems. Consider the following:

- The use of your home as collateral for a loan can put your home at risk if you find that you cannot make your monthly payments. Those loans that require a large final payment (or *balloon* payment) are particularly risky; you may have to take out another loan to pay off this obligation, and your home may be put in jeopardy if you cannot qualify for financing to make the balloon payment.

- Home equity credit lines allow you to continually tap into your loan to finance major purchases, without the additional paperwork, costs, and delays involved in taking out a new loan for each new expenditure. That convenience could lead you to borrow and spend money more freely than you might otherwise. And with an adjustable-rate credit line, you may end up paying higher interest rates than are available elsewhere. Again, if you cannot pay off your borrowings, your home can be put at risk.

If you decide that the tax advantages and comparatively low rates of a home equity loan are too good to pass up, shop around and compare loan packages with a variety of lenders. Loan terms can vary widely, even within one area. Also keep in mind the following tips from the Consumer Credit Institute and the Federal Trade Commission:

1. Because you are using your home as collateral and because of the extra costs associated with home equity loans, those loans should be used only for major purchases and expenses, such as a second home, college tuition, paying off high-interest consumer loans, or financing the down payment for a business investment.

2. Be sure that all the interest you plan to deduct is, in fact, deductible. Check with your tax adviser for details on the tax consequences of your loan.

3. Before deciding on a home equity installment loan, you may want to look into the possibilities of refinancing your existing home mortgage. Refinancing might permit a larger net loan, a lower interest cost, and a larger tax deduction.

4. Before establishing a home equity credit line, you may want to explore the possibilities of other types of loans that do not require using your home as collateral, including personal installment loans, your credit cards, and other unsecured lines of credit available from various lenders. The interest rates, however, are usually higher on unsecured loans.

5. Carefully compare the rates on home equity loans or credit lines offered by different lenders. Ask about the cap on adjustable-rate loans, and calculate what your monthly payments would be if rates were to rise to the maximum. Also ask about and compare all other costs and fees involved. Just as with a home mortgage, closing costs associated with an equity loan may include a loan application fee, home appraisal fee, title search, credit check, attorneys' fees, and points (one point equals one percent of the total amount you borrow). Costs that continue through the life of the loan may include an annual membership or participation fee, transaction fees, and/or inactivity fees for credit lines. These fees may run as high as $500 to $800, but many lenders waive some or most of them in special promotions of their home equity programs.

6. Ask whether it is possible that you will owe a large final balloon payment at the end of the loan term. If so, you may want to renegotiate your payment terms to avoid the balloon payment or ask the lender to agree ahead of time, in writing, to refinance your end-of-loan balance or extend your length of repayment, if necessary.

7. Also ask about the plan's policy on penalties for late payments and on conditions under which the lender can consider the borrower in default and demand immediate full payment.

8. Do not establish a home equity credit line for more than you expect to use; the points charged are usually calculated on the total loan amount.

9. Be absolutely certain that you can afford to make the monthly payments on your home equity loan, particularly if they will be in addition to monthly mortgage installments. Consider how you would handle sudden unexpected expenses or loss of income.

10. Read the loan document carefully and be sure you completely understand it before signing. You may want to ask your tax adviser or lawyer for information on your state's laws applying to home equity

loans, as well as for advice that can help you weigh the advantages and risks of home equity loans.

YOUR CREDIT RECORD

Although creditors usually consider a number of factors in deciding whether to grant credit, most rely heavily on your credit history. To learn how you have handled credit in the past, most creditors purchase a report from your local credit bureau. Your credit bureau report is based on information regularly reported to the bureau by the retailers and creditors with whom you have credit cards, a loan, or other financial dealings. It also contains matters of public record, such as bankruptcy and court judgments against you.

Under the federal Fair Credit Reporting Act, if you apply for a loan and are turned down because of information contained in your credit bureau report, the creditor must identify the credit bureau involved. At your request, which can be made by mail or in person, the credit bureau must provide a summary of your credit file. If you act within 30 days of being denied credit, there is no charge for this service.

You have the right to dispute any information in your credit record that you consider inaccurate, outdated, or incomplete. To register your objection, write the credit bureau, explaining why you believe the information to be incorrect. Unless your dispute is frivolous or irrelevant, the credit bureau must reinvestigate the matter and delete the information from your report if it cannot verify the disputed facts. If you disagree with the results of the reinvestigation, you are entitled to write a brief statement explaining your side of the story; your statement will become part of your credit bureau report.

If the negative information included in your report is accurate, however, only time can ensure its removal. Credit bureaus are generally permitted to report bankruptcies for 10 years and other negative information for 7 years. There is nothing that you (or anyone else) can do to remove accurate information from your credit file unless the reporting period has expired. Don't be misled by ads aimed at persons with bad credit histories, judgments, or bankruptcies. Promises to "repair" or "clean up" a bad credit history can almost never be kept.

DEALING WITH DEBT

Credit can be a valuable convenience. It can also become a heavy burden on the consumer who uses it indiscriminately. Following are some early warning signs from the Consumer Credit Institute of a credit situation that may be headed for trouble:

- Not paying your bills on time, or juggling bill-paying each month
- Making only minimum payments on large credit card bills
- Not knowing how much you owe
- Regularly using your overdraft credit on your checking account to pay bills
- Living up to your income, without saving anything for emergencies
- Being denied credit because of a negative credit report

If you recognize one or more of these warning signs, the following guidelines may help you get back on track:

1. Analyze where your money is going. Establish a budget and stick to it.

2. Contact your creditors if you are facing temporary problems in making payments. They may be willing to work out a modified payment plan that reduces payments to a more manageable level.

3. If you are thinking about turning to a company that offers debt consolidation loans, debt counseling, or debt reorganization, investigate the company thoroughly before signing any agreement. Check the company's complaint record with the local BBB and your state or local consumer protection office. And remember that some businesses offering debt "relief" charge substantial fees but fail to follow through on the services they promise. Be certain you understand exactly what services the business provides and what they will cost you, and do not rely on oral promises that are not spelled out in a written contract.

4. If you need help in dealing with severe or potentially long-term debt problems, you may want to contact your local nonprofit Consumer Credit Counseling Service (CCCS).* Counselors with the CCCS will try to work out a repayment plan that is acceptable to you and your creditors, and will also help you set up a detailed and realistic budget. Their services are offered free or for a minimal charge.

*For the address of your local CCCS office, contact the National Foundation for Consumer Credit, Inc., 8701 Georgia Avenue, Suite 507, Silver Spring, MD 20910, (301) 589-5600.

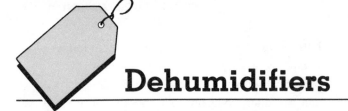

Dehumidifiers

Excess humidity in your home can cause damaging rust, warping, and mildew; give a musty smell to basements and other lower-level rooms; and make you feel even more uncomfortable on hot, sticky days. Air-conditioning does an excellent job of removing humidity as it cools the air. (See *Air Conditioners,* pages 8–16.) Improved ventilation also may help, if humidity is caused by indoor sources such as cooking, dish- or clothes-washing, or showering. And in areas where air-conditioning is undesirable and ventilation can't handle the job, electric dehumidifiers offer an effective alternative.

FUNCTION AND CAPACITY

Like an air conditioner, a dehumidifier contains a compressor or refrigerating unit, chilled evaporator coils, and warm condenser coils. Warm air is drawn into the dehumidifier by a fan and circulated over the cold evaporator coils, where the moisture in the air condenses and runs off into a drip pan or drainage hose; the heat from the air is absorbed by the condenser coils. The dry, chilled air then passes over the warm condenser coils and back into the room.

Thus, unlike an air conditioner, which uses outdoor air to cool the condenser, a dehumidifier actually returns dry, slightly *warmed* air to the room. Even so, the air processed by the dehumidifier usually feels more comfortable with much of its moisture removed, and the problems of rust, warping, and mildew are greatly reduced.

The most important feature to consider when selecting a dehumidifier is **capacity,** usually defined as the amount of water, in pints, that the unit can remove in 24 hours at a temperature of 80°F and a relative humidity of 60 percent. The capacity that you require depends on the size of the space to be dehumidified and the amount of moisture present. Most manufacturers determine their models' "certified" or "rated" capacity according to a standard established by the Association of Home Appliance Manufacturers (AHAM). The table on page 139 shows the capacity recommended by AHAM for particular areas and humidity levels.

RECOMMENDED DEHUMIDIFIER CAPACITY*

Humidity Level	Area (in square feet)				
	500	1,000	1,500	2,000	2,500
Moderately damp (room feels damp & smells musty in humid weather)	10	14	18	22	26
Very damp (always damp & musty; damp spots on walls & floors)	12	17	22	27	32
Wet (room feels wet; condensation or water seepage on walls or floor)	14	20	26	32	38
Extremely wet (wet floor, laundry drying)	16	23	30	37	44

*Source: Association of Home Appliance Manufacturers.

FACTS AND FEATURES

Once you have determined the capacity required for your particular space and humidity conditions, keep these additional tips in mind as you shop for and use your dehumidifier:

1. It pays to comparison-shop for prices. Dehumidifier prices may range from about $100 to $550, with a unit's price generally a reflection of its capacity and the number of convenience features it offers.

2. Deal with a knowledgeable, reliable retailer. If uncertain, check with your local Better Business Bureau.

3. You may want to look for the following convenience and performance features:
   - Easy-to-use controls
   - Quiet operation
   - An adjustable humidistat, which allows you to increase or reduce the amount of moisture removed from the air
   - A "fan only" setting for air circulation without dehumidification
   - A drip pan that is easy to remove, carry, empty, and replace and/or a hose connection to allow direct-to-drain connection
   - Rollers or casters on the bottom of the unit for increased maneuverability

4. Follow the manufacturer's recommendations for use and maintenance. Most dehumidifiers should not be used below 65°F; the condenser coil can ice over at lower temperatures. Maintenance is usually a simple matter of periodically cleaning the drip pan to prevent mold and bacteria growth, and dusting or vacuuming the coils once a year.

Dishwashers

[For information and advice on selecting a retailer, saving on energy costs, and appliance service and service contracts, see *Appliances,* pages 25–28.]

In many American homes, the freedom that dishwashers offer from hours at the kitchen sink makes them more a necessity than a luxury. Dishwashers today are more energy-efficient than the models of a decade ago. They clean dishes under more sanitary conditions than hand-washing and often use less hot water in the process. With costs ranging from about $150 to $800, they also offer a wide array of features that can make comparison-shopping a confusing process.

STYLES AND SIZES

Standard built-in dishwashers are designed to be permanently attached to water pipes, drains, and electrical lines. Most fit into a 24-inch-wide space under the countertop and between two kitchen cabinets; a few compact built-ins fit into an 18-inch space. All are finished on the exposed front only.

Convertible-portable dishwashers are finished on all sides and on the top, and are designed to be rolled to the sink and connected to the faucet and drain with hoses. Most can be later installed as built-ins, making portables a good choice for renters who plan to own a home one day and people who move often.

Undersink dishwashers are designed for small kitchens; they fit into a small space under a specifically designed shallow sink.

FACTS AND FEATURES

Wash systems. Every dishwasher has a rotating spray arm in the bottom of the tub that sprays hot water up over the dishes. Many models have an additional one or two spray arms, which ensure thorough washing of all dishes and odd-shaped items in all parts of the tub.

Wash cycles. Dishwashers clean according to cycles programmed into the appliance. A typical "normal" cycle consists of two washes and two or three rinses plus a drying phase. All other cycles extend or decrease one or more of these phases and/or change the water temperature. For example, a "light wash" cycle may have only one wash, while a "pots and pan" cycle might add a third wash and/or use hotter water.

Most economy models have "normal," "light wash," and "rinse only" cycles; these should be adequate for most families' needs. Some of the other cycles on more advanced (and more expensive) models include: "pots and pans" or "heavy soil," "china/crystal," "rinse and hold," "cool dry" or "air dry," and "delay-start" (which allows you to load the dishwasher and set it for washing several hours later).

Racks always include upper and lower racks plus one or two flatware baskets. Convenient variations on that standard setup include adjustable racks that can be raised to suit the contours of a particular load of dishes and fold-down racks that allow you to stack short items such as cups on two levels in one rack.

The **booster heater** available in some dishwasher models checks incoming water temperature and, if the water is not hot enough to effectively clean greasy dishes, automatically heats it to the proper temperature (140°F). This allows you to wash dishes when hot water is in short supply and/or to keep your main water heater set at a lower temperature, cutting the water heater's energy consumption.

Water usage varies considerably among makes and models, ranging in some machines from 8 to 14 gallons, depending on the cycle, and in others from 6 to 11 gallons. A dishwasher that consumes less hot water also consumes less energy. Water usage information usually can be found in the dishwasher's use and care manual or its specification sheet.

 DISHWASHER CHECKLIST

Following is a checklist of factors you may want to consider when selecting a dishwasher:

☐ Will the dishwasher fit in your available kitchen space?

☐ Is it energy-efficient? (Also see "Energy Costs," *Appliances*, pages 26–28.)

☐ Does it have at least two spray arms?

☐ Are spray arms located so that they do not interfere with easy loading of the machine or take up much of the washer's dish capacity?

☐ Is operating noise level acceptable?

☐ Will racks conveniently accommodate your plates, glasses, serving pieces, and cookware?

☐ Does the dishwasher have a booster heater?

☐ Does its water consumption in a typical cycle compare favorably to that of similar models?

☐ Does it have a liquid rinse aid or rinse-conditioner dispenser (useful if you have hard water)?

Drycleaning

*Dry*cleaning takes its name from the solvents it uses to remove soil and stains from fabrics. Because the solvents contain little or no water and do not penetrate fibers as water does, drycleaning is the only safe method for cleaning many fabrics that would shrink, bleed, or fade if washed in water. Still, it's not impossible for an expensive new outfit to come back from the drycleaner's irreparably damaged. How can you minimize that possibility? Your best bet is to avert problems before they begin. Keep these tips and precautions in mind when you shop for clothes:

1. Look for the care label. The Federal Trade Commission requires apparel manufacturers to attach permanent labels to most garments, supplying instructions for drycleaning or laundering. Exceptions may include totally reversible garments; hosiery, leg warmers, and similar items; very sheer, fragile, or small articles; clothing that can be washed by the strongest possible methods without damage; and articles that sell for $3.00 or less.

2. Watch out for "exotic" combinations of materials—for example, light-colored cotton with dark suede trim, or silk with decorative beads or silver-painted buttons. Cleaning the cotton can cause the dyes in the suede to run, and while the silk is being treated, the beads or decorative buttons can melt, bleed, or chip.

3. Be aware that some fibers and trims simply wear out faster than others and should be purchased with that understanding. Such items include cashmere, camel's hair, mohair, angora, lightweight and loosely woven wools and gauzes, suede and leather (both imitation and genuine), snakeskin, acrylic knits, bonded fabrics (which are held together by adhesive), pleated silk, sized (stiffened) rayon, and fake fur glued to cloth. Also keep in mind the short life expectancy and special care needs of painted and/or glued beads, buttons, and sequins; buttons or trim made of polystyrene; trim sewn on with a single continuous thread; belts or other items containing cardboard stiffeners or glues; and rubberized raincoats or raincoats coated with vinyl or polyurethane.

4. When buying a garment containing elastic, make sure it fits properly; stretched-out elastic may not spring back after cleaning.

5. Don't be misled by price. Cleaning problems occur just as often with high-fashion garments as with less expensive clothing.

6. If you are in doubt about the serviceability of a particular garment, show your purchase to a drycleaner before wearing it.

OUT, OUT #@!☆#?!! SPOT

The best first aid for any kind of spot is to blot up the staining substance at once. Never rub a stain; that can damage the surface fibers and color and make the stain penetrate farther into the fibers.

Next, when attempting do-it-yourself stain removal, proceed with care. Improper use of chemicals—or even water, if the garment's dye or sizing or stiffening agent is water-soluble—can damage or discolor fabrics. Keep a stain removal guide handy, or call your drycleaner for advice on removing a specific staining agent from a particular fabric. Take your better garments to the drycleaner as soon as possible—stains can set with age. At the cleaner's, point out any spots, including colorless spills such as sugary beverages that can stain when heated, and identify the source. Also point out potentially troublesome trims and items containing glues, plastics, or cardboard stiffeners.

DAMAGE AND DISPUTES

Examine your clothes when you pick them up at the drycleaner's and point out any problems right away. Some stains simply cannot be removed by any known method. Many problems, however, such as a spot that was missed or an inadequate pressing job, can be corrected by the cleaner, and most cases are satisfactorily settled at this level.

If a garment was damaged even though all care instructions were followed, the *manufacturer* is responsible. In such a case, your best recourse is to return the item to the store where you bought it. If the drycleaner failed to follow care instructions or did not exercise reasonable care, the *cleaner* is at fault, and you are entitled to recover the value of the garment's remaining life expectancy.

The International Fabricare Institute* publishes a guide assigning life expectancy ratings to all categories of textile products, and it also provides tables for determining the value of a product based on its remaining life expectancy and its condition at the time it was damaged or lost. Your cleaner should have a copy of this guide; it is up to you to negotiate a reasonable settlement.

If you are unable to reach an agreement with the cleaner, contact your local Better Business Bureau or consumer protection agency for advice. If there is a dispute over who is responsible for the damage, ask that the garment be submitted to the Textile Analysis Laboratory at the International Fabricare Institute for testing and determination of responsibility. You cannot send a garment directly—the laboratory will only accept items submitted by member drycleaners or by retailers, textile affiliates, consumer protection agencies, or the BBB.

*12251 Tech Road, Silver Spring, MD 20904, (301) 622-1900.

Exercise Equipment

Whether your goal is to lose a few pounds, build your muscles, or condition your cardiovascular system, getting started on a good fitness program need not require a major investment in a home gym. A highly motivated person can achieve all those goals with no more equipment than a good pair of sneakers, through jogging, calisthenics, push-ups, sit-ups, or any of a number of other fitness activities. The problem for most of us is that it is nearly impossible to find and maintain the necessary degree of motivation. Grinding out sit-ups on the bedroom floor is *boring;* jogging is no fun, either, when it's too hot or cold outside or the sky threatens rain. Health clubs (discussed on pages 186–88) offer the alternative of exercise in a social setting and the motivation provided by varied equipment, experienced trainers, and fellow fitness seekers. But it can be difficult to locate a club with the facilities and atmosphere you want at a price you can afford—and for some, finding time for health club workouts isn't always possible.

That's where home exercise machines come in. With the proper planning and the right equipment, exercising at home can offer convenience and privacy, while taking much of the boredom out of solo sweat. All home exercise machines are not created equal, however. Products vary in the type of conditioning they promise to provide and in how well they keep their promises, and prices can range all the way from under $100 for a simple stationary bike to $5,000 and up for a deluxe home gym with weight-training apparatus for the whole body.

The following guidelines can help you choose from among the array of home exercise equipment. Included are tips on establishing an effective exercise routine plus an overview of the relative advantages and disadvantages of the most common types of equipment.

AEROBIC VS. WEIGHT TRAINING

Before investing hundreds or thousands of dollars in a home fitness center, you'll want to take some time to sort out your exercise needs, goals, and preferences. The tips that follow can help you make some of those basic decisions. And the chart on pages 148–49 will point you toward the equipment best suited to your needs. Keep in mind that the type of equipment that's right for you depends on what you hope to achieve through exercise.

Exercise takes two forms: isometric/isotonic exercise and aerobic exercise. If your aim is to strengthen and define your muscles, you'll need to look for equipment designed for isometric and/or isotonic exercise; that is, a machine that makes you work your muscles against some form of resistance. In isometric exercise, you work your muscles by pressing against an unmovable obstacle; in isotonics, you move muscles through their entire range of motion while pressing against the resistance. Weight-training equipment, which can range all the way from inexpensive dumbbells and barbells to high-priced weight-training benches and home gyms, is designed to provide concentrated isotonic and/or isometric exercise.

The key to weight training is the slow, smooth contraction and relaxation of a muscle that is pressing against a heavy load. It is best to start a weight-training program with light weights and 8 or 10 repetitions of a movement and then slowly increase first the number of repetitions and then the weight. Each time another 2 to 10 pounds of weight are added, you should drop back to the lower number of repetitions and slowly build up again.

Weight training may give you the look and feel of good health—but if cardiovascular fitness, protection against heart disease, and/or weight loss are your objectives, you'll need to choose equipment designed to give you an **aerobic** workout. Regular aerobic exercise, provided by such activities as running or bicycling, conditions the body to extract and use oxygen more efficiently; increases the endurance, efficiency, and pumping capacity of the heart; decreases body fat; and can lower blood pressure and cholesterol levels.

Your Training Heart Rate Zone

Effective aerobic training is based on finding the right level of activity for your particular age group. The idea is to elevate your heart rate to a level high enough to induce a training effect but not so high as to put undue stress on your heart. Here's how to calculate that effective training heart rate zone: First, subtract your age from 220 to find your "theoretical maximum heart rate." Your ideal training heart rate zone is usually considered to be between 60 and 80 percent of that maximum rate. For example, if you are 30 years old, your most effective training range—the range within which you want to elevate your heart rate during the greater part of each exercise session—is 114 to 152 beats per minute, as demonstrated below.

$$220 - 30 = 190 \text{ (theoretical maximum heart rate)}$$
$$190 \times 60\% = 114 \text{ (lower end of training heart rate zone)}$$
$$190 \times 80\% = 152 \text{ (upper end of training heart rate zone)}$$

For best results, you'll need to exercise at your target heart rate zone for 15 to 20 minutes three or four times a week. Every-other-day workouts are ideal, because they give your body sufficient time to recover between sessions. To keep tabs on your heart rate, begin either by taking your pulse periodically as you exercise or by using a heart rate monitor, which may come as standard equipment on some more costly machines or can be purchased separately. Once you become accustomed to workouts, you will probably find that your body's own signals tell you when you are exercising at the right level. Also, you will find that elevating your heart rate to a training level requires increasing levels of exertion as you become more fit.

Less vigorous and/or less frequent exercise also carries health benefits, although results probably will be realized more slowly than they would be with a more vigorous exercise program. Also, if you are exercising to lose weight or to increase your fitness for a competitive event such as a marathon race, more frequent exercise sessions can help speed your progress toward fitness. Remember, though, that overtraining can cause injury. Whether your choice is aerobics or weight training and whether you are a beginner or an experienced athlete, it is important not to overdo it. Keep alert to your body's signals. If a particular activity hurts, discontinue it for a while. If your muscles ache between sessions or you feel constantly fatigued, cut back on your routine and give your body a chance to recover.

Of course, it is possible and often desirable to combine aerobic and isotonic/isometric exercise for a "complete" exercise program. Weight training alone does little for cardiovascular fitness, while running on a treadmill won't increase your muscular strength or upper-body muscle toning. A complete workout can help you increase both cardiovascular fitness and muscle strength and endurance. And the two forms of fitness can be complementary—muscular fitness can protect you against injury as you perform aerobic fitness activities.

Some types of exercise equipment, such as rowing machines and cross-country ski exercisers (see pages 148–49), are designed to give you a complete workout. Or you may choose to combine activities—to pump hand weights, for example, while peddling an exercise bike.

TIPS FOR FITNESS SHOPPERS

The chart on pages 148–49 details the form of conditioning and the advantages and disadvantages offered by several popular types of exercise equipment. As you shop for a home exercise machine, remember to keep your personal preferences in mind; working out on a treadmill can give you good aerobic conditioning, but if you hate running, the only workout provided will be to your wallet. Also be sure to carefully examine the equipment you are considering and give it an extensive tryout, either in the store or at a health club.

The quality and performance of particular models of exercise machines vary considerably, and so does the cost. A treadmill may cost anywhere from $300 to $5,000 or more, for example, and an exercise bike from as little as $60 to as much as $2,000 and up. Cost may be a reflection of quality of construction and/or of the number of high-tech electronic

Cutting The Fat

Exercise decreases body fat by burning calories. Fat is burned off throughout the body; no piece of equipment, despite advertising claims, can allow you to "spot-reduce," or exercise specific muscles to decrease fat in a given area. Each pound of fat that your body stores represents 3,500 calories of unused energy. The chart below shows the number of calories burned through various activities.

Obviously, the more vigorous or prolonged the exercise, the more calories you burn. But as the chart demonstrates, even moderate exercise can convey significant benefits over the long term. Adding just 15 minutes of daily moderate exercise such as walking can use up about 100 extra calories per day. Maintaining that schedule would result in the burning of an extra 700 calories per week, or about 10 pounds in a year, assuming food intake stays the same. On the other side of the coin, adding just one extra slice of bread or one extra soft drink a day—or any other food that contains approximately 100 calories—can add up to 10 extra pounds in a year if physical activity does not also increase.

ENERGY EXPENDITURE CHART*

Activity	Calories Burned per Minute	Activity	Calories Burned per Minute
Sitting quietly	84	Swimming (crawl, 45 yards/minute)	522
Lying down or sleeping	90	Aerobic dancing	546
Bicycling (5 mph)	174	Racquetball	588
Canoeing (2.5 mph)	174	Bicycling (13 mph)	612
Walking (2 mph)	198	Jogging (6 mph)	654
Swimming (crawl, 20 yards/minute)	288	Cross-country skiing (5 mph)	690

These *hourly* estimates are based on values calculated for a 150-pound person. Remember that the energy cost of activities such as walking or jogging which require you to move your own body weight are greater for heavier people, since they have more weight to more. Thus a person who weighs 150 pounds will use more calories jogging one mile than a person jogging alongside who weighs 115 pounds.

*Source: *Exercise and Weight Control*, The President's Council on Physical Fitness and Sports, Washington, DC.

features a machine offers. Construction quality is the more important consideration. If a machine is not well designed and built, it may be uncomfortable to use and/or may bend or break under your workouts. Poor design also can force you into awkward positions that can lead to injury or prevent your getting the aerobic training effect the machine is supposed to provide. As a general rule, you probably will need to pay at least $200 or $300 to get a well-constructed machine that will perform well and will hold up to several years of repeated use.

As you shop, look for sturdy construction and smooth, comfortable operation. You should feel confident that, with a little practice, you will be able to master the equipment. You may also want to consider how the size of the machine and its noise level will fit in with your living space. Finally, keep in mind that extra features such as leather seats, chrome plating, or electronic displays designed to show your target and/or working pulse rate, pace, number of calories burned, etc., can add considerably to the cost of a machine without making the workout any easier or the effects any better. There's nothing wrong with aesthetic or high-tech extras; in fact, interesting graphic displays can help fight boredom and spur you on to greater effort. But don't lose sight of the fact that no machine, no matter how fancy, will do the work for you.

A Quick Guide to Home Exercise Machines

Exercise bikes *[Note: Depending on model, provides either aerobic exercise/lower-body muscle training or both aerobic and isometric/isotonic exercise.]*

Advantages	Disadvantages	Features to Look For	Special Notes
Low-impact aerobic exercise. Relatively compact & easy to store.	Standard models provide no upper-body muscle toning. Relatively noisy.	Sturdy, stable construction. Smooth pedaling; no rocking motion. Comfortable, adjustable seat. Easy-to-use resistance controls. Quiet operation. Speedometer/odometer.	Some models have dual action handlebars for exercising the upper body as you pedal. Recumbent bikes, pedaled horizontally, may ease back stress for persons with lower-back problems. Costs may be twice as high as standard vertical cycles. Weighted metal flywheel provides smoother, more realistic cycling motion.

Rowing machines *[Note: Provides both aerobic exercise/lower-body muscle training and isometric/isotonic exercise.]*

Advantages	Disadvantages	Features to Look For	Special Notes
Low-impact total body exercise. Relatively compact and easy to store.	Can be stressful for persons with lower-back problems.	Sturdy, stable construction. Smooth, even rowing; no rocking motion. Comfortable, sliding seat. Secure, comfortable foot rests. Easy-to-use resistance controls. Quiet operation.	"Oars" may move back and forth on a single plane (on less expensive models) or pivot on brackets for motion more like real rowing. Weighted metal flywheel provides smoother, more realistic rowing motion.

Treadmills *[Note: Provides aerobic exercise/lower-body muscle training.]*

Advantages	Disadvantages	Features to Look For
Low-impact aerobic exercise. Exercising while standing can be easier on lower back.	No upper-body muscle toning. Heavy; require lots of space. Relatively noisy. Some people feel unsteady on moving floor.	Sturdy, stable construction. Belt that starts slowly & operates smoothly. Easy-to-use speed adjustment controls; adjustable incline. Quiet motor. Speedometer/odometer.

Cross-country ski machines *[Note: Provides both aerobic exercise/lower-body muscle training and isometric/isotonic exercise.]*

Advantages	Disadvantages	Features to Look For	Special Notes
Low-impact total body exercise. Exercising while standing can be easier on lower back. Folding models compact & easy to store.	Require relatively high degree of coordination & concentration to use properly. Some models noisy. Some people feel unsteady on sliding tracks.	Sturdy, stable construction. Smooth, even motion. Secure footholds. "Poles" adjustable for height. Easy-to-use resistance controls for both arms & legs. Quiet operation. Guardrail or hip pad to ensure proper posture.	Weighted metal flywheel provides smoother, more realistic skiing motion.

Stair climbers *[Note: Depending on model, provides either aerobic exercise/lower-body muscle training or both aerobic and isometric/isotonic exercise.]*

Advantages	Disadvantages	Features to Look For	Special Notes
Low-impact aerobic exercise. Easy to use. Quiet.	Can put strain on knees.	Sturdy, stable construction. Smooth operation. Secure hand grips and footholds. Hand grips adjustable for height. Easy-to-use resistance controls.	Models include "steppers," for aerobic and lower-body exercise, and "climbers," in which you "climb up" an inclined pole with your hands & feet in grips, for total body training.

Home gyms *[Note: Provides isometric/isotonic exercise.]*

Advantages	Disadvantages	Features to Look For	Special Notes
Safer than "free weights" because weights attached to steel cables.	No aerobic conditioning. Heavy; require lots of space.	Sturdy, stable construction. Ease of performing exercises to work different parts of body; easy to switch from one exercise to another. Even resistance throughout a movement. Comfortable, adjustable bench. Easy-to-use resistance controls.	Resistance usually provided by weights, springs, or pressurized cylinders. Most models have horizontal bench; some have slant board—you lie on an incline & pull up. Some models have vertical rather than horizontal bench for more economical use of space.

HOME FITNESS CHECKLIST

1. If you are over age 30 or have health problems, check with your doctor before beginning any new exercise program.

2. Start small, with short, frequent exercise sessions, particularly if you are out of shape. Nothing kills motivation more quickly than sore muscles or shinsplints resulting from an overambitious first workout.

3. Set specific, realistic, short-term goals. Losing 50 pounds can seem to take forever, and you are bound to get discouraged if that is your objective. A loss of 10 pounds in 12 weeks is more achievable, and reaching that goal can motivate you to strive for more. Similarly, simply "getting in shape" is too vague an objective to keep most people on track; training for improved endurance or performance in a particular sport can yield more tangible, rewarding results.

4. Take the boredom out of your exercise routine by varying activities. Alternate use of your exercise equipment with brisk walking, aerobics, or other fitness pursuits. Varying your routine also can help prevent the muscle strain or injuries that can result from overdoing one specific activity. Other tricks for reducing boredom include exercising to music or in front of the TV set.

5. Start each exercise session with a moderately vigorous warm-up session of four to five minutes, and end with a four- to five-minute cool-down. It is also a good idea to begin and end with a few minutes of stretching exercises.

6. It is important to breathe properly during exercise: Exhale during exertion; inhale during recovery.

7. Don't stop suddenly if you feel tired during vigorous exercise; slow the pace until you are ready to pick up the pace again, or gradually cool down with more moderate activity.

8. Carefully read and follow the instructions that come with your exercise machine. Achieving best results and avoiding injury depend on maintaining proper form during exercise. It can also be helpful to visit a health club to try out the type of equipment you are planning to buy—not only to find out whether you like the machine but also to get expert tips on proper exercise techniques.

9. Remember that you do not *need* a high-priced exercise machine to get in shape. Inexpensive and effective exercise aids, which can either supplement your equipment or add some variety to your exercise routine, include jump ropes, aerobic dance videotapes, arm and leg weights, and "free weights"—barbells and dumbbells, which may be sold as single units or in sets and as solid weights or with interchangeable plates.

Financial Planners

[Also see *Tax Preparers*, pages 317–22.]

Estimates on the number of financial planners in the U.S. range all the way from 50,000 to 250,000. While experts may disagree about the figures, all agree on one fact: Rapid growth and ineffective regulation in the financial planning field have created enormous opportunities for fraud and abuse. Most planners are legitimate, and many might do an excellent job of helping you properly manage your income and assets. But the large number of unscrupulous operators makes it imperative for you to observe the precautions detailed below before you place your financial future in the hands of a financial planner.

THE FACTS BEHIND THE PHRASE

Under existing law (the Investment Advisors Act of 1940), anyone who offers to furnish, for a fee, advice on the purchase and sale of securities is considered an investment adviser and is required to register with the Securities and Exchange Commission (SEC). In reality, only a small percentage of individuals providing investment advice actually comply with that requirement. And although those who do register must file an application disclosing any criminal background, *there are no educational or testing standards* for registration as an investment adviser.

Some states have adopted legislation requiring investment advisers to be licensed on the state level and, in some cases, to meet certain testing requirements. But in most cases, almost anyone can claim the title "financial planner," regardless of education, training, or experience.

In response to growing concern over abuses and the lack of effective oversight in the financial planning profession, some attempts at self-regulation have emerged. The International Board of Standards and Practices for Certified Financial Planners (IBCFP), a nonprofit, nonmembership, public-interest organization, has developed educational, testing, and professional standards for financial planners. Individuals meeting IBCFP requirements are licensed to use the trademarked title "Certified Financial Planner" or "CFP," and are subject to disciplinary actions if they violate the organization's code of ethics. Other titles, such as AFPS (Accredited Financial Planning Specialist), are granted by other professional organizations and reflect an investment adviser's compliance with varying standards of education, examination, and experience. But remember that neither membership in an organization nor initials after a name guarantee competence or integrity. Regardless of an individual's title, your best approach is to apply your own stringent standards to the selection of a financial planner.

CHOOSING A FINANCIAL PLANNER

A good financial planner can give you objective, reliable advice to help you develop a budget and an investment strategy tailored to your individual needs. But how do you find a competent, honest planner?

Your search might begin with a survey of friends, relatives, and colleagues who have had satisfactory dealings with their own investment advisers over a period of several years. Keep in mind the fact that a planner who has worked successfully for another person may not necessarily have expertise in the financial areas in which you have a need. Also ask for recommendations from your contacts in the financial community: your banker, broker, or accountant. Organizations that accredit financial planners should be able to provide the names of several planners in your geographical area; look in your phone book for organization listings.

Once you have the names of several prospects, check with:

- **Your state securities division:** A background check can reveal any noncompliance with state and federal laws.
- **The SEC:** Your planner should be registered with the SEC or registered under state laws dealing with investment advisers.
- **The BBB:** Ask for a reliability report on the planner.

Your next step is to schedule interviews with several prospects. There is usually no charge for these exploratory meetings, but ask about fees first. Then ask the following questions:

1. **What is your professional background?** Look for a strong track record of educational and job experience covering a broad spectrum of financial planning issues. Ask whether the planner also takes advantage of continuing education and training.
2. **How long have you been a financial planner?** Look for three or more years of experience as a financial planner and several more years of prior experience as a broker, insurance agent, accountant, or lawyer.
3. **How long have you been in the community?** One of the basic rules of investing applies here: Deal with individuals you either know personally or can check out through reliable references.
4. **Will you provide references?** Get the names of three or more clients whom the planner has counseled for at least two years. Ask them about their level of satisfaction, their investment returns, and their intentions of staying with the financial planner. Avoid planners who pressure you

to rely on the word of one or two new clients—these short-term clients may be victims (willing or unwitting) of a Ponzi scheme, in which early investors are paid handsomely in order to lure new investors, who end up losing most or all of their money when the scheme collapses.

5. **May I see examples of plans and monitoring reports you have drawn up for other investors?** Pay particular attention to the frequency and quality of the monitoring reports, since these updates will be vital to reviewing and recharting your financial objectives.

6. **Will I be dealing with you or with an associate?** If your planner will be turning over all or most of the day-to-day work on your financial plan to an associate, take the time to check out that individual as well.

7. **What professional/trade organizations do you belong to?** Membership in an industry group may indicate that the planner has met certain standards and may further signal a dedication to the profession. Ask for an explanation of any title used by the planner, and about the requirements for use of the title and membership in the organization. Call the organization to verify what you are told.

8. **What specific experience do you have in the areas that concern me?** Some planners specialize in one or more areas of financial planning or in a certain type of client. In such a case, determine whether an area of specialty matches your goals. Also ask whether the planner refers clients to another source of assistance if the need arises for services outside his or her areas of expertise.

FEES AND SERVICES

Financial planners are categorized by the manner in which they charge their clients.

- **Fee-only.** These planners charge either an annual fee based on assets and investment activity, or an hourly fee of $50 to $200 or more. Basically, they offer a financial plan and then refer clients to others who sell financial products such as stocks or mutual funds. Payment is required whether or not you choose to implement the suggested plan. The advantage to the client: The planner who does nothing more than give advice is not burdened by the potential conflicts of interest related to commissions earned on the sale of particular investment products.

- **Commission-only.** Some planners charge no fee but do earn a commission on the investment products they sell. The claimed advantage: The customer would have to pay a commission no matter where the product was purchased, and he or she benefits from the convenience of "one-stop" shopping by buying the investment products sold by the planner.

- **Fee/commission.** Some planners charge a fee for the financial plan and a commission for the sale of products. The claimed advantage: The fee usually is lower than that charged by fee-only planners.

A 1986 SEC study of the financial planning industry found that 85 percent of financial planners sold investment products, but *only 47 percent* told prospective clients that they did so. It is up to you to determine whether a planner is offering sound financial advice or is simply trying to earn a commission by selling a particular product. When you interview prospective planners, ask how they expect to be compensated. If the planner earns commissions, ask whether he or she offers a complete range of investments or sells only a specific type of product and, similarly, whether the planner offers investments from one specific company or from many providers. The answers are your clues to whether the "planner" is acting in your best interest or is primarily a salesperson pushing a particular product. Finally, ask for an estimate of the planner's bill before you commit yourself. According to the National Association of Personal Financial Advisors, a group of fee-only planners, the planner's bill should not exceed 3 percent of your annual income or investment base, regardless of whether compensation comes from fees or commissions.

SERVICE SPECIFICS

No matter what kind of fee arrangement your planner uses, you should expect to receive the following basic services:

1. A clearly written financial plan, including a balance sheet of assets vs. liabilities, a projected cash flow statement for at least one year, and a precise definition of your financial goals and the steps you will need to take to achieve them.
2. A discussion of the amount of risk you are willing to assume in pursuit of your financial goals.
3. Specific suggestions for improving your personal cash management.
4. Projections for shifts in the rate of interest, inflation, and other factors that will affect your plan.
5. Options and alternatives providing a range of investment choices, with a list of the pros and cons of each.
6. A plan for liquidation in the event of emergency, outlining ways to obtain reserve cash with the least possible cost and disruption.
7. Suggested sources of advice from other professionals; this is particularly important if you do not have a regular accountant, attorney, insurance agent, or stockbroker.
8. A specific schedule for monitoring your financial plan and periodically reviewing its performance and objectives.

"RED FLAGS"

Be on the alert for the following warning signs of fraud:

"No risk." Avoid a planner who urges you to put your money in any investment with a "guaranteed" short-term interest rate that is far above prevailing market rates. This is the number one sign of a possible Ponzi scheme.

No staff. Be wary of a planner whose "office" is a post-office box or whose "staff" is an answering machine. Visit your prospective financial planner's office, and make sure the planner has established ties with reputable professionals in the community.

Few or no alternatives. If one or two investment products are pushed, the planner may be trying to steer you into a fraudulent scheme, or may be more interested in a commission than in your financial future.

"Too complex." If the planner tells you that the investment strategy is too complicated for you to understand and urges total faith, take your money elsewhere.

Unclear or exotic. Watch out for a vaguely phrased or completely unstated investment purpose, such as a "blind pool," in which investment is allowed at the planner's discretion. Another warning sign is any "exotic" element in the plan, such as "top secret technologies" or "inside information from Wall Street."

Fire Protection

In 1988, according to the National Fire Protection Association (NFPA), an international nonprofit volunteer membership group, more than 5,000 Americans were killed and nearly 23,000 injured by home fires. As tragic as those numbers are, they represent a dramatic decrease in U.S. civilian fire death rates, which have declined at a fairly steady rate over recent years—by 19 percent from 1977 to 1982 and by 14 percent from 1983 to 1988. That decline may be the result of the increased use of smoke detectors, says an NFPA report, plus greater public awareness resulting from improved fire safety education efforts.

Protecting yourself and your family from the threat of fire involves three key steps: minimizing fire hazards, installing smoke detectors, and developing a family escape plan. Following is an examination of each of these critical and interdependent elements, along with guidelines for selecting and using a home fire extinguisher.

CAUSES AND CURES

It is always easier to prevent a fire before it starts than to detect and fight it once it has begun. Effective fire protection therefore begins with prevention—and that means understanding the primary causes of home fires and taking a few simple steps to reduce or eliminate those hazards.

Smoking. Careless smoking is the leading cause of fatal residential fires in the U.S.

☐ Never smoke in bed or when feeling drowsy.

☐ If you smoke, use a large, heavy ashtray designed to keep cigarettes from falling out.

☐ Empty ashtrays only when you are certain the contents are cold.

☐ After a party in your home, check behind and under furniture and cushions for smoldering cigarettes.

☐ Store matches and lighters out of the reach of young children, and teach children to bring any matches or lighters they find to an adult.

Heating equipment. Heating and cooking equipment together form the second leading cause of fatal residential fires. According to the NFPA, there has been a sharp rise in recent years in the incidence of home fires caused by portable and area heaters, particularly wood-burning stoves.

☐ Have your heating system professionally inspected at least once a year.

☐ Have chimneys and fireplaces inspected yearly for cracks, loose connections, and obstructions; clean and repair as needed.

☐ Check gas vents periodically for corrosion and obstructions.

☐ Keep combustibles such as clothes, furniture, and newspapers at least three feet away from the furnace, heater, and fireplace.

☐ Cover fireplaces with metal screens or heat-tempered glass doors.

☐ Conscientiously observe manufacturers' recommendations for use and care of portable and kerosene heaters; keep them out of "traffic" areas and at least three feet away from combustible materials.

☐ Provide proper ventilation when fireplaces and portable gas or oil heaters are in use.

☐ Never burn underseasoned or green wood.

☐ Allow ashes to cool completely before transferring them to a metal container for disposal.

Cooking equipment. Fire hazards in the kitchen are most often associated with negligence in the use and care of the stove and other appliances.

☐ Keep the stove free of grease and other combustibles.

☐ Do not store matches, a can of grease, or any other combustibles on or near the stove.

☐ Do not store food or other items above the stove; a child or adult can be burned while reaching over a hot stove to get them.

☐ Make certain window curtains cannot blow over the stove.

☐ Wear short or tight-fitting sleeves when you cook.

☐ Turn pot handles inward, away from the stove's edge.

☐ If the contents of a pan catch fire, turn off the heat and cover the pan with a lid or another pan to smother the flames.

☐ In case of an oven fire, close the oven door and turn off the heat.

Electrical hazards. Faulty or misused electrical wiring is a major cause of home fires.

☐ Make certain your home has sufficient electrical circuits to avoid overloading.

☐ Follow manufacturers' recommendations for connecting special appliances, such as air conditioners or large space heaters, to their own heavy-duty electrical circuits.

☐ Do not overload extension cords; have additional wall outlets installed instead.

☐ Do not run electrical or extension cords under rugs, behind radiators, through door jambs, or over hooks or nails.

☐ Periodically inspect electrical cords for cracks and broken plugs.

☐ If a fuse blows, determine the cause and correct the problem before replacing it; always replace with a fuse of the proper size.

Safety indoors and out. Follow these additional tips for minimizing fire hazards all around the house:

☐ Keep your basement, attic, and other work and storage areas clean of debris such as cartons, newspapers, rags, old clothes, furniture, sawdust, and wood shavings.

☐ Keep outdoor areas free of dry leaves and combustible rubbish.

☐ Allow enough space for proper ventilation around appliances, TVs, stereo equipment, etc.

☐ Store flammable and combustible liquids away from potential sources of heat or sparks. Store gasoline in a marked safety can in a detached garage or toolshed.

☐ Use flashlights rather than candles in emergencies. When using candles or oil-burning lamps, make sure they stand securely, and extinguish them if you leave the room for more than a few minutes.

☐ Keep the barbecue a safe distance from the house, and do not leave the fire unattended. Never use an outdoor barbecue indoors.

☐ Make a fire safety tour of your home at least twice a year, and immediately correct any problems you find.

INSTALLING A FIRE DETECTION SYSTEM

Most fatal residential fires strike at night, while their victims are asleep. Home fires often smolder for hours, producing large quantities of smoke and toxic gases, before bursting into open flames. A home fire detection system is designed to sound an early warning, giving you time to escape before the air becomes unbreathable or exit routes are cut off.

Residential fire detection systems range all the way from single $10 to $30 battery-operated smoke detectors installed in small apartments or mobile homes to whole-house fire alarm systems connected to a central receiving station. Whole-house systems often are combined with a burglar alarm system, with distinctive audible alarms enabling the homeowner to immediately tell the difference between a fire and a burglary. If you are considering the purchase of a household alarm system, see *Burglar Alarm Systems,* pages 60–64, for advice on choosing a system and selecting a contractor. This chapter focuses on the most commonly available fire detection devices, some of which may be installed as components in a household system and all of which you can buy and install on your own as part of your fire protection plan.

Smoke Detectors

Smoke detectors save lives, and in most states, they are required by law in new and/or existing residential housing. There are two basic types of smoke detectors:

- **Ionization smoke detectors** contain a small, carefully shielded quantity of radioactive material which "ionizes" the air in the detector's smoke chamber, generating a weak electrical current. When smoke particles drift into the chamber, they reduce the electrical current flow, tripping a horn or buzzer.
- **Photoelectric smoke detectors,** which are slightly more expensive than ionization models, use a light beam and a light-sensitive photocell to sense the light reflected by smoke particles. When smoke is dense enough to reflect a preset amount of light, the alarm is sounded.

There are slight differences in the kinds of fires to which each type of detector responds most quickly. Ionization models have a slight edge in giving early warning of open, flaming fires, while photoelectric devices are somewhat more likely to respond quickly to slow, smoldering fires. Tests have shown, however, that either type of smoke detector has a high probability of giving adequate warning for most residential fires. To be certain of covering all possibilities, you may want to consider installing both ionization and photoelectric models.

A more important question than which *type* of detector to buy is *how many* to install. According to the widely accepted *Standard on Household Fire Warning Equipment* (NFPA 74), minimum protection includes one smoke detector outside each sleeping area in the home, one on each habitable floor, and one in the basement. For extra protection, NFPA recommends that supplemental detectors be added as needed—inside each bedroom, for example, particularly if the family sleeps with the doors closed, and/or in the living room, family room, attic, furnace room, and hallways. Each additional detector provides more time for the family to escape; having more than one detector is also a wise precaution against the possible malfunctioning of a single unit. Be aware, though, that most models are not recommended for kitchens because of the possibility of false alarms caused by cooking vapors; for garages, where automobile exhaust might set off the alarm; or for attics or other unheated spaces, where temperature or humidity extremes might affect operation.

Shopping tips

Once you have decided on the type and number of smoke detectors you want, you are ready to shop for a specific model. You'll find a wide selection at most discount, department, and hardware stores. Keep the following questions and considerations in mind as you make your choice:

1. Look for the label of a recognized testing laboratory, such as Underwriters Laboratory (UL), to make certain the device meets minimum performance standards.
2. Check the installation, use, and maintenance instructions. Are they clear and complete?

3. Determine whether the detector operates on batteries or standard household current. Battery-operated detectors are usually easier to install. They typically operate for about one year on a nine-volt battery; make sure the model has an audible signal, which can be heard from behind closed doors, to tell you when battery power begins to run low. Smoke detectors that run on household electrical current continue to operate as long as there is current in the circuit. Installation of these units may be somewhat complicated, however.

4. If you are installing a number of smoke detectors in a relatively large home, you may want to consider buying *multiple station detectors.* These usually are arranged so that all of the alarm devices sound when any one of them detects smoke; alternatively, with some models, the alarm is sounded by the detecting device and a single receiver unit, usually placed in the homeowner's bedroom. The number of detectors that can be interconnected varies from model to model; some models also allow the connection of heat detectors.

   If you do not install multiple station detectors, be sure to test your detectors before final installation to make sure all family members can clearly hear the alarm from behind closed bedroom doors. If not, consider installing smoke detectors inside each bedroom.

5. You may also want to look for these additional safety or convenience features:

   • A "safety light," which can help guide the family's escape. Be aware, though, that in heavy smoke, even a very bright light won't be of any help.

   • An extra-loud alarm for heavy sleepers and the hearing-impaired, also useful when the detector is to be placed in a basement or other distant room.

   • A "silence" button, which lets you instantly silence a false alarm for a few minutes while you clear out cooking smoke or some other cause. The value of this feature is somewhat controversial—while a "silencer" can be a plus if it prevents you from removing the battery or the detector during false alarms and possibly forgetting to replace it, NFPA maintains that, for optimum safety, no detector should be "disarmable."

Installation and maintenance

Battery-powered smoke detectors are generally easy to install—you simply attach the unit to the ceiling or wall by means of screws, adhesives, or expansion fasteners, slip in the battery, test the alarm, and the job is done. A detector that plugs into a wall outlet can be a bit trickier. If the best location for the device does not have a convenient outlet, you may need to have an electrician install an outlet or hard-wire the unit into the electrical system. Never hard-wire a smoke detector to a circuit that can be turned off from a wall switch. And if the unit is plugged into a wall outlet, make sure it has a restraining device so it cannot be accidentally disconnected.

Be sure to follow the manufacturer's installation and maintenance instructions for whatever type of smoke detector you are installing, and also keep these recommendations in mind:

- Smoke and hot gases rise, filling the highest points in a room or house before moving toward the floor. Locating a smoke detector high on a wall or ceiling can take advantage of that fact, allowing an early warning while low-level air is still relatively clear. According to NFPA, the preferred installation point for a smoke detector is on the ceiling at least 4 inches from any wall, or on a side wall 4 to 12 inches from the ceiling to the top of the detector. In a basement, the detector should be located close to the stairway leading to the floor above but not at the very top of the stairs, where a "dead air" space may prevent smoke from reaching the unit.

- Air drafts and the temperature of the mounting surface can affect a smoke detector's performance. Locate detectors at least three feet away from air vents, and do not install on uninsulated exterior walls, ceilings below uninsulated attics, or ceilings containing radiant heating coils. (This is particularly important in mobile homes.)

- Test your smoke detectors regularly according to the manufacturer's recommendations. With an ionization model, testing usually involves holding a lighted candle about six inches below the unit; to test a photoelectric model, extinguish the candle and let smoke drift into the detector. Using real smoke is a more reliable testing method than the "test button" found on many older smoke detectors, which may simply indicate that the alarm works and not that the detector circuit itself is functioning. Some newer smoke detectors have a light-sensitive cell or other sophisticated mechanism which allows you to test battery, detector, and alarm without real smoke. Check the instructions to see if your detector has this feature.

- Never "borrow" smoke detector batteries for other purposes. If you remove a detector or its battery to stop a false alarm, keep it in a visible spot as a reminder to replace it.

- Clean smoke detectors according to the manufacturer's recommendations; this may involve simply holding the nozzle of your vacuum cleaner to the side slot openings.

Heat Detectors

Heat-sensing devices may be available either as part of a smoke detector or as a separate product. Most heat sensors are designed to trigger an alarm when the room temperature reaches a certain specified point (*fixed temperature detectors*) or when air temperature rises at an abnormally rapid rate (*rate-of-rise detectors*).

Heat detectors may provide some added protection, but their use is advised only when they are installed as part of a total system based on smoke detectors. It is the smoke rather than the heat in home fires that most often causes injury and death, and heat detectors may remain silent even in the midst of a deadly, smoldering fire. They can be useful, however, in certain spots where smoke detectors cannot be used—in a kitchen, where grease particles and cooking smoke might cause numerous false alarms, for example, or in areas such as a furnace room, basement, or attached garage which may be too cold or humid to allow proper functioning of a smoke detector.

A HOME FIRE ESCAPE PLAN

Your smoke detectors can give you precious extra time in the event of a home fire, but it's up to you to make the best use of that opportunity. Seconds will count if you and your family are threatened by fire. If you have established and practiced a plan for escape, you won't waste precious time trying to figure out the right course of action, and chances are that order rather than panic will rule in the reactions and actions of family members. Following is a step-by-step approach to developing a family escape plan:

1. **Draw a floor plan of your home.** Include windows, doors, stairways, and outside features such as a balcony, roof, or tree which might be used to aid escape. Involve all members of the family in this activity.

2. **Work out at least two escape routes from each room, and mark them clearly on the sketch.** Indicate a primary route as well as alternate choices to use if the first exit seems dangerous. Double-check each exit to make sure it really can be used in an emergency. Can all family members open and fit through the window? Are all exits free of furniture or other impediments? If you live in a multilevel home and upstairs windows are too high for safe use, are escape aids such as metal escape ladders kept near windows?

3. **Decide who will take charge of a young child or any other person who might be unable to escape alone.** Remember, though, that your route to a child's room may be cut off—at as early an age as possible, a child should be taught how to escape unaided. Also remember that young children often believe that they can hide from fire; make sure they understand that they must exit immediately in a smoke or fire situation.

4. **Agree on an outside meeting place where the family will immediately assemble following escape.** It will be vital to know whether everyone

has made a safe exit. Make sure each family member understands that no one is to reenter a burning house for any reason.

5. **Go over the entire plan with each family member.** Make sure everyone is familiar with the floor plan, and take the family through the escape routes for every room. Practice opening windows and using escape ladders. Teach children how to call for emergency help, and make sure they understand that they must use a neighbor's phone to make that call.

6. **Hold a fire drill at least twice a year, including some at night, when most fatal fires occur.** Home fire drills may sound like a silly idea—but they *do* save lives. Vary the drills by calling out different imaginary fire sources, forcing family members to choose alternate routes. After the drill, discuss what happened and how reactions might be improved.

7. **Make sure all family members are aware of these important facts and actions to take in case of fire.**
   - If you must go through a smoke-filled area, crawl on hands and knees, with head held low under the smoke.
   - Before opening an inside door, reach up high and feel the space between the door and the frame with the back of your hand; then touch the knob, again with the back of your hand. If either the opening or knob feels hot or if smoke is coming through the bottom or sides of the door, don't open it; use an alternate exit instead.
   - Don't stop to dress or to gather belongings during a fire; no possession is worth risking your life.
   - Sleeping with bedroom doors closed can slow the spread of fire and give you more time to escape. As you proceed through your escape route, close doors behind you to help keep the fire from spreading.
   - If your clothing should catch fire, the rule is, "Stop, drop, and roll." Stop running, cover your face with your hands as you drop to the ground, and roll to smother the flames.

HOME FIRE EXTINGUISHERS

A fire extinguisher can keep small fires from becoming major blazes—*if* you have the right type of extinguisher and *if* you know when and how to use it. To pick the right extinguisher, you must know something about the way fires are classified and what works against each type of blaze.

Class A fires involve ordinary solid combustibles such as paper, wood, fabric, rubber, and plastic.

Class B fires involve flammable or combustible liquids such as grease, oil, gasoline, tar, paint, and cleaning solvents.

Class C fires involve electrical equipment.

Fire extinguishers may be designed for use on one or more types of fire. The label will tell you which of the three classes an extinguisher can handle and how effective it will be in fighting each type of fire. For example, a unit labeled "1A" must be capable of putting out a blazing stack of 50 pieces of 20-inch-long wood two-by-twos, a "2A" model should put out a fire about twice that big, and so on. An extinguisher labeled "1B" can snuff 3¼ gallons of flammable liquid burning in a 2½-square-foot pan; a "2B" unit can handle twice that job. A "C" rating (never preceded by a number) means the extinguishing agent is nonconductive and therefore safe to use on electrical fires. The label also gives you operating instructions, both in words and pictures.

Here are some tips for selecting and using a home fire extinguisher:

1. Look for a label showing that the unit has been tested by an independent testing laboratory such as Underwriters Laboratory (UL) or Factory Mutual Research Corporation.

2. When deciding which type of extinguisher to buy, assess the potential hazards in your home. A unit rated for class B fires is usually the best choice for the kitchen. For protecting your workshop or garage, you might choose a multipurpose "A:B:C" model, effective against all three types of fire. It is a good idea to have an all-purpose extinguisher on each floor of your house for optimum protection. Some people also opt to buy an extra unit containing the gas halon for protecting prized stereo or computer equipment. Halon extinguishers are very effective against class B and C blazes and marginally effective against class A fires, and they leave behind no messy residue. On the other hand, they are relatively expensive and their use and disposal has been linked to damage of the earth's ozone layer.

3. Also consider these factors:

   - **Weight.** Home fire extinguishers may weigh anywhere from about 1 to 30 pounds; the greater the capacity, the heavier the unit. Make sure adult family members are able to easily lift and use the extinguisher.

   - **Capacity.** Units with greater capacity will discharge longer; however, any household extinguisher with a capacity of 10 pounds or less will discharge completely within a maximum of 30 seconds. Again, when deciding on capacity, take into account the weight of the unit and who is likely to use it.

   - **Ease of operation.** You may have to press a button or squeeze a pair of levers to discharge the extinguishing agent. How much strength is needed to discharge the unit?

   - **Instructions.** Are use instructions large and easy to interpret?

   - **Mounting.** Most fire extinguishers come with a wall mount. How easy is it to remove the extinguisher from its mounting for use?

- **Tamper seal.** Most models have a seal or pull pin to prevent accidental discharge and to show that the unit has not been used or tampered with. Is the seal or pin easy to remove for use of the extinguisher?
  - **Rechargeability.** Can the model be recharged after use or if it loses pressure? With some small, inexpensive units, replacing may be less costly than recharging.
4. Install extinguishers in plain sight, in a path of exit so there will always be an escape route if the fire cannot be controlled.
5. Familiarize yourself with how to use the extinguisher, and instruct all adult family members in its proper use and operation. Demonstrate how to hold and discharge the extinguisher; purchasing an extra unit to practice with may make sense for some families. Make sure everyone understands the following rules for fighting fire with an extinguisher:
  - Keep a safe distance from the fire.
  - Aim the unit at the base of the fire first, then use an upward sweeping motion.
  - Fight a fire only if:
    - ☐ You discover it in its early stages and it is small and confined to the area in which it started.
    - ☐ You are certain how to operate the extinguisher.
    - ☐ The unit is in good working condition and is rated for the type of fire you are facing.
    - ☐ You can fight the fire with your back to an escape route.
    - ☐ The fire department has been called.
6. Follow the manufacturer's maintenance instructions, and inspect fire extinguishers at least once a month to make sure they are fully charged. Remember that owning a partially used extinguisher is like having no extinguisher at all; if a unit has been used or tampered with, take it to a recharging service company. To locate a service dealer, look in the yellow pages of your phone directory under "Fire Extinguishers."
7. If you have further questions about fire extinguisher selection, use, or maintenance, contact your local fire department.

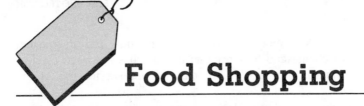

Food Shopping

A look at your budget and your weekly calendar no doubt will reveal that food shopping is a pretty big part of your life. No other category of products covered in this book is purchased so frequently; nowhere are the opportunities more favorable for either overspending *or* saving.

Building significant savings into your shopping bill can be child's play. But to successfully play the game, you have to know the rules. Following is a look at the ins and outs of the food shopping process from both your angle and the retailer's, along with guidelines that can help you plan a money-saving shopping strategy.

GUIDELINES FOR FOOD SHOPPING SAVINGS

1. **Your list is your most important ally.** Buying on impulse is costly. Not only can it mean spending more than necessary on individual items, but the impulse shopper also tends to buy wasteful items that may contain less food value (and more fat or calories) for the dollar. Further, shopping without careful advance planning can lead you to buy too much, with the excess ending up in the trash bin, or too little, which can translate into uneconomical extra shopping trips.

   When you make a shopping list:

   ☐ **Build it around a well-thought-out meal plan.** Plan your menus for a week in advance, keeping in mind the objective of adequately filling your family's nutritional needs while causing the least possible damage to your budget. (Also see "Dietary Guidelines," pages 167–68.)

   ☐ **Plan to buy only the amount of food that you can conveniently store.** Buying "extra" for leftovers can be wasteful and/or fattening.

   ☐ **List your needs in relation to the shopping pattern you prefer to follow in your favorite store.** For example, you might shop for heavy, bulky staples such as canned goods and detergent first, then more fragile fresh fruits and vegetables and other "squashables," and finally meats, dairy items, and frozen foods. The idea is to follow your *own* system for shopping rather than the one laid out for you by the merchandiser. (Also see "Stick to your list," page 169.)

Dietary Guidelines

The following dietary guidelines from the U.S. Department of Agriculture (USDA) and the U.S. Department of Health and Human Services are intended to advise basically healthy American consumers on the selection of foods that will help them stay healthy. Also included are recommendations from the American Heart Association (AHA) on healthy levels of fat, cholesterol, and sodium consumption. These guidelines do not apply to people who need special diets because of disease or conditions that interfere with normal nutritional requirements. Those people may need special instruction from registered dietitians, in consultation with their own doctors.

1. **Eat a variety of foods daily in adequate amounts,** including selections of:
   - Fruits and vegetables
   - Whole-grain and enriched breads, cereals, and other products made from grains
   - Milk, cheese, yogurt, and other products made from milk
   - Meats, poultry, fish, eggs, and dry beans and peas
2. **Maintain a "desirable" weight.** See "Desirable Body Weight Ranges" on page 355 of *Weight Loss Promotions*.
3. **Avoid too much fat, saturated fat, and cholesterol.** What is "too much" for one person may be acceptable for another, depending on blood cholesterol levels and other heart disease risk factors. In general, the American Heart Association recommends that you consume no more than 300 milligrams of cholesterol per day, that no more than 30 percent of your daily caloric intake come from fat, and that no more than 10 percent of your fat intake should be saturated fat. All fats in foods are mixtures of *saturated* and *unsaturated* fatty acids, but foods high in saturated fats are the real culprits as far as blood cholesterol levels are concerned. Saturated fats are found in larger amounts in foods of animal origin. However, *hydrogenation,* a thickening process, makes naturally unsaturated fats more saturated; hydrogenated oils are used in margarine, shortening, and many baked goods.

   To reduce your daily consumption of fat and cholesterol:
   - Choose lean meat, fish, poultry, and dry beans as protein sources.
   - Use skim or low-fat milk and milk products.
   - Moderate your use of egg yolks.
   - Limit your intake of oils and fats, especially saturated fats, such as butter, cream, lard, heavily hydrogenated fats, some margarines, shortenings, and foods containing palm and coconut

167

oils. Oils high in *unsaturated* fatty acids include *monounsaturated* fats such as olive oil and peanut oil and *polyunsaturated* fats such as safflower, sunflower, corn, soybean, and cottonseed oils.

4. **Eat foods with adequate starch and fiber.** Rather than adding fiber to foods that do not contain it naturally, eat more of the foods that are good sources of fiber and starch, such as whole-grain breads and cereals, fruits, vegetables, and dry beans and peas. To ensure a balanced diet, most Americans would be wise to substitute starchy foods for those high in fat and sugar.

5. **Avoid too much sugar.** Sugars provide calories but virtually no other nutrients and are a significant cause of tooth decay, particularly when eaten between meals. It is not possible to avoid all sugar, because most of the foods we eat contain some sugar in one form or another. But it is reasonable and desirable to keep the amount of sugars and sweet foods you eat moderate and to examine food labels with an eye for sugar in its many forms, which include sucrose, glucose, maltose, dextrose, lactose, fructose, honey, corn sweeteners, and syrups.

6. **Avoid too much sodium.** Table salt contains sodium and chloride, both of which are essential in the diet. In addition, salt often is required for the preservation of certain foods. However, sodium intake is one factor known to play a role in high blood pressure, and since most Americans eat more sodium than they need, it is a good idea to reduce your sodium intake. That can mean using less table salt, reading labels carefully, and eating sparingly those foods to which large amounts of sodium have been added. While there are no established daily recommendations for sodium intake, the AHA recommends that sodium intake should be limited to between 2,000 and 3,000 milligrams per day.

7. **If you drink alcoholic beverages, do so in moderation.** Alcoholic beverages are high in calories and low in nutrients, and excess alcohol consumption has been tied to nutritional deficiencies, diseases such as cirrhosis of the liver and certain types of cancer, and birth defects. One or two standard-size drinks daily appear to cause no harm in normal, healthy, nonpregnant adults, according to the USDA.

For further information on diet and health, see *Exercise Equipment,* pages 144–50; *Vitamins,* pages 348–49; and *Weight Loss Promotions,* pages 354–59. For a copy of the USDA booklet *Nutrition and Your Health: Dietary Guidelines for Americans,* send 50¢ to: R. Woods, Consumer Information Center–K, P.O. Box 100, Pueblo, CO 81002.

☐ **Add up the approximate cost of the items on your list to see if the total matches your food budget.** Referring to supermarket circulars and register receipts from past shopping trips can help you make this estimate. Some weeks you may find that you are over budget—making that discovery before you shop gives you the opportunity to make some changes in your weekly menu or to trim some nonessential, low-nutrition snacks or dessert items.

2. **Watch for specials and coupons, but make sure they really are a bargain.** There's no doubt that advertised specials and cents-off coupons can save you money. But at the same time, they may be no bargain if they influence you to buy a product you can't really use or to stock up on larger sizes or quantities than are practical. Also, if you must make a special trip to the store to take advantage of the price reductions, consider whether you will realize any savings at all, particularly if the store's prices on other items are high or if you must make a minimum total purchase in order to take advantage of the special.

3. **As you shop:**

   • **Take your time.** Try to schedule shopping trips for days when you can spend a little extra time and not for the hours when you are likely to be tired, rushed, or hungry.

   • **Stick to your list.** Remember that the floor plan and displays in supermarkets are the result of exhaustive market research and are geared to maximize sales in general and to boost impulse buying of high-profit items. You'll find low-profit staples such as potatoes or flour in out-of-the-way bins or on the bottom shelf. But items with a high profit margin, such as "gourmet" foods and magazines, will be on eye-level shelves, in eye-catching displays at the end or in the middle of aisles, or at the checkout counter. Further, commonly purchased items such as milk and bread are likely to be way back in the far corner of the store, meaning that you will have to walk past a lot of inviting merchandise on the way. Being aware of the planning behind store layouts and displays can help you resist the impulse to grab the most accessible item and instead stick to *your* shopping plan.

   • **Look beyond the packaging.** Like the layout of the store, most product packaging is planned to catch your eye and help a product find its way into your cart. Keep in mind that an elegant package or a mouth-watering food photo is no indication of the quality inside the package. Don't be afraid to try plainly labeled products. While in some cases you may find that you do prefer the name brand or gourmet item, you may also be pleased to discover that many less-costly store brand or local brand foods are just as good as the more familiar "name" products.

169

- **Read food labels.** Under federal law, the label on a food package must contain at least the following information: the name of the product, the net contents or net weight, and the name and location of the manufacturer, packer, or distributor. Most of the foods on the supermarket shelf also are required to include a list of ingredients, with the ingredient that is present in the largest amount listed first, and other ingredients following in descending order according to weight. Most of the items *not* required to carry an ingredient list are "standardized" foods such as jellies, ketchup, peanut butter, and milk, for which the Food and Drug Administration (FDA) has established a standard, accepted recipe. Even those products, however, generally must list which of the approved optional ingredients or optional forms of mandatory ingredients they include. A product that resembles a standardized food but is not as nutritious must be labeled "imitation."

Other information commonly found on food packages includes nutritional information, grades, and product dating.

Nutrition labeling is voluntary except in cases where the manufacturer adds a nutrient or makes a nutritional or dietetic claim, such as "low-calorie" or "low-fat." Nutrition labels must list the product's per-serving amounts of calories, protein, carbohydrates, fat, and sodium, as well as each serving's percentage of the U.S. Recommended Daily Allowance* for protein and seven essential vitamins and minerals. Manufacturers also have the option of listing cholesterol, fatty acid, and potassium content.

Grading information, such as "U.S. Grade A," has no relation to a food's nutritional content. Grade levels for meat and poultry, set by the USDA, are based on the quality of taste, texture, and appearance; inclusion of grade information on the label is voluntary. The National Marine Fisheries Service grades fish products according to similar standards. Milk and milk products in most states carry a "Grade A" label, based on FDA-recommended sanitary standards for production and processing.

Product dating generally is not regulated by the FDA. The product dating terms most commonly used are "sell by" or "use by"—those dates are intended to give the consumer an idea of how long an unopened product should remain wholesome and safe under normal storage conditions.

Clearly, there is a wealth of information to be found in the small print on a product package. Correctly interpreting what you read there is essential to understanding what you are buying and whether a product meets your nutritional needs and standards. But reading a food label sometimes seems to require a degree in chemistry and a

*Also see *Vitamins,* pages 348-49.

dictionary of marketing terms. The definitions below can help you uncover the facts behind the claims.

- **Look for unit prices.** Compare the price per measure—per ounce, pound, quart, etc.—of products in different sizes or brands. In most stores, you'll find unit prices on shelf tags or stickers, although in some cases you may have to search for that information and sometimes you may not find it at all. It isn't difficult to compute unit prices yourself, although it helps to bring along a pocket calculator. Simply divide the product price by the number of ounces, pounds, etc. Of course, if two products are the same size, their price stickers are your point of comparison. You may have noticed that even that piece of information is sometimes hard to come by, particularly in stores with registers that electronically scan for prices. Your best defense against a supermarket's policy of phasing out the use of individual product pricing is: (1) Ask for prices at the courtesy counter; (2) Complain, both in the store and through a call to the store manager; (3) If you see no change in policy, take your business elsewhere.

4. **Check your receipts** and/or keep an eye on the prices read by the electronic scanner. Mistakes are always possible, even when computers help to run the cash register.

5. **Keep your register receipts for a week,** and don't hesitate to return items that are damaged or aren't as fresh as they should be.

A DICTIONARY OF FOOD LABEL TERMS

To accurately interpret food labels, you'll need to focus on the ingredient and nutrition information listed. Following are some of the terms you will find, along with their plain-English definitions. Note that some definitions may change as the result of regulatory action by the FDA.

Calories

"Low-calorie." Contains no more than 40 calories per serving and no more than 0.4 calories per gram.

"Reduced-calorie." At least one-third lower in calorie content than the food to which it is compared.

"Light" or "Lite." A "light" product intended to be useful in reducing calorie intake must meet the FDA's requirements for low- or reduced-calorie foods and provide full nutrition labeling information. The problem is that manufacturers may use "lite" to mean light in color, texture, taste, sodium, fat, calories, etc., and which characteristic is being described may be unclear.

"Diet" or "Dietetic." Must meet the requirements for either low-calorie or reduced-calorie foods or must be clearly described as being useful for a special dietary purpose other than maintaining or reducing body weight.

Cholesterol

"No cholesterol." Cholesterol is found only in animal products, such as meat, poultry, cheese, butter, and eggs. Thus a "no cholesterol" label or any of the cholesterol-content labels defined below may be placed on any product made of grains or vegetables, even if the food naturally contains no cholesterol and *even if it is high in saturated fats.*

"Cholesterol-free." Contains no more than 2 milligrams of cholesterol per serving.

"Low-cholesterol." No more than 20 milligrams of cholesterol per serving.

"Cholesterol-reduced." Has been reformulated or processed to reduce cholesterol by 75 percent or more.

Fat

"Low-fat." There is no precise standard or definition for this term except when it is applied to certain meat, poultry, and dairy products. Low-fat dairy foods may contain no more than 2 percent milk fat. Low-fat or lean meat, other than chopped meat, may contain no more than 10 percent fat by weight; "lean" ground beef may contain no more than 22.5 percent fat.

Sodium

"Sodium-free." Contains less than 5 milligrams sodium per serving.

"Very low sodium." 35 milligrams or less per serving.

"Reduced sodium." The usual level of sodium has been reduced by at least 75 percent.

"Unsalted" or "No salt added." Can be used to describe foods once processed with salt but now produced without it. However, a food labeled "unsalted" may still contain other forms of sodium.

Sugar

"Sugar-free." A food can be labeled "sugar-free" and still contain calories from sugar alcohols, including sorbitol, xylitol, and mannitol. It may also contain artificial sweeteners such as saccharin, which has no calories, or aspartame, which has the same calories as sugar but is so much sweeter that only small amounts are needed.

"Naturally sweetened." A misleading term which may mean that a food has been sweetened with fruit, fruit juice, or even common table sugar.

Other Terms

"Serving size." The numbers in the nutrition label are based on the amount that the manufacturer defines as one serving. Thus it is possible for a manufacturer to make a product appear to be low in calories or fat by cutting the serving size. When reading the nutrition label, it's important to first take a look at the designated serving size and decide whether it is enough to satisfy you and other family members.

"Natural," "Organically grown," or "Organically processed." These terms appear on many product packages but have little meaning. There are no federal standards for food sold as "natural" or "organic."

"Refined" and "Enriched." "Refined" describes a type of flour produced by milling grains to a fine consistency. Refining removes bran, fiber, and some other nutrients. "Enriched" flour has iron and three B vitamins added to levels required by the FDA.

Funerals

The death of a loved one is a terrible experience that nearly all of us face at some time. Funeral arrangements are often made by people who are under emotional stress and time constraints—people who initially may not be concerned about expense. Still, with funerals frequently costing $5,000 and up, a funeral is the third most expensive single purchase most consumers ever make, after their home and car. And making hasty and uninformed decisions can lead you to pay thousands of dollars more than you need to, for a funeral that isn't exactly what you want.

Following is some information and advice on costs and alternatives that can help you make informed and thoughtful decisions about funeral arrangements.

PLANNING AHEAD

As difficult as it may be to talk about death, family discussion and prior planning of such matters as disposition of the body, preferences as to the ceremony, choice of the burial site, and sources of funds can both ease the burden of decision making for a grieving family and allow for the expression of personal preferences on all aspects of the funeral.

Before making decisions relating to the preplanning of a funeral, you may want to talk with your clergy and visit a number of funeral homes and cemeteries. Exploratory visits can allow you to compare various types of funerals and burials as well as the quality and cost of services offered.

You may simply choose to make a tentative list of your decisions and preferences and leave the document where it can be easily found and recovered by your family. (But don't record your wishes in your will, which will be read *after* your funeral, or leave instructions in a safe-deposit box, which will be frozen at your death.) Or you may choose to plan and pay in advance for your funeral.

In 1989, according to the American Association of Retired Persons (AARP), more than 900,000 prepaid funeral contracts were sold, most often by funeral homes or by sellers affiliated with either a funeral home or an insurance company. A number of experts, however, urge caution in the purchase of such plans. With some prepaid plans, it is possible that you may lose some or all of your money if you change your plans or move to another part of the country, or if the company selling the plan goes out of business before providing the service you paid for. If you are considering the purchase of a prepaid funeral plan, the AARP recommends that you ask these questions:

1. **Is the contract revocable?** With a completely revocable contract, you are guaranteed a refund if you change your plans or move to another state. Be sure to ask whether you would receive a *full* refund and whether you would receive any interest earned on your payments.

2. **Is the price guaranteed?** A price guarantee protects you against inflation; it ensures that you will receive the agreed-upon goods and services for your payment price, with the seller covering any increase in costs. If the price is not guaranteed, your estate or your survivors might have to pay the balance.

3. **What if the seller goes out of business?** Ask whether your money will be placed in a trust account (in some states this is required by law) and where the trust account will be held. If the money is in trust, you should be able to get it back if the seller goes out of business.

4. **What is the total payment and exactly what does it cover?** If you are offered the option of paying in installments, ask whether interest or a carrying fee is charged. Also, find out who would be required to pay the balance if you died before making all the payments.

As an alternative to investing in a prepayment plan, you may want to consider setting money aside to pay for the funeral either through a special savings account called a "totten trust" or "revocable living trust," which would pay funds for your funeral to a named beneficiary upon your death, or through an existing life insurance policy.

For information on state laws affecting the purchase of prepaid funerals, check with your state funeral board, insurance commissioner, or attorney general. And for further information on prepaid funeral plans or on buying funeral goods and services, you may want to send for copies of the free AARP booklets *Product Report: Prepaying Your Funeral?* (D13188) or *Product Report: Funeral Goods and Services* (D13496). To order, send a postcard to: AARP Fulfillment, 1909 K Street N.W., Washington, DC 20049.

Choosing the Type of Funeral

When you plan a funeral, you must first make some choices about the disposition of the body.

Interment (earth burial) in a cemetery is the most common form of burial. Another alternative is burial above the ground, or **entombment,** in a mausoleum, which may be a small, privately owned building housing the crypts for one family or a community mausoleum housing many crypts. Mausoleum burial is generally a good deal more expensive than interment.

Burial is usually accompanied by a funeral service, which may take place in the funeral home, at the gravesite, or in a church. Or you may select the alternative of "rapid" or "immediate" burial, in which the body is taken directly to the cemetery, usually within one day of death, without embalming or viewing. Immediate burial may be followed at a later date by a memorial service in the home or at whatever site you choose.

Cremation, in which the body is reduced to ash by a heating process, is a simple and inexpensive alternative to burial (although some religions have strictures against this practice). If you select **direct cremation** (cremation of the deceased without a viewing or other ceremony at which the body is present), a casket is not required; any inexpensive nonmetal container is permitted. Ashes may be scattered, disposed of by the crematory, buried in a cemetery, or stored in an urn. The family may keep the urn, or it may be placed in a mausoleum crypt or in a columbarium, a building containing many spaces or niches. Direct cremation may be followed by a memorial service or, if the ashes are to be stored in a cemetery, a committal service.

Donation of various organs or tissues or of the entire body to a hospital or medical school can provide a needed service to humanity and eliminate almost all funeral costs. (Again, however, for some persons religious strictures may apply.) Donation of the body usually must be arranged in advance with a medical school. Donation of organs can often be chosen by a survivor, even without prior instructions.

Under certain conditions, the body may not be in an acceptable condition for donation, so when planning ahead it is wise to make contingency funeral plans. And if only the organs or tissues are donated, you will still need to make arrangements for burial or cremation. If you wish your organs or body to be donated at your death, express your wishes to your family verbally and in writing. In many states, you can record your instructions simply by filling out the Uniform Donor Card attached to your driver's license.*

The Funeral Home

Once you have decided what type of funeral best suits your wishes and financial resources, you must choose the funeral home that will coordinate it. You might ask for recommendations from friends or from a memorial society (see page 178). Look for a funeral home that has been operating in the community for a number of years, and contact the local Better Business Bureau for a reliability report.

The Federal Trade Commission (FTC) Funeral Rule, which went into effect in 1984, has made it easier for consumers to compare the costs and services offered by various funeral homes and to select only the merchandise and services they want or need. The Funeral Rule requires funeral providers to give price information over the telephone and to

*For a Uniform Donar Card and further information about donation of organs or of the body, contact the Continental Association of Funeral and Memorial Societies, Inc., 7910 Woodmont Avenue, Bethesda, MD 20814, 301-913-0030.

make available a written price list itemizing each funeral item and service. Many funeral homes sell goods and services in various "package deals." The itemized price list lets you compare the cost of the total package with the cost of individually buying the specific products and services you want. Following is a look at what those products and services generally entail:

Regardless of the type of funeral you select, the **basic services of a funeral director and staff** usually include transportation of the body from the place of death, consultation with the family, preparation and filing of legal documents and notices, and care and shelter of the body before disposition.

If you choose **burial with a ceremony,** those services also commonly include cosmetic preparation of the body; embalming, if necessary (see page 180); direction of visitations and the funeral service; and transportation of the body to the church (if there is to be a church ceremony) and to the cemetery. You will also pay for use of the funeral home's facilities, vehicles (the hearse, limousines, and cars for family and flowers), and other equipment (such as tents and chairs for graveside services).

Funeral products or goods include caskets, outer burial containers, register books, acknowledgments, and burial clothing. The casket can be the most expensive part of a funeral, with costs ranging all the way from a few hundred to several thousand dollars. The outer burial container, which may be either a metal or fiberglass *vault* or a less expensive metal or concrete *grave liner*, is not required by law but is required by many cemeteries to prevent the grave from sinking. The outer burial container also may cost several hundred to several thousand dollars. The most inexpensive grave liner should be just as effective as the most costly vault in preventing collapse of the ground, although a more expensive airtight and watertight vault may be more effective at retarding deterioration of the casket.

Miscellaneous funeral expenses often include "cash advance" items, which are temporarily paid for by the funeral director on your behalf. These include flowers, fees for pallbearers, honoraria for clergy, and obituary notices. The Funeral Rule requires funeral directors to tell you in advance, in writing, if they charge a service fee for buying cash advance items.

Direct cremation costs typically cover the basic services of a funeral director and staff as described above, plus fees for transportation of the body to the crematory, the cost of the container in which the body is cremated, a cremation fee, placement of the ashes in an urn or other container, the cost of the container, and delivery of the container to the survivors. You'll also pay additional costs for the funeral home's services and use of its facilities and equipment if you decide on a viewing or other ceremony prior to cremation or a memorial service afterward.

Memorial Societies

Nonprofit consumer organizations, memorial societies charge a small lifetime membership fee, usually of about $25, in return for which they can assist members in arranging simple, dignified funerals. Memorial societies often are able to negotiate significant discount arrangements for members with specific funeral homes. They also can provide members with information and advice regarding funeral costs and alternatives, legal requirements, death benefits, and other matters. If you move, you can usually transfer your membership to the nearest local society, and if death occurs far from home, assistance is generally available from the nearest society. For a free list of memorial societies in the U.S. and Canada, contact the Continental Association of Funeral and Memorial Societies, Inc., 7910 Woodmont Avenue, Bethesda, MD 20814, 301-913-0030.

If the body is **donated** to a medical institution, virtually all costs are eliminated, as the institution usually assumes the responsibility for transportation within a specified distance and for final disposition by cremation. If organs or tissues are donated, however, you will still need to arrange and pay for the type of funeral you choose.

After you select the funeral goods and services that you want and before you commit to a purchase, the funeral director is required by the Funeral Rule to provide an itemized statement showing the prices of the individual items you are considering, a "good faith" estimate of the cost of any cash advance items, and the total price. This information gives you a final opportunity to add or subtract items and thus to be certain that you are arranging the funeral that you want and can afford.

Choosing a Cemetery

If the body or ashes are to be buried or stored in a cemetery, you will need to make additional arrangements with a cemetery director. If you are planning a funeral for a loved one, first find out whether the deceased owned a funeral lot. If not, look for a cemetery that has been in operation for a good number of years, and ask the local Better Business Bureau for a reliability report. Visit the cemetery—does it seem to be well cared for? Find out whether there is an endowment care fund to ensure that the cemetery grounds will be adequately maintained now and in the future.

Cemetery costs can range all the way from around $1,000 to $10,000 and up, depending on the particular cemetery you select, its location, the type of burial vault, whether you choose a lot or a space in a mausoleum or columbarium, and other factors. In general, cemetery costs cover the purchase of the lot or space, opening and closing the grave, the outer burial container, recording interment in the cemetery's books, and installing a monument or marker on the gravesite. The marker may be purchased from the cemetery or from a separate company; prices vary widely depending on size, material, and workmanship. Many cemeteries have regulations restricting the size and type of marker that may be used—make sure you look into these restrictions before purchasing a marker from an outside source.

Other cemetery costs may include separate fees for maintenance and care of markers (often called a "memorial fund" or "special care fund") and for flower and wreath placement.

Before purchasing a cemetery lot, find out exactly what services the price includes, and make certain the cemetery provides any special services (such as flower placement or availability of a chapel) that you might desire. If you are considering a pre-need purchase of a cemetery lot, also keep the following in mind:

- Before making a commitment, consider that circumstances may change by the time of your death. You might not live in the same area, for example, or the cemetery might experience unpredictable changes, such as new ownership or new legal requirements.

- If you are purchasing a lot under a preconstruction plan, ask what actions the cemetery will take if a death should occur in the family before the site is developed. Make sure those arrangements are included in the purchase agreement.

- If you purchase a lot on time payments, be certain the agreement clearly spells out the terms of the payment plan and the arrangements that would take effect in the event of a death before final payment.

TIPS AND PRECAUTIONS

Whether you are making advance plans about funeral arrangements for yourself or planning a funeral on short notice for a loved one, these recommendations can help you avoid making costly mistakes:

1. Phone or visit a number of funeral homes to inquire about services and costs. Ask for an itemized list of the specific services included in package deals and compare the package price with the cost of individual services.

2. Do not be afraid to ask questions at the funeral home—you have the right to know what you are paying for. Consider bringing along a friend or adviser who is not as emotionally involved with the death and who can help you make clear decisions about expenditures and additional services.

3. When visiting a funeral home, ask to be shown the full variety of caskets available (all of which may not be on display). If you prefer an

inexpensive casket, don't be embarrassed to ask for what you want.

4. Be aware that, except in certain special cases, embalming—the replacement of body fluids with chemicals—is not required by law and the funeral home is required to obtain permission before proceeding. Embalming is nevertheless often performed routinely unless the funeral director receives specific instructions to the contrary. Under the Funeral Rule, you are not required to pay a charge for unauthorized embalming unless it is required by state law. Many funeral directors can arrange a private family viewing, without the need for embalming; the additional alternatives of cremation, rapid burial, refrigeration, or a hermetically sealed casket also eliminate the need for embalming.

5. If you are making plans on a limited budget or for any reason wish to reduce funeral expenses, selecting from among the following alternative arrangements can offer equal dignity at less cost:

   • **Cremation** eliminates cemetery costs; an inexpensive alternative container may be purchased instead of a casket.

   • **Direct burial or cremation** eliminates the costs of cosmetic preparation and embalming of the body, as well as other expenses for use of the funeral home's services and facilities.

   • A **closed-casket funeral,** without a viewing, can save the costs of embalming and cosmetic preparation of the body as well as use of the funeral home's facilities for the viewing.

   • A **graveside service** eliminates the cost of using the church or funeral home for ceremonies.

   • A **memorial service** held after burial or cremation can cost much less than a funeral service, particularly if the funeral home's facilities and equipment are not used.

   • Choosing to perform any of the funeral home's standard services yourself—such as filing for death benefits, providing burial clothing, or using your own cars rather than the home's limousines—can reduce costs. But be certain to discuss your plans with the funeral director *in advance* to determine what the savings will be.

   • If possible, avoid scheduling funeral services on the weekend or a holiday, when funeral homes and cemeteries generally charge extra for certain services.

6. Look into the availability of death benefits, which can be used to pay for funeral expenses and which may be provided by Social Security (for persons who worked under the Social Security system), the Veterans Administration, and some unions, fraternal societies, pension plans, or insurance policies.

Furniture

When you make major purchases of furniture and accessories, you create a home environment that can bring you pleasure—or discomfort—for many years to come. Take the time to become sufficiently informed about your own needs and the products available in the marketplace, and you'll improve your chances of buying furnishings that will give you enjoyment *and* value.

PLAN BEFORE YOU SHOP

Before you visit a furniture showroom, do some realistic thinking about your needs and priorities. Consider these factors:

- **Lifestyle.** What activities will take place in the rooms you are furnishing? Will a living room, for example, double as a family room and a place for entertaining guests? Knowing how your furniture will be used and by whom can help you make wise decisions regarding its style and practicality.

- **Space.** Note the size and shape of rooms before you shop. Draw a floor plan to scale on a piece of grid paper and use paper cutouts of furniture to try out various arrangements. Take into account the location of doors, windows, and heating and electrical outlets. Don't trust your eyes to judge size; bring along a folding ruler or tape measure when you shop.

- **Function.** Don't forget the practical details. Will that new sofa fit through the hall door? How much storage space do you need in dressers and cabinets? Will you be moving in the near future, and if so, how will your furniture look and fit in a new house or apartment?

- **Color.** Your least expensive decorating tool, color can enlarge a small room or create a dramatic effect in a larger one. Bring along samples of your wallpaper, paint, and floor coverings when you shop. And keep practicality in mind: Pale colors will soon show wear on the family-room couch.

- **Style.** Take a look at how professional decorators handle a variety of spaces and lifestyles. Visit the model rooms in furniture or department stores and in model homes or apartments decorated by professionals. Look through home decorating magazines; the furniture ads in these magazines and in newspapers can give you an idea of available styles, materials, and prices.

- **Budget.** Set a budget before you shop and stick to it. Know how much you can comfortably afford to spend on each item and on your total purchase.
- **Where to shop?** Visit a number of stores and compare prices, services, and credit terms. Some retailers offer interior design consultations, custom coverings, or catalogs for furniture lines not carried in the store; shop around for the services that suit your needs. Ask about credit terms and delivery. An added charge for delivery or a comparatively high credit charge may mean that a "good buy" is not as good as it first appeared. If you have any questions about a dealer's reliability, check with your local Better Business Bureau.

FURNITURE TYPES AND TERMS

For the most part, furniture falls into two general categories: upholstered (sofas, chairs) and case goods (tables, dressers, cabinets). Both types of furniture can be constructed of any of a variety of woods and wood-composition materials. **Hardwood** includes mahogany, walnut, maple, oak, cherry, birch, teak, pecan, and others. **Softwood,** including such woods as pine, cedar, and redwood, is often used in ready-to-finish and outdoor furniture. Softwood is less expensive than hardwood and more subject to dents, deep scratches, and warping.

Veneering is a decorative process in which thin layers of decorative woods are bonded to other surfaces to create designs, inlays, and finishes. Veneering is found in all price ranges. Watch out for plastic "veneering," in which pieces of plastic molding are used to simulate wood.

Bonding is used to "build" large sections of wood from several small pieces. Plywood is one example of a bonded wood: Several layers of solid wood or particleboard are bonded one on the other to make a strong and rugged "ply"-construction wood product which is used to reinforce various types of furniture.

Printing and **engraving** are decorative processes used to reproduce the look of a fine wood-grain pattern on smooth panels.

Finishes can be *clear,* to allow natural wood color and grain to show through, or *tinted* or *opaque,* to change the color of a wood or to make two different woods that are used together look alike. The number of steps used to create the finish—ranging from fewer than 4 to more than 25, many done by hand—will be reflected in the price of the furniture.

JUDGING THE QUALITY OF CASE GOODS FURNITURE

Follow these guidelines from the Furniture Information Council when evaluating wood furniture:

1. Run your hand over the finish to check for rough areas that may have been inadequately sanded.
2. Look for uniformity of color and grain patterns.
3. Inspect the finish; is it streaked or applied too thickly in the corners? Are there cracks or bubbles?
4. Operate all moving parts—drawers, table leaves—to make sure they move easily and fit properly.
5. Check drawers for glides and stops. Drawer hardware should be sturdy and bolted from the inside.
6. Check interiors for areas that may snag clothing.
7. Inspect any glass shelves, decorative trim, lights, and other accessories to be sure they have been installed carefully and securely. Glass panels should be thick enough to resist cracking or chipping during normal use.
8. Look for any shortcuts or shortcomings in craftsmanship.
9. Check hangtags for the type of construction or the kinds of wood and veneer used in a particular item.

INSIDE UPHOLSTERED FURNITURE

With upholstered furniture, there's more than meets the eye. How can you judge the quality and value of the furniture beneath those cushions? It helps to begin with an understanding of the basic structural components of upholstered pieces.

Frame. This is the basic unit of all upholstered furniture. Frames can be made of kiln-dried hardwood, a combination of hardwood and plywood, steel, laminated boards, or strong rigid plastic. All-hardwood frames are rare and are used only in expensive furniture.

Supports. Webbing, straps, wood slats, or springs can be used to provide support, or firmness, in upholstered furniture. Springs can be coil, double cone coil, or zigzag, and are anchored to one another and to the front and back of the frame with metal clips. Supports that are too far apart or are not properly anchored together can reduce the comfort and durability of the furniture.

Cushioning. Cushioning materials can include cotton or polyester batting, springs, down, and polyurethane foam. Polyurethane is the most widely used cushion material; the higher the density of the foam in the seat cushions (up to four pounds per cubic foot), the longer the comfortable life of the cushion. Better-quality cushions—seat and back—contain a solid core of foam or springs rather than shredded foam.

Outer covering. Upholstery fabric is available in a wide variety of natural and man-made fibers, leather, and vinyl. The cost of a fabric plays a major role in an upholstered item's price, so keep your use and budget requirements in mind as you shop.

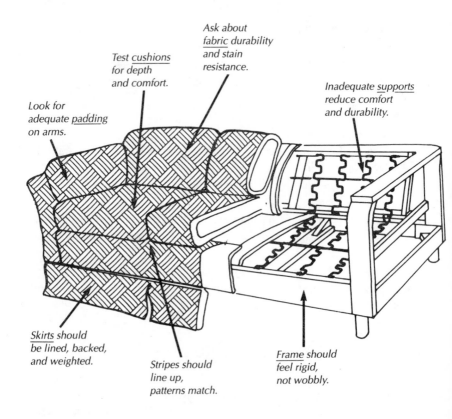

Look for
adequate padding
on arms.

Test cushions
for depth
and comfort.

Ask about
fabric durability
and stain
resistance.

Inadequate supports
reduce comfort
and durability.

Skirts should
be lined, backed,
and weighted.

Stripes should
line up,
patterns match.

Frame should
feel rigid,
not wobbly.

JUDGING THE QUALITY OF UPHOLSTERED FURNITURE

1. **Read the label and ask questions:** On upholstered furniture, labels are required to disclose the material used to pad the frame and fill the cushions. Federal Trade Commission guidelines also require manufacturers to state whether synthetic materials have been used to simulate natural wood, leather, or marble. If a tag or label carries the name of only one wood, all of the exposed surfaces must be made of that wood. Labels may also have information about flammability resistance, care recommendations, and any fabric pretreatment. Ask the salesperson for details on other quality features: frame materials, kind and number of supports, cushioning materials.

2. **Test the frame:** Lift one end; it should feel rigid and should not creak or wobble. Feel for frame edges beneath fabric-covered areas; poorly padded areas will wear quickly.

3. **Test the supports:** Sit down and bounce around. You shouldn't hear loud creaks and thumps, which can mean the springs are hitting the frame.

4. Examine the cushions: The comfort of cushions is a matter of personal preference. Sit down and bounce several times to test cushion height, depth, and degree of softness and personal comfort. Ask the salesperson for information on the density of foam, which is available from the manufacturer.

5. Test the padding: Squeeze the arms of sofas and chairs; you shouldn't be able to feel the frame through the padding.

6. Examine the fabric: Ask the salesperson for any information available from the manufacturer on the fabric's durability. Also ask whether matching protective arm covers are available. Check the fabric label for cleaning instructions and information on whether the fabric has been treated to resist stains.

Some retailers offer additional fabric finishing. Before purchasing such a service, determine whether the fabric has already been treated by the manufacturer, and read the retailer's agreement carefully to be certain you understand what is and is not covered by the warranty on the fabric finish.

7. Look at the detailing: Stripes should line up, patterns should match, and repeating patterns should be centered on the cushions. Seams should be straight and well finished, with tight stitches and no gaps or puckers. Make sure any buttons are evenly spaced, and check to see if furniture skirts are lined, backed, and weighted to hang straight—all signs of quality.

Finally, whether you are buying upholstered furniture or case goods, remember these guidelines:

- You can save considerably by looking for end-of-season sales and reduced prices on discontinued lines, display items, and as-is pieces.

- . . . but if you buy something at discount, make sure you know whether you have to give up anything (delivery? installation? warranty?) to get the lower price.

- Watch out for "bait and switch" schemes (see page 307) and promotions offering zero coupon bonds as a "free gift" or "bonus" with purchase. (Also see *Zero Coupon Bonds*, pages 360–61.)

- Imported woods, intricate coverings, and special finishes can be expensive. You may be content paying a premium price for these extras, but don't feel that you have to buy a very expensive item to get quality—furniture made without the extras can also be beautifully styled and durable.

- Read the warranty carefully and make sure you understand its terms. Also ask about the store's return policy, and get all specifics in writing.

- If you buy furniture on time, be sure you know the full terms and conditions of the seller's credit service. (Also see "Buying on Time," *Credit and Installment Buying*, page 133.)

Health Clubs

We all *know* that we should exercise, but finding the time and the motivation to make exercise a routine part of our lives can seem a nearly impossible task. For many people, a health club may offer a solution. Membership in a health club can help you establish a time and a place for exercise, in a setting away from the distractions and temptations of home. The company of people who share your interests and goals is a powerful motivating force, and a club's varied facilities and equipment can help conquer the most powerful enemy of exercise: boredom. What's more, experienced health club instructors can help you develop a personal exercise plan, set realistic, attainable goals, and pace yourself properly to avoid injury.

Along with these advantages comes one major drawback: cost. Depending on the health club's location and facilities, membership may cost anywhere from $100 to $1,000 or more per year. What you get in return can vary widely, depending on a club's atmosphere, staff, and equipment. It pays to shop around and ask questions before deciding which health club to join. Only at a club with inviting facilities and a knowledgeable, welcoming staff will your investment pay off in terms of a long-range program of physical fitness.

Following are guidelines that can help you evaluate and select a quality health club. You may also want to review the tips on starting and sticking with an exercise program found on page 150 of *Exercise Equipment*.

CHOOSING A HEALTH CLUB

1. **Check with your local Better Business Bureau** for reliability reports on the clubs you are considering. Thirty-three thousand consumers made that important safety check in 1987.

2. **Make an appointment to inspect the club,** scheduling your visit for the time of day when you would normally use the facilities. Talk with members and ask about their satisfaction with club services, and pay particular attention to the following points:

   - Are there long lines at the equipment?
   - Are facilities and equipment clean and in good working order?
   - Are workout and locker rooms a comfortable temperature and well ventilated?
   - Is the atmosphere friendly and welcoming?

- Do staff members seem knowledgeable, motivated, and interested in members' activities and progress?
- Does the club have amenities that suit your interests and needs?

3. Ask questions.

- How many members does the facility have and is there a limit on new membership? This can be an important consideration with a new club in a well-populated area.
- What are the qualifications of the staff? Do they have training in physical education, exercise physiology, or a related field? If you want help in a specific area, such as weight loss or instruction in a particular sport, are there staff members qualified to assist you?
- Is there an orientation session when you join to help you learn how to work out safely and to set up an individual exercise program tailored to your physical condition and your goals?
- Is a means provided for you and the staff to chart your progress?
- What are the club's hours, and what are the policies regarding scheduling use of facilities and services?
- Is there a trial period during which you may sample health club services without the obligation to join? Some clubs may allow you to try out the facilities for a week or two for a small charge; find out if this charge will be applied to your membership fee if you decide to join.
- You may want to ask if the club is a member of the International Racquet and Sports Association (IRSA), a trade association of owners and managers of fitness and racquet clubs; IRSA member clubs must subscribe to an established code of conduct. For information, contact: IRSA, 132 Brookline Avenue, Boston, MA 02215, 617-236-1500.

4. Carefully look over the agreement. It's a good idea to take a copy of the contract home with you and read it thoroughly before signing. Look for the following points:

- Are all the oral promises you received written into the contract?
- Are all services listed? In some states, clubs may be required by law to list all facilities and equipment, too.
- What is the term of membership? Many health clubs offer multiyear memberships; these usually are less expensive than a yearly or monthly term, but you must use the facility regularly to get your money's worth. Until you are reasonably certain that you like the club and have the motivation to stick with a long-term exercise program, a shorter-term membership may be a wiser choice.
- What is the total cost and the payment schedule? Are there penalties for late payment? Are all club features and services covered in the basic fee, or are there additional charges for some services?

- Is any part of your membership fee refundable if you decide to cancel? This can be a particularly important consideration if you are thinking of choosing a longer-term membership.
- Does the three-day "cooling-off" period apply? In some states, you are granted a period of up to three business days after you sign a contract during which you may cancel for a full refund.

Finally, keep these tips and precautions in mind when considering health club membership:

☐ You are more likely to get your money's worth out of club membership if the facility is conveniently located near your home or work.

☐ Don't sign up for membership in a club that has not yet opened for business, no matter how attractive the brochure or the offer. Remember, if the center is legitimate, there will most likely be attractive special membership offers at the opening.

☐ Be wary of special telephone offers for club membership, particularly if the caller offers you the "convenience" of charging your membership fee to a credit card. It is wiser to wait until you have read the contract before signing up.

Home Buying

Your home will probably be the largest single investment you ever make. And in the process of home buying you will be faced with some of the most important and complex decisions of your life.

In 1988, U.S. Better Business Bureaus received an estimated 130,000 requests for information relating to real estate sales and rentals—a reflection of the concern prospective homeowners feel when presented with such critical choices. In the pages that follow, we'll attempt to address that concern by presenting a basic, step-by-step guide to making prudent and informed home-buying decisions. We'll also refer you to some excellent sources of further information to assist you as you take the challenging but rewarding steps toward home ownership.

TO BUY OR NOT TO BUY

Ten years ago, deciding whether or not to buy a home was a relatively simple matter. Home prices were rising so fast that, for anyone who could afford it, a house was one of the best possible investments. Today, stabilized home prices in most areas have minimized the short-term investment factor in the home-buying decision, making it more important than ever to consider other factors—including finances, lifestyle, and personality—before rushing out to look for that "dream house."

Home ownership has many advantages: good *long-term* investment potential; the income tax deductions for mortgage interest and real estate taxes; the pride of having a place to call your own. But there are disadvantages as well, including the worries and responsibilities of mortgages, taxes, and repairs; unpredictable expenses; and decreased mobility. Before you make the decision to buy, you owe it to yourself to take a close look at these factors and to consider whether buying or renting is the right option for you.

To a large extent, your decision to buy or rent will be influenced by the relative costs of homes and rentals in your area. Calculate and compare the costs of both options over a number of years, taking into account closing and maintenance expenses, interest and property tax deductions, and the projected future value of your home, as well as rent on a comparable residence and your potential return from placing your savings in an investment other than a home.

Another valuable exercise in helping you determine whether buying or renting is the more attractive option is to shop for financing before you even begin shopping for a home. A "prequalifying interview" with a commercial lender (for more about potential loan sources, see "Financing

Your Purchase," pages 196–97) will tell you how much mortgage you will be able to carry, and a search of the classifieds will give you a good idea of whether that's enough to buy you a home that will meet your needs.

DEFINING YOUR DREAM

Assuming you've decided that home ownership is the right option for you, how do you go about finding *the* home that has everything you're looking for? Before you even begin to house-hunt, it's a good idea to make a list of the basic specifications you require in a home. Defining your "must-have" features, as well as those "extras" that are nice pluses but not essential, can save you time and possibly money, because you'll be able to focus on looking at the right homes in the right locations, and you'll avoid the risk of falling for a "dream house" that really doesn't suit your requirements. Consider the age and number of family members (be sure to keep the future in mind) as well as your family's lifestyle in making a list of your preferences in the following areas:

1. **Size.** Lot size; number of bedrooms/bathrooms; need for separate dining room, utility room, family room, workshop area, garage, fenced-in yard, other rooms.

2. **Floor plan.** One floor, split-level, or two or three floors? Consider ease of cleaning and maintenance, as well as any special needs of family members.

3. **Location.** Proximity to work; quality of and proximity to schools, stores, public transportation, church or synagogue, health care and recreational facilities.

4. **Type of home.** Detached home, multifamily dwelling, townhouse, condo, co-op, mobile home? There are pros and cons in each option. Condos and co-ops can be the right choice for people who want ownership without many of its problems and responsibilities. A detached home is usually the most costly of the options, but for many people it conveys advantages of privacy and convenience that outweigh the higher price tag. Only you can judge your preferences and your budget to arrive at the decision that's right for you. (Also see *Condos and Co-ops,* pages 112–15.)

5. **New vs. old.** Again, each option has its advantages and disadvantages. In new homes, systems and appliances are less likely to require costly repair and are more often still covered by warranties. Construction and building materials may also be under warranty. Stricter building codes could mean that a new house offers better insulation as well as energy-conserving materials such as thermal glass. Buyers of new homes usually can choose their preferred colors, carpeting, and fixtures, so decorating costs can be lower.

On the other hand, new construction tends to occur on the outer fringes of urban areas, increasing distance from work, schools, shopping, and other amenities. New homes may be smaller than older ones and may require landscaping, fencing, and possibly retaining walls to protect ground from erosion. The new home may be in a new neighborhood, without fully established schools and community services, and there may be assessments for sidewalks, storm drains, or other facilities.

An existing home may have larger rooms as well as interesting design, material, and functional features not found in a new house. Older homes are generally closer to the center of metropolitan areas, and real estate taxes may be lower because services have already been built and established. But the older dwelling may be in need of expensive repairs, replacements, or even remodeling or modernizing, and those costs can be difficult to predict. Again, only you can weigh all the options and choose the course that best suits your needs and preferences.

WHAT CAN YOU AFFORD?

An important companion step to defining your requirements in a home is figuring out how much house you can afford. As a rough rule of thumb, your monthly mortgage, insurance, and tax payments should equal no more than 28 percent of your gross household income. But to determine the level of expenditure and debt that's appropriate for your individual circumstances, there is no substitute for a careful examination of your own income and expenses.

First, to calculate your maximum down payment, figure out your net worth by totaling your available cash assets, including cash in savings accounts, checking accounts, money market funds, and other liquid investments; the value of stocks and bonds; the value of any assets you would be willing to sell; expected gifts or loans from relatives or friends; and collectible money owed you by others. Then subtract from this total an adequate cushion against emergencies. Also subtract the cash you'll need for closing costs (see "The Closing," pages 197–99), moving expenses, repairs to the home you would be selling, and new household items you'll need to buy as soon as you move. What you have left is the amount available for your down payment. The more cash you lay out for the down payment, the smaller the loan you'll need and the less you'll have to pay in monthly installments. On the other hand, there are certain situations in which it makes financial sense to put down as small a down payment as possible—for example, when one of your main priorities is reducing your federal income tax. Your tax adviser and/or accountant can help you make that determination.

To get an idea of what you can comfortably handle in those monthly payments, first calculate your annual *after-tax* income from salaries, commissions or bonuses, interest and dividends, gifts, and other sources. Divide the total by 12 to arrive at your monthly net income. Next, total your yearly living expenses (current and estimated for the future): car payments; life, health, and auto insurance; loan interest; food; clothing; health care; education; transportation; child care; entertainment; savings deposits. Divide by 12, and then subtract your monthly expenses from your monthly income to get an estimate of your maximum monthly housing budget. This is the amount you would be able to pay for your mortgage, taxes, homeowners insurance, utilities, and home repairs and maintenance.

Local utility companies, a real estate agent, and any previous homeowning experience can help you estimate costs for utilities, insurance (also see "Homeowners Insurance," pages 199–205), maintenance, and repairs, and the remaining total will give you an idea of the amount you can afford in monthly mortgage payments. You also may want to talk with your tax adviser about the possible benefits of adjusting your paycheck withholding allowances. Because of the tax deductions for mortgage interest payments and property taxes, you may be able to lower your withholding tax to increase your take-home pay, thus increasing the amount available for monthly payments.

Your figures may be higher or lower than a particular lender's computations; that's why it's a good idea to interview at least one prospective lender before you begin to house-hunt. You might also want to enlist the services of a certified public accountant to help you estimate what you can afford.

THE HUNT IS ON

You're ready to start the search for the house that best suits your needs and your budget—but where do you begin? If you are uneasy about the intricacies of the home-buying process, now is the time to select an experienced real estate lawyer, whose services you can call on during the negotiation and closing processes. You may choose to wait until you are ready to make a formal offer on the home you want before hiring a lawyer, but remember, you may need to move quickly at that point. (Also see Legal Services, pages 249–54.)

You may also want to enlist the services of a real estate agent. A good agent can save you time and can help guide you through the financial and legal maze of home buying. Ask for referrals from friends and colleagues who have recently bought or sold homes, and look for experienced agents who work for brokers with a proven track record in the areas in which you'll be looking. Don't be shy about asking prospective agents how many years they've been working in the field and how many homes they've listed or sold in your area of interest. Ask whether the broker participates in a cooperative listing service, in which a number of companies share information on all listed properties in a given geographical area. Find out whether the agent is a member of a trade association. The titles Realtor® and Realtor-Associate® indicate membership in the National Association of Realtors,® an organization whose members are required to follow a strict code of ethics. In any case, be sure to contact the local Better Business Bureau to check the reputation of agents and the brokers they work for. And remember that the real estate agent is working for the *seller*—so it's best to keep some critical facts, such as your top price limit, to yourself.

Of course, on your travels through the classified ads and along the streets of the neighborhoods you like, you'll come across homes directly for sale by the owner. When no real estate agent (and no commission) is involved, the cost of a house may be lower. But you'll also have to do without the services of a professional who is experienced in house sales— in such a case, the help of your real estate attorney or accountant becomes doubly important.

Whether your own efforts or those of an agent bring you to the front door of a home for sale, always take along a notepad and compare the house against your list of "must-have" and "extra" features. Keep a log of the homes you visit and how they measure up to your ideal. Ask questions and take a close look at the internal and external condition of the house—the House Condition Checklist on page 194 can help. If you're looking at a new home, check out the reputation of the developer, both with other homeowners in the development and with the local BBB.

The quality of the neighborhood deserves at least as much careful consideration as that of the house. Drive through the area and note the visual appearance of homes and businesses. How close are the police, fire department, hospitals, shopping, schools, public transportation? Visit the schools,* and attend a community gathering or read the local newspaper to get an idea of the concerns of local residents. Check with the local police precinct to find out whether the crime rate is rising or dropping, and visit the city or town hall for information on future anticipated growth. Keep in mind that the rate at which homes increase in value over time is greatest in the most desirable locations.

Once you've zeroed in on the home that comes closest to your ideal, it's wise to get expert advice before making an offer. First, you'll need to hire a building inspector to prepare a written report covering the major structural elements inside and outside the house, including the age and condition of systems, electrical wiring and plumbing, appliances, the roof, and other appropriate items, as well as a detailing of anticipated repairs. Building inspectors are listed in the yellow pages—look for a member of the American Society of Home Inspectors or a similar organization. As always, check references, and check the reputation of the inspector with the local BBB.

---

*You might also want to visit your local library for a copy of *Public Schools U.S.A.: A Comparative Guide to School Districts* by Charles Harrison (©1988 Williamson Publishing Co., Charlotte, VT). This reference source evaluates the performance of 500 school districts in major metropolitan areas—the criteria it uses can help you make your own evaluation of districts not covered.

House Condition Checklist*

This questionnaire was developed to help prospective home buyers gather information and to encourage sellers to disclose pertinent facts about the condition of their house.

Yes No

☐ ☐ 1. Has the basement leaked within the past two years? What basement waterproofing repairs have been made within the past two years? _____

☐ ☐ 2. Has the roof leaked within the past two years? What roof repairs have been made within the past two years? _____
What type of roof does the house have? _____
How old is it? _____

☐ ☐ 3. Has the plumbing backed up within the past two years? What plumbing system repairs or service have been made within the past two years? _____

☐ ☐ 4. Is heat provided to all finished rooms? How old is the heating system? ___
Is it _____ Gas _____ Electric _____ Oil _____ Other _____?
When was it last repaired or serviced? _____

☐ ☐ 5. Is there a central air-conditioning system?
☐ ☐   If so, is it provided to all finished rooms? How old is it? _____ Is it _____ Gas _____ Electric? When was it last repaired or serviced? _____

6. How much is the average monthly bill for: Electricity $ _____ Gas $ _____ Fuel/Oil $ _____ ?

☐ ☐ 7. Do any appliances, fans, motors, pumps, light fixtures, or electrical outlets need repairs?

☐ ☐ 8. Is the fireplace in working condition?
When was it last repaired, serviced or cleaned? _____

☐ ☐ 9. Are there any storm windows or screens on the premises that are not installed?

10. What type of flooring material is in each area covered by wall-to-wall carpeting? _____

☐ ☐ 11. Do gutters and downspouts need any repairs other than routine maintenance?

12. How old is the hot water heater? _____ What is its capacity in gallons? _____ When was it last repaired or serviced? _____

☐ ☐ 13. Do front, rear, or side yards ever have standing water more than 48 hours after a heavy rain?

☐ ☐ 14. Do fuses blow or circuit breakers trip when two or more appliances are used at the same time?

☐ ☐ 15. Are all exterior door locks in working condition?
☐ ☐   Will keys be provided for each lock?

☐ ☐ 16. Is there insulation in the ceiling or attic?
☐ ☐   The walls?
☐ ☐   Other places?

*Source: Montgomery County (MD) Office of Consumer Affairs.

Be wary if you are offered a **zero coupon bond** as a "free gift" or "bonus" with the purchase of a home. IRS regulations regarding the use of zeros with home sales are complex and contain provisions that might affect the deductibility of your annual mortgage interest. Consult your tax adviser for information and recommendations. (Also see *Zero Coupon Bonds*, pages 360–61.)

OFFER AND CONTRACT

Once the house has been inspected, you'll need to decide on the maximum price you're willing to pay, taking into consideration the price of comparable homes in the neighborhood as well as the cost of necessary repairs or equipment replacement and remodeling. You're ready to make an offer, which in home-buying terms means a written Offer to Purchase. This can be drawn up by the real estate agent and checked over by your lawyer, or prepared entirely by your lawyer. *Once your offer is accepted, it becomes a contract.* That's why it is critical that all the basic elements, as well as the qualifications you may wish to put in, protect your rights and interests. Among other elements your lawyer may suggest, the offer should include:

1. A legal description of the designated property.
2. Conditions under which the offer is void without penalty to the buyer. Your offer should be made on the condition that you can obtain satisfactory financing, that you receive all necessary assurances from home and termite inspections, and, if you are buying a replacement home, that you are able to sell your current home at a specified price.
3. A list of fixtures, furnishings, equipment, etc., that are to remain in the home and on the property.
4. A provision that the offer is contingent on a final inspection.
5. A provision in case of property damage between the contract signing and the closing.
6. The date on which you take possession.
7. The closing cost items (see "The Closing," pages 197–99) that you want the seller to pay and those that you will share.
8. A time limit of 24 or 48 hours for acceptance of your offer.
9. The amount of "earnest money," or deposit, required. The offer should specify that the earnest money be deposited with a neutral third party.
10. The selling price.

Your offering price will probably be somewhat lower than both the asking price and the maximum price you are willing to pay. Once your offer is made, the give-and-take of negotiation begins, until you and the seller arrive at a price and an agreement that satisfies you both and your offer is accepted.

FINANCING YOUR PURCHASE

[Also see *Credit and Installment Buying*, pages 125–37.]

All or part of your mortgage loan might be obtained from any of the following sources: savings and loans; commercial banks; mutual savings banks; mortgage banking companies; or the home seller. Seller financing is usually the least costly and most flexible option, but it is contingent on the seller being willing to partially finance your purchase through one of a number of different arrangements. In considering seller financing, you'll need a real estate attorney to advise you on potential risks and to help you negotiate the most desirable agreement.

A variety of different financing options are available from the other, more traditional loan sources, and a package available from one lender may not be offered by others. Surveying as many different lenders as possible can help you find the best rates as well as the package best tailored to your individual needs. Mortgage-reporting services, which list current terms in your area, can be a good investment—ask your real estate agent if there is a reporting service covering your area. Many newspapers publish a list of rates in the business or real estate section, and many local Boards of Realtors and other real estate agencies provide information to their members or subscribers. Again, check with your agent.

Among the most common types of loans available from conventional lenders, you'll find the following:

Fixed-rate mortgage: Both interest rate and monthly payment terms are fixed for the life of the loan. Each payment is applied to both interest and principal, with the proportions varying over the life of the loan.

Graduated-payment mortgage: Interest rate is fixed; monthly payments are smaller in the beginning, rise at a constant rate for the first few years, and remain constant at a higher rate in the later years.

Adjustable-rate mortgage: Interest rate varies based on a formula related to some measure of current interest rates; monthly payments also vary, depending on changes in the market. There may or may not be caps on the maximum interest rate and/or caps on how fast payments can rise or fall.

Assumable mortgage: Allows the buyer to assume, or take over, the seller's mortgage, at the same interest rate. You or your attorney should check with the lender to review mortgages that the seller claims are assumable at existing rates.

Shared appreciation mortgage: Lets the buyer obtain a reduced rate from the lender in exchange for a future payment to the lender. The payment gives the lender a share of the anticipated profit from the eventual resale or refinancing of the home.

Growing equity mortgage: Interest rate may or may not be fixed; monthly payments increase on a regular scale each year after the first six years, with the amount of increase deducted from the loan principal. The quick reduction of principal generally means a reduced loan term and reduced total interest payments.

Balloon mortgage: Interest rate is generally fixed; monthly payments also are fixed but usually apply only to the interest, not the principal. After a short term (3 to 10 years is common), a large final payment is required or the debt must be refinanced.

Check with your real estate agent or a local lending institution to see whether you qualify for a loan insured by the Federal Housing Administration (FHA) or guaranteed by the Veterans Administration (VA). FHA loans generally involve down payments of only 3 percent to 5 percent, interest rates at or below market level, and possibly a longer repayment period than may otherwise be offered. VA loans are available to qualified veterans and their widows or widowers. No down payment is required if the loan is for $144,000 or less; interest rates and repayment periods are usually the same as for FHA loans. In both cases a funding fee equal to 1 percent of the total loan must be paid by the borrower; this can be spread over the life of the loan.

If you don't qualify for an FHA or a VA loan, you may want to ask your lender about the availability and cost of private mortgage insurance. This insurance works much like the FHA program, but it must be purchased from a private company, and the borrower pays the premium.

Before making a choice among all these alternatives, you'll need to assess your own financial position and how your income is likely to grow over the coming years, as well as the real cost of the mortgage. Ask potential lenders to clearly explain the rates and terms of the loans they offer and to itemize all the fees that must be paid in connection with finalizing the loan. In turn, the lender will ask you for a financial statement listing all your assets and liabilities, several recent tax returns, a verification of current employment, and other information intended to confirm your ability to pay off the loan.

THE CLOSING

In the settlement or closing, the deed of ownership is transferred from seller to buyer. The closing should always involve a legally responsible third party, such as a real estate lawyer, who ensures that the terms of the contract have been met before money changes hands and the title is transferred.

Title Insurance

Most lenders require home buyers to purchase a title insurance policy at closing, but few buyers understand what they are buying, and many assume that their investment is protected by the title insurance required by the lender. In reality, a separate homeowners title insurance policy is also needed for full protection.

Title insurance provides a guarantee from the title company that you really own the property you think you own, under the rights and conditions of ownership and use that the seller has represented. The guarantee is based on the company's search of public records tracing the chain of ownership of the property. **Lender's title insurance** protects the lender's security interest—it is issued in the amount of the mortgage loan and it decreases and finally stops as the loan is paid off. **Owner's title insurance** protects the home buyer's interests and is usually issued in the amount of the purchase price. It guarantees that the insurer will pay any legal fees for defending against any challenge to the title and will pay any valid claims. A separate owner's title policy is needed even if your real estate lawyer has performed a title examination and assumed liability for his work. An independent attorney's liability is limited to negligence and does not include responsibility for many hidden title problems—problems that could end up costing you expensive legal fees or even loss of the property.

Title insurance is paid for at the time of purchase, and the one-time premium is usually included in the closing costs. The purchase is often handled by the real estate broker, the lender, or the settlement attorney. In some areas, the home buyer must specifically request an owner's title policy. Before purchasing title insurance, shop around to get the best policy and price. Also check the reputation and complaint record of the title company with your state insurance department and local BBB.

Closing costs can be significant, but who pays most of them—the seller or the buyer—is negotiable. That's why it's important that you have a reasonable estimate of those costs before drawing up a contract. Prospective lenders will be able to give you a preliminary idea during prequalifying interviews, and your attorney can further advise you as you prepare your offer. Many loans are covered under the Real Estate Settlement Procedures Act, including FHA and VA loans and loans made by lenders who have federally insured deposits. In such cases, the law requires that the lender supply you with a "good faith" estimate of closing costs when you submit a written loan application.

Settlement or closing costs fall into two categories: those associated with making the loan and those relating to the actual transfer of property.

The largest single item usually is the "points" (also called a loan origination fee); this is the fee that the lender charges for arranging your loan. One point equals 1 percent of the total loan amount. So if you're getting an $80,000 loan and the lender charges four points, you and/or the seller will be paying an extra $3,200 in points at closing.

Additional charges cover the house appraisal, credit checks, inspection fee, document preparation, your lawyer's fee and possibly that of the lending institution's lawyer, and other administrative items. If the loan is privately insured, the 1 percent premium is paid at closing. You may be able to trim some closing costs by asking the seller which companies were used when he or she bought the house; since much of their work has already been done, those companies may charge you less. However, if the house is old, prior reports and information may be outdated and of limited value.

All closing costs plus the balance of the down payment must be paid at the closing. Prior to closing, you'll have to determine how payment should be made—certified check, personal check, or cash—and arrange to have the required amount available. It's a good idea to ask your lawyer to explain in advance what you'll be signing at the closing. And if anything is unclear or you're presented with any unexpected extra fees, don't be rushed. Ask your lawyer for explanations and be sure you understand all the details before you sign.

HOMEOWNERS INSURANCE

[You may also want to review *Insurance*, pages 220–38.]

Homeowners insurance is really a package of policies. It not only protects your home and its contents but also covers your personal liability to others and pays your living expenses if your home becomes temporarily uninhabitable. Understanding what a homeowners policy covers and how much coverage you need can save you from the twin pitfalls of buying too little coverage or paying for insurance that you could do without.

There are basically six different homeowners policies, which differ both in the type of property insured and in the number of perils that the insurer agrees to cover. As with other types of insurance, you can purchase varying degrees of coverage with each of the packages.

HO–1 (The Basic Policy): Provides coverage against 11 specified perils, listed in the chart on page 201. This form of policy is gradually being phased out and replaced by:

HO–2 (The Broad Form): Covers the same 11 perils as HO–1, plus 6 others.

HO–1 and HO–2 cover your house, other structures on your property, and your personal belongings, such as furniture, appliances, clothing, and other possessions, excluding automobiles and pets. These policies also pay any additional living expenses you incur, within reasonable limits, if you are forced to live elsewhere while your home is under repair.

HO–3 (The Special Policy): Protects your home from all causes of loss except those specifically excluded in the contract, but limits coverage of personal property to the 17 perils included in HO–2. This is currently the best-selling form of homeowners insurance.

HO–4 (The Renter's Policy): Designed for apartment dwellers, tenants of a house, and owners of cooperative apartments, HO–4 does not cover the building itself but does insure your personal property against all the perils included in HO–2. It also provides liability insurance and coverage for additional living expenses.

HO–6 (Unit-Owner's Policy): Designed for condominium and co-op owners, HO–6 is similar to HO–4. However, it also covers any additions or alterations you make that are not insured by the condo or co-op association's policy.

HO–8 (Older Home Insurance): Insures your house against the same perils as HO–1, but for its actual market value rather than its replacement cost. Many older homes contain design and material features that would be prohibitively expensive to duplicate today. HO–8 pays for restoring the property but not necessarily with the same type and quality of materials as were used in the original.

A supplement to either HO–2 or HO–3 can be purchased by mobile home owners, providing the same basic coverage as HO–2 but at a higher cost.

What Your Policy Covers

The extent and amount of coverage that your homeowners policy provides is determined by which of the six policy forms you select and what inclusions or exemptions are specifically written into your policy. The coverage provided by each of the six forms is fairly standard throughout the insurance industry, although there are occasional variations in the names companies assign their policies and the limits on coverage provided even by seemingly similar packages. The only *sure* way to know exactly what your policy covers is to read it carefully and ask questions about any provisions that are unclear.

As a general rule, however, most homeowners policies cover the following:

1. **Structure.** You are insured against damage caused by a covered peril to your home and/or to detached structures such as a garage or storage shed. (This coverage applies only to the "true" homeowners policies HO–1, 2, 3, and 8.)

Covered Perils*

PERILS AGAINST WHICH PROPERTIES ARE INSURED UNDER THE VARIOUS HOMEOWNERS POLICIES

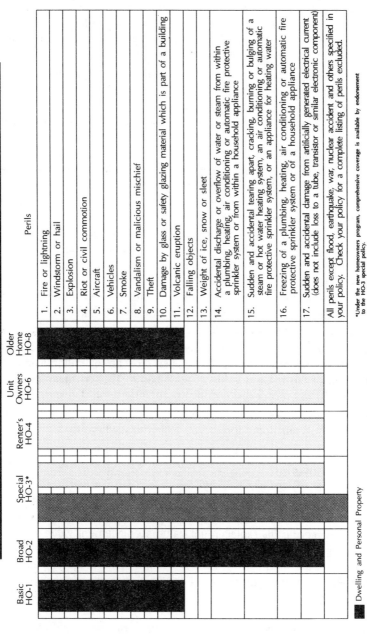

Perils	Basic HO-1	Broad HO-2	Special HO-3*	Renter's HO-4	Unit Owners HO-6	Older Home HO-8
1. Fire or lightning						
2. Windstorm or hail						
3. Explosion						
4. Riot or civil commotion						
5. Aircraft						
6. Vehicles						
7. Smoke						
8. Vandalism or malicious mischief						
9. Theft						
10. Damage by glass or safety glazing material which is part of a building						
11. Volcanic eruption						
12. Falling objects						
13. Weight of ice, snow or sleet						
14. Accidental discharge or overflow of water or steam from within a plumbing, heating, air conditioning or automatic fire protective sprinkler system or from within a household appliance						
15. Sudden and accidental tearing apart, cracking, burning or bulging of a steam or hot water heating system, an air conditioning or automatic fire protective sprinkler system, or an appliance for heating water						
16. Freezing of a plumbing, heating, air conditioning or automatic fire protective sprinkler system or of a household appliance						
17. Sudden and accidental damage from artificially generated electrical current (does not include loss to a tube, transistor or similar electronic component)						
All perils except flood, earthquake, war, nuclear accident and others specified in your policy. Check your policy for a complete listing of perils excluded.						

*Under the new homeowners program, comprehensive coverage is available by endorsement to the HO-3 special policy.

Legend:
- ■ Dwelling and Personal Property
- ▨ Dwelling Only
- ▒ Personal Property only

*Source: Insurance Information Institute

201

2. **Personal property.** Your personal articles are generally insured for at least 50 percent of the insured value of your home. If you suffer a personal property loss, most insurers will reimburse you for the "actual cash value" of an item (its replacement cost minus depreciation). **Replacement cost coverage** is generally a wise addition: It may add 10 to 15 percent to your premiums but will guarantee you reimbursement for the *actual cost* of replacing lost property.

3. **Liability coverage.** If a visitor is injured on your property or a tree in your yard falls on your neighbor's roof, the insurance company will pay the costs of defending you against a claim or lawsuit and will pay any damages for which you are legally liable. The maximum amount that the company will pay is usually $100,000. Additionally, most policies will pay up to $1,000 of medical bills for treatment required by a person injured on your property, regardless of who was at fault. Liability coverage extends beyond your own property, to cover up to $500 of accidental damage caused by a covered family member to someone else's property.

   More extensive liability coverage can be purchased through an "umbrella" policy, which generally expands the liability protection of both your homeowners and automobile insurance policies. Umbrellas often provide dramatic increases in coverage at very little additional cost. For example, you may be able to buy $1 million of liability protection for $150 to $200 a year. Consider making this investment if you have significant assets to protect.

4. **Landscaping.** Insurers commonly cover trees, shrubs, plants, and lawns up to a maximum of $500 per plant or an overall maximum of 5 percent of the insured value of your home. This coverage extends only to certain insured perils; it does not include wind damage.

5. **Loss of use.** Most policies cover reasonable extra living expenses if damage to your home forces you to live elsewhere for a time.

Are You Covered?

In order to receive full replacement payment for any partial loss or damage under a homeowners policy, you must insure your home for *at least 80 percent* of its replacement value. Replacement value is the cost of rebuilding or replacing the house—*not* its market value, which includes the value of the land and the cost of the foundation. Your insurance agent may be able to help you make an accurate determination of your home's replacement value, or you may want to hire a professional home appraiser.

It is extremely important to make sure you are not underinsured. A home valued at $80,000, for example, should be insured for a minimum of 80 percent of that amount, or $64,000. If a $5,000 damage to the home were to occur, the insurance company would pay $5,000, less the

"Disaster" Protection

No homeowners policy protects you from every risk. Notable exclusions are earthquake and flood damage.

Earthquake insurance is available through many private insurers, usually as an addition to a homeowners policy. And homeowners who live in flood-prone areas can purchase separate flood insurance from the National Flood Insurance Program administered by the Department of Housing and Urban Development's Federal Insurance Administration or from one of some 200 private insurers. To qualify for flood insurance, your property must be located in a community that meets federal standards for land use and flood plain management. For information, check with your insurance agent or call the National Flood Insurance Program at 800–638–6620.

deductible, to cover the cost of repairs. But if the home were insured for *less* than 80 percent—say, for $40,000—the insurer would pay a reduced benefit, which would equal either the actual cash value of damaged property (the replacement cost minus depreciation) or $^{40}/_{64}$ of the loss ($3,125), whichever was larger. Of course, in the event of total loss, the insurer pays the total amount of coverage—$40,000 in this example.

Many insurance experts recommend insuring a home for *100 percent* of its current replacement value—full coverage that would completely rebuild or replace the home. Often the cost difference between 80 percent and 100 percent coverage is not significant and the additional insurance can be a worthwhile investment.

A **replacement cost guarantee** can also be a smart investment for homeowners who choose to insure their homes for full replacement value. Under this guarantee, the *insurance company* is responsible for making certain your home is adequately covered. The amount of insurance is evaluated and updated each year, and the company pledges to cover the cost of replacing your home even if that cost comes to more than the face amount of your policy.

If you haven't updated your insurance coverage in several years, it's possible that the value of any home improvements plus the increase in construction costs in your area have increased your home's replacement value to the point where your homeowners insurance is below the 80 percent threshold. Make it a practice to review and adjust your homeowners coverage annually; you may save yourself an unpleasant surprise at claim time.

The amount of coverage you purchase on your home automatically determines the level of coverage of personal property (which is insured for 50 percent of the total house coverage), other structures on the property (10 percent), and loss-of-use expenses (20 percent, or 10 percent

Taking Stock

An inventory of your personal belongings can be a valuable aid in determining their value and making certain they are adequately insured. And if you ever need to file an insurance claim, an up-to-date inventory can help you establish the value of your property, identify exactly what was lost, settle your claim more quickly, and verify losses for possible income tax deductions.

To make an inventory, go through your house room by room and list all major items. Make a note of serial numbers, manufacturers, purchase prices, and approximate dates of purchase; attach any available receipts. You may want to supplement your written inventory by photographing or videotaping each room from several angles, with closets and cabinet doors open. On the back of photographs, jot down the date, location, and contents shown.

Store your inventory and photographs or videotapes in a safe place away from home, and be sure to update your inventory from time to time, especially when new items are purchased.

with HO–1 and HO–8). Personal property coverage also is subject to specific dollar limits on the amount that will be paid on claims relating to the theft of valuable items such as jewelry, watches, furs, antiques, camera equipment, and art pieces. If you want to raise the limits on protection of particular items, additional coverage can be purchased in the form of a separate "floater" policy. The floater can cover either a specific object (such as an oil painting) or a set of objects (such as jewelry). The cost of floaters varies depending on where you live and on the item insured.

Floater coverage applies wherever the object is located at the time of loss—that means the cost of your wedding ring can be recovered even if the ring is lost or stolen when you are on vacation a thousand miles from home. In most cases, you'll need to have items professionally appraised before purchasing a floater policy.

Shopping for Savings

Prices for equivalent homeowners policies vary from company to company, often by hundreds of dollars. To find the best deal, from a reliable source, follow the recommendations in "Your Insurance Provider," pages 236–37.

There are a few additional avenues of potential savings on homeowners insurance. If you have the assets to cover relatively small losses, raising the standard $250 deductible can substantially reduce your premiums. But be careful not to raise your deductible to a higher amount than you could comfortably afford to absorb if you suffered a loss.

Also ask your agent about the availability of discounts for:

☐ Brand-new homes
☐ Homes made of fire-resistant materials
☐ Homes equipped with smoke detectors, a sprinkler system, and/or burglar alarms
☐ The engraving of valuable personal property with identification numbers
☐ Policyholders who are 55 or older
☐ Policyholders who have several policies with the same company, or who have had their policy for several years

Filing a Claim

If you have a fire, theft, or other damage or loss in your home, the Insurance Information Institute recommends taking these steps:

1. Immediately report any burglary or theft to the police.

2. Phone your insurance agent or company as soon as possible. Ask these questions:

• Am I covered?
• Does my claim exceed my deductible?
• How long will it take to process my claim?
• Will I need to obtain estimates for repairs or other losses?

3. Make any temporary repairs needed to prevent further damage or to secure your home. Keep receipts and a record of the costs of those repairs and submit them to your insurance company for reimbursement.

4. Using your household inventory as a guide, prepare a list of lost or damaged items.

5. Save any receipts for additional living expenses you incur if your home is so severely damaged that you have to live elsewhere while repairs are being made.

If you live in a high-crime area, it may be impossible to find an affordable homeowners policy that provides coverage for losses due to theft. Under a program subsidized by the Department of Housing and Urban Development, you may qualify for federal crime insurance, which offers up to $10,000 of coverage for homes equipped with certain required locks on windows and doors. Ask your insurance agent for details, or write: Federal Crime Insurance Program, P.O. Box 41033, Bethesda, MD 20814.

FOR FURTHER ASSISTANCE

Home buying is a complicated and important step. If you feel you need further information or guidance, you may wish to contact the American Homeowners Foundation, a nonprofit educational and research organization which offers a detailed how-to book on home buying, a model home-purchase contract, and other helpful publications. For a free catalog, write: The American Homeowners Foundation, 1724 S. Quincy Street, Arlington, VA 22204. Also informative is the free *Home Guide* published by the National Association of Realtors—copies are available from member agents and brokers. For sources of further information on homeowners insurance, see pages 237-38 of the *Insurance* chapter. You might also check with your local Better Business Bureau for any additional information and advice contained in its consumer information booklets. Finally, a visit to your local library or bookstore can uncover a wealth of valuable information in the pages of financial and consumer magazines and books for the prospective homeowner.

Home Improvements

Home improvement and remodeling companies were the number one category of consumer inquiries received by U.S. Better Business Bureaus in 1988, and number four in consumer complaints. Over 45,000 consumers reported disputes with the company they had hired to repair, restore, or remodel their home. Yet many of these problems need never have occurred. The following tips on planning a home improvement project and choosing and working with a contractor can help ensure that a similar problem doesn't happen to you.

PLANNING THE PROJECT

Whether you are repairing your roof, insulating your home, or adding a room, it is easier to compare bids from various contractors if all estimates are based on the same criteria. That requires some planning and research to pin down what you want done and, if possible, the types of materials you want used. Try to get information from unbiased sources—organizations or individuals without a personal stake in selling you something. Your local library or state consumer protection office may be able to provide helpful publications; many trade associations also publish consumer-oriented literature on methods and materials. (Your library should have a copy of *National Trade and Professional Associations of the United States** or another resource providing the names and addresses of trade associations.)

Some home improvement topics are covered elsewhere in this book; see *Air Conditioners*, pages 8–16; *Burglar Alarm Systems*, pages 60–64; *Insulation*, pages 216–19; *Lawn Care Services*, pages 246–48; and *Pest Control*, pages 285–86.

You'll also find at your library or newsstand many home design and consumer magazines that can provide information and inspiration if your project involves remodeling the interior of your home. One planning exercise often recommended involves drawing a floor plan of your home using graph paper and patterns of your furniture cut to scale. Such a diagram can help you visualize changes and make optimum use of available space. Be sure to plan around traffic areas, furniture groupings, storage space, and lighting and electrical needs.

Once you have researched your project, put your needs in writing. Now you're ready to accurately and confidently discuss your project with a contractor.

*©1988 Columbia Books, Inc., Washington, DC.

Home Improvements: A Good Investment?

The most important reason for making improvements to your home is to increase your comfort and enjoyment. If you are planning to remodel in order to upgrade the price of your house, you should be aware that, when it comes time to sell, home improvements often do not pay back what they cost.

Keep these facts in mind when considering home improvements as an investment venture:

- Don't "overimprove"—buyers don't want the most expensive house on the block.

- The best home improvements in terms of investment potential are those that add to a home's practicality, such as adding a second bathroom or modernizing an out-of-date kitchen.

- "Cosmetic" improvements prior to sale of the home can also pay dividends. The idea is to make a good first impression; the means can be as simple as painting the shingles, replacing worn carpets, or tending the lawn and shrubbery.

- Before undertaking a major remodeling project, you may want to talk with an experienced real estate agent about its potential payback.

Following are average costs and returns for four typical home improvement projects.*

Project	Region	Average Cost	Estimated Percentage of Cost Recovered When Home Sold
Major kitchen remodel	Northeast	$21,302	95%
	South	$19,291	91%
	Midwest	$20,899	75%
	West	$21,071	91%
Remodel bathroom	Northeast	$ 8,293	80%
	South	$ 6,241	75%
	Midwest	$ 7,735	65%
	West	$ 8,003	71%
Add a bathroom	Northeast	$11,291	85%
	South	$ 8,534	90%
	Midwest	$ 9,234	83%
	West	$11,545	82%
Add a pine deck	Northeast	$ 5,615	81%
	South	$ 4,397	75%
	Midwest	$ 5,255	59%
	West	$ 5,170	55%

*From "1989 Cost vs. Value Report," *Remodeling* magazine, October 1989, ©1989 Hanley-Wood, Inc. The report evaluates the resale value of 11 popular remodeling projects in 40 cities nationwide. To purchase reprints, call 800-634-4773.

CHOOSING A CONTRACTOR

Personal recommendations from friends and neighbors are your best lead to a contractor who will provide quality work at a fair price. If personal referrals are unavailable, try looking in your local newspaper or the yellow pages of your phone directory.

Ask each contractor on your list for local references, and call or visit these homeowners to discuss their level of satisfaction with the contractor's work and to look at the finished project. Call your local Better Business Bureau and consumer protection office; ask for any available information on the contractor, including how long the company has been in business and whether there is any record of complaints or other relevant activities.

Ask the contractor if the firm is a member of the National Association of the Remodeling Industry, the National Association of Home Builders Remodelors Council,[TM] and/or any of the trade associations representing specific sectors of the remodeling industry. Most of these organizations require members to adhere to a code of ethics or standards and offer certification and continuing education programs, and some will act as an intermediary or arrange for impartial arbitration in case of disputes. Contact the local chapter of the association to confirm the information.

Some states require contractors to be licensed and/or bonded. Check with your state consumer protection office or state, county, or city housing authority to make sure the contractor meets all licensing and/or bonding requirements in your area. Remember, however, that in most cases bonds simply ensure compliance with local building codes or other regulations; they are no guarantee of integrity or competence.

Finally, ask the contractor if the company is insured against claims covering workers' compensation, property damage, and personal liability in case of accidents. In some areas, such insurance is required by law. You might want to ask to see a copy of the certificate of insurance, and ask for the name of the contractor's insurance carrier and agency so that you can verify that the contractor has adequate coverage.

It's a good idea to solicit more than one bid for your home improvement project. Ask contractors to come to your home to give their estimates in the form of written proposals. (There may be a charge for estimates; ask about this first.) Make sure all bids are based on the same set of specifications—it is difficult to compare price estimates unless you give each contractor the same description of the job you want done and each proposes to use the same methods and materials in carrying out the project. If estimates differ widely, discuss them in detail with the contractors and make sure you understand the reasons behind variations.

Price should not be the sole criterion for your final choice. Compare *all* factors, including the firm's references, reputation, and length of experience, plus how comfortable you feel with the contractor. Remember, during the duration of the project, the contractor will be an almost constant "living companion."

THE CONTRACT

A detailed, *written* contract is your best protection against annoying and costly disputes. Make sure the contract contains all the oral promises you've been given and that it spells out exactly what the contractor will and will not do. In general, a home improvement contract should specify the following:

- **The name and address** of the contractor and salesperson, and the license number, if applicable.
- **All financial terms,** including the total price, the amount of down payment, when further payments are to be made and in what amounts, and whether there is a cancellation policy. The down payment generally is about one-third of the total price; some state or local laws limit the amount of down payment that can be required. Try to negotiate a plan that schedules further payments at intervals as the work proceeds, with the amount of each payment based on the work that has been completed.
- **The work to be performed and the materials to be used.** If you intend to do some of the work yourself or hire another contractor to do it, this should be written into the contract. Make sure materials are precisely described, with quantity, quality, weight, color, size, and/or brand names.
- **An approximate starting date and completion date.** This schedule is generally contingent on factors such as the weather or the availability of supplies.
- **A statement that work is to be performed in accordance with all applicable building codes** and that the contractor is responsible for obtaining the necessary building permits. (Also see "Permits and Inspections," page 211.)
- **Any additional details** you consider important to completion of the job, such as cleanup and removal of debris and building materials, special requests for saving certain materials or appliances, or special instructions about areas where materials are not to be stored or precautions to be taken regarding children or pets.
- **The terms and conditions of any warranties** for materials and/or workmanship. The warranty should include the name and address of the party who will honor it, the duration of coverage, and whether it is full or limited. A full warranty guarantees repair or replacement of products or a refund of your money; "limited" means that certain restrictions and exclusions apply to repairs, replacements, or refunds.
- **If you plan to finance your project** through a personal loan from a bank, savings and loan, credit union, or other lender, the contract should include a clause stating that it is valid only if you are able to obtain financing at the rate you want.

The "Cooling Off" Period

When you sign a home improvement contract in your home and in the presence of the contractor or contractor's representative, you normally have three business days within which you are entitled to change your mind and cancel. Under the Federal Trade Commission's "Cooling Off" Rule, the seller must tell you about your cancellation rights both orally and in writing, and provide the forms that you would use in canceling. Contractors usually wait until the end of this cooling off period before starting work, so you may be asked to waive your three-day cancellation rights if you need immediate, emergency repairs.

The "Cooling Off" Rule applies to most other purchases costing $25 or more that you make in your home or somewhere other than the place of business of the seller. However, there are certain conditions under which the cooling off period does not apply. Check with your local consumer protection office or state office of the attorney general for a detailed explanation of your rights.

If you are undertaking a major remodeling project that will involve a substantial financial commitment, it is wise to seek legal advice before signing the contract. In any case, carefully read the contract and be certain you understand all its terms before signing. Never sign a contract until all the blanks have been filled in. And as soon as you sign the contract, ask for a copy and carefully file it away.

PERMITS AND INSPECTIONS

Building codes are established by most cities, towns, and counties, and vary considerably from one jurisdiction to another. As a general rule, a building permit is required whenever structural work is involved or when the basic living area of a home is to be changed. For example, if your home has an unfinished basement and you decide to finish off a portion for a family room, most jurisdictions would require you to obtain a building permit because you are planning to convert home storage space into "livable" space. In some cases, separate permits for electrical, heating, and plumbing work are also required.

Before proceeding with a home improvement project, you or your contractor should check with your area's zoning authorities to determine what permits or permissions are needed. Make sure it is the contractor who actually obtains the permit; the person who gets the permit is considered to be the contractor and is therefore liable if the work does not comply with the building codes.

When a government agency issues a permit for home improvement work, it inspects the work when it has reached a certain stage and/or

---

Emergency Repairs

The need for immediate repairs robs you of the time required to properly plan and research a project and comparison-shop among contractors. However, there are steps you can take to safeguard yourself, even in a home repair emergency.

1. Before calling a contractor, contact your local BBB and consumer protection office for complaint reports.
2. When you call the firm, describe the situation as precisely as possible, but let the contractor assess the problem and decide how to correct it.
3. Ask about minimum charges and labor charges. There is usually a minimum charge for the repairperson's visit to your home; if the work takes longer than a specified period, an additional hourly or half-hourly labor charge usually is added. Ask whether the minimum charge or labor charge includes travel time.
4. Before repairs begin, get a written estimate of costs, and insist on the right to approve any work that would raise the estimated bill.
5. After work is completed, get a detailed invoice that lists all charges for parts and service. Also ask for any parts that were replaced—these can be helpful in proving your case if you later suspect that repairs were unnecessary or were improperly performed.

---

when it is completed to ensure compliance with all codes and regulations.

WORKING WITH YOUR CONTRACTOR

It is important to establish a good working relationship with your contractor from the start. You've hired the firm to get professional assistance with your project, so it only makes sense to listen to the contractor's suggestions and advice. At the same time, though, you should not be embarrassed to ask questions, check the work in progress, voice your concerns if something doesn't look right to you, and insist that problems and mistakes be corrected.

The contractor is responsible for correcting his or her own mistakes, but any changes to the original plan that you request during the course of construction may cost extra. These revisions, commonly called "change orders," should be put in writing as an amendment to the contract, along with any agreed-upon additional costs. Many contractors require that the additional costs be paid at the time the change order is signed, in order to prevent disagreements at the end of the project.

Keep in mind that changing your plans may not only add to the cost of your project but can add to its length as well. Changes may require the contractor to order new materials or to reschedule work crews and subcontractors. The best way to avoid the necessity for changes is to make sure, before work begins, that the contractor has a clear understanding of what you want and has clearly diagrammed the plan so you can visualize the final product.

As work on your home begins, remember that the road to improvement is often paved with temporary inconvenience. Expecting problems and annoyances can help you cope with the noise, dust, confusion, and chaos. And keeping a careful eye on the project as it progresses can help you maintain a sense of control and catch minor problems before they become major conflicts.

It is a wise precaution, according to consumer affairs professionals, to withhold a negotiated percentage of the contract price (typically 10 percent) until the job is completed and you have had an opportunity to inspect the work. If a permit was required, do not make the final payment until the local building inspector's approval is given. If you borrowed money to finance the project, the lender generally will require a signed completion certificate before releasing the last payment. Never sign a completion certificate until all the work called for in the contract has been performed to your satisfaction.

RED FLAGS

Proceed with utmost caution if you encounter any of these warning signs of possible trouble ahead:

- You cannot verify a contractor's name, address, telephone number, and/or credentials.
- You cannot verify that the contractor is licensed, insured, and/or bonded as required.
- You are unable to obtain references, or the references have reservations about the contractor's work.
- The contractor offers you a "special low price" in exchange for the use of your home as a "model home" or "show house."
- You are offered an unbelievably low price for a repair job because, the contractor claims, materials are "left over" from another job.
- You are told that a "special price" is available only if you sign the contract *today.*
- The salesperson tries to pressure you into signing a contract by using intimidation or scare tactics. ("Your roof is about to cave in!" "Your furnace is ready to explode!")
- You are asked to pay for the entire job in advance or to pay in cash or in a check made out to the salesperson.

Humidifiers

A number of products are available for adding moisture to dry indoor air, ranging from central system humidifiers to small tabletop models. Central humidifiers are often installed by a contractor along with a central forced-air heating system (see "Choosing a Contractor," *Air Conditioners*, pages 14–15). They humidify an entire house by introducing moisture into the air as it passes through the heating/ventilating system on its way to the air distribution outlets.

When most people think of humidifiers, however, they mean the smaller tabletop or console units designed to add moisture to a single room or small group of connected rooms. These are generally available in four types: **ultrasonic** humidifiers, which use sound waves to break up water into mist; **cool-mist or impeller vaporizers**, which use an impeller to break up water into tiny droplets; **warm-mist** units, which boil water and dispense steam like a vaporizer but allow control of the level of humidity; and **evaporative** models, which blow air through a belt which is continuously cycled through water.

One of the most important considerations in selecting a humidifier is its capacity, or the amount of moisture the unit can dispense in a given time. To determine the capacity you need, calculate the volume of the space to be humidified by multiplying the total floor area in square feet by the ceiling height in feet. Then refer to the chart below.

HUMIDIFICATION SELECTION GUIDE*

Construction of Residence	Size of Residence in sq. ft.					
	500	1000	1500	2000	2500	3000
	(Water Output Capacity, Gallons Per 24 Hours)					
Tight (Well Insulated, Vapor Barrier, Tight Storm Doors and Windows with Weatherstripping, Dampered Fireplace)	**	1.4	3.2	4.9	6.6	8.3
Average (Insulated, Vapor Barrier, Loose Storm Doors and Windows, Dampered Fireplace)	0.5	3.0	5.5	8.0	10.5	13.0
Loose (Little Insulation, No Storm Doors or Windows, No Vapor Barrier, Undampered Fireplace)	1.0	4.0	7.0	10.0	13.1	16.1

NOTE: If there is uncertainty as to the type of home construction, the values shown in the average category (the unshaded area) may be used. An amount of approximately 2 gallons per 24 hours provided by internal sources of humidity (based on a family of four) has already been deducted from the above values.

*Source: Association of Home Appliance Manufacturers.

**Humidification not necessary to maintain conditions of 70°F (21.1°C) and 30%RH (relative humidity).

Besides selecting a unit with adequate capacity for the space to be humidified, keep the following tips in mind as you shop for and use your humidifier:

1. Look for easy-to-use controls and a water reservoir that is easy to fill and clean. You may also want to consider a model with a *humidistat*, a device that cycles the humidifier on and off as it senses moisture needs.
2. If your home's outside wall insulation does not contain a vapor barrier (see page 218), you should not use a humidifier—moisture buildup can damage walls and insulation.
3. Your humidifier may be placed in any living area where air circulates freely, but the ideal location is a spot within easy access of a water source and, in a home with central forced-air heating, near a return air register. For best results, do not place a humidifier near cold outside walls or in bathrooms, kitchens, or other areas where routine activities generate humidity.

BENEFITS AND RISKS

Officials at the Environmental Protection Agency and the Consumer Product Safety Commission (CPSC) recently announced the disturbing discovery that humidifiers, unless kept scrupulously clean, can raise the levels of airborne particles in a home, including bacteria, microorganisms, and molds, to as high as 10 times the federally accepted standards. Ultrasonic humidifiers kill microorganisms but may release fragments of bacteria and molds into the air. Warm-mist humidifiers and steam vaporizers kill most troublesome organisms by boiling the water.

The key to safe use of humidifiers is cleanliness—and that means conscientiously following the manufacturer's use and care recommendations. The CPSC advises consumers to use only distilled water (*not* tap water) to fill their humidifiers, to empty the units completely between uses, and to clean them frequently, as directed by the manufacturer.

The water in central system humidifiers also can become contaminated with bacteria, particularly if the unit remains inactive for some time. The Air-Conditioning & Refrigeration Institute, a manufacturers' trade association, urges thorough cleaning of central system humidifiers at the end of the heating system, plus inspection of the system once a month during winter, or according to the schedule recommended by the contractor or the owner's manual.

Another problem, unique to ultrasonic humidifiers, occurs when these units are filled with hard, or mineral-laden, water. A fine layer of white dust, composed of mineral particles, can be disbursed, aggravating respiratory problems while in the air and creating a cleaning nuisance once settled. The solution, again, is to use only distilled water; some manufacturers sell disposable demineralization filters intended to control the dust.

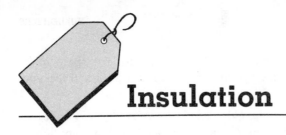

Insulation

In these energy-conscious times, installing home insulation can be a smart investment that makes the temperature of rooms more comfortable, deadens sounds between rooms, and lowers your heating and cooling bills.

Does your home need more insulation? The answer may be as obvious as the drafts around baseboards, cabinets, windows, and doors, or the outside cracks and gaps around the chimney or where pipes or wires enter the house. One quick check you can make in cold weather is to place your hand at several spots on an interior wall and compare its temperature with that of an exterior wall: If your home is adequately insulated, the exterior wall should feel only slightly cooler.

For a thorough assessment of the energy efficiency of your home, you'll need to call on a professional. Your best source of help may well be your local utility company. Under the voluntary Residential Conservation Service Program of the federal Department of Energy, most utilities will perform a whole-house energy audit for a small fee or at no charge. The energy audit will give you detailed recommendations on the costs and potential savings of adding storm windows or doors, caulking, weather stripping, and/or insulation. As part of the service, the utility also will provide referrals to contractors qualified to implement the recommendations of the audit, offer to arrange installation by a qualified contractor, assist you in securing financing, if needed, and allow you to repay the cost as part of your monthly fuel bill.

INSULATION TYPES AND TERMS

Manufacturers measure the ability of insulation to resist the flow of heat in terms of its "R" (resistance) value. The higher the R-value, the better a particular insulating material slows winter heat loss and summer heat gain. Under federal law, every package of home insulation must display its R-value rating, and all stores that sell insulation are required to have on hand the manufacturer's fact sheet, which identifies the type of insulation, its R-value, and its coverage area (the maximum area that the amount of insulation you purchase will cover while still achieving the R-value).

Insulation is made from a variety of materials and is sold in several different forms, including batts, blankets, loose fill, rigid insulation, foam, and foil.

- **Batts and blankets** are the familiar fluffy strips that are fitted between rafters and joists. Batts come in precut lengths and blankets in continuous rolls. Both are made of mineral fiber, which is commonly known as fiberglass or rock wool. Batts and blankets are lightweight and relatively easy to install, but they must be cut carefully to fit around obstructions such as pipes and electrical boxes.

- **Loose fill** comes in bags and is used mostly for attics and finished walls. It may be made of mineral fiber, cellulose (ground or shredded paper products or wood fiber, which must be treated to limit its flammability), perlite, or vermiculite. Mineral fiber and cellulose are blown into the space to be insulated; installation must be performed by a professional contractor. Perlite and vermiculite are poured, a process which most do-it-yourselfers can handle. Loose fill can be relatively easy to install in cramped spaces, but it can settle and lose its R-value if not properly installed or if it becomes wet.
- **Rigid insulation** comes in rigid slabs or boardstock in a variety of sizes, densities, and thicknesses. Made of polystyrene, polyurethane, or polyisocyanurate, these products are more useful in new construction than in existing buildings. Rigid insulation is combustible and must be protected by drywall or some other fireproof material.
- **Insulating foam** is pumped into a cavity or space, where it solidifies. It is most commonly used in the exterior walls of existing buildings and must be installed by a professional.
- **Reflective foil insulation** consists of one or more sheets of aluminum foil. Foil is the most effective insulator against radiant heat, and when more than one sheet is used, the air between sheets provides resistance to the transfer of heat. If foil is punctured or improperly installed, however, its insulating advantages are greatly reduced.

Obviously, no one form of insulation or insulating material is suitable for all applications. Choosing the proper form involves an evaluation of the area to be insulated, the local climate, the R-value needed, and your budget. The labels on most insulating materials provide some information that can help in the selection process. Your local utility, a knowledgeable retailer, or a qualified contractor can also provide valuable information and assistance.

PROFESSIONAL SERVICES OR DO-IT-YOURSELF?

If you are a handy person *who is willing to take the time to learn about proper installation measures and safety precautions,* it's possible to save some money by installing insulation yourself. For major insulation jobs, or when you haven't the time or expertise to tackle a do-it-yourself project, follow these steps to find a qualified insulation contractor:

1. Ask your utility company and friends and neighbors for recommendations.
2. Call your local BBB for a reliability report on each prospect.

Batts, blankets, and some rigid insulation can be bought with a **vapor barrier** on one side. These kraft paper or foil coverings protect the material from condensation, which can lower its R-value. If you are installing insulation with a vapor barrier, make sure the barrier is on the side of the insulation that will be heated. When adding new insulation over an existing layer that has a vapor barrier, either use unfaced material or, if that's not available, remove or thoroughly slash the vapor barrier of the new insulation.

3. Get at least three written estimates and compare more than just price. Each estimate should include the cost of materials and labor; details on the R-value of the insulation to be installed in each part of the house; types of material to be used; areas to be covered; thickness of insulation; and, in the case of loose fill, the number of bags to be used.

4. Ask the contractor you select for a written contract or receipt specifying the details listed in the estimate. Before you agree to the installation, ask to see the manufacturer's fact sheet, which confirms the information the contractor has provided about materials and coverage area.

5. Make sure either you or the contractor have adequate insurance in case of injury on the job.

If you decide to install insulation yourself, the following tips can help you shop for the most cost-effective materials:

1. **Determine the R-value you need.** This varies according to the part of the house you're insulating and the part of the country you live in. Your local utility company or energy office can help you determine the correct R-value.

2. **Decide what type of insulation to install.** See pages 216–17 for a description of the most commonly used forms of insulation. When deciding which form of insulation to buy, take into consideration ease of application and availability of installation instructions.

3. **Measure the area you're going to insulate.** Check the chart on insulation packages to figure out how much insulation you'll need to get the recommended R-value. Remember that installing more than you actually need is a waste of money.

4. **Shop for your best insulation deal.** Use the following formula:

Price of the package ÷ Square feet of insulation needed for the R-value you select ÷ R-value number you select = Cost of one unit of R-value

All the numbers that you need to plug into this formula are either on the package of insulation or can be provided by the retailer. Comparing the cost of one unit of R-value for each product you are considering helps you determine which gives you the R-value you want at the lowest cost.

SAFETY CONSIDERATIONS

Some insulating materials are combustible, and even those that are generally noncombustible can retain heat and present the risk of igniting combustible materials nearby. Furthermore, the installation of thermal insulation may increase the risk of fire in a home where the electrical system is deficient. Obviously, when insulation is added, every precaution should be taken to avoid the creation of a fire hazard. Homeowners and contractors are responsible for following all manufacturer's precautions and instructions regarding proper installation procedures, as well as for ensuring that there are no potentially hazardous problems in the home's electrical system.

The Insulation Contractors Association of America recommends the following specific precautionary measures:

1. Maintain at least three inches of clearance around all recessed light fixtures. (Listed or Insulated Ceiling fixtures, which are designed so that they can safely be covered with insulation, are marked "type IC.")
2. When installing insulation in an attic, take particular care to prevent damage to the electrical insulation on wiring. Avoid lifting, pulling, and twisting those wires.
3. Make sure properly sized fuses or circuit breakers are used, and that bulbs of proper wattage are used in all light fixtures. Oversized fuses and bulbs of too-high wattage can create excess heat and cause combustion.
4. If there is any possibility that the electrical system is defective, an electrical inspection should be conducted by an electrician, electrical inspector, or other qualified technician.

If you are installing insulation yourself, follow these additional safety tips:

• Make sure your work area is well lighted.
• Wear protective clothing, gloves, and a breathing mask, and wash that clothing separately when finished.
• If your attic is not floored, lay boards or plywood sheets over the tops of joists or trusses to make a safe walkway.
• Watch out for roofing nails protruding through the roof sheathing.
• Remember that your home's electrical system is a source of heat any time it is in use. Be sure to observe the fire safety precautions outlined above and on the product package.

Insurance

(Also see "Auto Insurance," *Automobiles,* pages 48–52; "Homeowners Insurance," *Home Buying,* pages 199–205.)

For the average American consumer, insurance is the fourth-largest expense of a lifetime, ranking right behind food, housing, and taxes. Yet most people don't understand how insurance works, how companies price insurance products, or what their policies cover. A majority buy coverage they don't need and/or don't buy the coverage they do need. And often they don't discover their error until it's too late, when the time comes to file a claim.

Becoming an educated consumer of insurance products can save you thousands of dollars—and untold misery at claim time. The following "quick course" provides the basic tools that should help most readers save money by making more informed and effective insurance-buying decisions.

Insurance is divided into two parts: life, health, and disability on one side and property/casualty (including homeowners and automobile insurance) on the other. Homeowners insurance is covered in the *Home Buying* chapter, on pages 199–205; for a discussion of auto insurance, see pages 48–52 of *Automobiles.* In this chapter, we'll examine life, health, and disability insurance and also take a look at Medicare supplement insurance, or "Medigap."

LIFE INSURANCE

Of all the types of insurance you buy, life insurance is likely to cost the most, according to the National Insurance Consumer Organization, a nonprofit public interest membership organization. Yet the availability of hundreds of different policies makes it extremely difficult for consumers to evaluate and compare the costs of various plans. Before you begin to comparison-shop, you should have an understanding of the basics: how life insurance works, the forms of policies available, and how much coverage you need.

Life insurance is a legal contract between a buyer and an insurer. Under the terms of the contract—your insurance policy—the insurer promises to pay, at the time of your death, a sum of money to the person or persons you name as beneficiary. This promise is given in return for your agreement to pay a sum of money (the premium) to the insurer over a specified period of time.

Insurance companies base their rates on a determination of the average lifespan of a group of people with similar characteristics, such as age, weight, family history, and smoking habits. Using information obtained from your application and, sometimes, from a company-paid medical exam, the insurer places you in a group of people with the same characteristics, and thus the same "level of risk." People with similar risks pay the same premiums.

Each year, your risk of death increases, and consequently the cost of insuring your life goes up. The two basic forms of life insurance—*term life insurance* and *whole life insurance*—take that fact into account in their use of two different methods of determining premiums.

With **term life insurance,** premiums rise according to age. Term insurance provides protection over a specified number of years—usually 1, 5, 10, or 20. After that term of years expires, protection ends, unless you renew the policy. The right to renew is usually granted only up to a specified maximum age, such as 65 or 70. With a renewable term policy, you do not have to undergo a physical exam or provide other evidence of insurability to renew, but each time you renew, the premium rate increases.

Here is how the premium on a typical policy providing $50,000 worth of one-year renewable term insurance might increase.*

	Man	Woman**
Age 30	$145	$138
Age 40	$190	$178
Age 50	$405	$328
Age 60	$925	$715

Most term life policies are **convertible;** that is, they can be exchanged for a whole life policy, without evidence of insurability, usually up to age 60 or 65. It's possible, however, that your insurance company's price on a whole life policy may be higher than you could obtain from another insurer at the time of conversion.

Whole life insurance (also referred to as permanent, cash-value, straight life, or ordinary life insurance) provides protection for as long as you live, without an increase in premiums. The costs of your policy are averaged out over your lifetime on a yearly basis; the premium during the early years of the policy is much higher than you would pay for renewable term insurance, and over the later years, much lower.

There is an added dimension to a whole life policy, which might be considered a type of insurance policy and savings plan all in one. Whole

* From *A Consumer's Guide to Life Insurance,* American Council of Life Insurance, Washington, DC.

** Rates for women are almost always lower than those for men, since women live longer on average.

life plans build **cash value**—a sum of money that increases over the years on a tax-deferred basis. Tax-deferred means that in most cases you are not required to pay income taxes on the increase in cash value until you withdraw the money. Even then, only the *taxable gain,* the amount by which the cash value exceeds the premiums you have paid, is taxable.

If you voluntarily cancel (or *surrender*) your whole life policy, its current cash value is paid to you in a lump sum. The cash value has other uses, including:

- You can take out a loan from the insurer for up to the amount of current cash value, using your policy as collateral. If you die before the loan is repaid, the amount owed, plus interest, is deducted from the death benefits paid to your beneficiary. Some insurers penalize policyholders for borrowing against the cash value by paying lower dividends to borrowers.

- You can stop paying premiums and use the accrued cash value to finance a "paid-up" policy, which provides a reduced level of protection.

- You can use the cash value to purchase an annuity that provides a guaranteed monthly income for life.

The table below* shows the increase in cash value for a hypothetical $100,000 whole life policy issued to a 35-year-old male, and compares the yearly premiums for that policy with those of an annual renewable term life policy.

	Whole Life Premiums	Cash Value	Term Premiums
Age 35	$1,100	$ 0	$ 140
Age 45	$1,100	$ 9,000	$ 210
Age 55	$1,100	$24,000	$ 590
Age 65	$1,100	$43,000	$1,600

Variations on Whole Life

The many forms of whole life policies include:

Limited payment whole life: Higher premiums are paid for a shorter period of time, such as 20 years, after which the policy is considered "paid up."

Single-premium whole life: The total premium is paid in one lump sum at the time the policy is issued. Until recently, these policies offered considerable tax advantages for policyholders who borrowed against the cash value; however, recent changes in the law have closed many of those loopholes.

* Statistics from *Taking the Bite Out of Insurance,* National Insurance Consumer Organization (NICO), Alexandria, VA, 1988.

Combination or economatic plans: These policies combine term and whole life in one contract; a typical combination is 60 percent of whole life and 40 percent of term. Through the years, dividends are used to buy additional paid-up whole life insurance, and the percentage of whole life in the policy increases as the percentage of term decreases. Premiums are generally lower than those of standard whole life policies and remain level throughout the life of the policy. However, they may be less than is needed to guarantee to cover the policy for the whole of life.

Universal life (or flexible-premium adjustable life): Under most forms of universal life, you can pay premiums at any time and in any amount, subject to certain minimums and maximums. Also adding to this plan's flexibility is the fact that you can increase the amount of coverage, if needed, without providing evidence of insurability; however, you will have to pay commissions and other charges for coverage changes.

The amount of cash value a universal life policy accumulates reflects the interest earned at prevailing interest rates. Rates are usually guaranteed for one year and are disclosed at the time of sale and in annual reports. With other whole life policies, it can be difficult for the policyholder to identify the current rate. Under an Option A (or I) universal life policy, death benefits remain constant unless you request changes; under Option B (or II), the death benefit gradually increases each year, equaling the policy's original face amount plus accrued cash value.

Interest-sensitive whole life: This variation of universal life offers *fixed* premiums and death benefits; its cash value growth is dependent on current interest rates.

Variable life: This form of insurance is actually a security; sellers must be registered representatives of a broker-dealer licensed by the National Association of Securities Dealers and registered with the Securities and Exchange Commission. With a variable life policy, you pay fixed premiums and your policy's cash value is invested in a separate mutual funds account managed by the company. The face amount and cash value of the policy increase or decrease depending on the success of the investments; death benefits, however, cannot fall below the original face amount. Before you buy a variable life policy, you must be provided with a prospectus detailing all expenses, including commissions, sales and administrative charges, and taxes.

Adjustable life: A combination of whole life and term, adjustable life allows you to change the face amount of the policy by changing your premium payments or the length of time the policy is in force.

Many life insurance policies pay annual dividends; such policies are known as **participating.** Dividends are actually a form of premium refund. When premiums exceed the insurer's estimate of what will be needed to pay death benefits and company expenses, some of that excess is refunded to policyholders. Dividends can be taken in cash, left to accumulate at interest, used to reduce premiums, or, in the case of whole life policies, used to purchase paid-up additional whole life coverage. Life insurance dividends are usually not taxable.

What Should You Buy?

With so many different policies available and so many different companies offering them, deciding which policy and how much coverage to buy is a difficult and complex process. The National Insurance Consumer Organization offers these recommendations:

1. Think twice about buying *any* life insurance if you are:
   □ single, with no dependents; or
   □ married, with no dependents, with a working spouse who earns wages comparable to yours.

Remember that the primary purpose of life insurance is to protect a family against the loss of income due to the death of a breadwinner.

2. Detailed formulas are available to help you calculate how much insurance coverage you need; check your library for books or periodicals containing such worksheets. Alternatively, you might use this simple rule of thumb: *The life insurance coverage you need is equal to five times your annual net income.* (If you are married and your spouse works, you would buy a total of five times the higher net income and split the total proportionately to your two incomes.)

Of course, in applying any general rule to your individual circumstances, a number of personal factors must be taken into account. These include the amount of any life insurance you already own, how many children or other dependents you have, your net worth and any prospects of inheritance, your spouse's employment status, your spouse's likelihood of remarriage, and your personal views and preferences (many people assign a high priority to the comfort of knowing that their family's future financial needs are well secured).

3. When choosing between term and whole life insurance, consider the following:
   • Annual renewable term insurance offers the most protection at the lowest current cost.
   • Due to the high premiums, many younger people simply cannot afford to buy adequate coverage through a whole life policy.
   • If you need to surrender a whole life policy in the first few years (and, according to NICO, roughly 50 percent of such policies are canceled within 10 years), you stand to lose a good deal of money, since the high premiums you have paid will not yet have had sufficient time to develop any significant cash value.
   • As you get older, your life insurance needs typically decrease. As an alternative to a whole life policy that continues in effect past your

retirement years, you might consider buying lower-cost term insurance while you are young and placing the premium savings in a long-term investment plan. Another alternative might be to choose a pension option that continues all or part of your pension to your spouse on your death.

- On the other hand, whole life insurance can be the better option if you are over 55 and want life insurance in force at your death in your 70s or 80s (as you might, for example, if you marry someone much younger than yourself and have children late in life).
- Also, if you are in the higher tax brackets in retirement, the tax advantages of whole life insurance can be substantial.

Comparing Costs

The costs of life insurance policies vary considerably, but those costs can be difficult to decipher and compare. The following tips can help you get the most for your insurance dollar:

☐ In comparing **term** insurance policies, ask for the annual cost per $1,000 of death benefits. Compare cost-per-thousand for the same kinds of policies, for the same age, sex, health status, and amount of coverage. If you expect to keep the policy for some time, look for a policy that is renewable up to at least age 65. However, before renewing your term insurance, check with competitive companies to make sure you still have the best rates.

☐ In comparing **whole life** insurance policies, ask agents for the *interest-adjusted net cost index,* which measures the cost of the policy if you surrender it after a specified number of years. The lower the index (down to negative numbers), the less expensive the policy. Also ask for and compare the *interest-adjusted net payment index,* which measures the ongoing cost of a policy if you don't cash it in or the cost if you die while holding it. Again, the lower the index, the less expensive the policy. These two indexes can only be used to compare similar policies, for the same type and amount of coverage and the same personal characteristics, such as age, sex, and smoking habits. *Since the indexes were developed several years ago, they factor in assumptions about interest rates that are no longer valid.* But even though their figures are no longer strictly accurate, they provide a good basis of comparison among similar policies.

　　Other factors to look for and compare include projections of: ☐ future cash surrender value (the amount the company will pay you at any time you wish to voluntarily cancel the policy); ☐ dividends (look for the *actual net,* not *gross,* figure); ☐ premiums; and ☐ total death benefits. One useful exercise suggested by NICO is to ask one company for a proposal showing its projected death benefit, premiums, and cash surrender value for a period at least 20 years in the future. Then ask other companies for proposals using the same death benefit and premiums—the company with the highest cash surrender value will probably give you the best return on your investment.

Finally, keep these facts and precautions in mind when you shop for life insurance:

1. Insurance agents are paid a high commission on the premiums you pay in the first year of coverage and lower commissions in later years. That may increase some agents' incentive to sell you a whole life policy. When listening to a sales agent's pitch, keep *your* best interests in mind.
2. Don't rely on the sales agent for tax advice—consult the company's published material and your own accountant or tax adviser.
3. Don't be swayed by currently advertised interest rates on whole life policies, and be wary of promises of exceptionally high returns. Rates can change at the discretion of the insurer. Also be aware that the dividend projections an insurance agent may show you are just that—projections, which may or may not prove accurate.

HEALTH INSURANCE

A health insurance policy protects you and your family from prohibitive expenses stemming from the medical treatment of illness, injury, or accident. The proportion of doctor, hospital, and pharmacy bills that the insurer will pay is dependent on the type and amount of coverage you buy.

Insurance companies determine the size of health premium payments by estimating the revenue they will require to cover benefits, operating costs, and other expenses. Estimates of benefit payments are based on

Mail Order Policies

Unsolicited mail offers of life, hospitalization, accident, and disability insurance often play heavily on consumer fears and confusion. While mail order insurance can be a worthwhile investment, it is vitally important to look carefully at terms and coverage, particularly when the solicitation promises acceptance regardless of health. Some of these policies pay small benefits for a high premium or may duplicate coverage you already have. Check with your state insurance department to determine whether the company is licensed to sell insurance in your state, and compare prices and benefits with those of policies available from other companies.

statistical projections of the number of policyholders who will become injured or ill in a given period and how much it will cost to treat them. Just as with life insurance, the premium you pay for an *individual* health insurance policy is also based on an evaluation of personal characteristics such as age, sex, smoking habits, and general physical condition.

About two-thirds of all Americans are covered by group health insurance plans offered through an employer. Group insurance is also available through various organizations such as fraternal societies, labor unions, college health departments, and rural and consumer health cooperatives. Because group plans insure many individuals under one contract, with consequent savings in sales and administrative expenses, premiums are usually significantly lower than with individual policies. Under a group insurance plan, the physical condition of the insured generally has no bearing on his or her eligibility for coverage, and an individual's coverage cannot be canceled unless employment or organization affiliation ends.

The protection provided by group health insurance policies varies from plan to plan. It is important to read and understand all information available from your employer or association about your policy. If the group health plan does not fully cover your health needs, you may need to supplement coverage with individual insurance. In that case—or if you are self-employed or work for an employer that either does not provide health coverage or offers a selection of coverage—you'll need a basic familiarity with the workings and relative merits of the various health insurance options.

Types of Health Insurance

Fee-for-Service: Under most traditional fee-for-service plans, the policy-holder pays a *deductible* (a fixed amount that may range from $100 to $250 for an individual, $500 to $1,000 for a family) and a share (or *copayment)* of the remaining costs of the health care bill, up to a maximum of perhaps $1,000 to $4,000 in a given year. There is generally both an annual and a lifetime ceiling on the amount of benefits that the insurance company will pay. Lifetime ceilings may range from as low as $25,000 to as high as $1 million.

The major advantage of a fee-for-service plan is that it allows you to choose your own doctor. On the other hand, you usually are also required to fill out and file claim forms to obtain reimbursement for medical bill payments.

Fee-for-service plans include these options:

☐ **Basic coverage** generally pays hospital, surgical, and doctor bills. Benefits may cover the costs of a hospital stay, X rays, lab tests, surgical procedures in the hospital or a doctor's office, prescription drugs, and in-office doctor visits.

☐ **Major medical** picks up where basic protection leaves off. Designed for the prolonged or catastrophic (rather than routine) illness, major medical pays large amounts for extensive treatment and/or hospitalization for long-term illnesses or injuries.

Increasingly, insurers are providing basic coverage and major medical in a single comprehensive package.

Fee-for service insurance usually does not cover routine medical care such as checkups, well-child exams, and immunizations. And insurance providers often reserve the right to judge the appropriateness of medical procedures, sometimes by requiring second opinions, as well as to set limits on reasonable charges beyond which they will not reimburse for particular medical services.

Health Maintenance Organizations (HMOs): In 1988, roughly 13 percent of Americans were members and patients of an HMO. HMOs operate somewhat like a combination insurance policy and doctor or hospital. Like an insurance policy, they cover health care costs in return for a monthly premium, and like a doctor or hospital, they furnish actual health care services. An HMO plan provides total health care coverage, usually with no deductible, few copayments, and no annual or lifetime limit on benefits; premiums are generally about the same as for fee-for-service coverage. Doctor and hospital bills, including those for routine and preventive care, are prepaid by the insurer, so there are no insurance claim forms to fill out. With an HMO, health care is provided not by the doctor of your choice but by one of the plan's "primary care physicians" (usually an internist, family practitioner, or pediatrician), and medical care is often provided in a clinic rather than in an office setting. If you require treatment that the primary physician is unable to provide, he or she assigns a staff specialist or, if needed, refers you to an outside specialist or places you in a hospital affiliated with the HMO. Most HMO plans cover emergency care provided by an unaffiliated physician or hospital outside the facility's geographical area.

An employer that provides traditional fee-for-service coverage and has 25 or more employees is required by federal law to offer HMO coverage as an option if requested by an employee.

There are a growing number of variations on the HMO prepayment concept, including **Preferred Provider Organizations (PPOs), Individual Practice Associations (IPAs),** and **Competitive Medical Plans (CMPs),** among others. Many of these plans allow you to choose your health care provider from a list of participating private-practice physicians who have agreed to treat members of the plan in their offices at a discounted rate. Often, you also are given the option of choosing to use your own doctor and pay the difference between his or her fee and the plan's approved discount charges.

Deciding which of these health insurance options is right for you is a matter of weighing your preferences and family needs. Fee-for-service plans allow you to choose your own personal physician and, when needed, medical specialists. However, they generally do not cover the costs of routine medical care. With an HMO or other prepayment plan, lower deductibles, fewer copayments, and coverage for routine checkups mean that you probably will pay less for medical care. But the decisions as to which doctors and hospitals provide that care will, to a great extent, be made for you.

How Much Coverage Do You Need?

The ideal health insurance program is one that prevents undue financial strain from an illness or injury, without requiring premium payments that are themselves a strain to maintain.

With an HMO or other prepayment plan, you generally receive total coverage for all your medical bills. But if you are buying a fee-for-service plan on an individual basis—whether as a supplement to your group policy or as your primary source of coverage—you'll have to make some decisions about the amount of coverage you need and can afford.

Fee-for-service plans vary as to the amount of copayments and deductibles *you* pay and the maximum lifetime benefits the *policy* will pay. Many insurance experts recommend that a health insurance policy cover a minimum of 80 percent of most doctor, surgical, hospital, and prescription drug bills, once the deductible has been met. That deductible can range from $100 to $1,000. If you have the cash reserves to cover

HMO Checklist

While the quality of medical service provided by HMOs is generally on a par with that provided by private-practice physicians, factors such as the individual doctor–patient relationship, the atmosphere of waiting and examination rooms, and the length of wait for treatment can vary from one HMO to the next. If you are considering enrolling in an HMO, taking the following steps can help you judge the quality of care provided by a particular organization.

1. Call several local medical groups and doctors and ask about the reputation of the particular plan.
2. Ask current subscribers how they rate the organization's service.
3. Contact the local BBB for a complaint report.
4. Read the HMO contract and discuss all details and questions with the plan representative before enrolling. Find out how long the HMO has been in business, and ask what the turnover rate is among plan subscribers. Think twice about enrolling in an organization that has been operating less than two or three years or has a turnover rate above 30 percent.

smaller medical bills, selecting a higher deductible can be a good way to trim your premium payments. Selecting lower maximum benefits can also reduce benefits. However, the Health Insurance Association of America recommends a lifetime maximum of no lower than $250,000.

You'll need to compare more than just the size of the premiums, though, in choosing health insurance coverage. It's possible for a higher premium to pay for itself in terms of extra services that meet your particular needs—for example, coverage of well-baby exams for a family with a new child; 100 percent coverage of major expenses such as hospital surgery or semiprivate hospital room and board for a person with large, foreseeable medical expenses; or coverage for specific medical services, such as psychiatric treatment.

In deciding how much insurance you need, consider your family's health history, the relative costs of medical care in your area, and the income and savings you have available to cover emergencies. Make sure you have enough coverage to protect yourself and your family from the high costs of a serious injury or illness. And be certain to check into any other health care benefits available under protection you may already have, such as workers' compensation, social security benefits, disability insurance, and life insurance disability provisions.

The High Costs of Individual Insurance

Approximately half of all U.S. employers pay the entire bill for insuring the health of their employees. According to the National Insurance Consumer Organization (NICO), an insurance policy purchased on an individual basis is generally more expensive than the same coverage purchased on a group basis—often as much as 50 percent more expensive.

Following are a few ideas that may help you save money when there's no employer to help foot the bill for insurance coverage:

1. In most cases, employers are required to continue your group coverage for 18 months after you leave a job. You may have to pay additional fees and the full premium, but you'll still save significantly on the group rates. The same rule often applies to other persons losing insurance, such as children who reach the maximum age of coverage or spouses who divorce. Ask your employer for details.

2. If you belong to a trade or professional association, ask about the availability of group health insurance. Also check with your state insurance office—it may be able to provide names of group plans available through clubs, unions, or other organizations which you may be eligible to join.

3. Some insurance companies offer group rates in special plans to self-employed individuals in similar occupations. The savings can be worth the effort of tracking down an agent offering such a plan.

Disability Income Insurance

Life insurance provides your family with replacement of your income if you die; health insurance pays your medical bills if prolonged illness or injury hits—the third factor in the equation is disability income insurance, which provides income if you are unable to work due to extended illness or injury.

According to NICO, about 30 to 40 percent of working Americans are protected by employer-provided group long-term disability insurance, which in most cases provides adequate coverage. In evaluating your group disability plan or shopping for individual disability coverage, keep the following tips in mind:

1. Social Security disability benefits provide income for the most severely disabled; the proportion of benefits to your former take-home pay decreases as family income rises. Contact your local Social Security office or your insurance agent for information on the amount and conditions of benefits.

2. Shopping around will give you a good idea of the monthly income benefits that various disability plans offer a person at your income level. Some experts recommend buying a policy that replaces at least 60 to 70 percent of your lost income.

3. Look for a policy that pays benefits when you cannot work at your own occupation, rather than one which pays only when you are totally disabled and unable to do **any** type of work.

4. Waiting periods and benefit periods vary considerably among policies and substantially affect the cost of coverage. **Waiting periods**—the amount of time you must be disabled before benefit payments begin—may range from a week to six months. If you have the cash reserves to cover emergencies, selecting a longer waiting period can mean big savings. **Benefit periods**—the length of time that benefits will continue—range all the way from 13 weeks to a lifetime. It's generally wise to look for a plan that pays benefits up to age 65.

5. Premiums for disability plans may remain level or, with "step-rated" policies, increase as you age. The distinction is somewhat similar to that between term and whole life insurance (see pages 221–22). Level premiums mean that you pay relatively high premiums in the early years of the policy so that you can pay relatively low premiums in the later years. As with whole life insurance, if you cancel the policy within the first few years, you lose the reserve buildup of your premium overpayments.

4. The expense of individual health care coverage makes it vital to shop around for the best rates and to buy only the coverage you really need. In some cases, the only way to bring the premiums for individual fee-for-service insurance down to an affordable level may be to select high deductibles and copayments. Again, carefully consider your individual health care needs—a family with several small children might be better served by an HMO covering the costs of frequent routine checkups.

MEDICARE AND MEDIGAP INSURANCE

The federal government's Medicare Program was instituted in 1966 to help elderly and disabled Americans pay for the rising costs of medical and hospital care. In 1988, Congress expanded the Medicare program with the Medicare Catastrophic Coverage Act, which, in exchange for higher premiums, provided new benefits intended to better protect the nation's 33 million Medicare beneficiaries from catastrophic hospital, doctor, and prescription drug bills. Late in 1989, however, Congress repealed the catastrophic health care law.

As the dust settles on catastrophic coverage, many older Americans may be confused as to exactly what Medicare now covers and whether they need a private insurance policy to fill the gaps between that coverage and the actual costs of medical care. Also, many persons who had already purchased a Medicare supplement, or **Medigap,** policy before the repeal of catastrophic care may have concerns over whether their coverage is still adequate.

Do You Need Medigap?

According to the U.S. Department of Health and Human Services, you should think twice before buying private health insurance in addition to Medicare if:

☐ You are enrolled in a prepayment plan, such as an HMO, that has a contract with Medicare.

☐ Your income is low enough to qualify you for the Medicaid program, which provides medical care for financially needy individuals of all ages.

☐ You are not eligible for Medicaid but meet certain other low-income and resource tests, thus qualifying for limited financial assistance through Medicaid. Your state or local Social Security agency can provide details on eligibility requirements.

Other Medicare beneficiaries should also weigh their options carefully before deciding to buy a Medigap policy. If you or your spouse are working or retired and the employer provides comprehensive health benefits, that insurance may adequately fill all or most of the gaps in Medicare coverage. And if your income or resources are substantial, you may want to consider filling the gaps yourself rather than buying private supplemental coverage. In deciding whether to supplement your Medicare coverage, you'll need to consider your personal financial situation as well as the size of the gaps in your health coverage. A logical first step is to familiarize yourself with the benefits Medicare provides. (See page 234 for an outline of 1990 Medicare benefits and pages 237–38 for sources of further information on Medicare coverage.)

Also keep these recommendations and precautions in mind:

1. Medigap insurance is not sold or serviced by the federal government or state governments. It is illegal for an ad or an insurance agent to suggest otherwise.

2. Most of the services not covered by Medicare are also not covered by Medigap policies. That includes long-term skilled care or custodial care in a nursing home. (Also see "The Costs of Care," *Nursing Homes,* pages 283–84.)

3. Don't look for a policy that will fill all the gaps. It is far more cost-effective to buy coverage for the most important gaps and to pay the less expensive medical bills yourself.

4. Many Medigap policies do not cover excess charges—the difference between the actual fees charged by health care providers and the amounts approved by Medicare. Excess charges are potentially the most expensive gap in Medicare coverage.

5. Consider all your alternatives before buying a Medigap policy. Continuing the group health coverage you have at work or joining an HMO or other prepayment plan participating in the Medicare program might better meet your health care needs.

6. If you decide to buy a Medigap policy, shop carefully and compare the costs and coverage of various plans. Be aware that model standards developed in December 1989 by the National Association of Insurance Commissioners (NAIC), which are expected to be adopted by all states, require Medigap plans to provide the following *minimum* benefits:

   ☐ Coverage of eligible expenses for hospitalization not covered under Medicare Part A, from the 61st to 90th day of hospitalization. Eligible expenses are expenses of the kind covered by Medicare and to the extent considered "reasonable" by Medicare.

   ☐ Coverage of either all or none of the $592 inpatient hospital deductible.

   ☐ Coverage of eligible expenses for daily hospital charges—for semiprivate room and board and miscellaneous services such as drugs, X rays, lab tests, and operating room use—if the beneficiary chooses to use Medicare's 60 nonrenewable lifetime reserve days.

1990 Medicare Benefits*

The Medicare coverage in effect before enactment of the Medicare Catastrophic Coverage Act was restored on January 1, 1990. If you are a Medicare beneficiary, or when you become eligible for the program, Medicare hospital insurance (Part A) is made available automatically and free of charge. However, to receive the benefits of Medicare medical insurance (Part B), which helps pay for doctor's services performed in a hospital, clinic, doctor's office, or at your home, you must enroll during the general enrollment period from January 1 through March 31 each year. You must pay a monthly premium for Part B coverage; most Medicare beneficiaries have that premium deducted from their monthly Social Security benefit payment.

Following is a summary of 1990 Medicare benefits:

Hospital Insurance (Part A)

- After you pay the first $592 of allowable charges, Medicare pays all other allowable charges for the first 60 days of inpatient **hospital care** during a benefit period. For days 61 through 90, you pay coinsurance of $148 per day. If you need more than 90 days of hospitalization in any benefit period, you may draw on your 60 lifetime reserve days. You must pay coinsurance of $296 per day for each reserve day used, and once used, they are not renewable.

- Medicare helps cover 100 days of inpatient, posthospital **skilled nursing facility care** per benefit period. Medicare pays all approved charges except daily coinsurance of $74, which you must pay for days 21 through 100. *Medicare does not pay for custodial care in a nursing home.*

- **Hospice care** is covered for up to 210 days.

Medical Benefits (Part B)

- You pay the first $75 in allowable charges; Medicare then pays 80 percent of all allowable charges for most services for the rest of the calendar year. You must pay the other 20 percent plus all charges in excess of Medicare's allowable amounts.

- **Home health care** services are covered at no cost to the beneficiary.

*Source: U.S. Department of Health and Human Services

☐ Coverage of 90 percent of all Medicare Part A eligible expenses for hospitalization, once all Medicare hospital coverage, including lifetime reserve days, is exhausted, up to a maximum lifetime benefit of an additional 365 days.

☐ Coverage under Medicare Part A of the costs for the first three pints of blood received in the hospital per year, unless replaced or paid for under Medicare Part B.

☐ Coverage under Medicare Part B of the costs for the first three pints of blood received as an outpatient per year, unless replaced or paid for under Medicare Part A, once a $75 deductible has been met.

☐ Coverage of the 20 percent copayment of Medicare Part B eligible expenses, whether the beneficiary is hospitalized or an outpatient, once a $75 deductible has been met.

Other important "extra" features that you might look for include coverage of private in-hospital nursing care and of medical services received outside the U.S.

7. In evaluating different policies, ask the following questions:

• How much of which deductibles and copayments does the plan cover?

• How much, if any, of the difference between actual health care fees and Medicare-approved charges is covered?

• Which, if any, health care services does the policy cover that are not covered by Medicare?

• Are there maximum dollar amounts or limits on the length of time for which benefits are payable?

8. Also consider and compare the following features:

• **Maximum benefits:** Some private health insurance policies pay less than the Medicare-approved amount, or may pay nothing at all, for medical services performed in a doctor's office or on a hospital outpatient basis.

• **Preexisting medical conditions:** Most state laws require Medigap policies to cover preexisting conditions (those for which medical advice was given or treatment recommended or administered before policy coverage began) once the policy has been in effect for six months. The NAIC model standards also prohibit a waiting period for new preexisting conditions in a policy you buy to replace existing Medigap coverage.

• The policy's **deductible,** if any.

9. Look for a policy that is *guaranteed* renewable for life.

10. Make sure the policy does not duplicate your existing coverage under private insurance; under federal and state laws, supplemental policies may not duplicate Medicare coverage.

11. If you purchased a Medigap policy prior to the repeal of the Medicare Catastrophic Coverage Act, you should have received notification early in 1990 from your insurance provider of revisions to the Medicare program, modifications made to your policy, and the effective date of any premium adjustment due to changes in Medicare benefits. Don't rush into increasing or replacing your Medigap policy for fear that you are no longer adequately covered. During the transition period in which insurers wait for state approval of their modified policies, most providers of supplemental insurance will revise their policies to restore benefits to the levels that existed before the enactment of the catastrophic coverage law. Once your insurer's policy is approved by the state and offered to you, however, you will need to consider all the questions that would apply to the purchase of a new policy, including comparison shopping for benefits and rates offered by competitive insurance providers.

12. If you discontinued a Medigap policy in 1989, in most cases you are entitled to reinstitute that coverage in 1990, with substantially equivalent coverage and without any waiting period for preexisting conditions, at terms at least as favorable as those you would have received if you had never terminated coverage.

YOUR INSURANCE PROVIDER

Whatever form of insurance you need, following these recommendations can help you find an agent and a company that will provide consistently reliable service:

1. If you have had prior satisfactory dealings with a particular company, start your search there. Also ask friends and colleagues for recommendations, and check the yellow pages for the names of insurance companies or representatives in your area. See pages 237–38 for additional sources of information on insurance and on the performance record of particular insurance providers.

2. Policies differ widely as to coverage and cost, and companies differ as to quality of service. Shop around and compare those three key factors before you buy. Ask for and compare quotes from three or more insurance companies.

3. When shopping for insurance, you'll find that there are two types of agents: *direct agents,* who represent just one company, and *independent agents,* who sell the insurance products of several different companies. Call both types of agents for quotes—but make sure you are comparing prices for the same coverage.

4. Don't buy more policies than you need. A single comprehensive policy is better than several policies with overlapping or duplicate coverage. Be particularly cautious about buying policies with strictly

limited coverage, such as cancer, travel, or contact lens insurance, which often either duplicate existing coverage or provide benefits too small to justify the cost of the premiums.

5. Don't be pressured into buying a policy the first time you meet with an agent. Insist on taking reading material home with you and making your comparisons and your decision at your own pace.

6. Be scrupulously accurate when filling out an insurance application; in some cases, providing false information can lead to denial of a claim or cancellation of coverage.

7. Read your policy carefully and, if necessary, ask your agent for a point-by-point explanation of the language. The time to eliminate coverage you don't want and to make sure you have the coverage you need is when you buy the policy—not when you file a claim.

8. Never pay premiums in cash. Pay by check, money order, or bank draft made payable to the insurance company only.

9. In most cases, federal law requires insurance companies to allow you a certain specified period of time during which you may change your mind about the purchase of a policy and return it for a refund of all premiums paid. With life insurance, that "free look" period ranges from 10 to 30 days if you buy the policy through an agent, 30 days if you buy it by mail. With health and disability insurance, you have 10 to 20 days if an agent is involved, 30 days with a mail order purchase. With Medigap, regardless of how you purchase the policy, the "free look" period is 30 days.

10. When you file a claim, keep complete and accurate records of all conversations and correspondence.

FOR FURTHER INFORMATION

Your local library shelves are no doubt filled with books and periodicals providing detailed information and advice relating to all forms of insurance. Particularly valuable are the monthly *Best's Review* and the book *Best's Insurance Reports,* both published by A. M. Best Co., which rate insurance companies and provide basic information on addresses, officers, financial soundness, and other data. Helpful, too, are back issues of *Consumer Reports* magazine, which provide rates and ratings on dozens of different companies.

Your local BBB can provide information on the number, type, and resolution of complaints against companies you are considering. In 1988, U.S. BBBs received nearly 280,000 requests for complaint records of insurance providers.

Finally, the following organizations provide consumer-oriented information and literature, often free or at minimal cost. (Toll-free consumer hotline numbers are given where available.)

American Council of Life Insurance
1001 Pennsylvania Avenue, N.W.
Washington, DC 20004–2599
202–624–2000
(Insurance industry association—life & Medigap insurance)

Health Care Financing Administration
Health and Human Services Department
200 Independence Avenue, S.W.
Washington, DC 20201
202–245–6113
(Medicare)

Health Insurance Association of America
1025 Connecticut Avenue, N.W.
Suite 1200
Washington, DC 20036
800–635–1271
(Insurance industry association—health insurance)

Insurance Information Institute
110 William Street
New York, NY 10038
800–221–4954
(Insurance industry association—send stamped, self-addressed envelope for free leaflets on auto and homeowners insurance)

National Association of Insurance Commissioners
444 North Capitol Street
Suite 316
Washington, DC 20001
202–624–7790
(Association of state insurance regulators—contact with problems or complaints relating to insurance providers)

National Insurance Consumer Organization
121 N. Payne Street
Alexandria, VA 22314
703–549–8050
(Nonprofit public interest membership organization—auto, disability, health, homeowners, life—send $3.00 and stamped, self-addressed envelope for NICO booklet *Buyer's Guide to Insurance*)

Social Security Administration
(Medicare)
800–234–5772

Your state Agency on Aging (Medigap)

Many **state insurance departments,** usually located in the state capital, provide complaint data for insurance companies operating in the state and publish consumer buying guides with cost comparison guidelines.

Jewelry

[Also see *Watches,* pages 352–53.]

Jewelry can be an elegant gift, a joy to receive, a delight to wear for years and for generations. It can also be an expensive mistake. How can you know which is which *before* you make a purchase? The following information on the fundamentals of classifying and evaluating gemstones and precious metals can help. And so can this most important piece of advice, which applies to every topic in this book but has particular relevance to a purchase so often based on whim, sentiment, and fashion: *If you don't know the merchandise, know the merchant.*

CHOOSING A JEWELER

Reputable, ethical merchants stand behind their products and services. A few simple steps can help ensure that you are dealing with a reliable jeweler and that you make informed and careful jewelry-buying decisions.

1. Ask friends and neighbors for recommendations on jewelers who offer competitively priced, accurately represented merchandise and courteous, knowledgeable service. Look for a firm that is well established in the community and has earned a reputation for service and reliability.
2. Contact the local Better Business Bureau for a reliability report on the seller.
3. Before buying, shop around for the best prices through newspaper ads and catalogs and, if possible, at several different stores.
4. Establish a budget before you shop, and stick to it.
5. If a salesperson cannot or will not answer reasonable questions about merchandise, ask if another salesperson is available who can supply the information you want. If you can't find the help you need, take your business elsewhere.
6. Learn which questions are reasonable and important by familiarizing yourself with the following facts and terms.

GEMSTONES

Most gemstones are minerals, formed as a result of varying natural pressures and temperatures on the rocks that make up the earth's crust. Of the more than 3,000 minerals found on earth, only a small percentage possess the color, beauty, and rarity to be characterized as gemstones. The "precious" gemstones—diamonds, emeralds, rubies, and sapphires—exhibit a phenomenal degree of these qualities. A second category of gemstones embody the same three qualities in varying degrees. These gems include, among others, such stones as agate, alexandrite, amethyst, aquamarine, bloodstone, carnelian, chrysoberyl, citrine, garnet, jade, jasper, lapis lazuli, moonstone, opal, peridot, sardonyx, spinel, topaz, tourmaline, turquoise, and zircon. Also in this category are a few gems that are not minerals: pearl, coral, jet, and amber.

Some gemstones in this second category (jade and opal, for example) sometimes exist in such fine quality that they can command higher prices than lesser grades of diamonds, emeralds, rubies, and sapphires.

The Gemological Institute of America (GIA) quality analysis system is the most widely used in the United States for grading gemstones. For most gems, four factors determine value and price:

☐ **Color.** There are literally thousands of shades of red, blue, green, and other gemstone colors. Of prime importance in grading a gem is the *strength* of its color. While color is virtually impossible for the layperson to identify, a reliable jeweler will tell you frankly where each stone stands on the color scale.

☐ **Clarity.** Completely flawless gemstones are extremely rare, and even the most expensive stones nearly always contain some external surface irregularities or internal "inclusions"—imperfections such as spots, bubbles, or lines. Clarity is graded according to the relative position of the stone on the GIA's Flawless-to-Imperfect scale.

☐ **Cut.** Proper cutting emphasizes the richness of the stone's inherent color and its "brilliance," the amount of light reflected back to the eye. Small, flat, polished planes or "facets" are cut into many types of gems to enhance brilliance. "Cut" also describes the shape of the stone; traditional shapes include round, oval, pear, emerald, marquise, and heart.

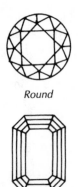
Round

Oval

Pear

Emerald

Marquise

Heart

☐ **Carat weight.** The size or weight of a gem also affects its value. A carat is equal to 200 milligrams; there are 142 carats to an ounce. Carats are further subdivided into points, with 100 points to a carat.

Diamonds

Diamonds that appear virtually identical to the eye may have a wide range of values. Only an expert can judge the true value of a diamond by evaluating its "four Cs"—its color, clarity, cut, and carat weight.

Color. Fine diamonds are characterized by the absence of color; completely colorless, icy white diamonds are rare and therefore more valuable. White diamonds with a tinge of blue—known as "blue-white"— are rarer still.

Clarity. The fewer the inclusions, the more valuable the diamond, even though inclusions that do not interfere materially with the passage of light through the stone do not affect its beauty. Under Federal Trade Commission rules, a diamond can be called "flawless" only when no imperfections are visible to a trained eye, in good light, under 10-power magnification.

Cut. A finished diamond has 58 facets. Small diamonds, usually under .05 points each, often have only 17 facets and are worth much less per carat than the 58-facet full-cut stones.

Carat. Since larger diamonds are quite rare, they have a greater value per carat. A setting with 10 diamonds of .10 carats each, for example, would have a *total weight* of one carat but would be worth considerably less than a one-carat diamond of the same quality.

Other Precious Gemstones

Emeralds are the green variety of the mineral beryl. The finest quality stones have a velvety grass green color. The emerald is a hard stone but it does fracture easily and it requires special care in wear and handling.

Rubies are a transparent to translucent variety of the mineral corundum and are red with limited traces of other tints or hues. Natural rubies contain what appear to be angular-shaped bubbles.

Sapphires are also varieties of corundum. They can be blue, yellow, green, orange, purple, or pink. Corundum of any of these colors which also exhibits a six-ray star when cut round without facets is known as a "star sapphire."

From Amethyst to Zircon

Among the many remaining gemstones, some, such as alexandrite, are extremely expensive, costing thousands of dollars per carat, while others,

Gem Substitutes

Federal Trade Commission rules require that all synthetic and imitation stones be identified and sold as such.

A *synthetic* gemstone has the same chemical composition and physical and optical properties as a natural gemstone but is made in a laboratory rather than found in nature. Among the synthetic stones readily available in jewelry are synthetic rubies, sapphires, emeralds, opals, alexandrite, and amethyst. Synthetics make beautiful jewelry and are markedly less expensive than the natural gemstones they replicate.

An *imitation* gem approximates the physical appearance of a natural gemstone but has a different composition and/or structure and thus different qualities of beauty and durability. The most common imitation "gem" is glass, which has been used in place of gemstones since ancient Egyptian times.

such as smoky quartz, are very low in price. Many less expensive gemstones are opaque and are therefore selected for their beauty of color rather than for their brilliance.

It is important to know how durable a particular gemstone is when making your selection. Some stones must be used with care. Zircon, for example, chips very easily when worn in a ring but is suitable for use in a piece that will receive less wear, such as a pendant or brooch. Some softer gemstones, such as peridot, opal, and amber, are easily abraded and need special care. And some gemstones, such as amethyst, are susceptible to fading upon exposure to intense heat or strong, direct sunlight.

Each gemstone has its own character, and the qualities that affect value must be judged and evaluated by an expert. A reliable jeweler can help you choose among stones for value.

Pearls

Cultured pearls are formed by a certain type of oyster when concentric layers of a crystalline substance called "nacre" are deposited around an irritant intentionally placed in the oyster's body. *Natural pearls* are formed when an irritant accidentally lodges in the body of the oyster; they are extremely rare. *Imitation pearls* are made by various different manufacturing processes and are found in all forms of inexpensive jewelry. According to FTC rules, they must be labeled "imitation" or "simulated."

Cultured and natural pearls are judged by their luster (also referred to as "orient" or "brilliance"), size, shape (the more symmetrical, the more valuable), color (pink are the most expensive, followed by white), surface perfection, and rarity (a perfect pair of pearls is very rare, since nature makes few pearls exactly alike).

Pearl matching is considered a fine art. All pearls in a strand should *appear* alike in color, luster, and size, and should be strung through their exact centers, with a knot between each pearl.

PRECIOUS METALS

The eight precious metals are gold, silver, and the six members of the platinum family (platinum, palladium, rhodium, ruthenium, iridium, and osmium). The last five metals are very rare and generally are used more for industrial purposes than for jewelry.

Gold

The amount of gold an article contains is expressed in *karats*. In its purest state, 24-karat gold (100 percent, or 24 parts, pure gold) is usually considered too soft for practical use in jewelry. Therefore, gold is alloyed (combined) with other metals to increase its durability and, sometimes, to produce variations in color. A gold/copper alloy produces a red-gold color, for example, while white gold is produced by combining gold with nickel or palladium.

The most common alloy of gold used in jewelry is 14k gold (14 parts of gold and 10 parts of one or more other metals). All jewelry containing 10 karat (10k) or more gold must be stamped with the karat designation and the manufacturer's trademark. Except on watch cases, alloys of gold less than 10k cannot legally be marked or sold as gold jewelry in the United States, unless the stamp carries a qualification such as "1/10 12k Gold-Filled" (one-tenth of the weight of the article is 12k gold).

Gold-filled or **gold-plated** means that an article contains a sheet or layer of gold mechanically bonded to a base metal, such as stainless steel. Gold-plated jewelry usually contains less gold than gold-filled pieces. **Gold-electroplated** items contain a very small quantity of gold, which is measured in millionths of an inch; **gold-washed** jewelry contains even less.

Silver

Like gold, silver is soft in its pure state and must be combined with other metals, usually copper, for use in jewelry and other items. **Sterling silver** contains 92.5 percent silver and 7.5 percent copper. The term "sterling" refers to the composition of the metal, *not* to the weight of the finished article. Sterling silver jewelry can be light and thin or very heavy.

Jewelry Appraisals

An appraisal is an opinion as to the authenticity, quality, design, and value of a piece of property. There are two general types of jewelry appraisals:

☐ An **insurance replacement value appraisal** gives the approximate cost, at current prices, of replacing the jewelry item or recreating it as closely as possible. This type of appraisal is generally needed to properly insure jewelry against loss, theft, or damage.

☐ An **estate evaluation** appraises the *cash value* of an item, or the price it would bring in an "unforced" sale. It does not consider current costs of labor, material, design, or marketing, and thus is normally lower than appraisals for insurance replacement value. This type of appraisal is usually necessary when jewelry is part of the probate procedure of a will.

Appraisers commonly charge a fee based on an hourly rate; the more intricate the jewelry, the more time needed to examine it. When selecting an appraiser, your first choice usually should be the jeweler who sold you the item and who therefore has the detailed information needed to give a full and accurate appraisal. If another source must be found, Jewelers of America, a trade organization of the retail jewelry industry, suggests that you take these precautions.

1. Contact the local BBB for a reliability report on the appraiser.
2. Ask to see certificates indicating that the appraiser has gemological training.
3. Determine whether the appraiser carries merchandise similar to your items. If not, he or she may not have adequate familiarity with your type of jewelry to develop an accurate appraisal.
4. Ask to see copies of previous appraisals, and make certain they contain the following vital information:

A listing of all major stones, with their identification, shape, dimensions, approximate weight, and quality; identification of the type of grading system used when referring to quality; a listing of all minor stones, with their identification, size, and total weight; a reference to the type or workmanship of the setting and metal stamping; a written description or photograph of the entire piece; an estimate of the item's value; and a list of the equipment used to develop the appraisal.

Some sterling silver articles, such as candlesticks, may have bases loaded with another material to give the article weight and/or balance. In such a case, the article is stamped "weighted" or "loaded."

Jewelry made of part silver and part gold must carry dual designations, such as "sterling and 10k." Jewelry and other items stamped "silver-plated" may contain as little as 1/100,000 of an inch of silver bonded to a base metal.

Platinum

Like pure silver and gold, platinum and palladium are alloyed for use in jewelry. However, these two scarce metals are alloyed with even less abundant precious metals, generally iridium and ruthenium. The resulting alloys contain little, if any, base metals and are very expensive.

There is no national stamping regulation for the platinum metals, although some states have laws establishing standards for platinum and alloys of platinum. The usual proportions for platinum jewelry are 90 percent platinum and 10 percent iridium or 95 percent platinum and 5 percent ruthenium.

Palladium is generally used to eliminate excess weight from such items as earrings or brooches; the usual alloy is 95.5 percent palladium and 4.5 percent ruthenium.

Jewelry made of platinum or palladium usually costs slightly more than 14k gold.

CARE AND CLEANING

Fine jewelry can last a lifetime and more *if properly cared for.* Some stones require special care and cleaning procedures. Your best course is to ask your jeweler for advice when purchasing the item. The following general guidelines from Jewelers of America apply to the care and cleaning of most gemstones and precious metals:

☐ Don't wear rings when you are doing rough work or using harsh household cleaners or chemicals.

☐ Keep your jewelry separated when you put it away, and always wrap items individually in soft fabric or tissue paper.

☐ Apply perfumes, colognes, cosmetics, hairsprays, and lotions *before* putting on jewelry.

☐ Clean your jewelry regularly. Ask your jeweler to recommend proper cleaning methods.

☐ Take your gemstones to your jeweler once a year for an expert cleaning and a check that stones are secure in their settings.

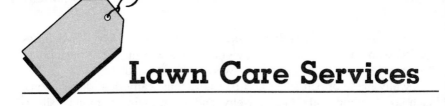

Lawn Care Services

A thick, emerald green lawn can be a very appealing part of a home. Not only is a well-tended lawn attractive, but it can add to the home's value, prevent erosion of the soil, and have a cooling effect during hot weather. Proper lawn care involves seeding, fertilizing, watering, mowing, weed and pest control, and a number of other chores. If you are a homeowner who lacks either the time or the inclination to tend your lawn, you may be considering hiring a lawn care service to help keep the grass green.

The basic services offered by lawn care companies typically consist of fertilizing the lawn and treating it for the control of weeds and pests. A series of four to six treatments usually are scheduled over the course of the warmer seasons, with the schedule based on the most effective time to target weeds and pests and the most appropriate time to fertilize. For an additional fee, most lawn care companies also will provide mowing, trimming, reseeding, aeration (providing a good flow of air and water into the root system), and/or tree and shrub care.

A relatively new type of lawn management offered by some lawn care companies, Integrated Pest Management (IPM), uses a reduced amount of pesticides to control pests at acceptable levels. The IPM system supplements limited pesticide use with "cultural tactics" such as monitoring trees, shrubs, and turf on a year-round basis for any signs of pests; carefully pruning trees to enable them to ward off predators; top-dressing the soil with organic matter; using genetically resistant grasses; and encouraging the presence of beneficial parasites which kill those that threaten plants and trees. Constant monitoring of the yard is required when the IPM system is used, and both the homeowner and the lawn care service must have a good understanding of total yard management.

CHOOSING A LAWN CARE SERVICE

Following are guidelines that can help you select and work with a lawn care company:

1. Ask friends and neighbors for recommendations, or look in the yellow pages of your phone directory for the names of nearby firms.
2. Ask several firms for free written estimates, and make sure you understand exactly what services are and are not covered by each bid. Don't let yourself be talked into paying for services you don't really want or need. At the same time, don't automatically accept the lowest

On Your Own

If you decide to tend your own turf, one good source of information on properly planting and maintaining your lawn, shrubs, and trees is your county Cooperative Extension Service. Your county agent often can provide information over the phone or send you brochures on various lawn care topics, and can also tell you how to have your soil tested so that you can pinpoint its needs and the best types of plants for your growing conditions. Another helpful source of information is The Lawn Institute, a nonprofit corporation that encourages and assists in research and public education efforts relating to the improvement of lawns and sports turf. The Institute publishes a series of fact sheets on topics of special interest to home gardeners. Write to: The Lawn Institute, County Line Road, P.O. Box 108, Pleasant Hill, TN 38578-0108, or phone 615-277-3722.

bid. Make sure estimates include a detailed list of services, such as how often the lawn will be mowed; whether clippings will be removed; a schedule for reseeding, fertilizing, and other treatments; the type of grass you have and the type to be used in reseeding; etc. Consider whether each company offers a soil test and lawn analysis before beginning service. And ask whether the estimate covers a blanket program, which treats every lawn alike, or custom care, which tailors treatment to the specific needs of your lawn.

3. Ask what products the company plans to use and what the purpose is of each application. If you are concerned about the safety of any of the products or application techniques the company uses, contact your county Cooperative Extension Service for information and advice.

4. Ask for customer references and contact them to ask about the service. Contact the local Better Business Bureau and consumer protection office for complaint reports.

5. Find out if the company is a member of a trade association with a professional code of ethics, such as a state turf association or the Professional Lawn Care Association of America.

6. Some states require professional lawn care services to be licensed; if that is the case in your state, ask for proof that the companies you are considering are in compliance. Also ask for evidence that the company carries adequate personal liability insurance in case of injuries.

7. Insist on a *written* contract and make certain it covers all the services you have been promised. Also make sure you understand all of the contract's terms. Are there extra charges for treating special problems such as fungus-related diseases or Japanese beetles? Will you be asked to renew the contract each year or is it of indefinite duration? (Most

lawn care companies continue treatment from year to year unless you cancel the contract.) Also carefully read the terms and conditions of any warranty. What must you do under the terms of the contract to keep warranty coverage in effect? For example, you may need to water the lawn according to a specific schedule after grass seed is applied in order for the company to accept responsibility for the results of the reseeding.

8. Finally, keeping the following tips in mind can help you obtain the most satisfactory service from the lawn care company you select:

- Don't expect miracles. If your lawn is in poor condition, it may take two or more seasons for it to become healthy and weed-free. And if your lawn is a disaster area, you may need to reestablish it first by completely resodding or reseeding, a job you can take on yourself or hire the lawn care company to perform.

- Keep yourself, your family, and your pets off the lawn during chemical applications and afterward until the grass is dry. Ask the technician if any further precautions should be taken.

- Good results will depend on your keeping the lawn properly watered between visits from the lawn care service. Ask the company for advice on watering needs in your region and remember these tips: (1) Follow a regular watering schedule (once a week is commonly recommended); (2) water deeply enough to soak the soil; (3) water in the morning.

- Some disease and insect problems can do serious damage in a very short time; it's up to you to report the first sign of a problem to the lawn service.

- For further information on lawn care services, send a self-addressed, business-size envelope to: The Professional Lawn Care Association, Dept. FH, 1225 Johnson Ferry Road N.E., Suite B-220, Marietta, GA 30067.

Legal Services

At one point or another, most of us require professional legal counsel, yet selecting and working with a lawyer can put us on unfamiliar terrain. The following advice can help demystify the process. Included are tips on deciding when you need a lawyer, selecting legal counsel suited to your needs, negotiating legal fees, and working with the attorney you hire.

DO YOU NEED A LAWYER?

Often, even seemingly complex legal matters or conflicts can be handled without the intervention of a lawyer. You'll need to use your own judgment, of course, in determining whether outside legal counsel is required in your particular case. Begin by asking yourself these questions:

1. **Are there alternatives to seeking a lawyer that might be appropriate in this situation?** These alternatives might include:
   - Consulting a good do-it-yourself legal guidebook.
   - Talking over a dispute with the parties involved and trying to reach a compromise.
   - Seeking the assistance of an impartial third party such as a family counselor or religious adviser who might help mediate the conflict.
   - Seeking the advice of your banker, insurance agent, tax adviser, or other appropriate professional.
   - Taking the problem to your local Better Business Bureau or consumer protection office; a news media "action line"; the appropriate federal agency, trade or professional association, or occupational or professional licensing board; or small claims court. (See *If You Have a Complaint*, pages 362–67.)

   If you are still uncertain whether your particular situation calls for professional legal help, consider consulting a general practice attorney for advice on all the available alternatives. An hour's worth of legal counsel early on in a situation sometimes can keep sticky problems from growing into costly legal disputes.

2. **Is the dispute likely to be taken to court? Does it involve a substantial amount of money or property? Is it a complex legal matter requiring the filing of complicated legal documents?** If the answer is "yes" to any of these questions, you probably need an attorney. Among the situations in which you almost always should seek legal counsel are buying or selling a house, signing a contract involving a substantial

249

sum of money, seeking damages or contesting claims following accidents involving personal injury and/or major property damage, drawing up a complex will, resolving estate or tax problems involving substantial amounts of money or property, settling a contested divorce, establishing a new business, and filing for bankruptcy.

SHOPPING FOR LEGAL ADVICE

In order to select a lawyer who will give you competent, cost-effective service, you must know your alternatives and be prepared to seek out and interview suitable prospects.

Legal assistance resources. Personal attorneys may practice alone or as part of a small or large legal firm. In general, sole practitioners and lawyers who work for small firms charge lower fees than large-firm lawyers and may have greater experience in handling individual and family matters. You also are likely to receive more personalized attention from a sole or small-firm practitioner. In some situations, however, you may want to consider a large firm—for example, when the firm's staff includes specialists in a particular field of law whose services could be advantageous in your case.

If you cannot afford or prefer not to pay the fees charged by a personal attorney, you might consider a legal clinic. These operations do a high-volume business in handling routine, standardized legal procedures. Because they usually advertise extensively, employ paralegal assistants (persons who are not lawyers but are trained to perform routine legal work under the supervision of an attorney), and use cost-cutting efficiencies such as programmed word processors and standard forms, legal clinics may charge substantially lower fees than private attorneys. A legal clinic may be an appropriate choice if you require assistance in handling a simple will, an uncontested divorce, an uncomplicated trust, or a similar standardized procedure. Even if you decide to turn to a legal clinic, however, it is still important to follow the steps outlined below under "Interviewing candidates," "Negotiating fees," and "Working with your lawyer."

If you simply cannot afford legal fees, several legal assistance resources are still available. These may include the federal government's Legal Services program, the Legal Aid Society, or other programs providing free or low-cost services to low-income clients. Consult your local phone directory, consumer affairs office, district attorney's office, or bar association for information on services available in your community.

A list of prospects. The careful search for a personal attorney begins with the compiling of a list of appropriate candidates. Here are some suggestions for assembling that list:

- Ask for recommendations from friends, neighbors, and business associates who have had legal problems similar to yours.
- Seek referrals from the legal department or outside legal firm employed by the company you work for.
- Talk with professionals in fields connected with your case: your banker, if you have a financial problem; a marriage counselor or social worker for marital and family disputes; your doctor in a case of personal injury.
- If you live or work near a law school, contact the dean's office and ask for the names of faculty members who teach courses in the area of law that concerns you; then contact those individuals for recommendations.
- Contact your city, county, or state bar association and ask for the names of lawyers who handle cases in your area of concern. Be aware, though, that some of these bar association referral services simply refer members on a rotating basis. Ask a few questions about the referral process: What qualifications are required of listed lawyers? How are names selected for referral? Are referrals matched to the particular legal problem?
- Check the yellow pages of your phone directory as well as attorneys' ads in newspapers, radio, and TV.

Once you have the names of several prospects, check out their credentials. A useful publication for this purpose is the *Martindale-Hubbell Law Directory*,* available in most public libraries, which details attorneys' educational and professional background, association memberships, and areas of expertise; it may also include brief biographical sketches and representative listings of clients.

Interviewing candidates. Many lawyers will agree to meet with prospective clients one time without charge, as long as it is clear that the intent is simply to get acquainted and not to solicit specific advice about a case. When setting up these exploratory sessions with the candidates on your list, be sure to ask whether there will be a charge and, if so, whether that sum will be credited toward fees if you decide to hire the attorney.

It's best to enter these meetings prepared with a list of questions, plus copies of documents relevant to your case, which you may want to leave with the lawyer you decide to hire. A checklist of suggested questions is presented below. As you weigh and compare the answers you receive, also consider your personal reaction to each candidate. You will want to find a lawyer with whom you feel comfortable, who listens attentively and courteously to your concerns, who does not intimidate you with "legalese," and who is open in providing references and talking about fees.

☐ **Are you a general practice lawyer or do you specialize in a particular area of law?** Most general practice attorneys are able to

*©1989 Martindale-Hubbell, Inc., Summit, NJ.

handle a variety of routine legal matters. If your case is particularly complex, however, a specialist may handle the job more efficiently. Specialists usually charge higher hourly fees than nonspecialists, but because they are more familiar with the relevant areas of the law, they may take less time to handle the case and thus may end up costing less.

☐ **What experience do you have in cases like mine?** Ask for examples of recent cases similar to your own. What was the outcome, time spent, and fee? Ask for the names and phone numbers of these clients so you can call on them for references.

☐ **Do you have any other experience or qualifications which make you particularly qualified to handle my case?** Ask for details of any special distinctions or activities relevant to your situation, such as membership in an organization or committee, a teaching position, or publication of papers or books.

☐ **Will you personally perform all the work related to my case?** In large and small law firms, attorneys often turn over much of the detail work on client cases to junior associates or paralegals. This practice may save you money, but you should ask for assurances that work performed by others will be adequately supervised by the experienced attorney whom you interview and that you will be billed at a lower rate for that work. Also ask to meet the other person(s) who will be doing most of the work on your case.

☐ **How long do you estimate it will take you to complete my case, and what is the estimated total cost?** Cost will be a major factor in your decision, of course, but it should not be the sole criterion. The lawyer's experience and credentials are also critical elements, as is your level of comfort and confidence.

☐ **Will you itemize your bills?** Ask whether all bills will identify the date and nature of services performed and the names of the persons rendering services, and will include a detailed list of out-of-pocket costs.

☐ **Will you keep me informed about the status of my case?** You have the right to expect periodic written reports of progress. You may also want to ask when and how you can contact the lawyer. Is he or she readily accessible by phone and in person at hours convenient for you?

☐ **What is your billing schedule?** Some lawyers may ask for a retainer, others may bill in periodic installments, and others may charge the entire fee in advance. (Also see "Negotiating fees," below.)

Negotiating fees. Most legal fees are determined by arrangement between client and lawyer. Before work on your case begins, it is important both to discuss the system by which your lawyer's fee will be determined and to ask for a written estimate of all fees and services. If you cannot afford the lawyer's estimated fee, don't be embarrassed to say so—you may be able to negotiate a lower fee or a more manageable payment plan.

The standard systems for determining legal fees include the following:

- **Hourly fees.** Under this most common of all legal fee arrangements, you are charged for your lawyer's time at an agreed-upon hourly rate. Ask about your lawyer's per-hour fee as well as that of junior associates, paralegals, or any other staff members who may render services. Also ask about the *minimum billing period*. Most lawyers measure billable time by a specified fraction of the hour; that is, if your attorney spends five minutes on the phone on your behalf, he or she may charge you for the nearest tenth or quarter of the hour. The smaller the increment, the more you're likely to save.

  When you are paying an hourly rate, it is particularly important to have an estimate of the total number of hours your matter will take. You may also want to ask the lawyer to establish a fee ceiling which cannot be exceeded without your written approval.

- **Flat fees.** For the performance of routine legal tasks, some lawyers may charge a flat or fixed fee. Make sure you understand exactly what the flat fee does and does not cover. Also ask for a comparison estimate of what you would pay on an hourly rate basis.

- **Retainers.** Some lawyers require a retainer, or down payment for services to be performed. If you are asked to pay a retainer, insist on a receipt and a written agreement specifying which services are and are not covered by the retainer. The agreement should also pledge that when your case is concluded, you will be refunded any amount that has been paid in excess of actual fees and costs.

- **Contingency fees.** If you cannot afford to hire a lawyer to help you seek damages in, for example, a personal injury suit, you might consider a contingency fee arrangement. Under such an arrangement, your lawyer receives a specified percentage of the damages you are awarded. If you do not win the case, the lawyer does not receive a fee, but you are still liable for paying court costs and the attorney's out-of-pocket expenses. Most contingency fee arrangements are negotiated on a sliding scale; the lawyer's percentage decreases as the amount of the award increases and is also dependent on how long it takes to settle the case. For example, the lawyer may receive 25 percent of the settlement if the case is settled out of court, 30 percent if the case goes to trial, and 40 percent if there is an appeal.

  Before agreeing to a contingency fee arrangement, ask the lawyer for an estimate of the total cost based on an hourly fee and also request a realistic appraisal of your chances of winning the case; then compare total costs under both arrangements. If you decide to accept a contingency fee arrangement, make sure the lawyer's fee is based on the amount of money you are actually able to collect. Also ask whether out-of-pocket expenses are deducted from the settlement before or after the percentage is figured—you will pay less if expenses are deducted **before** the contingency fee is computed.

- **Percentage fees.** Commonly associated with cases involving the sale of a house or the settlement of an estate, percentage fees are based on a percentage of the total value or amount of money involved rather than on an appraisal of the nature or duration of the services provided. Be sure to compare proposed percentage fees with hourly or flat rates; the latter two arrangements are usually less costly options.

WORKING WITH YOUR LAWYER

Once you have selected a lawyer, ask that your arrangement be put in writing, in an agreement that details the services to be performed; the estimated number of hours involved; the system by which the fee will be determined; the total estimated fee, including hourly rates, if applicable, plus an estimate of additional costs and expenses; the details of any retainer or contingency fee arrangement; the system according to which you will be notified of progress; and the billing schedule. Read this contract carefully before signing it, and make sure both you and the lawyer hold on to a signed copy.

As your case progresses, remember that you are entitled to reasonable access to your attorney, preservation of your confidences, periodic updates on both positive and negative developments, and the right to make the final decisions that determine the objectives to be pursued in your case. In turn, you have the obligation to give your lawyer a truthful accounting of all the facts, including any new developments that might affect your case.

If at any point you find yourself dissatisfied with your lawyer's work, your best course is to first present your grievances to the attorney, in writing, and ask for an explanation. If you are unable to reach a satisfactory resolution, you have the right to dismiss your lawyer. However, to ensure that your case will proceed smoothly, never take that step without consulting another attorney first. If you believe your lawyer has neglected your interests or acted unethically, you may choose to file a formal grievance with the local bar association or, if the lawyer agrees to participate, to take the matter to binding arbitration through the state bar association or a consumer agency.

Long-Distance Phone Service

[Also see **Telephones—Conventional, Cordless, and Cellular,** pages 323–32.]

Which long-distance phone company offers the best rates? The answer depends on your personal calling habits. Since the breakup of the Bell system in 1983, American consumers have been faced with the necessity and the opportunity to choose the company that will handle their long-distance calls. In this new, competitive market, a number of companies promote a variety of discount calling plans. But the company with the largest discounts may not necessarily offer the greatest savings on *your* phone bill. Following is a two-part plan for analyzing your phone habits and choosing the company that offers the package best suited to your calling patterns.

Step # 1: Analyze Your Calling Needs and Habits

Assemble your long-distance phone bills for the past six months or so, and make a note of the following:

1. **The average number of long-distance phone calls you make each month.**
2. **The average length of those calls.**
3. **When you place your calls.** Chart the number of calls you make on weekdays, Saturdays, and Sundays. Then note the time of day—daytime, evening, or night.
4. **The distance of calls.** Use an atlas to calculate the approximate number of miles between your home and the locations you call most often.

Step # 2: Compile and Compare Phone Company Rates

With your calling habits analysis in hand, phone the long-distance companies that serve your area. If you have been asked by your local phone company to choose a "primary carrier" (see page 257), you should have been provided with a list of possible choices. Otherwise, you might look in the yellow pages of your phone directory for the toll-free numbers of long-distance carriers.

Ask each company to send you information on services and rates. Also ask what the charge would be for a few typical calls from your list; for example, what would each carrier charge you for phoning the folks in

Omaha for 20 minutes on a Saturday evening? Besides comparing the prices quoted for these representative calls, you'll also need to consider the following variables as you determine which company's rates and services offer the greatest savings and convenience:

1. **What is the discount calling plan?** Discount plans commonly entail a flat monthly rate charged for a certain volume of long-distance calls placed during specified times of the day or week. For example, you might pay $8 a month for the right to make an hour of calls on weekday nights or on weekends. Different companies use different systems to determine the rates charged for calls above the specified maximum volume; some may charge a per-minute rate based on calling distance, others a flat hourly rate for calls to anywhere in the U.S., prorated by the minute. For calls placed at times of the day or week other than the period covered under the discount plan, you may receive varying discounts—per-minute or hourly rates may be lower for weekday daytime calls, for example, and even lower for weekday evening calls.

   The key to evaluating discount plans is comparing them to your personal phone usage. Which plan most closely matches your calling patterns? If a carrier's lowest rates are offered at hours when you rarely make long-distance calls, for example, the package is not for you. And if you generally make few long-distance calls, a company's basic service plan may suit you better than any discount package.

2. **Is there a monthly minimum usage fee?** If a minimum fee applies, you will be billed each month either for that specified minimum charge or for your actual usage, whichever is greater. Do you make enough long-distance calls to offset the minimum monthly fee? If not, you may want to look for a package with no minimum fee; however, these usually also include higher per-minute rates.

3. **Are volume discounts available?** If you use long-distance extensively, you may qualify for additional discounts, which generally rise along with the dollar amount of your total monthly usage. For example, you might receive a 5 percent discount on $100 to $200 of monthly calls, an 8 percent discount on $200 to $500, and so on. Be sure to ask about any restrictions as to the time periods or types of calls qualifying for volume discounts.

4. **How is call duration measured?** Does the company round up phone time to the nearest minute or the next six seconds? If you make a good number of short calls, that billing increment can significantly affect your bill.

5. **Are long-distance calls within the state priced differently from calls placed to other states?** If so, also compare sample charges for calls to in-state locations you phone frequently.

6. **Is there an enrollment or sign-up fee?** This fee is usually small and some companies waive it entirely.

7. **How extensive is coverage?** Does the company provide service to all the areas you commonly phone, including international locations?

8. **Is a "calling card" available?** Will the carrier provide a phone credit card so you can place calls when you are away from your home phone? You will generally pay a surcharge, the amount of which varies from company to company, for each credit card call.

9. **Are "special" services available?** Services you might want to look for include operator assistance, collect calls, and third-number billing. What are the charges for the use of special services?

10. **What is the cancellation policy?** Is there a free trial period? Are you locked into using the service for a specified period? Will your enrollment fee be refunded if you are dissatisfied with the quality of service?

"Equal Access"

The "easy dialing" or "equal access" program, a result of the deregulation of the telephone industry, is designed to provide consumers of long-distance services with equal access to high-quality long-distance connections. Implementation of equal access by the country's local telephone companies began in the summer of 1984 and will continue through the 1990s. If equal access has not yet reached your exchange, here's what you may anticipate.

When equal access is implemented in your area, or if you move to an area that has already been converted, the local phone company will ask you to choose your "primary carrier" from a list of long-distance companies. Once your choice is made and the phone company makes the necessary adjustments to its switching equipment, you will simply need to dial 1 + the area code + the seven-digit phone number on either a pulse or tone phone to place a call through your chosen carrier. If you decline to select a primary carrier, the local phone company will randomly assign one to you. During a six-month "free choice" period beginning with the conversion to equal access, you will have the option of switching carriers as often as you like free of charge or, after your first free switch, for a $5 fee.

Even after you have chosen a primary carrier, you will be able to use other long-distance companies when you so choose, simply by dialing their five-digit equal access code.

Don't Forget The Local Calls

As you shop around for the best value in long-distance phone rates, you may want to examine the service you are receiving from your local phone company as well. In most areas, your monthly charge for local phone service is based on the type of service plan you select: flat rate, measured rate, budget rate, or Lifeline.

- **Flat rate** allows you to make an unlimited number of calls within the phone company's service area.
- **Measured rate** costs less but allows fewer local calls; there are extra charges for calls above the limit.
- **Budget rate** (not available in all states) costs even less, but there is a charge for each local call you place.
- **Lifeline** provides discounts on phone service for low-income households.

When making your choice, examine several recent phone bills and note the number of local calls you typically make each month. Then call your phone company for information on the service rates charged in your area and recommendations on the plan best suited to your calling patterns.

"CUSTOM CALLING"

A number of the special features built into well-equipped modern telephones and answering machines may also be available through your local phone company, for a one-time registration or connection charge plus a monthly service fee. Your phone company may also offer custom calling features not available on standard telephone equipment. Custom calling features may include:

- **Repeat call,** which will keep trying a busy line and let you know when the call goes through.
- **Speed calling,** which lets you push two or three keys to automatically dial a prearranged number. The more phone numbers you "store," the higher the fee.
- **Call waiting,** which "beeps" you when another caller is trying to phone in on a busy line.
- **Call forwarding,** which transfers incoming calls to another number when you are not at home to answer your phone. Some services will forward only calls from specified numbers.
- **Return call,** which dials the number of the last person who phoned you.

- **Priority call,** which signals calls from specified numbers with a distinctive-sounding ring.
- **Call block,** which allows you to block out calls placed from specific originating numbers. The caller will hear a recorded message saying that you are not taking calls at the moment.
- **Call trace,** which traces an incoming call and reports the number to the phone company, which in turn reports it to the police.

If you are thinking of signing up for any of these custom calling services, be sure to carefully consider whether its use and benefit will justify its expense. Also, compare the total cost of the service, including registration and service fees, with the cost of these extras purchased as features on a telephone or answering machine. Remember, too, that when you own the phone or answering machine, you can take the features along with you if you move.

Mail Order and Telephone Shopping

Nearly 92 million Americans ordered a product or service by phone or mail in 1989, according to the Direct Marketing Association. For those millions of consumers who need or prefer to shop at home, mail order catalogs, book and record clubs, magazine subscription offers, toll-free order lines, and other direct marketing services are an important and appreciated convenience. And most consumers—90 percent, according to a 1989 U.S. Postal Service study—report themselves satisfied with the merchandise they receive through the mail. As with any field, however, the shop-at-home industry has its share of unreliable businesses and unscrupulous operators. In 1988, in fact, U.S. Better Business Bureaus received 58,200 complaints relating to merchandise ordered by mail or phone. Further, the U.S. Postal Inspection Service warns that consumer losses due to mail fraud amount to millions of dollars per year.

While the actual number of cases of mail order fraud represent only a small fraction of the total of all mail order and phone transactions made each year, it pays to know how to recognize a reputable offer and how to help keep your name off the list of the dissatisfied. Following are tips from the Council of Better Business Bureaus and the Direct Marketing Association (DMA), the largest organization of direct marketers world-wide, which can help you avoid problems when you place an order by phone or mail:

1. Before placing an order with an unfamiliar company, check out the firm with your local Better Business Bureau.
2. Guarantee and return policies differ considerably from one mail order company to the next. Before you order, make sure you understand the company's policies regarding returns and product guarantees. That information generally is found in the customer service section near the order form in a catalog. Or you may call or write mail order companies with your questions and ask them to send copies of product warranties before you make a purchase.
3. Never send cash through the mail; use a check, money order, or credit card instead.
4. Fill out order forms carefully and completely. Photocopy the form and your check or money order before mailing, or make a note of the company's name, address, and phone number; item inventory numbers; sizes and colors ordered; the date of the order; your method of payment; etc. When placing a phone order, keep a record including all those details plus the name of the person you speak with. Also ask that your order be read back to you and/or confirmed

How to Get Your Name Off a Direct Mail List

If you are tired of receiving unsolicited mail or telephone sales calls, there is a way to have your name taken off national advertising sales lists. The Direct Marketing Association provides two no-charge consumer services: Mail Preference Service and Telephone Preference Service. You may write either or both services in care of: Direct Marketing Association, 11 West 42nd Street, P. O. Box 3861, New York, NY 10163–3861. Upon receipt of your request, DMA will send a form for you to complete and return. The organization will then contact its more than 3,500 member companies and request that they remove your name from their lists.

in writing. Whether you order by phone or mail, hold on to all information regarding your order, including the catalog or ad and your canceled check or charge account records, until the merchandise has been delivered in satisfactory condition or the service has been used.

5. You often can save money by using a toll-free 800 number when placing a telephone order. If you are not sure whether the company you are calling has a toll-free number, check an 800 directory or call the toll-free 800 information number, 1-800-555-1212.

6. If you receive telephone sales calls that you consider inconvenient or annoying, follow these steps:

- If you are interested but do not want to talk at the time you are called, ask the caller to mail you information or call back.
- If you simply are not interested, say so.
- If the caller persists unreasonably, hang up.
- Report harassing, annoying, or obscene calls, which may begin under the guise of a sales call, to the business office of your local telephone company.

7. Know your rights under the law when you place an order by mail or phone. See "Know Your Rights," page 263.

8. Open and inspect merchandise as soon as possible after receiving it to make sure the item is what you ordered and that it is in satisfactory condition. If you wish to return a product, you usually will find return instructions in the order section of the catalog or on the back of the package slip; you may also find a return form and/or a shipping label enclosed with the order. If return information is not available, follow these steps:

- Write the company, specifying what you are returning and why, the method you used to make payment, and your full name and address. Carefully package the merchandise and return it by insured mail, parcel post, or regular mail with return receipt requested.

- If the merchandise was sent to you in error, the mail order company is responsible for the cost of return. Contact the company for instructions.
- If you received damaged merchandise, write the company for instructions. Keep all packaging material plus a copy of your letter, and do not return the merchandise until you hear from the company.
- If you request a refund, under the Federal Trade Commission (FTC) Mail Order Merchandise Rule (see page 263) the company must issue you a check within seven business days if you paid by check or money order or must credit your charge account within one billing cycle if you charged the order.

9. If you have a problem relating to a mail order transaction and cannot reach a satisfactory agreement with the company on your own, the following organizations and agencies may be able to help. (Also see *If You Have A Complaint,* pages 362–67.)

- The DMA's Mail Order Action Line (MOAL), 11 West 42nd Street, P. O. Box 3861, New York, NY 10163–3861. MOAL will contact the mail order firm directly and attempt to reach a resolution.
- Your local Better Business Bureau.
- Your local or state consumer protection office.
- The U.S. Postal Inspection Service; contact your local post office and ask for the name and address of the nearest postal inspector. The Postal Inspection Service may contact the firm and attempt to help settle your problem and/or may investigate if the case seems to involve mail fraud.
- The Federal Trade Commission (FTC), 6th & Pennsylvania Avenue, N.W., Washington, DC 20580. The FTC may be able to take action if the case involves widespread mail fraud.

  When contacting any of the above, put your complaint in writing and specify the item or service ordered, the date of the order, and all other pertinent information; enclose photocopies of any materials that substantiate your complaint, such as your canceled check, credit card invoice, etc.

10. Do not give out your credit card number, bank account information, or other confidential personal information over the phone unless you initiated the call and you know the company with which you are dealing.

11. The DMA offers a number of free informational booklets, including *Shopping at Home, A Consumer Information Guide, Guidelines for Telephone Shopping, How Did They Get My Name?* and *Make Knowledge Your Partner in Mail Order Shopping.* Send your request for any of these booklets to: Consumer Services Department, Direct Marketing Association, 11 West 42nd Street, P. O. Box 3861, New York, NY 10163–3861.

Know Your Rights

The Federal Trade Commission (FTC) **Mail Order Merchandise Rule,** often called the "30-Day Rule," requires mail order companies to ship merchandise to you within the time period specified in their ad/catalog or, if no shipping date is given, within 30 days of receipt of payment and a correctly completed order form.

If the company cannot meet its shipping date, it must notify you of that fact and give you the option of either agreeing to a specified delay, which may be up to 30 days, or canceling the order for a full refund. In notifying you, the company must provide a cost-free means, such as a postage-paid card, for you to reply if you wish to cancel. If you do not respond to this notice, your order will be considered still in effect. A second delay notice must be sent if the company cannot meet the new shipping date; if you do not sign and return this notice within the stated time period, your order will be considered canceled.

When an order is canceled because of delayed shipment, the company is required to issue you a check or money order within seven business days or, if you paid by credit card, to credit your charge account within one billing cycle.

Some mail order sales are exempt from the Mail Order Rule, including:

- Magazine subscriptions and similar serial deliveries, such as book and record clubs, except for the first shipment
- Sales of seeds and growing plants
- Mail order photo-finishing
- C.O.D. orders
- Orders placed over the phone and charged to a credit card account

The FTC is currently considering expanding protection to the latter category of telephone orders charged to credit card accounts. Even now, consumers who order by phone and use their credit cards have some protection under the FTC Fair Credit Billing Act. Under this act, if a charge appears on your credit card account for merchandise that you have returned or that you did not order, or if you are billed for merchandise that you ordered but did not receive, you are entitled to contest the charge by writing the credit card issuer and the mail order company. The card issuer must investigate the charge and, if warranted, remove it. However, you must make your complaint *within 60 days* of the first appearance of the charge on your bill.

Mattresses and Foundations

Your bed is the single most-used piece of furniture in your home. The average person logs over 2,700 hours of sleeptime a year, and a good mattress/foundation set should last from 8 to 10 years (that's at least 22,000 hours of wear and tear!). So in shopping for bedding, it's smart to look not only for initial comfort but also for maximum quality and durability.

UNDER THE COVERS

Bedding can be constructed in a wide variety of ways, using many different materials. Here's a quick overview of what you'll find when you visit the furniture store or specialty sleep shop.

Innerspring mattresses (the choice of about 75 percent of today's sleep-set seekers) are made of tempered steel coils set between layers of upholstery materials, which provide insulation and cushioning.

Foam mattresses consist of a solid core of foam (usually polyurethane or, less commonly, latex) or of several layers of different types and densities of foam laminated together.

Box spring foundations are made of steel coils mounted on a wooden base, topped by padding and covered with fabric. Some foundations are simply polyurethane foam attached to a wooden frame.

Mattresses and foundations are often sold in sets; otherwise the retailer generally charges the same price for the mattress and its matching box spring. Innerspring and foam mattresses of the same size, style, quality, and manufacturer also often cost the same. Costs for mattresses and foundations run the gamut from $100 to $1,000-plus, depending on size and quality of materials and construction. A low-cost mattress generally will have fewer coils and less upholstery; a deluxe mattress often will have many extra layers of very fine-quality upholstery material. (Also see page 265 for quality guidelines.)

Waterbeds (about 15 percent of the bedding market) are available in two basic styles. The more traditional "hardside" type is a vinyl watermattress, a liner, and a heater in a rigid frame. The newer "softside," a waterbag and liner contained in a quilted casing, looks much like a conventional bed. Both types offer different degrees of movement, from "full-motion" to "waveless" models. Waterbeds may cost anywhere from about $200 to $1,000, depending on size and the degree of movement (the less movement, the more expensive the bed).

HOW TO JUDGE QUALITY

The wrong bedding purchase can literally be a pain in the neck (and back) for years to come. Here are some tips to help you distinguish better quality in bedding:

1. **How does it feel?** The only way to find a comfortable sleep set is to "rest-test" a variety of styles and models. Don't be shy! Lie down, roll over, try out your usual sleeping position. You're looking for *gentle* support at the shoulders, hips, and lower back. Product labels are not a reliable guide to finding the mattress that will give you the right support—one manufacturer's "firm" may be another's "extra firm."

2. **How does it sound?** A good-quality mattress/foundation set will not creak, bump, or make other suspicious sounds when you lie down and roll around on it (but an occasional "ping" is normal with innerspring bedding).

3. **How does it look?** Like the tailoring of a well-made suit, the look and feel of fabric and stitching can provide a clue to the quality of bedding. Mattress corners should have weight and substance; edges should be solid but resilient. And beware of mattresses that are less than six inches thick.

4. **Does it have the quality basics?** Study the information on display, read the labeling, request literature, and ask the salesperson to tell you about product features. The Better Sleep Council, a nonprofit organization of bedding manufacturers and suppliers, recommends that consumers use the following guidelines when shopping for mattresses and waterbeds.

   Innerspring sets: Look for more than 475 coils in a king-size model, 375 in a queen-size, and 300 in a full (double). If you can feel the coils through the cover, keep shopping.

   Foam mattresses: Make sure the mattress density is at least two pounds per cubic foot of foam (generally, the higher the number, the better the foam).

   Waterbeds: The mattress vinyl should be at least 20 millimeters thick. Any seams should be lap seams, in which the vinyl is overlapped and heat-sealed, rather than butt seams, in which the pieces of vinyl meet and are attached much like the pieces of cloth in a shirt or blouse. Ask to see verification that the product meets the state of California's waterbed standards, whether you live in California or not. Several other states have also established waterbed standards, but California's are the most comprehensive and exacting, and they are generally accepted as industry guidelines.

SHOPPING TIPS

- Prices for identical products will vary from store to store and from season to season. You may find special sales or promotions any time of the year, but watch for them especially in August, September, and October. Be sure to compare the labels of similarly priced items for information on construction and materials used.

- Standard mattress sizes are twin (38″ x 75″), full or double (54″ x 75″), queen (60″ x 80″), king (76″ x 80″) or California king (72″ x 84″).

- If you share a bed, you and your partner should do the comfort-testing together.

- When buying a mattress, you may be wise to also spring for the foundation designed to go with it. Putting a new mattress on an old foundation can reduce comfort and shorten the useful life of the mattress.

- If you're also buying a bed frame, look for a center-rail support for queen-size or king-size mattress sets. Carpet rollers on the frame are another sign of quality.

- Prolong the comfort and life of your purchase: Turn your mattress over and end-to-end regularly (every few weeks at first, then every couple of months) to equalize wear and tear. And don't let the kids use it as a trampoline!

- Mattress/foundation warranties protect against product defects but do not assure comfort and support until the end of the warranty period. Most mattress warranties are prorated (proportioned to the amount of time you own the product) after the first year.

Microwave Ovens

[For information and advice on selecting a retailer, saving on energy costs, and appliance service and service contracts, see *Appliances,* pages 25–28.]

Even though about three-quarters of all American homes have a microwave oven, a good deal of mystery still surrounds the selection and use of this relatively new type of cooking aid. There are more makes and models of microwave ovens on the market than of any other major appliance. And since many purchasers aren't quite sure how the oven works or exactly how they'll use it, selecting among all the available models and features can be a real challenge.

HOW THEY WORK

Microwaves are short, high-frequency, electromagnetic waves similar to radio waves, which can be generated inside a microwave oven by a vacuum tube called a magnetron. A wave guide distributes the microwaves throughout the oven cavity, and the metal walls and doors of the oven keep the waves inside. Microwaves are reflected by metal, transmitted through glass, paper, and most plastics, and absorbed by food. They cause the molecules in food to vibrate rapidly, and the friction caused by the molecules rubbing against one another generates the heat that cooks the food.

Microwave cooking is fast and convenient. Defrosting can take minutes instead of hours, and leftovers, beverages, and single meal portions can be reheated easily and quickly without wasting energy. (Microwave ovens typically consume one-third to one-half as much electricity as conventional ovens for cooking the same item.*) Microwave cooking results for many foods, particularly those high in moisture such as vegetables, fruits, fish, and sauces, are as good as or better than conventional cooking. And since many foods can be cooked and served in the same container, cleanup often is easier.

On the other hand, many foods, including roasts, chops, steaks, and pancakes, do not brown as well in the microwave oven as in the conventional oven. (But see "Micro/convection ovens," page 269.) And cooking certain foods in the microwave oven should not even be attempted; these include eggs in the shell, very large items or quantities such as a 25-pound turkey or a dozen potatoes, deep-fried foods, popcorn

*Source: American Council for an Energy-Efficient Economy.

in a brown paper bag, yeast breads, and any food that requires dry heat to cook properly.

Many people believe that the advantages of microwave cooking outweigh any disadvantages. But even the most enthusiastic supporters of this cooking method agree that, since microwave cooking is so different from the conventional methods most of us are familiar with, successful use of a microwave oven requires some adjustment of food preparation and cooking habits. Knowing a few basic facts about the way food cooks in the microwave can help.

1. **Speed of cooking.** Microwave cooking is *fast,* particularly when food is cooked in small quantities—a few seconds can mean the difference between dinner and disaster. The best rule for avoiding overcooking is to set the timer for the minimum amount of cooking time, then check for doneness. Knowing the wattage of your oven is also important; most cookbook and food package recipes are developed for higher-wattage ovens (600 to 700 watts or higher), so you may need to adjust cooking time or power level for best results.

2. **Cookware.** Most glass, paper, plastic, and ceramic cookware is suitable for use in the microwave oven. Metal, which reflects microwaves, may be used only sparingly and in accordance with the oven's owner's manual. Plastic wrap may be used to cover foods, but to avoid the possibility of chemicals from the wrap leaching into the hot food, don't let the wrap come into direct contact with the food as it cooks; also be sure to fold back an edge or poke holes in the wrap to allow steam to escape. (Also see *Cookware,* pages 120–21.)

3. **Food quantity.** The more food you put in the oven, the longer it will take to cook. If you double the quantity, cooking time will increase by about 50 to 75 percent.*

4. **Food thickness.** Microwaves enter food from all sides to the depth of about one inch. Foods thicker than one inch are cooked in the center by the heat that is conducted from the outer layer, just as in a conventional oven. However, since cooking is so much faster in a microwave oven, it is often necessary to allow intervals of "standing time" in which heat can spread to the center. Heat will continue to conduct even after the food has been removed from the oven; it is important to keep this in mind when checking doneness.

5. **Food density.** Dense foods take longer to cook in the microwave oven than more porous items, because it takes the microwaves longer to penetrate the denser substance. That's why it takes longer to cook a two-pound roast than a two-pound meatloaf.

6. **Food shape.** Uniformly shaped foods cook more evenly than items of varying sizes and shapes. For example, a meatloaf will cook more evenly if shaped into a circle than a rectangle, while the thin edges of

*Source: The General Electric Company.

wings and legs on poultry will cook more quickly than the bulk of the bird.

7. **Food composition.** Foods high in fat and sugar cook faster, since fats and sugars absorb microwaves more quickly than most other food components.

STYLES AND SIZES

Microwave ovens range in price from less than $200 for a small, basic model to over $1,500 for a deluxe range/microwave combination. Most microwave ovens fall into one of the following general categories.

Countertop microwave ovens come in small, midsize, and full-size versions. The interior size of the oven, which determines both the amount of food and the size of cooking utensil it will accommodate, generally varies from 0.5 to 1.6 cubic feet. Outside dimensions, which can be an important consideration when space is limited, run from about 20 to 27 inches in width, 16 to 21 inches in depth, and 13 to 16 inches in height.

Under-the-cabinet microwave ovens may be used on the countertop or may be hung from the cabinet above to free up counter space.

Over-the-range microwave ovens often have a built-in vent hood and light for the conventional cooktop below. Some over-the-range units are sold as part of a "cooking center"—a combination range, cooktop, and microwave oven.

Built-in microwave and micro/convection ovens are designed to be installed in a wall or cabinet. Some countertop models also can be built into a wall or cabinet with an optional accessory kit.

Micro/convection ovens combine microwave power and convection heating in a single cavity, allowing the oven to cook with the speed of a microwave oven and to brown and crisp like a conventional oven. In convection cooking, air is heated by a concealed electric element and circulated inside the oven by a fan. A micro/convection oven allows you to cook with either method separately or to combine microwaves and heat for fast baking and roasting. However, micro/convection ovens are more complicated to use than simple microwave ovens, and for quantity baking or broiling, your conventional oven, with its larger capacity, often will do a better job.

FACTS AND FEATURES

Capacity. Consider the amount of space you have available and the way you plan to use the oven (for occasional reheating or to prepare entire meals?) when deciding what size oven to buy. Small microwave ovens may be called "compact" or "subcompact," but the way manufacturers define those terms varies. In general, small ovens have a capacity of less than 0.8 cubic feet; some compact or subcompact ovens, with capacities of 0.3 or 0.4 cubic feet, may be too small to hold even an ordinary dinner plate or TV dinner. Midsize ovens, with a capacity of about 0.8 to 1.0 cubic feet, are roomier than small ovens and usually have greater power and more available features. Full-size ovens generally have a capacity of over 1.0 cubic feet; wattage and features may not be significantly different from those available on midsize ovens.

When deciding how large an oven you need, remember that microwave ovens with the same total number of cubic feet can have differing interior dimensions. Width is usually a more critical dimension than height when using the oven, so be sure to measure and compare "floor" space.

Wattage. Wattage determines the amount of microwave power available for cooking—the higher the wattage, the faster food will be cooked. Small ovens usually have from 400 to 500 watts, midsize ovens from 600 to 700 watts, and full-size ovens from 650 to 750 watts. If you plan to use the oven mainly for defrosting and reheating small items, a small oven's power should be adequate. If you expect to be taking on more ambitious cooking projects, you probably will need a more powerful oven.

Power levels. In some inexpensive ovens, the power remains constant; the only variable you control is the cooking time. Variable-power ovens, which come in all price ranges and oven styles, allow you to adjust the power to tailor it to the particular cooking operation. For example, you might use one setting to cook potatoes, a lower setting to reheat leftovers, and an even lower power level to defrost. Variable power ovens can have as many as 99 power levels, but 5 settings are sufficient for most cooking needs.

Controls. Microwave ovens are operated by either mechanical or touch-pad controls. Mechanical controls—often an "on/off" switch, a timer dial, and perhaps a "high/defrost" power level switch—are easy to use. They give you fewer cooking options than touch-pad controls, however, and cooking time settings can be imprecise. Touch-pad controls are available on all styles of microwave ovens. They allow you to set time and power level as you would touch the numbers on a calculator, and they may allow you to program two or more cooking stages, so that, for example, you can set the oven to first defrost and then cook. Most models equipped with touch-pad controls also display information about settings and cooking status on a lighted display panel. When the oven is off, the lighted display shows the time of day.

Some electronic touch pads are easier to program than others; some even come with display "prompters" to guide you from step to step. Before you select an oven, look through the owner's manual and ask the salesperson to demonstrate the setting of a few programs.

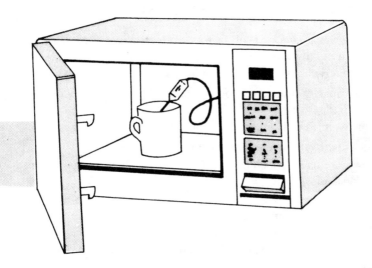

Programmed cooking. Many ovens equipped with electronic controls also have preset cooking programs that adjust both cooking time and power level for specific cooking jobs. Some of the more common programs include automatic defrosting, automatic reheating, preprogrammed recipes, and one-touch cooking (through which the oven calculates the proper cooking time and setting for a particular standard food item, such as a four-ounce hamburger patty).

Sensors. An automatic sensor monitors the humidity, heat, or odor of food and adjusts time and power level to cook the item properly. Some ovens equipped with an automatic sensor require you to program in the type of food being cooked, the doneness desired, and/or the food's approximate weight.

Temperature probes. A temperature probe monitors the internal temperature of a roast, casserole, or cup of soup and either turns off the oven or switches to a lower "keep warm" setting when food reaches a preset temperature.

Turntables. A turntable rotates the cooking utensil so food will cook more evenly. That can be a nice convenience; however, a turntable cannot substitute for stirring, rearranging, or turning over the food itself. Also, turntables on some models take up a good deal of usable oven space.

Cookbook. A good manual is an essential introduction to microwave cooking methods and to the features and operation of the particular oven model. It's a good idea to look through the owner's manual and cookbook that come with the oven both before making your purchase and after you have brought the oven home. Make sure all family members who will be using the oven read and understand use and care instructions.

✓ MICROWAVE OVEN CHECKLIST

Following is a checklist of factors you may want to consider when selecting a microwave oven:

☐ Will the oven fit in your available space?

☐ Is its capacity sufficient to accommodate the types of foods you will be cooking?

☐ Is its wattage sufficient to suit your anticipated cooking needs?

☐ Does the oven have at least five power levels?

☐ Does it have touch-pad controls? Are they easy to read and understand?

☐ Does it have any extra features you might want, such as programmed cooking, an automatic sensor, a temperature probe, a turntable, or a shelf or rack that allows two-tier cooking?

☐ Are the owner's manual and cookbook clearly written and well organized?

☐ Can you see clearly into the oven while food is cooking?

Moving

- Each year, one out of every six families moves.
- The average American moves 11 times in his or her life.
- Some 40 million Americans will change addresses this year.*
- U.S. Better Business Bureaus received over 58,000 requests for information on moving and storage companies in 1988, and nearly 4,000 moving- and storage-related complaints.

Moving is unavoidably inconvenient and typically stressful for the millions of Americans who endure it each year. If you are about to join their ranks, careful planning and knowledge of your rights and responsibilities can minimize the confusion. Here is a step-by-step overview of the moving process, along with some advice and recommendations from the American Movers Conference, a trade association of the household goods moving industry, that can help ensure you the smoothest move possible.

CHOOSING A MOVER

This critical first step—your choice of a mover—can make the difference between a smooth move and a disaster. The following advice can help you find a mover who is experienced and reliable and who will give you good service at a reasonable price.

1. Begin planning your move and selecting a mover six to eight weeks before your anticipated moving day.
2. Ask for recommendations from friends and business associates who have moved recently. Other sources to check: reputable real estate agents or the relocation manager of a real estate firm in your area.
3. Check with the BBB for a reliability report of companies you are considering.
4. Ask for a copy of the moving company's Annual Performance Report, which interstate movers are required by law to provide to prospective customers.
5. Ask two or three movers for a written cost estimate. Never accept an estimate over the phone—to give you a valid figure, the mover must survey your household goods as well as consider your destination and the timing of your move. You can ask for either a **binding** or **nonbinding** estimate.

*Statistics from the American Movers Conference.

Binding estimates (for which there may be a charge) are guaranteed final prices; they cannot be changed unless you add to the shipment or request services additional to those included in the estimate. To get a valid estimate and avoid extra costs later, you'll need to show the mover exactly which pieces are to be transported. Don't forget items under beds and in the closets, basement, attic, garage, and yard—anything omitted from the estimate can add significantly to your final costs. Make sure you also reach a clear understanding about additional services you'll require, such as packing, storage, or appliance servicing. And tell the mover about any conditions that could trigger additional charges, such as a "long carry" (when the truck cannot get within 75 feet of the door), more than one set of stairs, or a narrow doorway that will necessitate bringing in large items through a window.

Nonbinding estimates are the estimator's best guess as to the cost of your move. There is no ceiling on the final charges. On interstate moves, those charges will be determined by the actual weight of your belongings. On local moves, cost is determined primarily by handling time and manpower, but may also take into account volume (the space your belongings take up in the van) plus the distance of your move and the services provided.

6. Compare estimates, but remember that while cost is certainly a major factor, the company with the lowest estimate may not necessarily do the best job. If one estimate is significantly lower than the others, find out why. It's possible that the company's rates are simply lower in general. It's also possible that the mover has mistakenly or deliberately underestimated the time needed for your move or the weight of your goods, in which case your final bill may far exceed the estimates of the other movers.

7. Whatever type of estimate you ask for, be sure the mover specifies the services you'll require, and ask about any miscellaneous additional charges.

8. The mover you select will prepare an **Order for Service** detailing, among other items, estimated charges, terms and method of payment, all special services ordered, and agreed pickup and delivery dates (or the period of time within which pickup and delivery must be accomplished).

9. Interstate Commerce Commission (ICC) regulations require interstate carriers to give customers a copy of *Publication OCP–100, Your Rights & Responsibilities When You Move*. Be sure to read this booklet before you begin your move; if you have additional questions, call the nearest office of the ICC.

PACKING AND LOADING

The services movers provide can be costly. If you're prepared to invest time and effort, it's possible to save hundreds of dollars by packing and/or unpacking your belongings. Your mover can advise you on the purchase of adequate packing materials and on proper packing procedures. Ask about the company's policy on liability for self-packed cartons, and remember that if you do your own packing, it will be more difficult to prevail on a claim if goods are damaged.

If you decide to have the carrier pack your belongings, schedule a packing day one or two days before the van is due to be loaded. At that time, the mover will prepare an inventory of your household goods and their condition. Arrange to be present during the packing and make sure that all copies of the inventory are legible and accurate and that all household items are numbered, listed, and described correctly. If you disagree with the mover's assessment of the condition of any item, note your exceptions on the inventory before signing it.

If you received a nonbinding estimate for an interstate move, the van driver will weigh the van on a certified scale before and after your shipment is loaded. The difference—the net weight of your goods—determines your final charges. You can arrange to observe this official weighing. If you cannot witness the weighing and the figures seem high, you can request that the shipment be reweighed in your presence, at no charge, before delivery.

LIABILITY OPTIONS

Before your belongings are loaded on the van, the mover will give you a copy of the **Bill of Lading**. This is your contract for transportation and your receipt for your belongings—read it carefully before signing. The Bill of Lading takes precedence over the Order for Service and includes much of the information listed on that earlier document. It also outlines the extent to which the carrier is responsible for lost or damaged goods. Moving companies usually do not sell insurance, but they do offer a variety of liability options.

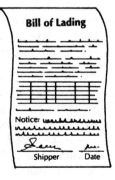

- **Limited liability** is provided at no extra cost. Under this option, interstate movers are responsible for damages or losses only up to 60¢ per pound per article, regardless of an item's value.
- **Added valuation protection** lets you seek recovery based on the *actual value* of a lost or damaged item computed at its current replacement cost *less depreciation* (the item's decrease in value during each year of

---

Storage

If you're not planning to move into your new home right away, you may need to have your household goods moved from your present residence and held in storage for later delivery.

Storage-in-transit can be provided by the mover at an additional cost for no more than 180 days. During storage-in-transit, the mover's liability coverage remains in effect. After 180 days, storage-in-transit is automatically converted to **permanent storage.** With permanent storage, your goods are stored under a separate contract with a warehouse, and the mover's liability ceases. The cost for permanent storage is based on either the cubic footage or the weight of the shipment.

If possible, inspect the warehouse beforehand. Be aware that the warehouse's liability may be much less than the coverage you purchased from the mover, and that most contracts of storage do not provide coverage for damage caused by climatic conditions such as humidity. It can be a good idea to have goods professionally packed when they are destined for storage.

---

use). Under this option, the mover's maximum liability is ordinarily set at $1.25 times the total weight of your shipment in pounds. The cost to you is 50¢ for every $100 of coverage. You can also select a higher dollar amount of coverage at additional cost.

- **Full value protection** covers the *full current cost, without depreciation,* of repairs to damaged items and replacement of or cash settlement for lost or irreparably damaged items. These liability plans vary among moving companies but costs generally range from 75¢ to 85¢ for every $100 of coverage. Ask your mover for details on the particular plan offered and on any restrictions in coverage.

Before buying additional coverage from the mover, check your homeowners insurance policy to see whether you are already covered. Most homeowners policies do not cover property while it is being moved, but you may be able to add a rider to your policy at a lower cost than the coverage provided by the mover. Also, if your employer is paying for your move, special insurance policies may be available to cover you. Make sure that any protection obtained through an insurance company covers the *full actual replacement value* of the goods being shipped.

DELIVERY AND CLAIMS

Movers are not required to make delivery on an exact date but rather within a reasonable time period after loading. If you require pickup and delivery on a specific date, ask the mover about any special conditions and fees for this service.

The mover is required to notify you by phone or telegram or in person if pickup or delivery will not be on schedule. Once you have left your residence, make certain the mover knows how to reach you. Contact the company's agent at your destination and make sure that office has your current phone number. If you cannot be reached when the mover is ready to deliver, your shipment may be placed in storage and you'll be forced to pay substantial storage and redelivery costs.

Unless you have arranged for the mover to extend credit, you will be required to pay the van driver before your goods are unloaded. Most movers require cash, a money order, traveler's checks, or a certified or cashier's check. If you received a nonbinding estimate, it's usually a good idea to have a check made out for 75 to 80 percent of the estimated moving charges and to have cash ready for the balance (which can be up to 110 percent of the estimated cost, with any balance payable within 30 days). If you are unwilling or unable to make the payment required, the driver has the right to put your shipment in storage rather than unload it, and you will be required to pay storage and redelivery fees.

As your belongings are unloaded, check them off on your inventory. Assign a family member or friend the job of supervising an "inventory control point"—an area where every item or container must be placed as it is taken off the truck so that it can be checked off and inspected for damage. *Make sure any damage or loss is noted on the copy of the inventory or delivery receipt that both you and the driver sign.* Do not sign the receipt until you have inspected your belongings. If you do not want cartons unpacked, inspect them carefully, and if you find any indications of damage, make a note on the inventory. If you discover damage after the driver has left, leave the item in the original carton and immediately contact the moving company's local agent.

A claim for loss or damage must be filed within nine months of the date of delivery, but it is to your advantage to notify the mover as quickly as possible, *in writing,* of the nature and extent of loss or damage. You may also seek compensation for expenses such as motel, food, and clothing bills if late pickup or delivery was the fault of the mover. Save receipts for all such expenses—some movers will reimburse you for actual costs, while others will pay a fixed dollar amount per day, regardless of what you spend.

ICC regulations require the mover to acknowledge your claim within 30 days of receipt, and to pay, decline to pay, or make an offer for settlement within 120 days. If the mover fails to respond to your claim, contact the nearest office of the ICC for advice.

CUTTING THE COSTS OF MOVING

The following tips can help trim the fat from your moving bill:

- If it's at all possible, avoid scheduling your move for the summer months, when 45 percent of all moves take place. Service may be slower during peak moving periods, and carriers are likely to charge higher prices.

- On interstate moves, weight is money. Consider leaving heavy or bulky items behind—they may be cheaper to replace than to transport. If you donate items to charity, remember to get a receipt for their fair market value to help you deduct donations from your federal income tax.

- Get a floor plan of your future home and discard any of your items that won't fit. Take a practical look at your belongings—clothes, tools, records, toys, hobby equipment—and get rid of anything you no longer use or need.

- Keep all moving-related receipts so that you can deduct allowable moving expenses from your federal income tax.

- If you are moving at your company's request, make sure you find out what portions of your expenses will be paid by your employer.

- If you are thinking of saving money by renting a truck and doing the packing and hauling yourself, first consider whether the savings are worth the expenditure of time and energy. Then shop for and compare truck and van rental services and read rental agreements carefully. Ask your insurance agent about the availability of insurance on your furniture in transit. If your homeowners policy will not cover a do-it-yourself move, a "floater" policy may be available for this special need.

Nursing Homes

In 1985, 1.3 million elderly Americans were living in nursing homes, along with 156,000 persons under the age of 65. Health experts expect those numbers to soar as the senior population continues to grow and the parents of younger disabled persons die or grow too old to care for them. The cost of nursing home care also is expected to skyrocket, from a yearly average of $22,000 in 1985 to just over $141,000 30 years from now.*

It follows that one day a good many of us will be seeking—and struggling to finance—nursing home services for ourselves or for a family member. How can you be certain of selecting a facility that will provide high-quality physical and emotional care in a clean, comfortable, pleasant environment? The search begins with an understanding of the types of care that nursing home facilities provide.

THE TERMINOLOGY OF CARE

In general, there are three different levels of nursing home care.

- **Skilled nursing care** offers nursing service on a 24-hour basis provided by registered nurses, licensed practical nurses, and nursing assistants, with treatment prescribed by the patient's physician. The emphasis is on nursing care, with restorative, physical, and occupational therapies available.

- **Intermediate care** offers less intensive nursing care, with services performed by or under the supervision of skilled medical personnel. Some medical, rehabilitative, and posthospital services are included.

- **Personal care or custodial care** provides round-the-clock assistance with such personal activities as dressing, eating, walking, bathing, and taking medicine; services can be provided by persons without professional medical skills but must be based on a doctor's orders.

Until recently, the above types of care were provided by three different categories of nursing homes—skilled nursing, intermediate care, and custodial care facilities. However, under the Omnibus Budget Reconciliation Reclamation Act of 1987, which took effect in 1990, the terminology and requirements for nursing homes have changed, eliminating intermediate care facilities and requiring those homes to "staff up" in order to provide skilled nursing and rehabilitation services that better meet the needs of an aging and increasingly frail nursing home population.

*Source: The Brookings Institution.

Custodial care services are now commonly provided in "personal care," "board and care," or "assisted living" homes.

For some senior citizens or disabled persons, care at home might be a less expensive and more personally satisfying alternative to nursing home care. Many communities offer services providing transportation, counseling, therapy, emergency medical treatment, and home-delivered "meals on wheels." A paid homemaker or companion can help with the cooking, laundry, and cleaning; a home health aide or trained nurse can provide part-time or intermittent nursing care. In some areas, adult day care centers offer reasonably priced daytime care and supervision while family members work. Before deciding that nursing home care is the only option, it makes sense to explore these alternatives. You may want to check with your area's Office of Aging, listed in the phone book, for help in locating these types of long-term-care services.

QUALITY CONSIDERATIONS

There are times, of course, when a nursing home is the only viable answer to a patient's needs. In such a case, your search should begin with an appointment with the prospective resident's personal physician to determine the level of care needed. Information on the nursing homes in your area may be obtained from the physician, your local health department and Social Security office, and local social agencies or senior citizens' groups. If the patient is being discharged from the hospital, a hospital social services director or discharge planner can work with the family to locate an available facility.

Phone each of the homes on your list to confirm the level of care provided and the availability of any special services prescribed by the patient's physician. Ask whether the home is licensed by the state, and whether licensed homes have chosen to participate in Medicare and/or Medicaid programs. The decision not to participate in these programs is not a reflection on the home's quality or reliability. However, if patients are eligible for this financial assistance or are likely to become eligible, they should consider a home that is certified for the program.

Also ask about the level of care required by the majority of the home's patients. Due to the recent changes in categorization of nursing home facilities, it is more important than ever to find a good "match" for the prospective resident's general condition and needs. A home that was previously classified as a skilled nursing facility may have a number of older, more frail residents requiring more intensive nursing care, while residents of a home that was formerly an intermediate care facility may be generally healthier and more active. Consider how comfortable the prospective resident will feel with the patients in the homes you are considering.

Once you have eliminated those nursing homes that do not meet your needs, careful inspection of the facilities remaining on your list is a must. It's a good idea to try to make exploratory visits to several homes, and to visit each home more than once.

Call the facility to make an appointment; try to schedule your visit during lunch or dinner hours so you can observe meal service. Ask to be permitted to tour the facility first, before talking with the administrator. See as much of the home as possible, and be suspicious if parts of the home are closed to you. Ask residents how well the home meets their needs. As you look through the facility, the Nursing Home Advisory & Research Council recommends that you pay particular attention to the following points:

- Are **recreation areas and physical therapy rooms** being used? If not, do they look as though they are used regularly? (Dust on the equipment in the therapy room should tell you something.)

- Are the **patients** out of bed, dressed, well groomed, and clean? Do they have their teeth in and eyeglasses on? Are they doing something appropriate for the time of day? Do they talk to one another or is there a general silence?

- Do **bedrooms** have telephones, radios, TV sets? Are there personal knickknacks around patient rooms and draperies by beds for privacy?

- Do **bathrooms** offer convenience and privacy? Are there grab bars around toilets, tubs, and showers? Look for towels, washcloths, toilet paper, soap.

- If you visit around **mealtime,** is there evidence that a meal has just been served or is about to be served? Has the food been eaten? Are patients encouraged to eat in the dining room? Do meal trays have patients' names on them, with special dietary needs noted? Do aides assist patients in eating; what is their attitude as they perform this service?

- Has the **staff** been cooperative with you? Do staff members seem to work well with patients, with one another, and with the administrator? Make a note of the number of staff members you see, and whether they are performing appropriate activities (aides with patients, food handlers in the kitchen).

- Is the **building** in good condition? Look for safe, clean furnishings, good lighting throughout, and sturdy handrails along obstacle-free hallways. Is there wheelchair access to all rooms, including bathrooms? Also ensure that the home meets fire code standards, that exits are clearly marked and unlocked on the inside, that there are smoke detectors, and that fire drills are held periodically.

When you make your exploratory tours, come prepared with a list of questions. Bring along a checklist or writing pad and make a note of the answers you receive, as well as the observations you make as you view the home. Your questions should include the following:

1. **Medical services.** Who is the staff doctor? How often does the doctor visit and how closely does he or she supervise patient care? What hospital does the home use and who decides whether a resident needs to be hospitalized? Does the home arrange for services with local dentists, optometrists, podiatrists, audiologists?
2. **Nursing services.** How many RNs (registered nurses), LPNs (licensed practical nurses), and nurse aides are there on staff?
3. **Physical therapy.** How often is therapy given? Are there a sufficient number of qualified physical therapists on staff or available on a consulting basis?
4. **Diet.** When are meals and snacks served, and how are special dietary needs handled? Are substitute foods allowed for menu items?
5. **Activities and social services.** Is there a regular activities program, including outdoor activities? (Ask for a copy of the program.) Are patients encouraged but not forced to participate? Are religious services held, and if so, in what faiths? Can residents continue to attend their own place of worship, if their physical condition permits and the church or synagogue is located near the nursing home? Is there a social worker on staff or on call to help patients handle adjustment to the home's environment and other personal problems? Does the home attempt to match interests and personalities when assigning roommates? Can arrangements be made for the services of beauticians or barbers? How will the resident handle his or her personal funds? What are the visiting hours?
6. **Money matters.** What is the basic monthly charge and what does it cover? What, if any, are the additional charges for services not covered in the basic rate? Are these extra charges itemized on the bill?

Once you have made your own observations, there are a number of sources you can and should check to confirm your findings. Many communities keep tabs on nursing homes through city and county welfare agencies, social service departments, and senior citizens' centers. The local Better Business Bureau can provide complaint records on the homes you are considering. Also available is a new resource compiled by the federal Health Care Financing Administration which evaluates and gives important statistical information on the 15,000 nursing homes in the U.S. Titled *Medicare/Medicaid Nursing Home Information*, the 75-volume guide is updated annually. Look for a copy in your local library, Medicaid and Medicare offices, state welfare agencies, or other agencies that serve senior citizens.

THE ADMISSIONS AGREEMENT

When you have decided on a home, you will be asked to sign an admissions agreement, which is essentially a service contract. As with any contract, read this document carefully and make sure you understand all the terms before signing. You also may want to ask your lawyer or the local Legal Aid Society to review it.

Watch out for institutions that require the payment of a large deposit. This may "lock in" a resident, depleting the funds he or she might need to go elsewhere. If a deposit is mandatory, explore the possibilities of arranging for monthly installments paid into a deposit fund; this can prevent the complete liquidation of the patient's assets. Nursing homes are prohibited from requiring admissions deposits if Medicaid will be paying the bill. Also be aware that federal law permits a resident's spouse to keep a portion of their joint income (at least $786 per month and $12,000 in assets in 1989, with those figures scheduled to increase annually). Seek legal advice if you have any questions about the rights of the patient and his or her family.

THE COSTS OF CARE

In 1988, private savings paid for roughly half the nation's $38 billion nursing home bill; the bulk of the other half was picked up by Medicaid. Under Medicaid, Americans are required to pay all the bills until their income and assets nearly run out. After that, the federal and state governments step in, paying the difference between the resident's income and the nursing home's rate, less a small personal needs allowance. Responding to the concerns of thousands of aging Americans who fear the prospect of exhausting their life's savings through a long stay in a nursing home, many private insurance companies have begun to offer a new kind of policy—long-term-care insurance. This new area of coverage should not be confused with Medicare supplemental insurance (Medigap), another form of private insurance, which is designed to help cover some of the gaps in Medicare coverage—but not long-term care (see "Medicare and Medigap Insurance," *Insurance,* pages 232–36).

Is purchasing a private long-term-care insurance policy a smart investment? The answer is—maybe. Here are some tips on this new and sometimes confusing area of coverage:

• Unless a long-term-care policy offers a good plan for keeping current with rising costs, you may be buying less coverage than you will need. For example, you may buy a policy today that pays benefits of $70 per day; if you need nursing home services 10 years from now and the cost of those services has risen to $150 per day, you will be responsible for the difference.

- Some policies require a prior hospital stay before benefits will be paid, although this practice is not permitted in some states. A prior hospitalization provision can be a serious concern for persons afflicted with Alzheimer's disease, arthritis-related problems, or other conditions that usually do not require hospitalization before the need for nursing home care arises.

- Many policies include an "elimination," "deductible," or "waiting" period (lengths vary) before payment of benefits will begin. In general, the longer the elimination period, the lower the premium.

- Before buying long-term-care insurance, shop around and compare the prices and terms of various policies. According to the Health Insurance Association of America, individual policy premiums in 1989 ranged from about $480 to more than $4,000 per year, depending on several factors that included age, the policy's elimination period, the amount and duration of benefits, and the availability of inflation protection. Read policies carefully, and ask for a summary of the policy's benefits or a disclosure form outlining its features. Pay particular attention to these points:

  What does coverage cost and are you guaranteed the right to renew at the same price, regardless of health? Is there a maximum lifetime benefit? A maximum length of coverage per "spell of illness"? What types of care, in what types of facilities, are covered? Is home health care covered, and if so, is a prior hospitalization or nursing home stay required? Is Alzheimer's disease specifically covered? What are the benefits (the policy's "indemnity value") and how long do they last ("duration of benefits")? Will the policy cover you if you move to another area?

For more on dealing with insurance providers, see "Your Insurance Provider," *Insurance*, pages 236–37. And for further guidelines on selecting long-term-care facilities, you may wish to contact the American Association of Retired Persons, (202) 728–4450; the American Association of Homes for the Aging, 1129 20th Street, N.W., Suite 400, Washington, DC 20036 (send stamped, self-addressed envelope), and the American Health Care Association, 1201 "L" Street, Washington, DC 20005.

Pest Control

More than 86,000 species of insects have been identified in North America, but only about 1 percent can hurt you or damage your belongings. Of those household pests that do qualify as troublemakers, you may be able to get rid of some yourself, and in some cases you may need to hire a trained exterminator. According to the National Pest Control Association, the nine most common household pests are cockroaches, termites, dog ticks, ants, fleas, mice, rats, spiders, and silverfish. Each has a different habitat and different eating habits, and each requires different eradication tactics.

Even if you start with a do-it-yourself approach to eradication, it's a good idea to check with a pest control company for up-to-date information on which pesticides are most effective against your particular problem. Read the label before buying or using pesticides, and use them only for the purpose listed and in the *exact* manner directed. Store unused pesticides in locked cabinets, and follow the instructions on the label when you dispose of leftover pesticides and pesticide containers.

Some pests can develop biological resistance to pesticides, and some, particularly termites, are almost impossible to control without the help of a professional exterminator. When the job gets too big for home remedies—or if you prefer not to handle and store pesticides—it's time to call in a pest control company.

CALLING THE EXTERMINATOR

Federal regulations require individuals involved in the commercial application of "restricted-use" products to be certified by state regulatory agencies. Structural pest control operators (the companies that provide pest control services to homes and businesses) are licensed and regulated by state agencies. Always deal with a licensed exterminator. You may also want to look for a member of the National Pest Control Association or a state or local pest control association. To find an exterminator, ask friends and neighbors to recommend companies they have used successfully, or look in your phone directory. Then follow the example of the more than 55,000 prudent consumers who last year called the Better Business Bureau to check the reputation of the pest control company they were considering.

Some reputable pest control companies sell their services door-to-door; however, you should be wary of the freelance exterminator who arrives at your door uninvited and offers a free inspection of the house. Don't let a con artist scare you into agreeing to immediate and costly treatments.

Always ask for a written estimate of fees and get all the facts before you sign a contract or authorize work. Ask the pest control operator to identify the pests and the extent of infestation. Ask for an explanation of the work necessary to solve the problem, how long the treatment will last, and what the results will be. Ask about the residual effects of chemicals, and discuss any special health considerations of family members—a pregnant woman, children, an elderly person—and of pets. Find out if the company has liability insurance to cover any damage to your house or furnishings during treatment. Understand the terms of any guarantee given: what it covers, how long it lasts, what you must do to keep it in force, and what kind of continuing prevention and control are necessary.

Don't hesitate to get bids from several pest control companies. Even termite damage will not get significantly worse if you wait a week or two before authorizing work. Don't rush your decision—you are paying for professional knowledge as well as skillful application of pesticides, so you owe it to yourself to look for someone whose judgment you can trust.

Get Them Out/Keep Them Out!

Once you've given your uninvited guests the boot, follow these tips to help avoid a repeat visit.

1. Frequently clean hiding places, such as cracks and crevices in floors, baseboards, and vents.
2. Seal kitchen cracks and close up any holes in walls. Seal breaks around pipes or wires.
3. Install or repair screens on outside windows and doors.
4. Get trash out of the house every day. Make sure garbage cans are properly sealed.
5. Don't leave pet food out any longer than necessary.
6. Keep food stored in tightly closed containers, and clean up spills and crumbs quickly and completely.
7. Inspect incoming grocery bags and soft drink containers.
8. Keep your pets insect free.
9. Outside the house, clear away debris and clutter, such as piles of cardboard boxes and lumber.
10. Visit your library or contact your county Cooperative Extension Service office for copies of the series of booklets and bulletins issued by the U.S. Department of Agriculture on home and garden pest control.

Prescription Drugs

Prescription drugs are powerful chemicals. It's not enough to simply visit your doctor, drop off a prescription at the nearest pharmacy, and take your medicine. Medication that is taken in the wrong doses, at the wrong times, or in combination with the wrong foods or drugs can be ineffective or even dangerous. It's up to you to protect yourself by learning as much as possible about every aspect of your health care. That includes being an informed consumer of prescription drugs by:

- Asking your doctor or pharmacist for the information you need to take medications safely and correctly
- Learning the facts about generic drugs
- Shopping for service and savings in getting your prescriptions filled
- Knowing where to go for additional information on drug actions, side effects, and interactions

THE INFORMATION YOU NEED

Your physician is your first and best source of information about prescribed medication. But when you are unable to get all your questions answered in the doctor's office, your pharmacist can provide important, possibly life-saving advice. Either your doctor or pharmacist may give you consumer information pamphlets, usually published and distributed by pharmaceutical firms, that explain medical problems and treatments. Remember, if the literature and/or the oral instructions provided by your doctor or pharmacist leave you with questions, do not hesitate to persist until you get the answers you need. Following is a checklist of questions to ask—and information that *you* must provide—in order to be certain of getting the greatest possible benefits with the least possible risks from the drugs that are prescribed for you:

☐ **What is the name of the drug and why has it been prescribed?**

☐ **What is it supposed to do and how long will it be before you see results?** You need to know what to expect from a drug in order to be able to tell your doctor if it is not working properly.

☐ **When and how should you take it and in what doses?** Does "four times a day" mean four doses throughout your waking hours, or must you get up during the night to take the medicine? Should it be taken before, with, or after meals? If you miss a dose, should you double up on the next one or pick up the schedule as prescribed?

The Facts on Generic Drugs

When a pharmaceutical firm develops a new drug, it applies for a patent, which gives the company the exclusive rights to manufacture and market that drug, usually for a term of 17 years. The drug is given two names when it is patented: a generic name, identifying the chemical compound that makes up the drug, and a brand name. Once the patent expires, competitive companies have the right to manufacture and sell the drug under its generic name or a different brand name. With competition in the picture, these generic drugs usually sell for less than the original product—often as much as 30 to 70 percent less.

You have probably heard debate over the question of whether generic drugs are as safe and effective as brand-name pharmaceuticals. The controversy began in the summer of 1988, when three officials at the Food and Drug Administration (FDA) pleaded guilty to accepting gifts from generic drug manufacturers in exchange for speeding new products through the agency's approval process. Further investigation revealed that several generic drug manufacturers had falsified test results submitted to the FDA. Late in 1989, the agency launched a major investigation into the testing, manufacturing, and marketing of generic drugs.

Despite this scandal, the fact remains that as this book goes to press, no generic drug on the market has been shown to be less safe or effective than the brand-name original. Most of the problems uncovered to date have dealt instead with illegal payments and discrepancies in recordkeeping and in applications for drug approval. Many physicians and other health professionals maintain that most generic drugs provide consumers with a less costly and just as effective alternative to brand-name drugs. The possible exception—certain "critical" drugs, required in very precise doses to treat hard-to-control diseases such as epilepsy, heart problems, or diabetes.

The bottom line is that it is important to be an informed consumer of every product you buy, including prescription drugs. When your doctor prescribes a medication for you, ask whether a generic version is available and whether in your case it is a safe and effective alternative. When your prescription is filled, make sure the pharmacist is aware of your doctor's instructions and your preferences; while pharmacists in most states are legally permitted to substitute a generic drug for the brand-name product prescribed unless the doctor specifies otherwise, not all druggists make such substitutions. And if you do *not* want a generic drug, make sure you speak up each time you fill or refill a prescription.

☐ **What side effects might occur?** Side effects are usually mild reactions such as a headache, nausea, drowsiness, or a slight rash, but they can include more serious warning signals such as prolonged vomiting, bleeding, marked weakness, or impaired vision or hearing. It is important to tell your doctor if you have had severe reactions to any drugs or foods in the past.

☐ **Are there any foods, beverages, or other medicines you should avoid while taking the prescribed medication?** Certain foods can interact with certain drugs, making them work faster or slower or even preventing them from working at all. Two or more drugs taken at the same time may interact and affect the way one or the other behaves in the body. And alcohol or other drugs taken in combination with some prescription or over-the-counter medications can affect performance skills, judgment, and alertness.

It is important to tell your doctor and pharmacist if you are taking any prescription or nonprescription drugs on a regular basis and if you are on a special diet or are taking food supplements. Also, you should tell the doctor if you are a smoker or a chronic user of alcohol, since smoking and prolonged alcohol use can affect dosage needs and/or increase the risk associated with the taking of certain drugs.

☐ **Should you avoid any particular activities while taking the medication?** Obviously, if a drug will make you drowsy or otherwise diminish your performance, you should not be driving, operating heavy machinery, etc.

☐ **Are there any special precautions for pregnant women or nursing mothers?** Some drugs can be passed on to a fetus through the placenta and/or secreted in breast milk, with possible harm to the baby. Tell your doctor if you are pregnant, trying to become pregnant, or nursing.

☐ **How long should you take the medication and can it be refilled?** In most cases, even if your symptoms seem to disappear, it is advisable to finish the medication; otherwise the symptoms and the disease may recur. Some prescriptions, such as those for long-term treatment of high blood pressure or diabetes, can be refilled without another doctor's appointment. In other cases, the doctor may want to see you again and possibly make some changes in your treatment.

☐ **How should the medicine be stored?** Some drugs should be refrigerated; others must be protected from light.

SHOPPING FOR SERVICE AND SAVINGS

Not long ago, if you needed to have a prescription filled, you took it to the corner pharmacy. Today, consumers have additional options. Many chain drugstores and supermarkets have prescription drug counters, and mail order catalogs or even your doctor may offer to save you time and money by filling your medication needs. Which of these options is right for you? What criteria should be used in selecting the source of your prescription drugs? Following are some facts and tips to help you make those sometimes difficult decisions.

Medications From the Pharmacy

Prices for the same medication can vary considerably from one local pharmacy to the next. Comparing prices is simple: Make a note of the name, dosage form (capsule, tablet, liquid), quantity or amount (number of capsules or fluid ounces, for example), and strength (such as 200 mg.) of your prescription drugs, and call a number of area stores for prices. It is a good idea to include independent pharmacies as well as small and large chains in your survey.

Price, of course, is only one of the many factors you take into account when choosing to deal with one retailer instead of another. As you shop for a pharmacy, also look for the following convenience and service features. You may decide to pay somewhat higher prices at a particular store in exchange for the services that matter to you.

☐ **Convenience.** Is the store conveniently located near your home? What are the hours? Are credit cards accepted, or can you open a credit account with the store? Is delivery to your home available? At what hours and at what cost?

☐ **Service.** Is service prompt and courteous? Is the pharmacist available and willing to answer your questions by phone and in person? Does the store offer extra service features, such as easy-to-open containers, if you have no young children at home; large-print labels; or confidential patient files, which keep track of all your medications and/or food or drug allergies, enabling the pharmacist to spot potential drug interactions or reactions?

☐ **Facilities.** Does the store have any other features you might need, such as a wide selection of reasonably priced nonprescription drugs and health aids, convalescent care items, a weighted scale, a blood pressure monitoring device, etc.?

Medications by Mail

Today, many prescription drug purchases can be made by mail, with your medications delivered right to your door. That can be a great convenience, especially for the bedridden or housebound person. It may also save you money, although it still pays to shop around and compare the prices in a mail order catalog with those of local pharmacies.

It can take two or more weeks to have a prescription filled by mail, so purchases are necessarily limited to "maintenance" drugs taken for long periods to treat conditions such as high blood pressure or diabetes rather than medications needed for immediate treatment of a new illness or infection. Most mail order firms require you to send them your prescription form; some will call customers' doctors for authorization. Some firms offer only prescription drugs, while others carry a broad line of nonprescription drugs and other health care items as well.

To buy from a mail order drug firm, you usually must belong to a membership group. Membership may be available through your employer, union, health insurance plan, or organizations such as the Veterans Administration. Or you can join an association that offers a mail order pharmacy plan, such as the National Council of Senior Citizens (800–631–7780) or the American Association of Retired Persons (call your local chapter for information). A few mail order pharmacies serve the general public; look for these in the yellow pages of your phone directory.

Medications at the Doctor's Office

A small but growing number of doctors not only write prescriptions but also dispense drugs directly to patients in their offices. That can be a welcome convenience. At the same time, you should not hesitate to compare prices and to use your local pharmacy or a mail order firm if you prefer.

TIPS FOR SAFETY AND SAVINGS

Keep the following recommendations in mind when buying and taking medications:

1. Carefully follow all instructions provided by your doctor and/or pharmacist.
2. Check the label each time you take a medication. Never take medicine in the dark, when you cannot read the label and be certain of what you are taking.
3. Do not transfer drugs from their original containers, which may be designed to protect the medicine.
4. Do not take someone else's prescribed medication. Your symptoms may look the same, but you may be suffering from an entirely different problem.
5. If a drug is not doing what it is supposed to do, check with your doctor. You may need a different dosage or a different drug.

6. Keep a list of all the medications you are taking, to show to your doctor and/or pharmacist as needed.

7. If you buy medications by mail, leave adequate time for delivery. Also, since mail order shopping means foregoing the services of a pharmacist, make doubly certain you get all your questions answered in the doctor's office and that the doctor knows about all the medications you are taking.

8. Keep all medications tightly covered and store them out of the reach of children.

9. Dispose of any unused portions of medicine by flushing them down the toilet, and dispose of containers carefully so children cannot get hold of them.

10. Remember these money-saving tips:
   - Ask your doctor whether free physicians' samples are available of medicines you'll be taking for only a short time.
   - If you are following a long-term treatment program, ask your doctor whether buying your medicine in larger quantities might cut costs.
   - Look for a pharmacy that accepts Medicaid, if you qualify. Some pharmacies will "accept assignment," allowing you to make no initial payment or only partial payment of your drug bill, with the store collecting the balance due from your insurance plan.

11. Remember that over-the-counter (OTC) medications are still *drugs*. Observe the same safety precautions that you would when taking prescription drugs, plus these:
   - Read and carefully follow product labels.
   - Never take a drug unless you need it.
   - Never take several OTC drugs simultaneously or in combination with prescription drugs without consulting your doctor.
   - Clean out your medicine cabinet every six months or so, and flush old OTC products down the toilet.
   - If your symptoms continue, *see your doctor.*

Radon Testing

Radon is a colorless, odorless, radioactive gas that occurs naturally as a by-product of the breakdown of uranium in certain soils and rocks. In outdoor air, radon is diluted to such low concentrations that it rarely poses a health risk. Inside an enclosed building, however, the gas can accumulate to harmful levels that increase the occupants' risk of lung cancer. According to government estimates, about 5,000 to 20,000 lung cancer deaths in the U.S. each year may be attributed to radon exposure.

Chances are that your home is among the majority that do not have a radon problem. But the dilemma is that unless radon levels are tested, there is no sure way to predict whether a particular house has high concentrations; it's possible for your next-door neighbor to be living in a safe environment while your own home has potentially dangerous radon levels. Furthermore, in 1988 a seven-state survey of 11,000 homes conducted by the Environmental Protection Agency (EPA) found that fully one-third of the homes tested had radon accumulations above safe levels. In announcing its findings, the EPA concluded that radon is a nationwide problem, and advised all persons living on or below the second floor of a detached house or apartment to have their home tested for radon.

RADON DETECTORS

Fortunately, testing the radon levels in your home is a simple and inexpensive process. In some areas, radon detectors are provided free of charge by the state or local government. These easy-to-use devices may also be purchased through the mail and in many local hardware stores, department stores, and drugstores.*

The two most popular commercially available radon detectors are the **charcoal canister** (costing roughly $10 to $25 per canister) and the **alpha track detector** (approximately $20 to $50 for one detector, with discounts generally offered for multiple purchases). Both devices must be exposed to the air in your home for a specified period of time (three to seven days for the charcoal canister, two to four weeks for the alpha track detector) and then sent to the manufacturer's laboratory for analysis.

Your state radiation protection office or regional EPA office can provide information on the availability of detection devices and can tell you

---

*Other techniques are available for measuring radon levels, but these usually require operation by trained personnel and are more expensive than the simpler devices described above.

whether a particular device is on the list of companies and products approved under the EPA's Radon Measurement Proficiency Program.

The EPA recommends testing for radon in the winter, when windows and doors are generally kept closed, thus reducing radon level fluctuations due to changes in ventilation and temperature. However, a 1989 Pennsylvania State University study concluded that radon levels in the soil can be 3 to 10 times higher in the summer than in the winter, with a possible consequent rise in indoor radon levels. The solution may well be to test your home both in winter and summer, even if the initial test indicates no radon problem is present.

Many people use the quicker and less expensive charcoal canister for their first test, or "screening measurement." This single, short-term measurement is not a reliable measure of the average radon level to which you and your family are exposed from room to room and from season to season; rather it gives an indication of the highest radon level in the home and can point out the *potential* for a radon problem.

Measurement is made in the lowest livable area of the home, since radon usually seeps in from the soil. Windows and doors are kept closed for at least 12 hours prior to the test and as much as possible during the test. Follow the manufacturer's instructions regarding the correct testing procedure and the proper exposure period for the device you are using.

Once you have mailed the sealed testing container to the laboratory for analysis, results are usually available within one or two weeks. The lab will report its findings in terms of either "Working Levels" (WL) or "picoCuries per liter" (pCi/l)—"pico" means "one-trillionth" and a "Curie" is a unit of radiation. In general, if your test results are above 0.02 WL or 4 pCi/l, follow-up testing using two or more of the longer-term alpha track detectors is advised in order to get a more accurate picture of the average radon level throughout the house. Levels higher than 1.0 WL or 200 pCi/l indicate a serious problem calling for immediate follow-up tests and short-term actions to reduce the radon level in the home.

REDUCING THE RISK

If test results indicate that you are being exposed to high levels of radon in your home, the EPA suggests the following steps to immediately reduce your risk:

- Stop smoking and discourage smoking in the house. (Smoking significantly increases your overall risk of lung cancer and may increase the risk of exposure to radon.)
- Spend less time in areas with higher concentrations of radon, such as the basement.

- Whenever practical, open windows and turn on fans to increase air flow into and through the home. This is especially important in the basement.
- If there is a crawl space underneath the house, keep all crawl space vents fully open.
- You may want to consult with your state or local health or radiation protection officials to determine whether temporary relocation is advisable until radon levels can be reduced.

While these actions will help reduce your risk from high levels of radon, they generally do not offer a long-term solution. For that, the EPA recommends, first contact your state radiation protection office for any advice or assistance it may be able to provide. If you decide that you need to hire a professional contractor or "radon mitigator," that office may be able to provide lists of contractors. It can also inform you of any relevant state regulations: Some states require companies offering radon screening to be licensed, and a few require certification of radon mitigators.

Before hiring a contractor, ask for and check references, and contact the local Better Business Bureau for a complaint report. Request written estimates from at least two contractors, and make sure you get any verbal guarantees in writing. Any corrective measures taken to reduce radon levels in your home should be followed by further testing to ensure that results are satisfactory.

Finally, watch out for door-to-door solicitors and con artists who may offer to:

- Use a Geiger counter to test your home for radon. (Geiger counters cannot measure radon levels.)
- Give you immediate test results. (It takes time to assess radon test results legitimately.)
- Sell you an air cleaner. (The EPA has concluded that air cleaners have not proven effective in reducing radon levels.)
- Install high-priced units to measure radon levels. (You'll probably pay less for the same devices at your local department store.)

Ranges

[For information and advice on selecting a retailer, saving on energy costs, and appliance service and service contracts, see *Appliances*, pages 25–28.]

Today's cooking center may consist of a single basic range or a series of high-tech, touch-controlled appliances. The selection is vast and the choice highly personal, a question of the cooking style you prefer, the configuration of your kitchen, the type of fuel source available in your home, and the convenience features of particular models. You probably will own your range for a good number of years and it may cost anywhere from about $300 to $1,200 or more, so you'll want to choose carefully. But the varied and sometimes confusing selection of brands and styles on the market can make that difficult—unless you take the time to sort out the available options and make some basic decisions before you shop.

STYLES AND SIZES

There are four basic types of ranges.

Free-standing ranges, the most popular style, stand between two base cabinets or sometimes at the end of a line of cabinets. They are usually 30 inches wide, although 20- to 21-inch and 24-inch "apartment-size" models are available, as well as 30- to 36-inch gas and 40-inch electric models. The wider ranges may have two side-by-side ovens below the cooktop or one oven plus a storage compartment. Other options include "high-low" or "tri-level" ranges, which have a second, smaller oven mounted over the cooktop. The upper oven can be a conventional bake and broil oven or a microwave oven.

Built-in ranges separate the oven(s), which are built into a wall, from the cooktops, which are recessed in a countertop in another part of the kitchen. Built-in ovens can be 24, 27, or 30 inches wide; height varies depending on whether the oven is a single- or double-oven unit. Cooktops come in many sizes, from 15 to 48 inches wide. Built-ins can give a custom look to your kitchen; however, unless you are putting a new kitchen in a new home or simply replacing an older built-in, installation requires extensive and costly remodeling.

Drop-in and **slide-in ranges** are a version of free-standing ranges designed to look like built-ins. A drop-in range hangs from a countertop or sits on a low cabinet base; a slide-in range sits on the floor. Drop-ins

296

Gas or Electric?

The choice between a gas and an electric range usually is determined by the fuel/power availability in your home as well as your local utility rates. Electric ranges require a special 208- or 240-volt line. Gas ranges require a professionally installed direct gas line and a 115-volt electrical circuit. Electric ranges consume less energy than gas ranges but generally cost more to operate because of the higher cost of electricity.

The relative advantages of gas and electric ranges are largely a matter of personal preference. Gas cooktop burners provide visual clues to the amount of heat and allow finer temperature control; further, the cooktop remains usable even during a power outage. However, the broiler in an electric range provides better browning over a wider area than most gas broilers. Also, self-cleaning features often are more effective on electric than gas ranges.

and slide-ins may be 27 or 30 inches wide, and they can be installed so that they are flush with the surrounding counter or so that they overlap the adjacent countertop edges, eliminating dirt-accumulating gaps.

FACTS AND FEATURES

Cooktop Choices

Whatever style of range you choose, you will find an assortment of available cooktop arrangements and features.

- **Conventional cooktops.** Most free-standing ranges and built-in cooktops have four electric elements or gas burners; some built-ins have a fifth element or burner.

  Electric cooktops usually have both six-inch and eight-inch coil elements. Extra features you may find include one eight-inch element with higher wattage for stir-frying or faster heating of large pans; a power-saving control that lets you reduce the heated portion of the eight-inch coils for use with smaller pans; elements with a thermostatic control in the center for "automatic" cooking; and solid disk elements. Solid disks, also known as hobs, heat up and cool down more slowly than coil elements and must be conditioned before use to prevent discoloring. On the plus side, solid disks allow more precise control of lower cooking temperatures and keep spills from dripping under the cooktop.

  Gas cooktops have burners with "infinite" flame adjustment, covered by round or square grates; some burner controls have handy click-stops at various settings. Many of the newer models of gas ranges have electric ignition rather than a pilot light, cutting gas consumption by about 40 percent.* Extra features you may find include one high-energy burner for faster heating and/or a thermostat-controlled burner for "automatic" cooking.

- **Convertible cooktops.** Some electric and gas ranges have cooktops with removable, interchangeable surface units, so that you can replace two burners with a griddle, a barbecue grill, a deep-fat fryer, a rotisserie, and/or a wok.

- **Induction cooktops.** A relatively new feature available on a few electric range models, induction cooktops consist of a smooth cooktop, with the cooking surfaces outlined, concealing an electromagnetic coil, which acts as the element and generates a magnetic field. When a ferrous metal (steel or iron) pan is placed on the cooktop, heat is generated in the pan itself; the rest of the cooktop stays cool. Pots and pans must have a completely flat bottom for food to cook evenly.

  Induction cooktops cut electricity consumption by 10 to 20 percent* and allow quicker heat-up and cool-down plus more precise temperature control than conventional electric cooktops. However, at present, their high cost more than outweighs the savings on energy consumption and puts these innovative cooktops out of the reach of many consumers.

- **Convenience features.** A number of design features can simplify the task of cleaning the top of the range. These include lift-up or removable cooktops; recessed tops, which prevent spills from running down the sides of the range; "seamless" edges and corners; removable drip bowls; and porcelain rather than shiny metal drip bowls. Features to avoid: dirt-catching chrome trim and unreachable nooks and crannies.

Oven Options

- **A second oven.** If you have a large family, do a lot of cooking or baking, or if there are two cooks in the family, you may find a second oven handy. A second, smaller oven can cook small portions of food more efficiently than the larger conventional oven. If you don't already own a microwave oven, you might appreciate the countertop savings offered by a free-standing high-low range or a double oven built-in with a microwave oven at the top. (Also see *Microwave Ovens*, pages 267–72.)

- **Combination ovens.** Some manufacturers make a combination oven, which allows microwave cooking and conventional heat cooking in a single, large oven cavity. You can cook with either method alone or combine them for faster cooking, along with browning and crisping.

*Source: American Council for an Energy-Efficient Economy.

Most combination ovens are electric, but a gas range with an oven that combines microwave and convection heat is also available.

- **Convection ovens.** Convection ovens, which cook by fan-forced hot air, are available in full-size gas and electric ranges and in gas micro/convection ranges. (Also see "Micro/convection ovens," *Microwave Ovens*, page 269.)

Conventional Oven Features

Oven capacity varies considerably among various range styles and models, with the greatest difference usually found in interior height and depth. Be sure to compare interior dimensions before making your selection.

Oven controls are usually dials, with either a single temperature dial or separate bake/broil and temperature controls. Electronic controls let you set the oven by touching a numbered pad. When the oven is on, a digital readout displays the oven temperature or, if you are using a temperature probe inserted in the food, the actual food temperature. When the oven is off, the electronic display shows the time of day.

Broiling in an electric range is performed by an element at the top of the oven cavity. Gas ranges have either a broiler compartment under the main oven or a separate "waist-high" burner at the top of the main oven cavity. Some models have a variable heat control, which allows you to raise or lower broiler temperature. Broiler capacity can vary, so be sure to compare dimensions before buying.

A **self-cleaning** gas or electric range eliminates a tough kitchen chore. The self-cleaning feature generally adds about $50 to $100 to the purchase price of the range; operating costs are usually only pennies per use.

There are two different self-cleaning systems.

☐ The **catalytic** or **continuous cleaning system** uses a rough porous coating on the oven walls designed to partially absorb and disperse grease and soil while the oven is in ordinary use at ordinary temperatures. Because of its special coating, a continuous cleaning oven never has as clean a look as a true self-cleaning oven, and racks and door parts must be cleaned by hand. Also, heavy spills must be wiped up immediately or they can become glazed over. Cleaning the oven with soap, detergent, or a commercial oven cleaner can permanently damage the surface.

☐ The **pyrolytic** or **true self-cleaning system** incinerates grease and food soil during a clock-controlled self-cleaning cycle of one to three hours in which the oven temperature reaches 800°F or more. The oven walls, racks, and door (except for a small area outside the door gasket) are completely cleaned; all that is left after cleanup is a white, ashy residue, which can be easily wiped away with a damp cloth.

Separate vent hoods come in many sizes and styles, from wall-mounted canopy hoods to shallow hoods that tuck under an upper cabinet or top off a high-low range. Vent hoods create drafts that pull smoke and odors through the range or cabinets to the outside via exhaust ducts. Nonvented hoods are available for use in kitchens where ductwork is not possible; they simply filter and recirculate the air. **Built-in venting**, which eliminates the need for an overhead hood, is available on many high-low ranges and as an integral part of many over-the-range microwave ovens.

In choosing a vent hood or venting system, look for:

- *Capacity* (measured in cfm's, the number of cubic feet of air moved in one minute; 200 to 400 cfm is standard)
- *Filters* that are easy to remove and clean
- *Fans* that are quiet and have two or more speed settings
- A *hood lamp* that lights the cooktop below

☑ RANGE CHECKLIST

Following is a checklist of factors you may want to consider when selecting a range:

- ☐ Is the range's energy source—gas or electric—the right choice given the available utility connections, your utility rates, and your cooking preferences?
- ☐ Will the range fit in and make optimum use of the available space?
- ☐ Does the cooktop have any special convenience features that you might want for cooking or cleanup?
- ☐ If it is a gas range, does it have electric ignition rather than a pilot light?
- ☐ Are oven and broiler capacity sufficient to meet your needs?
- ☐ Are electronic displays clear and readable?
- ☐ If you choose a self-cleaning oven, does it use the true (pyrolytic) self-cleaning system?
- ☐ Does the venting system have adequate venting capacity and other quality features (two or more fan speeds, easily cleaned filters, etc.)?
- ☐ Can you see clearly through the oven-door window?

Refrigerators And Freezers

[For information and advice on selecting a retailer, saving on energy costs, and appliance service and service contracts, see *Appliances,* pages 25–28.]

A refrigerator/freezer can cost anywhere from about $80 for a basic top-freezer to $3,000 or more for a large-capacity built-in model. When you are shopping for a major appliance with such a wide range of prices and available features and options, it makes sense to do some homework before making your selection.

STYLES AND SIZES

There are five basic types of refrigerators on the market.

Compacts or portables (capacity 1.5 to 6 cubic feet, width 12 to 24 inches*) are often used as a supplementary model in family rooms, offices, dorms, vacation homes, etc. Many fit under or on top of a cabinet. Compacts usually have a small freezer compartment; a few models also have an optional icemaker and/or an automatic defrosting feature.

Single-door models (capacity 9 to 14 cubic feet, width 23 to 30 inches) have one outer door plus a small inner door for the freezer compartment at the top of the unit. Frozen food can be stored for only a few days to one week, and the freezer compartment must be manually defrosted.

Top-mount refrigerator/freezers (capacity 10 to 25 cubic feet, width 24 to 33 inches) have two outer doors, with a separate freezer compartment at the top.

Bottom-mount refrigerator/freezers (capacity 18 to 20 cubic feet, width 32 to 36 inches) have a freezer compartment at the bottom of the unit; availability of this type of refrigerator is limited.

Side-by-side refrigerator/freezers (capacity 17 to 30 cubic feet, width 30 to 48 inches) typically have two side-by-side doors, with about one-third of the interior space devoted to the freezer compartment. (Some side-by-side models have a third, smaller door at the top of the freezer, covering a freezer compartment with a small shelf and/or an automatic icemaker.) The freezer section is more convenient to organize and use in a side-by-side model than in a top-freezer, and the narrower doors require less clearance in front for opening. On the other hand, side-by-side

*Dimensions provided by The General Electric Company.

refrigerator/freezers typically use about 35 percent more energy than top-freezers, and in the smaller-capacity units, the narrow freezer compartment can limit storage of large items.

Built-in refrigerator/freezers (capacity and width vary widely, depending on refrigerator style) are designed to be installed flush with the surrounding base cabinets, giving the kitchen a custom look. Built-ins generally are wider than free-standing models; some have greater depth as well. The energy consumption of a built-in usually is greater than that of a conventional refrigerator/freezer of the same capacity. Also, unless you are replacing an older built-in, installing a new kitchen, or completely remodeling, installation can be a major expense.

No-freezer refrigerators have almost vanished from the market because of a lack of consumer demand.

FACTS AND FEATURES

Capacity. One of the most important considerations when shopping for a refrigerator/freezer is selecting the right capacity for your needs. Too large a model will cost more than you need to spend and will waste space and energy. Too small a model will mean frequent extra trips to the supermarket. According to one rule of thumb, you should allow a minimum of 12 cubic feet for the first two persons in your household, then add 2 cubic feet for each additional person.* You may need less capacity if you often eat away from home or if you store the bulk of your frozen items in a separate freezer. On the other hand, if you entertain often or if your family will be expanding, you may want to buy a larger-capacity unit.

Be sure to shop with the future in mind—the average lifetime of a refrigerator/freezer is 20 years.** Also remember that it is generally much less expensive to buy and operate one large-capacity refrigerator than two small ones.

Defrosting. There are three basic methods of defrosting a refrigerator/freezer:

☐ **Manual defrosting**—defrosting by hand—can be a chore. But manual-defrost models typically use about half as much electricity as automatic-defrost models.** Compacts and single-door units are usually the only types of refrigerator/freezer that come in manual-defrost models.

☐ **Partial automatic defrosting** or **cycle-defrost** models automatically defrost the fresh food compartment when the refrigerator cycles off; the freezer must be manually defrosted. This system is most commonly available on single-door and top-freezer models.

*Source: The General Electric Company.
**Source: American Council for an Energy-Efficient Economy.

☐ The **frost-free** or **no-frost** systems automatically defrost both the freezer and fresh food compartments. Some newer models save energy by regulating defrosting time through sensors that respond to frost build-up. Frost-free defrosting is often available as a basic feature or as an option on compact, top-freezer, bottom-freezer, and side-by-side models.

Doors. Reversible doors, available on many top-freezers, allow you to reverse the direction in which the door opens. This can be an important option if you remodel or move.

Shelves. Top-freezers usually have several adjustable full-width refrigerator shelves, at least one half-width shelf for added flexibility in food storage, and one adjustable freezer shelf. Most side-by-side models have a number of adjustable full-width refrigerator shelves and fixed freezer shelves, plus a pull-out drawer at the bottom of the freezer section. Refrigerator shelves may be the traditional open-wire design and/or tempered glass or plastic. Glass and plastic shelves are breakable; however they are better at containing spills and are generally easier to clean than wire.

Door storage bins. These compartments may be fixed or adjustable; some are removable for easy cleaning. Other door storage features may include egg storage trays or covered egg bins, covered butter or dairy compartments, retainers for stacked frozen food packages, and/or a dispenser for frozen-juice cans.

Food storage pans. Most refrigerator/freezers have separate drawers for storing fresh vegetables and meat under prime conditions of temperature and humidity. Some storage pans have separate controls that let you vary temperature, humidity, and airflow.

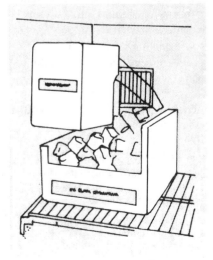
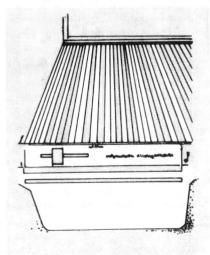

An automatic icemaker   *Fresh food storage pans*

Automatic icemakers. An icemaker may come already installed in the freezer or, in many models, may be purchased as an optional kit for later installation. You may want to hire the dealer or a plumber to handle the installation. An icemaker typically holds about six pounds of ice and keeps producing ice cubes until the bin is full. If you use a lot of ice, an icemaker can be a welcome convenience. However, it usually takes up more freezer space than ice cube trays and a storage bin would require, and the ice that sits at the bottom of the icemaker's large bin can absorb odors and an off taste from frozen food.

Other features. You will find a number of additional convenience features available, usually on the more expensive models. These include through-the-door ice and/or chilled water dispensers (some with a "nightlight"), wine racks or wine storage compartments, automatic ice cream makers, storage carousels, and custom trim kits that accept custom door panels matching the surrounding cabinets. Also available on some higher-priced, high-tech models are electronic controls, which allow you to program the refrigerator to perform a number of functions, such as to operate at a colder, "fast-freeze" temperature for a period of hours. Electronic controls also sound an alert when the temperature drops or the door is left open, and can guide service technicians in diagnosing the cause of malfunctions.

Selecting a Freezer

A food freezer can be a handy convenience, but to be economical, it must be kept at least two-thirds full at all times and food must be properly wrapped to prevent "freezer burn," or dehydration. There are two basic styles of home freezer: chest (top loading) and upright (front loading). Large models have a capacity of about 15 to 16 cubic feet. Compact freezers, with a capacity of less than 10 cubic feet, may be a more practical alternative for some families. While automatic-defrost freezers are available, most models require manual defrosting.

Key considerations in the selection of a freezer include size, capacity, and energy efficiency. Make sure that the unit will fit in your available space and that it has adequate storage capacity for your needs. Refer to the Energy Guide Labels when you shop, and remember that chest freezers are typically 10 to 15 percent more efficient than upright models, and manual-defrost freezers generally consume about 40 percent less electricity than automatic-defrost models.* (Also see "Energy Costs," *Appliances,* pages 26–28.)

*Source: American Council for an Energy-Efficient Economy.

☑ REFRIGERATOR/FREEZER CHECKLIST

Following is a checklist of factors you may want to consider when selecting a refrigerator/freezer:

☐ Will the refrigerator/freezer fit in and make optimum use of your available space? (Be sure to take into account necessary clearances for door swing and air circulation.)

☐ Is it energy-efficient? (Also see "Energy Costs," *Appliances,* pages 26–28.)

☐ Is its capacity sufficient to suit your present and future needs?

☐ Does the defrosting system suit your preferences and your budget?

☐ If the unit is a top-freezer, does it have reversible doors?

☐ Do doors have a stop to keep them from hitting cabinets?

☐ Are shelves durable, well supported, and easy to use and clean? Are they adjustable and removable?

☐ Do storage bins or pans have adequate capacity? Are they durable and easy to remove and clean?

☐ Are there glide-out rollers under the refrigerator so you can move it for easy cleaning beneath and behind?

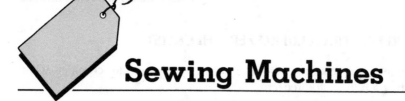

Sewing Machines

Shopping for a sewing machine is a balancing act: It involves making a realistic assessment of your needs and then finding the machine that has neither *more* than you need nor *less* than you want. If you are a fashion-sewing enthusiast, one of the more expensive computerized sewing machine models may be right for you. Computerized models can sew a wide variety of decorative stitches, allow you to memorize and repeat your own newly developed stitches, and have a variety of extra features, such as automatic stitch length and width selection, which make sewing more precise and convenient. Costs range from about $600 to $2,000. If you're among the majority who use a machine only for occasional sewing and mending, you will probably be well satisfied with a less costly (about $100 to $500) basic model. The following list, from the American Home Sewing Association, covers the basic features you should look for in any sewing machine:

- Machine starts and stops smoothly and is jamproof if you sew off edge of fabric.
- Bobbin doesn't vibrate while sewing and feeds thread evenly.
- Bobbin is simple to wind and easy to insert into case.
- Thread guides are easy to follow.
- Needle is easy to install.
- Fabric feeds evenly under needle.
- Variety of utility stitches.
- Variety of throat plates and feet attachments for utility stitches.
- Needle plate markings to guide seam widths.
- Accurate reverse stitching.
- Controllable stitch lengths and widths.
- Adjustable tension and pressure knobs.
- Variations in speed controls for stitching accuracy.
- Light that illuminates needle area.
- Foot or knee pedal is easy and comfortable to operate.
- Sturdy one-piece body construction.
- Easy to clean; limited oiling needed.
- *Instruction book you can understand.*

Extra features, such as a childproof power switch, stitch memory, or fancy decorative stitches may be important to you, as may such dealer extras as free lessons for beginning sewers. But remember that in general, more elaborate features mean a more expensive machine.

SHOPPING TIPS

1. Don't rush into a purchase. Take time to look over your library's files of consumer reporting publications and to ask the opinion of friends who own machines.
2. Compare the features of at least three models, and "test-drive" the machines yourself on fabrics of different weights and textures. Look for even stitches with good tension control—the stitches should look the same on both the top and bottom of the fabric, with no puckering.
3. Buy from a reputable dealer; if in doubt, check the reputation of dealers with your local Better Business Bureau. Watch out for high-pressure sales tactics, contests or "free" gift promotions that may have strings attached, and bait and switch sales tactics. (In bait and switch, a product is advertised at a "bargain" price in order to lure customers to the store, where a salesperson runs down the quality of the advertised model and "switches" the customer to a higher-priced item.)
4. Make the terms of service and the warranty part of your buying decision. How long does the dealer offer free service, and is it transferrable to another city if you move? How long is the warrantor responsible for repairs and replacement of defective parts? What are the conditions associated with the warranty?

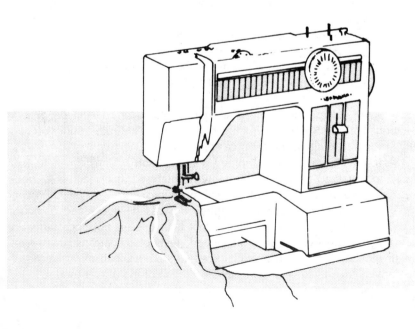

Stereo Systems

We hear with two ears, and depending on our position relative to the sound source, one ear receives sound a little sooner than and a little differently from the other. A stereo music system aims to recreate that three-dimensional listening experience.

Stereo is produced in the studio by the recording of instruments and vocalists on several channels, which are mixed electronically into the two channels put onto record, compact disc, or tape. When the recording is played back on stereo equipment, the channels are separated again. Thus the ears receive sound waves from two locations, which the brain translates into one rich, composite sound.

A stereo system has three major components: a music source, an amplifier, and a pair of loudspeakers. The **music source** may be a turntable, a cassette tape deck, and/or a compact disc player. The **receiver** might also be considered a music source, since it includes an AM/FM radio tuner, but it is primarily an amplification unit which enlarges the electrical signals received from the music source and powers the loudspeakers. Those **loudspeakers**—whether a pair of speakers in cabinets or a set of stereo headphones—are responsible for reproducing the sound on the recording.

For as little as $200, you can purchase the three main components of a stereo system in a single, **compact** package including turntable, amplifier, receiver, and loudspeakers. A compact system, however, usually cannot come close to matching the sound quality of a system made up of components purchased separately.

It's possible to spend anywhere from about $300 to $100,000 or more for a stereo component system. But if you know which features are important and take the time to comparison-shop, you should be able to put together a good single-music-source (turntable or CD player) system for about $500 to $600. And with a budget of $1,000 to $1,500, you can take home an excellent multisource stereo system.

The following look at terminology, features, and options can help you select moderately priced, high-quality turntables, receivers, and loud-speakers. You may also want to review *Audio and Video Equipment*, pages 29–30, and the separate chapters on cassette decks and compact disc players. As you shop, remember that high price is not necessarily an indicator of quality. Today's advanced technology means that even low-priced equipment can deliver excellent sound, albeit minus some of the convenience features and electronic "frills" of the pricier models.

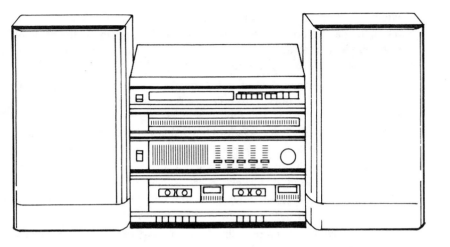

TURNTABLES

More and more recordings today are coming out on both compact disc
(CD) and LP record or on compact disc alone, and the CD has several
advantages over the traditional record album. So if you are new to music
collecting, you may want to invest in a CD player rather than a turntable.
(Also see *Compact Disc Players*, pages 90–94.) Of course, if you already
own a collection of LP records, you'll want to build your new stereo
system around a good turntable, either as your single music source or in
combination with a CD player. In shopping for a turntable, consider the
following features, options, and specifications:

☐ **Degree of automatic operation.** *Manual and semiautomatic turntables*
require you to place the tone arm on the record by hand; a
semiautomatic model will return the arm to its slot and turn off the
motor after the record has been played. *Automatic models,* or *record
changers*, allow you to place a stack of records on the turntable; the
records are automatically dropped down and played one at a time.
Some fully automatic models have additional convenience features,
such as a sensor that can judge the size of the record on the platter
and place the tone arm accordingly or a control that lets you
automatically replay one side of a record. Single-play turntables are
more popular than record changers as part of separately purchased
component systems, mainly due to the possibility of records being
scratched during the automatic play process. In making your choice,
consider both your music listening habits and the premium you place
on convenience.

☐ **Drive system.** A *belt-driven* turntable uses a belt or wheel to connect
the platter to the motor; on a *direct-drive* model, the platter and motor
are directly connected. There is some debate over the question of

whether either method has any inherent superiority. Some sources maintain that belt-driven models are more reliable than direct-drives, others believe that direct-drive models allow smoother, more precise rotation, and still others see no performance difference at all.

☐ **Rumble.** *Signal-to-noise ratio* is the measure of how well a turntable isolates mechanical noises (rumble) from the loudspeakers and thus its quietness in relation to the electrical signal. The Professional AudioVideo Retailers Association (PARA) recommends that you look for a model with a signal-to-noise ratio of 50 decibels (dB) or higher.

☐ **Wow and flutter.** If the speed at which a record rotates is inconsistent, you will hear sound distortions such as "sour" notes and wavering pitch. The percentage of wow and flutter in high-fidelity equipment should be less than 0.08 percent, according to PARA.

☐ **Cueing control.** This feature, standard on most models, lets you raise or lower the tone arm without touching it, thus minimizing potential damage to the record or cartridge.

☐ **Antiskating device.** The tone arm has a natural tendency to slide inward, which can wear down the side of the record groove and distort the sound. An antiskating device counteracts this tendency.

☐ **Speed control.** Turntables with speed control allow you to make fine adjustments in the speed at which a record is played. There is usually a strobe indicator which shows you when the turntable is turning too fast or too slow.

☐ **Cartridges.** The cartridge plays a key role in determining the quality of stereo sound. Look for a cartridge that can handle a wide range of frequencies, from the deepest organ notes to the highest harmonics of cymbals or violins, without underemphasizing or overemphasizing any—the measure of these characteristics is called "frequency response." PARA recommends a frequency response of 20–20,000 Hertz (Hz) ± 2–3dB.

Mounting and attaching a standard cartridge is a painstaking task. *Plug-in cartridges,* or *P-mounts*, are easier to install—they simply plug into the tone arm. You may also want to look for a cartridge with a built-in *damper brush*, a helpful feature that can minimize the distortion in playing a warped record.

RECEIVERS

A stereo receiver is an all-in-one unit combining an **AM/FM radio tuner**; a **preamplifier**, which lets you adjust volume, tone, speaker balance, and other characteristics of sound; and an **amplifier**, which increases the strength of the electrical signal sufficiently to activate the loudspeakers. Each one of these three components can be purchased separately, or you can buy an **integrated amplifier**, with a preamp and amplifier but no tuner. Some serious audiophiles believe that separate components allow greater control and flexibility; most people, though, prefer the convenience of owning a receiver.

Quality variations among receivers in the same price range are not significant. However, when shopping for a stereo receiver, you should look for these characteristics, features, and options:

☐ **Power.** The amount of power that an amplifier can deliver, expressed as *watts per channel*, is one of the major determinants of the price of the receiver. The greater the number of watts per channel, the stronger the signal output and the louder the sound your stereo can deliver without distortion. This does not mean that a more powerful (and more expensive) receiver is right for you; that choice is a matter of your personal music listening preferences and the size of your listening room. A knowledgeable retailer can help you determine how powerful an amplifier you require. In general, you'll need at least 20 to 30 watts per channel to achieve respectable volume levels in an average-sized living room. But keep in mind that your power needs will increase if you want to install extra speakers in a separate room, if your listening room is either uncommonly large or filled with sound-deadening furnishings such as overstuffed chairs and heavy draperies, or if you like your music loud—particularly if you like to turn up the volume on compact discs. Also remember that small gradations in power make little difference in the sound you hear; a 30–watt amp probably will sound the same to you as a 60–watt model.

The power of the receiver need not only be adequate for your room and your listening preferences; it must also be properly matched to the needs of the loudspeakers. An amplifier without sufficient power to drive the loudspeakers can cause sound distortion or even speaker damage. When matching amplifier to loudspeaker, look for the recommended minimum amp power the speaker requires. Also check the speakers' *impedance*—the level of resistance to electrical current from the receiver. Impedance is usually from four to eight *ohms* (a measure of electrical resistance); the lower the number, the lower the impedance and the more current the speaker will draw from the receiver. If you are considering buying low-impedance speakers, make sure the receiver is rated to handle them.

☐ **Versatility.** A receiver has input and output jacks for connecting the loudspeakers, turntable and/or CD player, cassette deck, and possibly other components such as a second set of loudspeakers, a second tape deck, a stereo TV set, or a video system. In selecting a receiver, consider which components you may want to connect to your system, both now and in the future, and make sure the model you buy has the capabilities you require.

☐ **Total Harmonic Distortion (THD).** This is a key measure of signal distortion; according to PARA, 0.1 percent THD is good, 0.05 percent or less excellent.

☐ **Controls.** Look for a simple, uncluttered, easy-to-use control panel.

☐ **Tuner.** An AM/FM tuner receives radio waves and turns them into electrical impulses, which are then amplified and reproduced as sound. The quality of a receiver's tuner is likely to vary more than the quality of its amplifier. Look for these key specifications, as recommended by PARA:

  • **Usable sensitivity**, how well the unit pulls in and reproduces weak or distant station signals, should be 4μV or lower.

  • **Frequency response**, the range of frequencies from low to high that a unit can process, is combined with the figure for Total Harmonic Distortion (THD) (see above) to indicate how accurately a unit receives a signal. In a quality unit, the distortion at 1,000 Hz should be less than 0.05 percent.

  • **Signal-to-noise ratio**, the difference between the pure signal and noise or interference, should be 70dB or higher.

  • **Selectivity**, the unit's ability to receive stations without interference from others on *nearby* frequencies, should be 70dB or more.

  • **Capture ratio**, the unit's capacity to prevent distortion by selecting the stronger of two signals received on the *same* frequency, should be 2.0 dB or lower.

  • **Separation**, how well each stereo channel holds its own programming without interference from the other, should be 40dB or higher.

☐ You may also want to look for a tuner with **quartz digital tuning,** which allows more precise and convenient location of stations than the traditional tuning knob. Quartz tuning allows you to preset a number of radio stations and to automatically scan for listenable stations.

☐ **Other performance and convenience features** you may want to look for in a receiver include a subsonic filter for reducing low-frequency interference, a sound enhancer for a "surround sound" effect, and a remote-control device. The number of functions you can perform with a remote varies from model to model; volume control can be a particularly handy feature.

LOUDSPEAKERS

A loudspeaker is actually a "system" all its own. Inside each loudspeaker cabinet, several speakers—usually two or three—share the task of converting the electrical signal received from the amplifier into sound waves. In a "three-way" system, those speakers within the speaker include a **woofer**, which reproduces the low or bass notes, a **tweeter** for the high or treble notes, and possibly a **midrange** for the in-betweens. A "two-way" system has only a woofer and a tweeter. "One-way" speakers, usually the lowest-priced variety, generally are not as accurate in delivering the lowest and highest sounds of the spectrum.

Your primary consideration when selecting loudspeakers should be compatibility with the receiver (see page 311), sound fidelity, and price. The speakers are the key element in your stereo system. Only if they reproduce sound accurately will you be able to hear the full spectrum produced by the system's other components. Be prepared to allocate one-third to one-half of your entire stereo budget to the loudspeakers. But at the same time, be aware that high price is not necessarily a guarantee of quality. The key to finding speakers that match your needs and budget—Listen.

Begin by listening to several models of speakers within your price range; if none suit your personal tastes, you may need to consider moving up in price. Bring along a record, CD, or cassette when you shop so that you can hear familiar music, and try out speakers at all volume settings. Keep your ears tuned for:

- **The bass notes.** Most speakers do a good job of reproducing the treble and midrange notes, but it is the ability to deliver the deepest bass frequencies clearly and powerfully that distinguishes a first-class loudspeaker.

- **The treble notes.** The high notes should be clear and distinct.

- **Freedom from coloration.** Watch out for subtle distortions in the midrange frequencies.

- **Loudness.** How high can you turn the volume without the sound breaking up or becoming "muddy" or distorted, or the speaker cabinet buzzing or rattling?

Also keep these facts in mind as you shop for and use your loudspeakers:

☐ Once you have selected a pair of speakers, listen to each one individually to make certain they produce the same quality of sound.

☐ Be sure to ask about return and exchange policies before you buy, particularly if you are unable to give speakers a thorough tryout in the store.

☐ The placement of the loudspeakers and your room's furnishings affect the way sound reflects off the floor, walls, and ceiling. Speakers usually should be placed away from corners, about 10 feet apart, and at ear level. But you may need to try them out in several different spots in the room to find the arrangement that gives the most natural and pleasing sound reproduction.

Tanning Salons

Despite scientific evidence linking suntanning to premature aging of the skin and an increase in the risk of skin cancer, many Americans continue to seek that sun-bronzed glow. And with the growth of the indoor tanning salon industry over the past decade, natural sunlight is no longer the only significant source of tanning rays. Before you decide to visit a tanning salon or buy a sunlamp for use at home, you should know some important facts about the myths and perils of indoor tanning, as well as some steps you can take to minimize the risks.

INSIDE THE SALONS

The device most commonly used in tanning salons is the tanning bed. Sunlamps above and below this clamshell-like support emit ultraviolet lights; the customer lies on a Plexiglas surface and relaxes as the lights tan the body on both sides. Until a few years ago, most tanning beds used shortwave ultraviolet B (UVB) rays. However, as concern mounted over the harmful effects of UVB radiation, which include sunburn and the increased risk of skin cancer, many salons switched to longwave ultraviolet A (UVA) rays.

Both UVA and UVB radiation are found in natural sunlight, but while UVA rays are present in nearly equal amounts throughout the day and throughout the year, UVB rays are more prevalent during the middle of the day, from about 10 A.M. to 2 P.M., and during the summer. The sunburn you suffer after lying on a hot beach at noon in July is the result of UVB rays penetrating the outer layer of your skin and damaging cells near the skin surface. When your skin reacts by producing the brown pigment melanin to protect itself from further damage, you end up with a tan.

UVA rays are weaker and work more slowly than UVB rays, thus lessening the risk of sunburn. That fact has led some tanning salon operators to claim that tanning beds using UVA radiation provide a safe, healthy tan. However, according to concerned physicians and federal agencies including the Food and Drug Administration and the Federal Trade Commission (FTC), such claims are false. Long-term exposure to the sun and/or to any artificial source of ultraviolet light, the FTC warns, contributes to your risk of developing skin cancer, premature skin wrinkling, brown "age spots," and skin rashes. UVA radiation in particular, because it penetrates the skin more deeply than UVB rays, can slowly break down the skin's inner connective tissues, causing skin to weaken and sag. Studies also show that overexposure to ultraviolet rays, including UVA rays, can damage the eye's retina and burn the cornea; repeated exposure over many years can lead to the formation of cataracts. While eye damage can result from long-term exposure to sunlight as well, the risks are far greater with indoor tanning devices, due to the intensity of the lights they use and the lack of one "warning sign" that natural sunlight provides: heat.

If you are thinking of overlooking these risks in pursuit of a "healthy glow," consider the following additional health hazards associated with indoor tanning:

1. Year-round tanning increases your skin's exposure to the dangers of ultraviolet rays.

2. Exposure to tanning salon rays increases the damage caused by sunlight, thinning the skin and making it less capable of healing.

3. Your age at the time of exposure to UV radiation is a critical factor relative to burning. Studies suggest that children and teenagers suffer greater harm than adults from equivalent amounts of UVB rays.

4. Whether you tan indoors or out, the combination of ultraviolet rays and some medications, cosmetics, and soaps may accelerate skin burns or produce painful rashes. In addition, tanning devices may induce common light-sensitive skin ailments such as cold sores.

5. Because the newer UVA tanning devices work more slowly than the older UVB models and usually do not cause sunburn, tanning salon customers tend to use the newer devices more often, increasing their risk of skin damage. Some also are tempted to stay in the tanning bed longer than recommended, which can result in serious burns.

MINIMIZING THE RISKS

If you do choose to tan at a salon or to use a tanning device at home, the following checklist can help you minimize some of the risks:

Exposure Limits

☐ Follow the recommended exposure limits for your skin type provided by the tanning device manufacturer or the salon staff.

☐ Make sure there is a timer on the tanning device that you can set to automatically shut off the lights or sound a signal when exposure should end.

☐ Never sunbathe outdoors on the same day that you visit a tanning salon.

Eye Protection

☐ Always wear protective eye goggles; ordinary sunglasses or cotton balls are not adequate protection against intense artificial UV lights. And make sure the goggles fit snugly.

☐ Ask whether the salon sterilizes goggles after each use to prevent the spread of eye infection.

Medical History

☐ Consult your doctor before using any type of tanning device if:

- You are taking antihistamines, tranquilizers, birth control pills, or any other medication that might increase your likelihood of developing a rash, a sunburn, or another allergic-type reaction when your skin is exposed to the sun or artificial light.

- You are undergoing treatment for lupus or diabetes, or are susceptible to cold sores. Ultraviolet radiation can severely aggravate these conditions.

- You sunburn easily but do not tan.

☐ Make sure the tanning salon maintains a file of information on customers' medical histories, including any medications or treatments being received, and that those files are updated periodically.

Tax Preparers

[Also see *Financial Planners,* pages 151–55.]

Each year, American taxpayers scramble to file their income tax forms before April 15. And each year a significant number of those taxpayers seek paid help in dealing with a maze of deductions, restrictions, requirements, and paper, paper, paper. The services and fees of tax preparers vary widely. To find competent assistance suited to your particular situation, you must first know your options and then be prepared with questions to ask and criteria to apply.

OPTIONS IN ADVISERS

Free Tax Assistance

Several programs funded by the Internal Revenue Service (IRS) are available to persons who have neither a lot of money to spend on tax advice nor particularly complex returns to file.

☐ **Tax Counseling for the Elderly** (TCE) offers free services provided by trained volunteers to taxpayers 60 years or older who need help preparing and filing their tax forms. Centers are located in central sites in cities and towns across the U.S.; many of these centers are operated by the American Association of Retired Persons (AARP) and are called "Tax-Aide Sites." Counselors also will make home visits to shut-ins and disabled persons unable to travel. For information, contact your local IRS office or AARP Tax-Aide, 1909 K Street, N.W., Washington, DC 20006, 202-662-4871.

☐ **Volunteer Income Tax Assistance** (VITA), with centers across the country, trains volunteers to provide free tax preparation services primarily to low-income, elderly, non-English-speaking, and disabled citizens. For information, contact your local IRS office.

☐ **A complete list of free IRS services and publications** may be found in IRS Publication 910, *Guide to Free Tax Services;* to order, call 1-800-424-FORM. Recorded information on about 140 topics of tax information is available through the IRS's toll-free Tele-Tax system. Tele-Tax telephone numbers and covered topics are listed in several IRS tax publications and tax form instructions; in most areas, the number is 1-800-554-4477. The IRS also has a toll-free hotline number that connects callers with agents who will answer specific tax-related questions. In most areas, that number is 1-800-424-1040; in some areas, you'll need to look in the white pages of your telephone directory under U.S. Government, Internal Revenue Service, Federal Tax Assistance. Keep in mind that during the tax season, those phone lines are almost constantly busy. Also remember that these IRS employees do not necessarily qualify as income tax preparers. If the answers you receive are later discovered to be wrong, you will still be responsible for the payment of the correct tax but will not be charged any penalty.

Written tax questions may be sent to your IRS District Director; for that address, call your area's toll-free IRS hotline number. Most local IRS offices provide walk-in tax help. Many also have lending libraries of informational audiocassettes and videotapes and conduct education programs for specific groups of taxpayers, such as farmers and small-business owners.

Finally, in some cases, the IRS will help you finish your partially completed tax return. For details on any of these services, contact your local IRS office. You may also want to ask for copies of the free IRS publications *Taxpayer Bill of Rights* and *Tax Guide;* to order, call 800-424-FORM.

Tax Preparation Chains

High-volume tax service companies generally charge a modest fee for the preparation of relatively simple tax forms, with the fee schedule usually based on the number of forms and lines to be filled. Offices may be open year-round or at tax time only. In general, customers "drop in" and are taken on a first-come, first-served basis. At least one chain also has a "by-appointment-only" service for middle- or high-income clients seeking to maintain a continuing one-on-one relationship with their tax preparer. This more private service, which often also includes year-round tax planning tips, costs about twice as much as the services of the standard drop-in outlets.

Employees of tax service chains are usually hired on a seasonal, part-time basis and provided with basic tax preparation training. Most chains will send a preparer to accompany you free of charge if your return is audited. The preparer can help explain how your return was completed but cannot speak on your behalf nor legally represent you before the IRS; you'll need to hire an attorney, an enrolled agent, or a CPA for that.

If your tax return is relatively routine, featuring mostly salary income and simple deductions, you may find that a tax preparation chain can give you competent service at a good price. However, if you are filing a business return or a complicated personal return, you may want to consider hiring an enrolled agent, a public accountant, a certified public accountant, or a tax attorney.

Enrolled Agents

To qualify as an enrolled agent, a person must either have worked at least five years as an auditor or in a similar position for the IRS or must pass a comprehensive IRS-administered examination in federal taxation and related subjects. To maintain professional accreditation, an enrolled agent must complete 24 credit hours each year in college-level continuing education courses on tax regulations and accounting methods. Enrolled agents are approved to represent taxpayers before the IRS; they also may provide assistance in financial planning. The services of an enrolled agent usually cost more than those of a national tax preparation service but less than those of a CPA; however, fee structures, usually calculated on an hourly basis, can vary.

If you have a relatively complex return to file and/or need tax advice or help in financial planning, you may want to consult an enrolled agent. There are about 40,000 enrolled agents currently practicing in the U.S.; 7,000 of these are members of the National Association of Enrolled Agents (NAEA), which imposes continuing education requirements on members beyond those prescribed at the state level. For the names of enrolled agents in your area, call NAEA at 800-424-4339.

Public Accountants

Many people confuse the titles "public accountant" and "certified public accountant" (CPA), but the two terms are worlds apart. A public accountant may be anyone who is in the public practice of accountancy—in many states, there are no minimum educational or testing requirements for use of the title. Thus it is particularly important, when considering hiring a public accountant as a tax preparer, to inquire about and verify the individual's educational background and training as well as membership in any state society with a mandatory continuing education program. Some public accountants are also enrolled agents and thus are well qualified to prepare your forms. Public accounts generally charge about as much as enrolled agents but less than CPAs.

Certified Public Accountants

A CPA has a college degree or its equivalent in work experience, has passed a rigorous two-day professional qualifying exam in accounting practices, and, in all but a few states, is required to take annual refresher courses to maintain certification. CPAs are legally permitted to represent you before an IRS auditor. If your return is particularly complex, you are in the upper-middle to upper income level, and/or there has been a major change in your life such as divorce or retirement which may have substantial tax consequences, a CPA whose practice is devoted to taxes can be a good choice for a preparer. CPAs may work for large or small firms or as individual practitioners. In general, the larger the CPA's firm, the more you will pay. Unless you are filing a business return for a company with annual sales of over $1 million, you probably will receive better, more personal service from a small firm or solo practitioner.

In exchange for fees that are usually higher than those charged by enrolled agents or the national tax preparation chains, CPAs should be able to provide solid tax planning and financial advice. To find a CPA, you might contact your state society of CPAs for a list of members in your area.

Tax Attorneys

Tax lawyers generally charge the highest fees of all tax professionals. They do not routinely fill out tax returns but may be the best choice for advice in handling complicated situations such as divorce settlements, estate planning, and serious disputes with the IRS.

CHOOSING A TAX PREPARER

If you have decided that your tax situation calls for the services of an accountant, enrolled agent, or other tax professional, be prepared to spend some time searching for the right person to handle the job. The best tax preparers may also be the busiest, so it's wise to start your search well before the start of "tax season"—the first of the year. Ask for recommendations from friends or colleagues whose financial situation is similar to your own and/or from the professional associations mentioned above. Then schedule an interview with the preparer; remember to ask if there is a charge for this initial consultation. Bring along samples of your current records and several recent tax returns, as well as a list of questions, which might include the following:

1. **What is the tax practitioner's educational background and experience, and how does he or she keep current with tax law changes?** If your situation requires specialized knowledge—if you are self-employed, a physician, or a small business owner, for example—also make certain the preparer has adequate experience in dealing with tax matters specific to your field.
2. **Will the interviewer also be the person who prepares your return?** If an associate will fill out your forms, ask about that person's credentials, too.

3. **Can the preparer be reached during the year or at tax time only?** Remember that you may need tax advice or help with questions from the IRS at any time during the year.
4. **How is the accuracy of the preparer's work checked?** Will your return be reviewed by one or more persons, and will it be checked for mathematical errors only or for mistakes in the interpretation of tax rules as well?
5. **Will the preparer accompany you to the IRS in the event of an audit?** Is he or she approved to legally represent you before the IRS? Is there an additional charge for this service? If you are assessed interest and/or a penalty because of an error in the preparer's work, who pays those expenses?
6. **How many tax forms does the preparer complete each year?** You will need to judge whether he or she has sufficient time to devote to your particular needs; one clue can be the number of extensions the preparer had to file for in the preceding year.
7. **How is the fee determined?** Ask for an estimate of the total bill and be sure you understand what services, if any, are included beyond the preparation of your return, and what services are excluded. The fee should be based on the complexity of your return, *not* on the size of your anticipated tax savings or refund.
8. **Will the preparer provide references?** Ask for and check references from two or three clients with tax situations similar to yours, and contact the local Better Business Bureau for a reliability report on the practitioners you are considering.

TIPS FOR TAXPAYERS

As you search for and work with a tax professional, keep these recommendations and precautions in mind:

- According to the IRS, an income tax preparer may be anyone who receives compensation for the preparation of all or a substantial portion of any tax return for another person, or who provides detailed information and advice that make the completion of the return largely a mechanical or clerical process. There are *no* educational or professional requirements for use of the title "tax preparer." However, tax professionals such as enrolled agents, CPAs, and tax attorneys must meet the educational and ethical standards of their profession, and employees of most national tax services are required to undergo thorough tax training.
- Even if you pay someone to help you prepare your tax return, you are still legally responsible for the information included in the return and for its timely filing. It's also up to you to compile and organize your

records in order to qualify for all the tax savings to which you are entitled. Your responsibilities include:

☐ Keeping careful records and saving all receipts that document the deductions you will claim.

☐ Organizing your documents. Categorize and list all the documents and figures you will be turning over to the preparer; this can translate into substantial savings if you are paying an hourly fee.

☐ Giving your preparer sufficient time to file a proper return. That not only means dropping off your records well before April 15 but also thinking ahead—phoning your preparer in the fall or early winter, for example, to discuss changes in your tax situation since last year or year-end moves you might make to cut your taxes for the current year.

• Make sure your tax practitioner is aware of and comfortable with your preferences regarding "gray areas" in which IRS rulings are ambiguous and you may or may not be entitled to deductions. Whether your stance is conservative or aggressive, you want to be certain your tax adviser is in agreement.

• Try to read and keep abreast of tax changes so that you can ask your preparer how they apply to you.

• Read your return carefully before signing it. Never sign a blank return or one filled out in pencil. And remember, no matter who prepares your return, you are the one whom the IRS will ultimately hold responsible for its accuracy.

• Retain a copy of your completed return and all related documents.

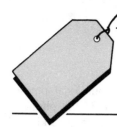

Telephones — Conventional, Cordless, and Cellular

[Also see *Answering Machines*, pages 17–20; *Long-Distance Phone Service*, pages 255–59.]

Not long ago, your telephone was *one* household appliance you never had to think about. Your choices were limited, and the equipment the phone company provided seemed to last forever. Those days of few concerns or options in telephone equipment are gone forever. Today consumers are faced with unfamiliar choices. They must decide whether to buy or lease their home phones, and if they buy, they may select equipment from among an abundant and varied assortment. The styles and functions of telephones keep changing; besides the traditional corded phone, there are now cordless and cellular models, combination phones with a built-in calculator, clock/radio, or answering machine, and even phones that can "remember" the numbers of your friends or dial by the sound of your voice. Further, telephones are no longer all created equal. The "wrong" phone may offer fewer features or poorer quality than you might find elsewhere in a comparably priced model.

Clearly, getting your money's worth out of telephone equipment today requires some research as well as some strategic shopping. The "phone survey" that follows can help in both areas: It includes a look at the relative advantages of leasing and buying phones, a catalog of features and options commonly available on corded, cordless, and cellular models, plus checklists of shopping tips and precautions.

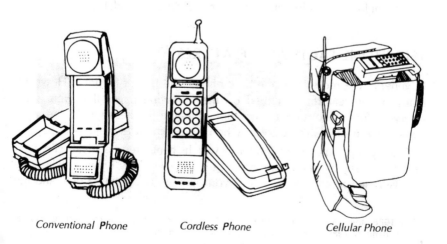

Conventional Phone   Cordless Phone   Cellular Phone

LEASING VS. BUYING YOUR PHONES

When you lease your telephone equipment, you pay your local phone company a monthly charge for the use and maintenance of the phones, jacks, and wiring. Depending on the type of phone you lease and the rates in your area, that charge may come to anywhere from about $20 to $60 a year. (For local rates, check your phone bill or call your local phone company.) Compare the monthly leasing charge with the cost of buying your own phone,* and you can see why, in most cases, owning your phone can be the more cost-effective option in the long run. Of course, costs for different phone models vary widely, depending largely on the extent of electronic gadgetry built into the unit. And the key to long-term savings is buying a *reliable* phone—when you lease, the phone company usually takes care of repairs and replacement, but those costs are *your* responsibility when you own the phone.

Installing and maintaining your own inside phone jacks and wiring may also save you money. Again, when you own the jacks and wiring, you are responsible for the costs of repairs and service. According to a report in *Money* magazine,** studies show that wire problems occur about once every 14 years, and the typical repair cost is $65; phone company wire-service fees average 89¢ per month. Thus, in the long run, owning the wires yourself can be less costly than leasing.

If you decide to buy your own phone, your simplest course may be to purchase the leased equipment already in your home. Most older-model phones were manufactured by Western Electric, a subsidiary of AT&T, in the days before deregulation of the phone industry, and they were built to last. Because the equipment is used, you should be able to get it for a good price. If buying rental equipment is not an option, however, or if you want to sample a different color or style or some of the extra functions performed by the newer phones, the catalog of features and options below can help you zero in on a style and model.

TELEPHONE FACTS AND FEATURES

In general, the more "capable" the phone, the higher its price. However, many of the features described on the following pages that were once reserved for office phones or top-of-the-line home models are now commonly available on less costly home equipment as well.

Dialing options. *Pulse phones*, which generate electrical clicks or pulses to signal the numbers you dial, come in two styles: the old-fashioned rotary phone, which you operate by rotating a dial, and the

*In 1988, the average telephone cost under $35, according to a report in *Consumer Reports* (January 1989, Consumers Union, Mount Vernon, NY).
**Money*, July 1989, Time Inc., New York, NY.

newer pushbutton models. *Tone phones,* which create different musical tones when you dial, come only in the pushbutton style. Tone dialing is faster than pulse dialing, and it is an essential feature if you want to use a long-distance company other than AT&T Communications (except if you reside in an "equal access" area—see page 257), or if you want to connect with "bank-by-phone" or other computer services.

Tone dialing requires Touch-Tone®* service, which is not available in all areas and which costs more than standard pulse service. There are two ways to avoid the additional monthly service fee charged for a Touch-Tone line.

☐ A **switchable pulse/tone phone** lets you dial a long-distance company or computer via your pulse line and then switch the phone to tone to complete the call.

☐ A **Touch-Tone adapter** is a separate device that is held up to the phone's mouthpiece or screwed on in place of the mouthpiece; once you have made your connection via pulse, you "dial" the adapter to generate the tone sounds.

Remember that many pushbutton phones are actually pulse dialers. If you want a tone phone: (1) Look for the phrase "Touch-Tone" or "true tone" on the phone's brochure or carton; (2) Listen for the musical tones as you dial; or (3) Look at the Federal Communications Commission (FCC) registration number on the bottom or back of the phone. A number ending in "T" indicates tone dialing; "E" indicates the capability of both tone and pulse dialing.

Other popular dialing options include the following:
- A **rapid dial pulse phone** dials twice as fast as the standard pulse model. Check with your phone company before buying this feature to make sure it will work in your service area.
- **On-hook dialing** lets you dial without picking up the handset.
- **Automatic or last-number redial** automatically redials the last number you punched in; some models will keep trying a busy number until the call goes through.
- **Memory or speed dialing** lets you program in emergency phone numbers or numbers you frequently call; these numbers may then be dialed at the touch of one or two buttons. With some models, you must press a "Memory" button and then punch in the programmed code, using the regular dialing pushbuttons. On *one-touch-dialing* phones, you simply press the assigned number on a separate keypad. The number of possible stored numbers may range all the way from 9 to 200.

When considering a phone with the memory dialing feature, make sure it has the capacity to handle all the digits you normally dial, including, for example, your long-distance carrier's phone number plus

*Touch-Tone is a registered service mark of AT&T.

your long-distance access code and the area code and number of the parties you call. You might also look for these additional memory dialing features: a *"Pause"* button, which allows you to insert a few seconds of silence in a programmed number to give a long-distance company or a computer time to respond; *alphanumeric memory*, which lets you dial by calling up a preprogrammed personal name on a digital display; and/or a *battery backup*, which preserves the phone's programmed memory in the event of an interruption of electrical power.

- **Voice dialing**, available on a few newer models, lets you dial your phone simply by speaking the previously entered name of the party you are calling. Quality and ease of use of these phones varies from model to model. Be sure to give a voice dialer a good tryout in the store, and carefully check the warranty and return policy before making your purchase. Voice dialers may cost five or six times as much as conventional phones.

Speakerphones. A speakerphone allows you to dial and carry on a conversation without lifting the handset; a microphone built into the phone picks up your words and a loudspeaker transmits the caller's voice. On some speakerphone models, your voice may sound distant or tinny to the caller. Also, carrying on a conversation over this type of phone can be awkward—each party has to wait for the other to pause completely before speaking. Again, it's important to give the phone a thorough tryout before you buy.

Keyset or multiline phones. Multiline phones can handle two or more phone lines, enabling you to switch between calls or to set up a conference call among yourself and two callers. Some models have a *call waiting* feature, which "beeps" when you are on the phone and another caller wants to break in.

Plus these additional performance and convenience features:

- A **digital display or readout** can show the number you dialed, how long you've been talking, or the time of day.
- A **ringer selector** lets you adjust the volume of the phone's ring or turn it off completely; when the ring is switched off, some models will alert you to incoming calls with a blinking light.
- An **intercom** lets you talk to someone else in your home over an extension phone.
- A **mute** or **privacy** button lets you talk to someone in the room without the person on the phone overhearing; you must keep pressing the button to keep the mute feature on.
- A **hold** button does the same thing but lets you walk away from the phone; it may also beep periodically to let the caller know you are still connected.

- A **flash** or **cancel** button terminates dialing or cuts the connection.
- **Lighted keys** can be handy when you are dialing in the dark.

TIPS FOR TELEPHONE SHOPPERS

1. **Before you buy a phone, ask to try it out in the store.** Make sure you can live with the sound of its "ring"—phones may beep, chirp, or ring like a bell—and that it rings loud enough to be heard over household noise. Phone a friend to check out the volume and clarity of voices at both ends of the line; listen particularly for static, echoes, or a tinny quality to sound. Make sure the pushbuttons or dial operate smoothly, and examine the phone's look and feel. Does it seem to be solidly constructed? Is the body smooth and well finished, with cushions on the bottom? Is the handset comfortable to hold and to cradle between shoulder and ear? If you wear a hearing aid, be sure to try out the phone with your hearing aid in place. According to FCC regulations, the hearing aid compatibility of all new phones must be noted in a conspicuous place on the outside of the box or package.

2. **Make sure your sole phone or the "main" phone that gets the most use in your home is well constructed and reliable, and that it is designed to work even during a power failure.** A somewhat less sturdy and less costly model with fewer convenience features may serve you well as an extension phone.

3. **Look for a phone with a modular cord, which can be easily replaced, rather than a permanently wired cord.** If a permanently wired cord breaks, the whole phone must be brought in for repairs.

4. **Be sure to check out the retailer before you make your purchase, through a phone call to the local Better Business Bureau.**

5. **Compare warranties and service policies before you buy.** Phone warranties generally cover from one to five years, depending on the manufacturer. With a *full warranty*, a defective phone must be repaired or replaced free of charge or your purchase price must be refunded. If the phone is covered by a *limited warranty*, be sure to read the fine print for answers to these questions: Does the warranty cover both parts and labor? Are service and replacement parts available locally, or must you send the phone back to the factory for repairs? (This question is particularly important if you are buying a nonstandard "novelty" phone, such as a designer or cartoon-character model; replacement parts and service can be difficult to obtain for some of these.) Who pays the costs of shipping? How long do repairs take and will you be provided with a "loaner" phone in the meantime? After the warranty expires, are repair costs based on a flat charge or on repair time? Is there a minimum repair charge?

6. **If you are leasing your phone and decide to buy a new one, return your old phone to your telephone service center and make sure the**

phone company stops the monthly leasing charges. Then call your local phone company before connecting your new equipment. When you call, you will be asked for two numbers that are usually printed on the bottom or back of the phone: the *FCC registration number*, which certifies that the phone will not damage the telephone network, and the *ringer equivalency number*, which indicates how much electrical power the phone requires. If you install too many phones on the same line, they may ring softly or not ring at all. The phone company can help you determine the maximum number of phones your line will bear.

7. **Special telephone equipment is available for persons with hearing, speech, vision, or motion impairments.** These **assistive devices**, some of which may be offered free of charge, include amplifier handsets for persons with hearing and speech impairments, "hands-free" dialers for persons with severe motion impairment, and computer-generated synthesized voice systems for deaf persons. In some states, assistive devices are available through the local phone company; in other areas, your source is the AT&T National Special Needs Center (NSNC). For information, contact your phone company, your public service utility commission, NSNC (800–233–1222), or the Electronic Industries Association's Assistive Devices Division (202–457–8719). You may also want to contact the Tele-Consumer Hotline, operated by the Telecommunications Research & Action Center and the Consumer Federation of America, at 800–332–1124 (483–4100 in Washington, DC) for a free copy of the fact sheet "Special Needs," which covers, among other topics, the special exemptions on phone service for which customers with disabilities may qualify.

8. **Other fact sheets** available from the Tele-Consumer Hotline cover how to choose a telephone and a long-distance company and what to do when your phone doesn't work. Another helpful publication, *How to Buy a Telephone*, is available from the Electronic Industries Association. Write: EIA, Telephone, P.O. Box 19100, Washington, DC 20036.

CORDLESS PHONES

Cordless phones are made up of two main components: a **base station**, which plugs into any standard phone line and an AC electrical outlet, and a battery-powered portable **handset.** These two components operate like two-way radios, sending signals back and forth to dial a call, trigger the ringer, and relay conversations. Calls are transmitted via low-level broadcast signals.

Following their introduction in the 1970s, cordless phones experienced numerous problems: poor connections, limited range, interference from the neighbor's phone, and even the possibility of phone "pirates" tuning in on a cordless phone owner's channel to make unauthorized free calls. However, improvements in the phones themselves, along with an increase in the number of channels allotted by the FCC for cordless phone operations, have reduced or eliminated many of these problems. And with prices ranging from about $50 to $300, increasing numbers of consumers are cashing in on the convenience of a hand-held phone that lets them chat with friends while roaming about the house or yard.

As is true with nearly all products, the quality of different models of cordless phones varies, and so do the variety and usefulness of available features. The following overview of the cordless phones on the market today can help you shop wisely for a product that should deliver satisfactory performance and the features that suit your needs.

Channel selection and security. Some cordless phones operate on only one built-in channel. That can be a problem if your neighbor's phone operates on the same channel—your phone may ring in error, you may encounter interference or eavesdropping on the line, and you may even be unable to use your phone when the channel is tied up. Possible solutions to the problem include asking your dealer to change your phone's channel or exchanging your phone for one that operates on a different preset channel. Alternatively, you might buy a *multichannel* or *channel-switching* phone, which lets you select the channel yourself; different models give you the option of selecting from among 2 to all 10 channels. For additional protection, you might buy a phone with one of the following security features:

- **Lockout security** and **guard tones** prevent another cordless phone user from dialing into your base station and placing unauthorized calls when your handset is in the base station.

- **Digital coding** prevents unauthorized access by means of a coded signal that is transmitted from your handset to the base station. Some models come with one built-in security code, while others let you select from among hundreds or thousands of possible codes.

Range. *Short-range* cordless phones may only operate up to 100 feet away from the base station; *long-range* phones may cover up to 1,000 feet. A phone's range for ringing and for conversation can differ; that is, the phone may ring for an incoming call at a certain range but be unable to transmit conversation at that distance from the base station, or vice versa. Also, actual range is affected by materials inside the building, electrical and electronic interference both inside and out, the area's terrain, and other factors. In general, a range of 500 to 1,000 feet should be perfectly adequate for most settings.

Battery chargers. The nickel-cadmium batteries in a cordless phone's portable handset must be periodically recharged by placing the handset on the base station. Some models, with a *portable charger*, let you recharge the batteries without returning to the base station, a convenience that gives you the option of storing the base station in an out-of-the-way spot. After prolonged use, cordless phone batteries may have to be replaced; most models have a "low battery" indicator to alert you to the need. Look for a phone with easily changed batteries rather than one that will require you to take the entire unit to the retailer or repair shop for battery replacement.

Antennas. Most cordless phones have a collapsible metal antenna, which may be susceptible to breakage. Some newer models have a rubber antenna or an antenna completely enclosed in the handset. Look for a model with an antenna you can replace yourself rather than one that requires servicing of the entire handset if the antenna breaks.

Plus these extras. Most of the convenience features popular on conventional corded phones are also found on various cordless models. As always, the general rule is that price climbs along with the number of available performance and/or convenience features. Cordless phone features may include:

- **Pulse/tone switching**
- **Rapid dial pulse**   (see page 325)
- **Automatic or last-number redial**
- **Memory or speed dialing**
- **Speakerphone capability**
- **Multiline capability**   (see page 326)
- A **ringer selector**
- An **intercom** between the handset and base station
- **Mute, hold**, and **flash** buttons
- **Originate/answer** or **base-mounted keypad**, which lets you dial out without the handset
- **Paging**, which allows you to "beep" the handset user from the base station
- **Two-way paging**, which also allows you to page from base station to handset

And these tips. Following are a few shopping and usage tips and precautions specifically related to cordless phones:

1. If you are considering buying a cordless model for use as your main or only phone, look for a phone designed to remain operational during power outages.
2. Follow the recommendations on shopping for conventional corded telephones given on pages 327–28. As you try out different models in the store, pay particular attention to the quality of speech you hear, and ask your phone partner about the sound on the other end of the line.
3. For optimum range and sound quality, install your cordless phone close to a window and extend the antenna fully during use.

4. Even with a multichannel phone, there is the possibility of someone listening in on your conversations by means of another cordless phone or a walkie-talkie. Therefore it is a wise precaution to avoid divulging confidential information over a cordless phone.

CELLULAR PHONES

Thanks to technological advances and mass-market production, the cellular phone is no longer a luxury available only to the wealthy or to the top business executive. Today, with prices for some cellular phone equipment starting as low as $150, more than a million Americans are placing calls to home and office from behind the wheel. If you are thinking of investing in cellular phone equipment, here are some of the options you will want to consider.

Mobile, portable, and transportable models. Mobile cellular units, the least expensive variety, are permanently installed in your car. Transportable models are powered either by your car's battery or by the battery in a specially designed shoulder bag. Portables contain a rechargeable battery and are small and light enough to fit into a briefcase or even a shirt pocket. When choosing among these three types of cellular phones, consider your budget and intended use. Is a model designed just for the car enough, or do you need a more versatile phone companion? If you are going to carry the phone with you, consider its weight—five pounds can be a remarkably heavy burden over the long haul. If you are looking at portable models, also take into account the amount of conversation time the battery allows between rechargings; that period can vary from thirty minutes to two hours or more.

Cellular carriers. When you place a call from your mobile phone, it is transmitted by means of radio signals to one of the many receivers placed in varying parts, or "cells," of major metropolitan areas. The receiver passes along your call to another cellular system or over the regular phone lines to a home phone. As you drive, your call is transferred from one cell to another; in general, the more receivers in an area, the better the reception.

The FCC permits only two cellular carriers in a given service area. You must sign up with one of these carriers in order to be able to place and receive calls; the company you select will assign you a cellular phone number, usually for a small registration fee. When making your choice, ask about the number and density of each company's receivers, the extent of its service area, and whether there are plans to expand coverage. Also ask friends and business associates who own cellular phones about their experience with a carrier's service. Finally, compare service fees and user charges. Most cellular carriers charge a monthly service fee plus a per-minute charge for all calls placed or received.

Features and fancies. A variety of performance and convenience features are available on cellular phones, some similar to the features on conventional phones and some specific to cellular units. Features may include:

- **Automatic or last-number redial** (see page 325)
- **Memory or speed dialing** (see page 325)
- **Voice dialing** (see page 326)
- **Speakerphone capability** (allows hands-free answering) (see page 326)
- **Lighted keys** (see page 327)
- **Hookups for facsimile and answering machines**
- **Multiple number capacity** (allows you to register two or more cellular phone numbers with different carriers, so you can place and receive calls in frequently traveled areas outside your primary service area)

Before you buy. It's a good idea to try out a cellular phone before buying one. Most dealers will lease phones for a short period, or if you are planning to rent a car, you might request one equipped with a mobile phone. Don't forget to ask about the warranty before making your purchase; be sure you understand exactly what it covers and for how long. Finally, phone the local Better Business Bureau for reliability reports on both the retailer and the cellular carrier.

Television Sets

[Also see *Audio and Video Equipment*, pages 29–30.]

In keeping with the "electronification" of America, the old-fashioned television box with its simple knobs and dials that once brought Milton Berle and Rin Tin Tin into the family room has changed. TV sets are available today in a variety of sizes and with a hodgepodge of features certain to bewilder the casual shopper. Prices range all the way from about $50 for small, simple, black-and-white sets to $4,000 or more for mammoth "big-screen" models, with the most commonly purchased 25- to 27-inch consoles starting at about $400.

What, besides a bigger screen, does a higher price tag bring you? As is often the case with consumer electronic equipment, the answer is features, features, and more features—some which may add considerably to your viewing pleasure and convenience and others which you might just as easily (and economically) live without. The following stroll down the aisles of the TV retailer's domain can help you sort out the available options, interpret the promotional jargon, and draw up a basic buying blueprint before you begin to shop.

TV SET FACTS AND FEATURES

Screen size* and picture quality. There are three major categories of TV sets: miniature, tabletop, and big-screen models.

- **Miniature TVs,** designed to fit into a briefcase, purse, or jacket pocket, may have a screen as small as two to five inches. These tiny entertainers usually run on AA batteries and come in both black-and-white and color varieties. The picture of even the best miniature sets cannot compare to that of a regular TV, and that picture becomes even less distinct when viewed in bright light or at an angle. Even so, the price of these portable models can run as high as $600.

- **Tabletop and console TVs** come in several different sizes; most common are 10-inch, 12-inch, 19- to 20-inch, and 25- to 27-inch models. In general, the larger the set's screen, the steeper its price; also, color sets cost considerably more than black-and-white models. Nearly all modern midsize and full-size TV sets can deliver a picture of respectable quality, although the better sets offer optimum *clarity* (sharp, crisp image), *contrast* (sharp blacks and whites, even in a brightly lit viewing room), and *color fidelity* (realistic color tones).

*TV picture screen size is always measured diagonally, from corner to corner.

When choosing the size of your tabletop or console TV, consider the dimensions of your viewing room and how close to the TV you customarily sit. If your room is very large or you want to duplicate the movie theater experience, you may want to consider the next category of sets.

- **Big-screen and projection TVs** match a big picture with a big price— about $1,000 to $4,000 or more. Big-screen TVs typically come in 30–, 32–, 35–, 40–, 50–, and 52–inch sizes. *Rear-projection* sets look like conventional TVs; *front-projection* models may come as two-piece units, with a separate screen, or may project onto a wall or roller screen.

Picture enhancements. Here are the terms you'll encounter in the ads or on the sales floor relating to improved picture quality:

- **A black-matrix or dark picture tube** reflects less room light, improving the contrast in bright-light viewing conditions.

- **High-resolution monitors** produce a sharper, clearer picture. In general terms, *resolution* is a measure of the number of lines on the picture tube that the set can display; the more lines, the sharper the picture. However, there is a limit to the amount of picture detail that most home video formats can reproduce, and most modern TV sets far exceed that limit. A standard VHS videocassette recorder, for example, may be able to resolve only about 260 lines. All other factors being equal, when you play a tape through that VCR, a TV with 500 lines of resolution will produce just as sharp a picture as a high-resolution model capable of reproducing 700 lines.

- **Improved-definition TV** (not to be confused with *high-definition TV*, a technological improvement yet to take root in this country) doubles the number of horizontal lines shown at one time on the screen, making for a smoother, line-free picture, particularly at closer viewing range.

Stereo sound. A stereo-capable TV set may have its own stereo speakers or may be connected to your home stereo system or loudspeakers, enabling you to receive stereo TV broadcasts or to enjoy stereo sound in videotapes played through your VCR. The improved sound quality of stereo TV generally carries over even into single-channel broadcasts.

Stereo TV sets contain built-in MTS (multichannel television sound), a stereo decoder, and at least two speakers. If your TV has an MTS adapter jack, you can install stereo capability by hooking up an optional stereo decoder.

Stereo TVs are capable of receiving a third channel called *SAP* (Separate Audio Program), which many stations in areas with large ethnic populations use for bilingual broadcasts. SAP-only models are also available; these allow you to choose between the regular monaural audio and the SAP audio signal.

Channel tuning. The traditional click-stop channel selector knob is found only on less expensive TVs today. More common is the *electronic tuner*—buttons or a touchpad that allows you to punch in a channel number (*direct access*) or scan up and down the band until you zero in on the channel you want. Some TV sets come with a certain number of channels preset at the factory; changing the preset channels can be a tedious process involving adjustments of tiny wheels or buttons. The number of channels you can receive without having to reset the tuner varies from model to model, from as few as 12 to as many as 180 for cable TV subscribers. *Quartz tuners* simplify the process of resetting the tuner by allowing you to touch a keypad to lock in channels within your viewing area.

Cable-compatible. Most large TV sets are equipped with a *coaxial cable jack* for connecting the set to the cable company's wires. Modern TV sets equipped with electronic tuners are usually capable of *direct tuning* of cable TV channels, as long as those channels are not "scrambled" by the cable operator. To receive scrambled programming, or if your TV is not equipped with direct cable tuning, you will need a set-top converter/decoder provided by the cable company. Once installed on most TV models, that converter/decoder becomes your channel tuner—you can no longer use your remote control to change channels, although it will still perform other functions such as on/off, sound level control, etc. TV sets with two antenna inputs allow you to retain full remote control; some other models achieve the same end by giving you the option of installing an optional signal-splitter.

Remote control. A remote-control device is standard equipment on most TV sets today; however the number of functions you can perform via remote varies from model to model. Better-equipped remotes let you not only turn the TV on and off, change the channels, and adjust the volume but adjust the picture and sound quality as well and perform a variety of other tasks. Some offer a "menu" of *on-screen graphic readouts* to guide you in adjusting color, contrast, tint, tone, and many other functions. A *unified remote* lets you control both TV and VCR with a single device.

As you shop, look for a remote with easy-to-read, well-spaced controls that will give you convenient control over the functions you perform most frequently.

Component TV systems. A TV set is actually an enclosed package of components, including the monitor or monitor/receiver, tuner/amplifier, and speakers. It's possible to purchase these components separately, much as you purchase the separate elements of a high-fidelity stereo system. A component TV system is "expandable"—you can add extra components such as a stereo VCR, personal computer, or videodisc player. However, a component system typically is more expensive than a conventional TV set, and you generally can duplicate the better sound and increased flexibility it offers by purchasing a high-quality stereo-capable TV with adequate input and output jacks for connecting other home entertainment components.

Warranties. TV set warranties usually extend from one to two years but vary from model to model. There is often a different, longer warranty period for the picture tube than for other parts.

Plus these extras. You may want to look for one or more of the following performance and convenience features, commonly available on midpriced to higher-priced TV sets:

- **On-screen displays** can show you the channel you are watching, the time of day, or other data.

- **Automatic color control** corrects variations in color accuracy at the touch of a button.

- **Last-channel recall** lets you automatically switch back and forth between two channels.

- **Channel block-out** lets you censor your family's TV viewing by preventing access to certain channels.

- **Picture-in-picture (PIP)** displays a small, inset picture anywhere you choose on the screen, so you can keep an eye on the ball game while watching the news.

- **RGB (red-green-blue) inputs** improve picture quality when you use your color TV set as a computer monitor.

- **Headphone jacks** let you tune in while tuning others out.

Toys

Play is a child's work, providing opportunities for physical, mental, social, and emotional growth. Toys are the tools that children use in play. Both friend and teacher, properly chosen toys help the child develop skills and confidence and provide an atmosphere for self-expression and creativity.

Selecting the "right" toy for a particular child involves a consideration of these criteria:

- Appeal and interest to the child
- Suitability to the child's physical capabilities
- Appropriateness to the child's mental and social development
- Safe, durable construction

The following tips from the Consumer Product Safety Commission (CPSC) can help you select toys suitable for the abilities and interests of children in various age groups. Remember, though, that these are simply brief, general guidelines. No two children are exactly alike in their time schedule of developing skills and interests, and no rule of thumb can adequately substitute for personal study and knowledge of a child's individual likes and dislikes, limitations and abilities.

TOY SELECTION GUIDE

From birth to 6 months, infants use toys primarily for looking, listening, sucking, and fingering. They like bright primary colors, simple designs, clear lines, and human-face features. Toys for watching are more appealing if they move and make noise (but movement should be slow and noise not too loud or sudden). Toys for holding should be light and easily graspable.

From 7 to 12 months, babies are capable of longer and more extensive exploration of toys. They like to bang, twist, drop, shake, bite, throw, open and shut, and empty and fill. Infants 10 to 12 months begin to master objects—to stack boxes, nest cups, push balls and cars, operate levers. Objects that appear and disappear, bright two- or three-piece "pre-puzzles," and picture books are favorites.

For 1-year-olds, action toys that produce movement or sound by the child's own efforts are a good choice. In play, the child is always on the move; running and climbing tend to dominate over exploring objects or constructing. Toys to satisfy this need include stable ride-ons propelled by pushing with the feet, push-and-pull toys, low climbing structures, and crawl-through tunnels. The child also enjoys small, light building blocks, simple stacking toys, and shape sorters.

For 2–year-olds, who love physical, active play, look for action toys that produce movement or sound by the child's own efforts and realistic-looking toys with working parts. You might satisfy the child's growing interest in pretend play with realistic dolls, stuffed animals, and hand puppets. Other favorites include familiar, realistic scenes (garages, airports, farms) and toy vehicles with moving parts and removable figures and accessories.

From 3 to 5 years, children are interested in dramatic and pretend play, with all sorts of props, including dolls and accessories, puppets, and dress-up costumes and equipment (cooking and housekeeping equipment, doctor's kits). Good construction toys include interlocking blocks and building systems. Dominoes and simple board games can aid in learning; so can simple electronic and teaching toys for shapes, colors, numbers, and letters.

From 6 to 9 years, children begin to show increasing variations in their interests and abilities. They are able to use reading, writing, and simple arithmetic in playing with games and toys. The child can perform simple sewing, weaving, braiding, and ceramics, and follow simple directions in science, craft, and model kits. Interest is high in the line between fantasy and reality (magic tricks and disguise kits) and in toy "collections."

From 9 to 12 years, there is a great variety in individual abilities and interests. The child may be interested in reading, science, computers, hobbies, crafts, building models, collections, specific arts and crafts, and athletics and/or competitive sports.

SAFETY AND AGE LABELS

U.S. hospital emergency rooms treated 113,000 children for toy-related injuries in 1986. Clearly, safety should be a major consideration in the selection of toys.

CPSC mandatory safety regulations require toys to meet the following standards:

Toys for All Ages

- No shock or thermal hazards
- Lead content severely limited
- No toxic materials

Toys for Children Under Age Three

- Unbreakable—will withstand use and abuse
- No small parts or pieces that could become lodged in the throat

• Rattles large enough not to present a choking hazard; will not separate into small pieces

Toys for Children Under Age Eight

• No heating elements in electrically operated toys
• No sharp points or edges

Nearly all American toy manufacturers also adhere to a voluntary product safety standard developed by the Toy Manufacturers of America (TMA), the industry trade association. You may find notification of adherence to this voluntary standard on a product package or label. The TMA Safety Standard, known as ASTM F:963, requires manufacturers to:

• Put age and safety labels on toys
• Put warning labels on crib gyms advising that they be removed when the baby can get up on hands and knees
• Make squeeze toys and teethers large enough to prevent a choking hazard
• Ensure that the lid of a toy chest will stay open in any position
• Make strings on crib and playpen toys no longer than 12 inches to prevent a danger of strangulation

But regulations and standards are only the beginning. Safety depends on parental care in selecting toys, and proper supervision once the toy is in the home. Parents and others responsible for a child's care should follow this checklist of safety suggestions from the Toy Manufacturers of America and the CPSC:

☐ Read age and safety labels on toys.
☐ Look for the words "nontoxic" on painted toys, "flame retardant" or "flame resistant" on fabrics, "machine/surface washable" on stuffed and cloth toys, and "UL (Underwriters Laboratory) Approved" on electrical playthings.
☐ Check for sturdy, securely fastened features on stuffed animals and cloth dolls.
☐ Make sure rubber rattles, squeakers, and teething toys are too large, even in their most compressed state, to fit into a baby's mouth.
☐ On arrows and darts, look for securely attached tips made of rubber, cork, or other protective material or flexible plastic suction cup tips.
☐ Always remove and immediately discard all plastic wrapping before giving a toy to a child (especially a baby or toddler).
☐ Read all instructions and make sure the child understands how a toy is to be used and any possible dangers that might result from misuse.
☐ Store toys safely. Teach children to put toys away so they aren't tripping hazards, and periodically check toy boxes and shelves for

safety. Keep toys intended for older children out of the reach of younger siblings.

☐ Periodically spot-check toys for minor damage and potential hazards and immediately repair or discard damaged toys.

TIPS ON TOYS

Finally, keep in mind these recommendations and precautions from the CPSC and the Toy Manufacturers of America when selecting toys:

1. Playing with a child is the best way to learn about his or her interests, abilities, and level of development.

2. If you are choosing a toy for someone else's child, consult the parents. This can help you avoid giving a toy the child already has or one that's inappropriate because of space limitations, and it almost guarantees a selection suitable to the child's interests and capabilities.

3. Whenever possible, involve the child in the selection and purchase of toys.

4. Determine a buying plan and budget before you step into a toy store. Don't forget to factor in the costs of accessories, replacement parts, and batteries. Also ask yourself whether the toy has *repeat* play value and whether it is durable enough to pass on from child to child.

5. Resist the urge to buy a toy labeled for an older child, even if you think your child is smarter or more advanced than the "average" child. Remember that age labels are based on physical, mental, and developmental needs as well as safety considerations. A toy that is too advanced will simply frustrate your child, and it may pose a safety hazard.

6. For information on toy safety or for a free copy of *Which Toy for Which Child*, a booklet containing comprehensive information on the functions of toys and which types are appropriate for which ages, contact the U.S. Consumer Product Safety Commission, Washington, DC 20207, 800–638–CPSC. The Toy Manufacturers of America also publishes a free booklet, *The ABC's of Toys & Play*, with information on proper toy selection, safety, and age labels on toy packages. To order, send a postcard to: Toy Booklet, P.O. Box 866, Madison Square Station, New York, NY 10159.

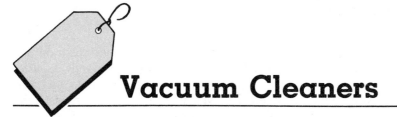

Vacuum Cleaners

[Also see *Appliances*, pages 25–28.]

There are three basic styles of vacuum cleaners, each with its own advantages and shortcomings.

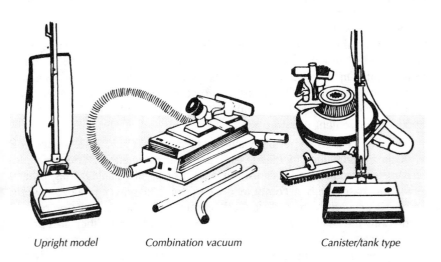

Upright model   *Combination vacuum*   *Canister/tank type*

Upright models, currently the most popular style of vacuum cleaner in the U.S., are specifically designed for cleaning rugs and carpets. Revolving beating brushes or bars in these units "agitate" the carpet surface, loosening dirt and dust lodged in the nap. Mild suction then carries the loosened dirt into the dust bag. Uprights are far less effective than canisters on uncarpeted surfaces; some models, in fact, can damage bare floors. A few machines address that problem by allowing you to switch off the beater brushes for bare-floor cleaning. In most cases, however, to clean uncarpeted surfaces with an upright, you'll have to use separate tools, which are usually sold as optional attachments. Hooking up those accessories can be troublesome. And even fitted with hoses and tools, an upright is likely to be less effective at bare-floor and above-the-floor cleaning than a canister model, largely because of its milder suction.

Canister vacuum cleaners do their job by means of strong suction produced by a motor-driven fan contained in the tank, or canister. These machines excel at bare-floor cleaning and above-the-floor dusting. They generally come equipped with several attachments, which may be

341

storable in the canister top. Those attachments typically include a dusting brush; crevice, upholstery, and floor tools; and two steel wands. Canister vacuum cleaners are usually somewhat lighter and easier to use than uprights; you simply push the lightweight wands and tools while the canister tags along behind you. They're also better at balancing on stairs and getting into tight corners and under furniture. However, while canisters may perform satisfactorily on dense, low-pile carpet surfaces, they are far less effective than uprights at removing soil embedded in medium- or deep-pile carpets and rugs.

Combination canister and power-nozzle vacuum cleaners mate the upright and canister designs. The basic style is that of the canister model, but the addition of a powered rug nozzle equipped with beater bars or brushes makes this style of vacuum cleaner suitable for both carpet and bare-floor cleaning. On some models, in order to clean bare surfaces, you have to disconnect the power nozzle and replace it with a floor attachment. On other units, you simply switch off the beater brushes for suction-only cleaning. Like canisters, combination models are better than uprights at reaching under furniture; some models, however, may be too wide for convenient use on stairs.

Deciding which type of vacuum cleaner to buy is a matter of evaluating your cleaning needs and personal preferences. Some people buy both an upright and a canister model, to suit all cleaning tasks; others cover the bases with a combination canister and power nozzle. If your home is covered in wall-to-wall carpet or, conversely, in mostly hardwood, tile, and low-pile rugs, you may decide that either an upright or a canister model alone will do the job. In any case, once you have made your choice among the three basic styles, the shopping guidelines below can help you find a model with the performance and convenience features that suit your needs and budget.

SHOPPER'S CHECKLIST

Plan to invest a few hours in trying out several different vacuum cleaner styles and models in the store. Test the cleaners on both carpeted and bare surfaces, and be sure to try out all the separate attachments. Bring along your own sample "debris" typical of the types of cleaning problems you encounter at home, whether that includes lint, dog hairs, or ground-up cereal. How easily does each model pick up dirt? Do particles stick in the brushes? Also pay attention to the width of the area cleaned in each pass of the machine; a wide swath can save you time and effort. Don't forget to run vacuum cleaners into corners, along walls, and under furniture to see how they perform in tight quarters.

Remember to choose your dealer as carefully as you choose your appliance. If unfamiliar with a retailer, contact the local Better Business

Bureau for a reliability report. And if you buy a vacuum cleaner from a door-to-door salesperson, remember your rights under the three-day "cooling off" period (see page 211). Finally, keep these questions and considerations in mind as you shop:

☐ Are the vacuum cleaner's controls conveniently placed and easy to operate?

☐ Does the model come equipped with all the attachments you want? Are wands and tools sturdy, secure when attached, and easy to assemble and detach?

☐ Is the hose flexible, for convenient cleaning in tight spots?

☐ Is the cord easy to pull out, rewind, and store? Is it long enough to reach all the outlets you'll need to use in your home?

☐ Is the dust bag easy to remove and replace? Does it have adequate capacity so you won't have to change it too frequently?

☐ Can the rug nozzle be easily adjusted for carpet pile height?

☐ Is the suction of a canister or combination model adjustable, either by a multispeed motor or vent control, to allow easy cleaning of draperies or light rugs?

☐ Is motor power adjustable to allow you to increase or reduce speed and suction to suit the cleaning task?

☐ Is operating noise level acceptable?

☐ Does an upright model glide smoothly and evenly over carpeted surfaces? If equipped with a "self-propelling" feature, is it easy to maneuver? Can its beater bars or brushes be turned off to allow bare-floor cleaning?

☐ Is a combination model easy to switch from carpet to bare-floor cleaning?

☐ Does the vacuum cleaner's weight make it convenient to use and easy to transport when not in use? Does it have a carrying handle?

☐ Are the vacuum cleaner and accessories relatively convenient to store?

☐ Does the model's price fit your budget? Prices for vacuum cleaners cut a wide swath, with the least expensive uprights and canisters starting at about $60 and the upper limit for uprights and combination models hovering at about $700. As a general rule, with a budget of about $300 to $400, you should be able to buy an efficient and convenient vacuum cleaner for moderate to heavy usage. If your cleaning needs are more modest, you might expect to spend about $100 for either a basic upright or canister alone, or $300 for a combination power-nozzle canister.

Videocassette Recorders

[Also see *Audio and Video Equipment*, pages 29–30; *Camcorders*, pages 65–68.]

Approximately 68 percent of all U.S. households have at least one VCR, according to the Electronic Industries Association. These button-studded metal boxes bring sophisticated technology to the fingertips of TV viewers across the land, enabling them to virtually write their own programming schedule: to "time-shift," or tape a show for viewing at a more convenient hour; to fast-forward through commercials and pledge breaks; to gather the family around the TV set to enjoy rented movies in the comfort of the living room. Along with the pleasures of this home video revolution comes a new terminology, a nomenclature of electronics that can baffle shoppers trying to select among the wide variety of VCRs available today. To make a wise choice, you'll need to understand some of these terms and decide which features are appropriate for your personal viewing habits.

VCR FACTS AND FEATURES

Price. VCR prices may run anywhere from $200 to $1,500 or more. At the upper end of the scale, you will find models equipped with S–VHS, for greatly enhanced picture quality; hi-fi sound, for superior sound clarity and accuracy; and a number of convenience features of varying usefulness. At the lower end, you'll find that most models deliver a good picture and have the basic features needed to record and play back. The major differences among low- and mid-priced models are ease and versatility of programming, ease of channel selection, number and variety of convenience extras, and reliability. The following synopsis of major features can help you pinpoint your needs and shop for the model that offers the best price on the features you require. You may also want to review the repair history of various brands, as compiled by *Consumer Reports* magazine,* for guidance in selecting a brand that has proven reliable.

    Format. VCRs are available in four basic formats: Beta, VHS, S–VHS, and 8mm. Each of these formats is incompatible with the others; you cannot play a tape recorded in VHS on a Beta machine, for example.

Consumer Reports, March 1989, Consumers Union, Mount Vernon, NY.

☐ The Betamax or *Beta* format, used in the first VCRs introduced to the U.S. consumer market, has dwindled in popularity to the point where today many rental tapes simply are not available in Beta. If you use your VCR primarily to record and play back TV programs or to view tapes created with your Beta camcorder, a Beta machine may suit your needs. Beta offers somewhat better picture quality than VHS.

☐ The *VHS* (Video Home System) format has been responsible for Beta's near-demise; most VCRs and camcorders sold today use the VHS format.

☐ A relatively new format, Super VHS, or *S–VHS,* offers improved picture quality. You won't be able to enjoy that sharper picture, however, unless your TV set is equipped with a special S–VHS (y/c) connector and you play tapes recorded in S–VHS. Although those tapes may include your own creations filmed with an S–VHS camcorder, very few rental tapes are available at this point. S–VHS VCRs typically cost several hundred dollars more than VHS models.

☐ The *8mm* (eight-millimeter) format uses very small tape cassettes and allows longer recording time than the VHS or Beta formats. An 8mm VCR may suit you if you mainly watch your own video creations or taped TV programs but not if you like to watch prerecorded tapes, which are not yet widely available in this format.

Programmability. All VCRs can be set to automatically record a number of different TV programs or "events" over the course of several days. The number of possible programs and days varies from model to model; so does ease of programming. In making your selection, consider your intended use. Will you only occasionally record a TV program or late-night movie, or do you plan to build a video library by asking your machine to record several shows over the course of a weekend or week? Keep in mind the recording time limits of videotapes: At its slowest speed (which produces the lowest-quality picture), a VHS machine can hold only eight hours on one cassette, a Beta recorder only five hours. Also take a look at the owner's manual to determine how easy or difficult a particular model may be to program. Some VCRs offer features that can help you perform that sometimes tedious process, including, most notably, *on-screen programming,* which guides by means of prompts on the TV screen or the remote control.

Of course, if you use your VCR mainly to watch rental tapes, you needn't invest in a high-priced model with sophisticated programming capabilities.

VHS HQ or SuperBeta. HQ (high quality) is a common feature on VHS VCRs sold today; its Beta counterpart is called "SuperBeta." Both systems offer a noticeable improvement in picture quality.

Sound enhancement. Most VCRs record and play in single-channel sound. If you own an older-model television set with one speaker, that's fine. But if you have a stereo TV or the capability of hooking up your TV to your stereo system and you like to record stereo TV broadcasts or to enjoy stereo sound in rental tapes, you may want to look for one of these sound enhancement systems found in the more expensive models:

☐ **Linear stereo,** found in VHS and Beta models, offers a slight enhancement in sound but can also deliver background noise and other distortions.

☐ **Hi-fi sound,** also found in VHS and Beta, offers greater improvement in sound quality with far less distortion than linear stereo. However, it can only deliver stereo sound when playing tapes that have been recorded in stereo. To make your own stereo TV recordings, you would need a VCR equipped with hi-fi sound and MTS (multichannel TV sound) stereo reception, connected either to your home stereo system or a stereo-capable TV set.

☐ **PCM recording** employs digital technology such as that used in making compact discs (see "Analog vs. Digital Recording," *Compact Disc Players,* pages 90–91) to deliver the highest-quality stereo sound possible from a VCR. PCM is available only in 8mm models.

Search methods. To locate a particular segment on a videotape, such as the beginning of a recorded TV movie, it's possible to simply fast-forward and rewind until you zero in on the spot. That method, however, can be annoying and time-consuming, and it can wear down both the tape and the VCR. Various features available on some VCRs help reduce wear on both your patience and your machine.

☐ **High-speed search** allows you to view a speeded-up version of the picture as you scan for a particular scene. The drawback: Running the tape through the playback heads at fast speed for more than a few minutes can damage both tape and heads.

☐ **Index search** lets you automatically fast-forward to the beginning of each separately recorded program on the tape, or fast-forward to any scene that you have indexed for quick call-up.

☐ **Skip search** also fast-forwards to indexed segments, but rather than stopping when it reaches an indexed point, the VCR shows a few seconds of the scene. If you decide that's not the right segment, the machine moves on and previews the next indexed point.

☐ **Address search** lets you assign index numbers to specific taped scenes. To call up a scene, you simply punch in its number in the TV channel selector.

☐ **Real-time search** lets you locate a segment by entering its position on the tape according to recording time. If you enter "60," for example, the machine fast-forwards to the segment recorded 60 minutes into the tape.

Channel tuner. Some VCRs let you select from only 12 preset channels; bringing in more requires tedious adjustments. Others offer the convenience of either a greater number of preset channels or easy selection of any channel at all.

Number of heads. A minimum of two heads are required for video recording, but some extra functions require additional heads. The number of heads is often used as a selling point; you're better off looking at the types of performance features the machine offers.

Tape counter. The tape counter provides a numerical display that tells you how long the VCR has been playing or recording; those numbers can help you quickly locate a particular scene. Some counters display actual hours and minutes, others a slightly less helpful set of arbitrary figures. Some have a handy "time remaining" feature which tells you how much space remains available on the tape for recording.

Remote control. The remote is a basic feature on nearly all models, but the number of functions you can perform by remote control varies from model to model; so does ease of use. Look for a remote that lets you perform the tasks you'll most commonly require and has easy-to-read, adequately spaced buttons. A *unified remote* lets you control both VCR and TV with one unit.

Plus these extras. Among the more common and/or more useful of the many convenience features found on VCRs today are the following:

☐ **One touch recording** allows you to start recording at the touch of a button.

☐ **Slow motion, freeze-action,** and **frame advance** are a few of the features that let you play around with the action on the screen—freeze a quarterback in midtackle, for example, or study a golf swing.

☐ **Simulcast recording** allows you to combine a television picture and an FM radio simulcast in the same recording.

☐ **Picture-in-picture,** found in the more expensive models, lets you view two or more scenes at once, so that, for example, you can watch a prerecorded movie while keeping an eye on the local news.

☐ If you often use your camcorder to make home movies, helpful VCR features include **audio and/or video dub,** for inserting new material into an existing tape, **edit/backspace,** for smoother incorporation of that new material, and **edit switch,** for better picture quality in added material.

Videotapes. When recording your own home movies with a camcorder, you may want to look for a videotape labeled "high grade" for clearer picture and better sound; "standard" tape can be fine for recordings you don't plan to save. Be aware, though, that there is no industrywide standard for this grading terminology. Also be wary of low-priced tapes that carry no brand name; these may be so inferior in quality that they can damage the VCR.

Finally, tape heads are extremely sensitive to dust; protect your VCR with a **dustcover** when not in use.

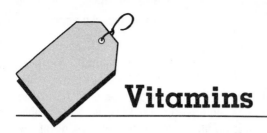

Vitamins

An estimated 4 out of 10 Americans routinely take a vitamin or mineral supplement, according to the Food and Drug Administration. Yet the debate continues among scientific panels, consumer groups, nutritionists, and vitamin makers over whether food supplements offer any health benefits to the average consumer.

ARE SUPPLEMENTS FOR YOU?

Organic compounds necessary in small amounts in the diet of all animals, including man, vitamins transform food into energy and body mainte-nance. There are 13 major vitamins: vitamin A (retinol), vitamin B_1 (thiamin), vitamin B_2, niacin, pantothenic acid, folic acid, vitamin B_6 (pyridoxine), vitamin B_{12}, biotin, vitamin C, vitamin D, vitamin E, and vitamin K. If any one of these vitamins is missing from the diet, a deficiency disease will develop.

Since vitamins are present in foods in very small quantities, extremely sensitive methods of measuring their potency or quantity have been developed. Some vitamins are measured in I.U.s (international units), an indication of biological activity; others are expressed by weight, in micrograms or milligrams. The initials "U.S. RDA" (United States Recommended Daily Allowances) were adopted by the Food and Drug Administration for use in nutritional labeling and dietary supplement programs. The RDA represents the highest amount needed of a particular vitamin, mineral, or protein. A generous safety margin is built into the determination of RDAs, which are set at levels up to 70 percent beyond the average American's needs.

In a March 1989 report, the National Research Council (the research arm of the federally chartered National Academy of Sciences) advised against the general use of dietary supplements. The report, based on a comprehensive review of studies on American nutrition and health, concluded that there was no evidence to support claims that vitamin and mineral supplements provide health benefits. A number of other organizations, scientists, and consumer groups agree, maintaining that, for most people, a balanced diet is the best source of nutrients and that dietary supplements are unnecessary for the so-called "average" eater.

On the other side of the issue, vitamin makers and a number of doctors and nutritionists assert that most Americans fail to eat a balanced diet supplying all their nutritional requirements. Dietary supplements, accord-ing to this group, are simply sound "insurance" against a nutritional deficiency. Further, some vitamin supporters point to studies that seem to indicate a health benefit from use of a specific nutrient in certain cases, such as calcium supplements for women to prevent osteoporosis or niacin to lower cholesterol levels.

There are areas of common ground as well in the vitamin debate. Most parties agree that people known to have deficient diets and those recovering from certain illnesses or nutritional deficiencies do require supplemental nutrients. And while there is disagreement on the value of vitamin and mineral supplements, nearly everyone agrees that supplements do no harm *as long as they do not exceed the RDA for any one nutrient.*

The danger arises when people self-prescribe large doses, or "megadoses," of particular nutrients. According to the National Research Council, the Department of Health and Human Services, and other authorities, the use of excessive amounts of some vitamin and mineral supplements can cause serious side effects. Excess vitamin D, for example, can cause nausea, weight loss, weakness, and the more serious conditions of hypertension (high blood pressure) and calcification of the blood vessels and kidneys.

FACTS AND MYTHS

Before deciding to take a nutritional supplement, remember that the best, most effective, and least expensive way to get the vitamins and minerals you need is to eat an adequate and reasonably varied diet. Consult your doctor before beginning a program of nutritional supplementation and *never* self-treat with doses beyond the Recommended Daily Allowances of vitamins or minerals. Finally, you may be interested in the following facts and myths about vitamins, compiled by the federal Department of Health and Human Services.

MYTH: Vitamins give you pep and energy.

FACT: Vitamins yield no calories; in and of themselves, they provide no extra pep, vitality, nor unusual levels of well-being.

MYTH: Vitamins must be taken in precisely formulated amounts and ratios to each other in order to have best effects.

FACT: Intake should be adequate but not excessive for each. No precise ratios are required.

MYTH: Organic or natural vitamins are nutritionally superior to synthetic vitamins.

FACT: Synthetic vitamins, manufactured in the laboratory, are identical to the natural vitamins found in foods. The body cannot tell the difference and gets the same benefits from either source.

Washing Machines

[For information and advice on selecting a retailer, saving on energy costs, and appliance service and service contracts, see *Appliances*, pages 25–28.]

Although washing machines come in a wide range of prices—from about $300 to $1,000 and up—nearly any model you select will do a good job of washing your clothes. The key differences among various makes and models include style, capacity, and energy efficiency.

STYLES AND SIZES

Washers come in two basic styles: top loading and front loading.

Top loading washers, the choice of most American consumers, use a central agitator to draw water through clothes. They usually come in compact, standard, and large capacities; however one manufacturer's "large capacity" may be another's "super capacity." A better point of comparison is the load size, usually given in number of pounds of clothes, for which each washer is designed. A capacity of about 10 to 12 pounds is usually considered adequate for a small family's needs; a larger family might look for a model that can handle 15 or more pounds of laundry.

Front loading washers, in which the entire wash basket revolves, require you to stoop to load and unload clothes and generally have a smaller capacity than top loaders. However, front loading washing machines use considerably less hot water—and thus less energy—than top loaders.

Compact washers range from 24 to 27 inches wide and come in both built-in and portable models, with the portables set on casters so that they can be rolled to the kitchen sink for use. Most compacts handle loads from about 5 to 10 pounds.

FACTS AND FEATURES

Wash cycles. Washing machine cycles consist of variations on a series of operations—fill, wash, rinse, and spin—which are performed automatically in sequence. The "permanent-press" cycle, for example, typically is programmed to include a slower-than-normal spin than the "regular" cycle, plus an additional cold rinse to minimize wrinkles. Most washers offer "regular," "permanent-press," and "delicate" cycles, a selection which should be adequate for most people's needs. Models with extra features may include "prewash/soak," "short," "heavy soil," "knits/woolens," and/or "extra rinse" cycles.

Controls. On most washer models, dials, pushbuttons, and levers allow you to select the basic cycle plus options such as time, water temperature, water level, and wash and spin speeds. More expensive models often include touchpad controls, which can provide greater control over selection of wash options, for example allowing you to program the washer to turn on hours later.

Temperature options. Most washers offer a choice of hot, warm, and cold washing, and warm and cold rinsing. The temperature setting you select will depend on the fabrics you are washing. Using warm or cold wash water rather than hot whenever possible can save considerably on energy costs and may prolong the life of some fabrics. Controls that allow you always to select a cold-water rinse can also mean energy savings; the temperature of the rinse water does not affect cleaning.

Water level control. Matching water level to load size saves water and energy. Washing machines are generally available with one to five water levels, and some allow "infinite" control so that you can match the amount of water used to the size of each wash load.

Wash and spin speeds. Speed controls may be built into the wash cycle, or a separate control may be provided to allow you to control wash and spin speed, so that, for example, you can reduce the action to gentle agitation for delicate fabrics or slow spin for permanent-press or delicate loads.

Dispensers. Bleach and fabric softener dispensers let you add these products at the start of the wash cycle; they are then automatically diluted and added at the proper time in the cycle. Some washers also provide a detergent dispenser system.

Lint filters. Filters keep lint from settling on clothes. Some models come with a self-cleaning filter that flushes collected lint down the drain; others require you to clean the filter manually.

☑ WASHING MACHINE CHECKLIST

Following is a checklist of factors you may want to consider when selecting a washing machine:

☐ Will the washer fit in your available space?

☐ Does it have at least three wash cycles ("regular," "permanent-press," and "delicate")?

☐ Does it have a water temperature control allowing you to select warm washes, when appropriate, and cold rinses?

☐ Does it have a water level control?

☐ Does it have a self-cleaning filter?

Watches

[Also see Jewelry, pages 239–45.]

The watches on today's market range all the way from remarkably accurate $10 digital timepieces in plastic cases to extravagantly designed jewelry items encased in precious metals and encrusted with gemstones that can cost as much as $100,000 or more. Regardless of price, though, watches fall into two general categories:

☐ **Mechanical watches.** These traditional "wind-up" watches operate by means of a mainspring inside the watch, which turns tiny interlocking wheels as it gradually unwinds; the wheels move the watch hands. *Automatic* or *self-winding* watches "wind themselves" as the wearer's wrist movements cause a weight behind the movement to rotate.

☐ **Quartz** or **electronic watches.** Powered by batteries, quartz watches are generally more accurate than mechanical watches, in part because of unique properties of the quartz crystal and in part because they have fewer moving parts and thus less friction from the interaction of parts. The watch battery sends electronic impulses through a small bar of synthetic quartz crystal, which vibrates more than 32,000 times per second. These vibrations are channeled through other watch parts to result in one impulse per second, enabling the watch to measure the second with unprecedented accuracy. Batteries generally must be replaced every 18 to 24 months. However, some batteries may last as little as 6 months if the wearer frequently uses extra features such as a game or calculator, and some are designed to last as long as 5 years.

The terms **analog** and **digital** refer to the way time is displayed on the dial. Analog watches have the traditional time-telling "hands." Digital watches display the time with digits, or numerals, which are created by either light-emitting diodes (LED) or liquid crystal displays (LCD). With an LED watch, you must push a button to light up the watch dial; these watches can be easily read in the dark but not in bright outdoor light. LCD watches show the time continuously. They cannot be read in the dark unless an extra, button-activated light source is built in. All mechanical watches are analogs; quartz watches may be either analogs or digitals.

Special feature watches perform a variety of tasks. Some tell the month, day, and year; some give the phases of the moon or the time in other countries or time zones. **Chronograph** watches measure small fractions of a second; some may be used to calculate speeds, distances, and altitudes. There are even specialized watches for astronauts, pilots, parachutists, skin divers, and the blind.

TIMELY TIPS

Watches are generally considered not only timekeepers but also fashion accessories, and their selection is largely a matter of personal taste and budget. There are simple guidelines, however, that you can follow to take much of the risk and guesswork out of purchasing a watch. The following shopping tips are provided by the American Watchmakers Institute, the national association of professionals who service timepieces, and Jewelers of America, Inc., a national trade organization of the retail jewelry industry:

1. Buy from a reliable jeweler, watchmaker, or established retailer. (See "Choosing a Jeweler," *Jewelry*, page 239.)
2. Buy a watch with a familiar trademark or one whose performance has a good reputation; beware of deceptive trademarks that sound similar to familiar brand names.
3. Avoid street peddlers or questionable mail order promotions offering huge discounts on so-called designer or "famous name" watches.
4. When purchasing a mechanical watch, other than an inexpensive fashion "throw-away" model, be sure to buy a jeweled lever movement. Watch jewels guard against wear by replacing metal with more durable materials at the contact points of constantly moving parts.
5. If the watch will be subjected to rough wear, consider a stainless steel case.
6. Before purchasing a watch, ask about the availability of replacement parts and ask for and record the name of the U.S. agent responsible for the distribution of these items. If problems arise, this agent should be able to supply the technical information and spare parts needed for service.
7. Check the warranty before you buy. What parts of the watch are covered and for how long? Will the seller perform repairs or must the watch be sent away for service?
8. Follow these tips in caring for your watch:
   - A mechanical watch should be checked regularly and serviced according to the manufacturer's recommendations.
   - Wind a mechanical watch at about the same time each day. Take off the watch before winding to avoid placing undue pressure on the stem.
   - Replace the battery in a quartz watch before it runs out; dead batteries can leak or corrode.
   - Immediately replace broken or scratched crystals. Even a hairline crack can let dust or moisture into the mechanism.
   - For a free pamphlet on watch care, send a self-addressed, stamped envelope to: Watch Care Brochure, American Watchmakers Institute, P.O. Box 11011, Cincinnati, OH 45211.

Weight Loss Promotions

So you think you need to lose a few pounds? Well, you're in good company. According to the American Dietetic Association, the professional organization of dietitians, nearly one of every three Americans is dieting. And those numbers promise to increase along with the growth of the over-40 population. The reason: People tend to put on weight as they get older, and those extra pounds can be harder to shed, due to a slower metabolism and, in many cases, a less active lifestyle.

A number of different weapons are wielded by combatants in the battle of the bulge. In their efforts to slim down, Americans try calorie counting, exercise, various "diet aid" products, and weight loss clinics. For a look at the role of calories and exercise in a weight control program, see "Cutting The Fat," *Exercise Equipment,* page 147. This chapter focuses on the concerns of people who feel that they cannot lose weight successfully on their own, and thus become customers of the diet-help industry.

ARE YOU OVERWEIGHT?

Most people who long to lose weight simply want to look and feel better; many also hope to improve their health and live longer. It's not surprising that so many Americans share these goals. Too much body fat can be both a physical and psychological burden. Further, excess body fat has been linked to health problems such as coronary heart disease, high blood pressure, osteoporosis, diabetes, arthritis, and certain forms of cancer.

Even given those facts, the question remains: Do *you* need to lose weight? The tables commonly used to judge an individual's ideal weight have come under frequent criticism from health professionals. First, they do not take into account the fact that *overweight* and *overfat* are not necessarily the same thing. People who are quite muscular may weigh more than the average for their age and height even if their body composition—the amount of fat versus lean body mass—is within a desirable range. Further, those height/weight tables, which were developed to predict longevity as it is affected by weight and thus help create standards for insurance premiums, are based mostly on studies of white, middle-class males aged 25 to 59. Thus they are not representative of the American population as a whole, and they make no allowance for the fact that people naturally tend to gain weight as they age. In fact, a debate is raging today among health care experts over the question of

DESIRABLE BODY WEIGHT RANGES

Height* (ft. & in.)	Metropolitan Life Insurance Company: 1983 Weights for Ages 25–59**		Gerontology Research Center: Weight Range for Men and Women by Age**				
	Men	Women	25	35	45	55	65
4–10	—	100–131	84–111	92–119	99–127	107–135	115–142
4–11	—	101–134	87–115	95–123	103–131	111–139	119–147
5–0	—	103–137	90–119	98–127	106–135	114–143	123–152
5–1	123–145	105–140	93–123	101–131	110–140	118–148	127–157
5–2	125–148	108–144	96–127	105–136	113–144	122–153	131–163
5–3	127–151	111–148	99–131	108–140	117–149	126–158	135–168
5–4	129–155	114–152	102–135	112–145	121–154	130–163	140–173
5–5	131–159	117–156	106–140	115–149	125–159	134–168	144–179
5–6	133–163	120–160	109–144	119–154	129–164	138–174	148–184
5–7	135–167	123–164	112–148	122–159	133–169	143–179	153–190
5–8	137–171	126–167	116–153	126–163	137–174	147–184	158–196
5–9	139–175	129–170	119–157	130–168	141–179	151–190	162–201
5–10	141–179	132–173	122–162	134–173	145–184	156–195	167–207
5–11	144–183	135–176	126–167	137–178	149–190	160–201	172–213
6–0	147–187	—	129–171	141–183	153–195	165–207	177–219
6–1	150–192	—	133–176	145–188	157–200	169–213	182–225
6–2	153–197	—	137–181	149–194	162–206	174–219	187–232
6–3	157–202	—	141–186	153–199	166–212	179–225	192–238
6–4	—	—	144–191	157–205	171–218	184–231	197–244

*Values in this table are for height without shoes and weight without clothes.
**The weight range is the lower weight for small frame and the upper weight for large frame.

whether a few extra pounds may actually be *beneficial* for older people, providing helpful energy reserves.

Despite this controversy, nearly all medical experts agree that obesity—being 20 percent or more over your ideal body weight—has a negative effect on both health and longevity. And the standard weight tables remain the reference most commonly used by doctors and health professional organizations to determine that ideal weight. Appearing above are two of those recommended weight tables: the standard height/weight table developed by the Metropolitan Life Insurance Company and a relatively new table developed by the National Institute on Aging's Gerontology Research Center to reflect the institute's recommendations regarding age-related changes in desirable weight ranges.

In referring to these tables, keep in mind that the amount of body fat you are carrying around is an even more important consideration than your total weight. A certain amount of body fat is necessary for everyone. Most experts agree that for women, about 20 percent of total weight should be made up of body fat; for men, the ideal is about 15 percent body fat. Determining how much of your weight is fat requires special tests, which can include underwater (hydrostatic) weighing, skin-fold thickness measurements, and circumference measurements. You'll need to see a doctor or dietitian to have those measurements made. But an easy test you can perform yourself is to pinch the fat folds at your waist and abdomen. (Make sure no muscle is included.) If you can pinch an inch or more, chances are you have too much body fat.

DIET PROMOTIONS

If you have decided that you really do need to lose weight but are convinced that you lack the willpower or the know-how to go it alone, a multibillion-dollar industry is eager to help. Players in that diet industry include the promoters of special "fad" diets, the makers of diet formulas and pills, and the operators of weight loss clinics. Before you decide where to invest your time, energy, and money, it is essential to carefully consider a weight loss plan's effectiveness, cost, and any potential health risks.

"Fad" Diets

The popularity of fad and novelty diets rises and falls with the position of the latest "self-help" title on the best-seller lists. These diets usually focus on one food or a limited combination of foods or other substances. Some advise eating only high-protein foods with few, if any, carbohydrates; others promote the reverse. Grapefruits, bread and butter, yogurt, and ice cream are just a few of the many "magical" foods that have been heralded over the years as the key to easy weight loss.

According to the Food and Drug Administration, any weight loss achieved through this type of diet is usually the result of a simple reduction of caloric intake, *not* of any special property of the substances consumed. Because variety in food selection is so restricted in these diets, they quickly become boring, and dropout rates are high. And because they do not emphasize lifestyle changes that can support the maintenance of a desired weight, any weight loss is likely to be temporary.

"Crash" and "Formula" Diets

Formula diets and crash diet plans are often based on a food supplement—a powdered "meal" mixed with water or skim milk, a nutritional "liquid food," an herbal blend, etc.—which is consumed either with meals or in place of some or all of the dieter's normal caloric intake. Some of these very-low-calorie diets may result in noticeable weight loss in a short time. Much of that loss, however, will be made up of water weight, and it usually will be quickly regained when normal food intake resumes.

Crash diet plans are often expensive and can be dangerous, causing serious illness or even death. They should *never* be undertaken without prior medical consultation and concurrent medical supervision. Further, like fad diet plans, crash diets are seldom helpful in promoting long-term maintenance of weight loss.

Diet Pills

Most over-the-counter diet pills and their cousins the diet gums, mints, candies, and similar concoctions, contain phenylpropanolamine (PPA), a chemical related to amphetamine, which suppresses the appetite. PPA has been labeled safe and effective by the Food and Drug Administration. However, it can cause side effects such as nervousness, dizziness, and sleeplessness. And it should not be taken by persons with high blood pressure, heart disease, diabetes, thyroid disease, or kidney disease; by pregnant or nursing women; or in combination with other medications containing PPA or with drugs prescribed for the treatment of depression.
Other "diet aids" include:

- **"Natural" bulk producers or fiber products.** Taken before meals, these pills absorb liquids, swelling in the stomach. A variation is "high-fiber bars," which are eaten between meals or with skim milk as a meal replacement. The claim for these products is that they create a feeling of fullness so that the user is satisfied eating less food. Their value in reducing weight has not been established.
- **Diuretics.** Diuretics, which rid the body of excess water by increasing the flow of water, may help some dieters shed a few pounds. However, any weight loss will be of water, not fat, and will most likely be temporary.

The precautions relating to fad and crash diet plans apply equally to diet pills and similar products. If you decide to use them, see your doctor first to rule out health risks. And be aware that even quick and dramatic weight loss is likely to be temporary—and may even be dangerous—if unaccompanied by a healthy, balanced diet and permanent changes in eating and exercise habits.

Commercial Weight Loss Clinics

From small, privately owned operations to major nationwide chains, weight loss clinics offer a variety of different plans for losing weight. Some are informal, some highly structured. Some feature group meetings, others one-on-one counseling. Some provide diet guidelines using ordinary store-bought food, while others may either encourage or require you to buy food and/or food supplements through the program. Medical and/or psychological evaluation, an exercise plan, and cooking and shopping lessons may or may not be included.

Just as the methods of diet centers vary, so do the fees they charge. Costs may include either a basic weekly fee and/or registration fee or a total up-front charge based on the number of pounds you want to lose. The total fee may cover special food and food supplements or you may have to purchase those separately. In the final analysis, a clinic's program can cost hundreds or even thousands of dollars.

Dropout and success rates vary, too, but those numbers are harder to compare, since most plans do not divulge that information. How then do you go about choosing among diet centers to find the program best suited to your needs? Following is a list of questions to ask in making that decision:

1. **Do you feel comfortable with the center's staff and its program?** Attend a meeting to evaluate the atmosphere and decide whether the center's approach—loosely structured meetings or individual counseling, diet guidelines or a "prepackaged" menu—suits your personal preferences.

2. **Is the center conveniently located to your home or work?** An out-of-the-way location can become an excuse for joining the dropouts.

3. **What are the experiences and qualifications of staff members?** Few or no restrictions apply to the use of the title "nutritionist." A registered dietitian, on the other hand, must have completed at least a bachelor's degree, an internship, or equivalent experience, and must have passed a professional qualifying exam.

4. **Are you required to see your own physician before beginning the program?** What evaluations does the center perform before and during membership? Many centers use body fat measurements, weigh-ins, and blood tests to chart members' health and progress.

5. **What will your daily caloric intake be?** Experts recommend that your daily intake remain at least 1,200 calories unless you are under a doctor's supervision.

6. **Does the plan include a specific program to help you keep off the pounds you lose?** Unless the center helps you learn healthy habits for eating and exercise and provides a means for reinforcing those long-term changes in lifestyle, chances are good that any weight loss will be temporary.

7. **What is the total cost of the program, including services and food or food supplements?** Make sure all costs and services are clearly spelled out in any contract you sign. And do not sign the contract until you have read it carefully and are certain you understand all its provisions.

Weighing Alternatives

A number of free or low-cost programs are available across the country which may offer healthful, effective alternatives to diet aids and commercial clinics. These include programs administered by community health centers, hospitals, universities, some religious organizations, and nonprofit groups such as Overeaters Anonymous. For advice on weight loss or for help in locating alternative programs in your area, contact your local or state health department, an extension agent with the U.S. Department of Agriculture, your nearest FDA office, or a local hospital or university.

Your own physician or a dietitian or psychotherapist may also be able to guide you in a safe and effective weight loss program. Be sure to check your health insurance policy to see whether it covers a medically prescribed and administered weight loss program.

FACTS ON FAT

Here are some additional tips and precautions for dieters past, present, and future:

- Significant weight loss should not be attempted without competent medical supervision. This is especially critical if the amount of weight loss desired is more than 10 percent of your total weight.

- Check with the local Better Business Bureau for reliability reports on any commercial weight loss program you are considering.

- Most studies confirm a sad fact that will come as no surprise to dieters: Keeping off the pounds you lose is just as hard as losing them in the first place. According to the American Dietetic Association, 90 percent of adult dieters later gain back the weight they lose, and only 5 percent successfully maintain their ideal weight. The most reliable and healthful way to escape that cycle is to combine dietary modification with exercise. Dieting alone can result in the loss of valuable body tissue along with the loss of fat. But decreasing your caloric input while increasing your daily physical activity can allow you to shed fat, not muscle, for the most efficient, healthful, and long-lasting weight loss.

- Research suggests that where your weight is located may be as important as how much you weigh. "Apple-shape" or "male-type" fat, which is carried in the abdomen above the waist, seems to pose more of a threat to health than "pear-shape" or "female-type" fat collected around the hips, thighs, and buttocks.

- Be on the alert for these signs of fraud in weight loss promotions:
  - ☐ Promises of immediate, effortless, and/or guaranteed weight loss.
  - ☐ Claims that any food or product can "burn off" fat.
  - ☐ Vaguely worded "testimonials" from "graduates" of the weight loss plan; testimonials should not be taken as a substitute for scientific proof of a plan's or product's effectiveness.
  - ☐ High-pressure sales tactics and one-time-only deals offered by door-to-door or telephone solicitors or by self-proclaimed health advisers who sell their product at public lectures.

Zero Coupon Bonds

State securities regulators and Better Business Bureaus are observing a disturbing trend in house, car, and furniture sales campaigns using zero coupon bonds as "free" or "bonus" traffic builders to entice customers.

"Zeros" are deeply discounted bonds that can be purchased for a fraction of their face value at maturity. For example, an investment of $40 today might buy you a bond that will be worth $1,000 in 30 years. The $1,000 would be "locked in"; that is, you are guaranteed the stated yield. But unlike many other bonds, zeros pay no (zero) periodic "coupon," or interest.

According to the North American Securities Administrators Association (NASAA), investors have purchased zero coupon bonds with a total face value of more than *$100 billion* since the fall of 1982, when zeros first appeared. The bonds are often promoted as good buy-and-hold securities for retirement plans and education trusts. But the problem troubling NASAA and the Council of Better Business Bureaus (CBBB) is that some retailers and home developers are using zeros as sales gimmicks without informing customers of the current value of the bonds, their tax consequences, possible liquidity problems, and the fact that the value of zeros redeemed prior to maturity fluctuates substantially along with interest rates.

CONSUMER CHECKLIST

With any investment, you need to have all the facts before you can make a wise decision to buy or sell. If you are considering acquiring zero coupon bonds—either by purchase from a broker or as part of a sales promotion—NASAA and CBBB recommend that you consider these facts and follow these steps:

1. **Determine the current price of zeros offered as sales promotions.** Do not be swayed by the long-term face value of the bond. Remember that the retailer or promoter paid just a fraction of the maturity amount for the bond, and that it will not be worth its face value for years or decades.

2. **Find out about the tax consequences of the zero offered.** Check with your tax adviser. Zero coupon bonds backed by the U.S. Treasury are subject to yearly federal income taxes, even though no interest payments are received by the bond holder, unless the zeros are placed in an IRA or other tax-deferred retirement plan. Municipal zeros are not subject to annual federal income tax prior to maturity

and usually are also exempt from most state and city income taxes, but tax laws vary from state to state.

3. **Don't be misled by the words "government-guaranteed" or similar phrases in advertisements.** Even with Treasury zeros, if interest rates rise, the value of the bonds will drop. And a zero with a locked-in rate lower than prevailing interest rates might be difficult to sell *prior to maturity* at anything near the original price.

4. **Remember the truism that there is no such thing as a free lunch.** Be cautious of retailers who offer zero coupon bonds as "free gifts" or "bonuses." For example, if you are buying a car, ask yourself whether you could get a better deal somewhere else and avoid the hidden cost of the bond.

5. **If the zero is offered in a sales promotion, take the time to look into the rules governing such promotions in your area.** Contact your state securities regulator and make sure the retailer is giving you all the facts that the law requires.

6. **If you are getting a zero with a new house, contact a tax adviser.** IRS regulations on zero coupon bonds involved in home sales are complicated, and they could translate into serious tax problems for you. Seek professional tax advice about the latest legal developments in this area.

7. **If you are buying a zero from a broker, ask about the markup.** The broker may not come right out and tell you how large a commission he or she is making on the sale, but if you ask, you are entitled to an answer. Markups can vary considerably; shop around among several zero coupon brokers to find the best deal. You might also consider buying shares in a mutual bond fund investing in zeros; this can be less expensive and bonds can be easier to sell. However, bond funds are still subject to substantial price fluctuations.

8. **If you are planning to sell prior to maturity, check your local newspapers or ask a broker for information about the resale market for zeros.** These bonds are a relatively new investment vehicle. While brokerage houses have indicated they will maintain an active resale market, that market remains relatively small.

9. **Remember that some bonds carry the risk that the bond issuer may not be able to pay the face value 10 or 20 years down the road.** Especially with corporate or municipal zeros, satisfy yourself as to the creditworthiness of the issuer.

10. **Before putting money in an investment plan, contact your local BBB for a reliability report on the company you intend to deal with.** If you have additional questions about zero coupon bonds, contact your state's securities administrator.

If You Have A Complaint

As a consumer, you have the right to expect that you will receive full value for every dollar you spend. But rights carry responsibilities, and to secure your fundamental consumer rights, you must be willing to accept responsibility for taking the following precautions and actions:

- **Shop with care.** Analyze what you need and which product or service features are important to you. Read labels, and read and evaluate consumer information. Choose dealers as carefully as you choose products and services. Make sure you understand warranties and contract terms, and ask about return or exchange policies before making a purchase.

- **Follow manufacturers' use and care instructions.** Keep all sales receipts, warranties, and instructions.

- **If a problem develops, speak up.** Complain when products fail to perform or when service is inadequate. Think of consumer inquiries and complaints as a form of public service. The results of your effective communication with the business community go beyond the obvious personal benefits of getting an answer to your question or resolving your individual complaint. To responsible manufacturers and retailers, consumer complaints point out problem areas in production, distribution, or communication. To consumer service organizations, including the Better Business Bureau, complaint correspondence can signal the need for industrywide improvements in advertising and selling standards.

GETTING RESULTS

Most products meet consumer expectations most of the time. But when something goes wrong, here are the steps you can follow to seek a satisfactory resolution of your complaint:

1. **Identify the problem.** What is wrong, what (if anything) have you already done to try to correct the problem, and what do you think is a fair settlement (refund, repair, exchange)?
2. **Gather records.** Collect the sales receipts, repair orders, warranties, canceled checks, and contracts that back up your complaint.
3. **Start where you made the purchase.** Contact the person who sold you the item or performed the service. Calmly and accurately explain the problem and what action you would like taken. If that person is not helpful, ask for the supervisor or manager and restate your case. Keep a

written record of your efforts and include notes about whom you spoke with and the results. A large percentage of consumer problems are resolved at this level—chances are good that yours will be, too.

4. **Put it in writing.** If talking with the salesperson or company representative does not lead to resolution of the problem, write a letter to the company. (The company's address may be listed on product packaging; if not, you can find it in the reference section of your library.) Make your letter brief and to the point, and include the following information:

- The date and place of purchase and any information you can give about the product, such as a serial number or model number. If your complaint relates to a service, describe the service and who performed it.

- Your method of payment—cash, check, credit card, or money order. Include copies (*not originals*) of receipts, canceled checks, sales contracts, warranties, etc.

- What you want done about the problem and a reasonable period of time you are willing to wait for resolution.

Type your letter, if possible, or make sure a handwritten letter is neat and easy to read. Resist the temptation to use angry, sarcastic, or threatening language—imagine that you are speaking face to face with the recipient, who probably was not responsible for causing your problem but may be very helpful in resolving it.

Keep a copy of all correspondence to and from the company. You should expect some response within three weeks, whether that involves resolution of the complaint or simply an indication that the matter is being investigated.

The Next Step

If your complaint letter to a company fails to elicit action, a number of sources of assistance are available.

Better Business Bureaus are nonprofit organizations sponsored by local private businesses. They offer a variety of services (also see "About the BBB," pages 1–3). In 1989, U.S. BBBs handled an estimated 2.5 million consumer complaints. Bureaus *do not* handle complaints about the price of goods and services, unless the price has been misrepresented. They also do not appraise, compare, or evaluate products nor do they give legal advice or recommendations. But Bureaus *can* attempt to resolve consumer complaints through BBB CARE$_{sm}$, a voluntary program supported by BBB member firms. BBB CARE$_{sm}$ is a three-step process:

Step #1: Communication. When you contact your local Bureau about a problem, you are put in touch with the company representative responsible for resolving customer complaints.

Step #2: Mediation. If you're unable to work out a solution with the company on your own, the BBB can join in as a neutral third party to help negotiate a mutually agreeable settlement.

Step #3: Arbitration. If informal mediation efforts fail, a BBB arbitrator can be brought in to reach a final binding decision. The arbitrator is an impartial third party, chosen from a pool of trained community volunteers, who will listen to both sides and make a fair and equitable decision.

Another program, BBB AUTO LINE, is targeted toward the resolution of automotive complaints resulting from manufacturing defects. (See "BBB AUTO LINE," *Automobiles,* page 56.)

Trade and professional associations represent a variety of interests, including banks, insurance companies, manufacturers of many different products, and professionals such as doctors, lawyers, and accountants. Some of the nearly 40,000 U.S. associations and their members have established third-party dispute resolution programs to handle consumer complaints that cannot be resolved at the point of purchase. If you choose a third-party dispute resolution program, ask for a copy of the rules of the program before you file your claim. The decision of the mediators may be binding upon both the consumer and the business, upon the business alone, or upon neither party. Check your local library for *National Trade and Professional Associations of the United States,** a reference source that provides a description of the consumer functions of associations. A list of trade associations and third-party dispute resolution programs can be found in the *Consumer's Resource Handbook,* published by the Office of the Special Adviser to the President for Consumer Affairs and the U.S. Office of Consumer Affairs.

City, county, and state government consumer protection offices may be able to help you resolve your problem or may refer you to the proper agency for assistance. If you have a consumer problem with a business transaction outside the state in which you live, contact the consumer protection office in the state where you made the purchase. Many states also have special commissions and agencies that handle consumer questions and complaints about banks, insurance companies, utilities, vocational and rehabilitation services, and weights and measures. Government consumer offices and special commissions are listed in the *Consumer's Resource Handbook.*

Federal agencies may have enforcement and/or complaint-handling responsibilities for products and services used by the general public, or they may only take action for the benefit of the public as a whole, not for individual consumers. Most agencies have publications, fact sheets, and other information that may be helpful in making purchase decisions and dealing with marketplace problems. If you need help in determining

*©1988 Columbia Books, Inc., Washington, DC.

which federal agency to contact with your particular problem, call the nearest Federal Information Center (see pages 366–67).

News media programs across the U.S. offer "Action Line" or "Hot Line" services through which consumers with problems may seek help. Some Action Lines select only the most severe problems or those most representative of a number of complaints and so may not be able to handle every complaint. Check with your local newspapers, radio and television programs, or library.

Occupational and professional licensing boards license or register members of more than 500 professions and service industries, from doctors and lawyers to employment agencies and TV repair shops. In addition to setting licensing standards, these boards also set rules and regulations; prepare and give examinations; issue, deny, or revoke licenses; bring disciplinary actions; and handle consumer complaints. To locate the local office of an occupational or professional licensing board, check your phone directory or contact the state consumer protection office.

Legal recourse may be your last resort if you encounter an "impossible" situation in which you have sustained a loss and the businessperson responsible refuses to respond to your requests for resolution. Small claims court can be the simplest and least expensive legal option. State laws vary on the maximum amounts of money that can be claimed or awarded in small claims court. Procedures generally are quick and informal; lawyers usually are not needed and in some states are not permitted. Check your local phone book for small claims court listings, and when you contact the court, ask the clerk for information on how to use the court. You might also want to contact the local Legal Aid Society for information. In order to better understand the process, it can be helpful to sit in on a court session before taking your own case to court.

If you win your case and the party you sued will not obey the decision, you can go back to court and ask that the order be enforced. Depending on local laws, the court may, for example, order the party's employer to garnish or deduct money from his or her paycheck and give it to the winner of the lawsuit.

If the amount in dispute is larger than the maximum your state allows in a small claims court suit, you may need to hire a private lawyer. (See *Legal Services,* pages 249–54.)

FEDERAL INFORMATION CENTERS

Federal Information Centers (FICs) help consumers find information about federal services, programs, and regulations. FICs also direct individuals to the correct Federal agency for help with problems.

Alabama
Birmingham (205) 322-8591
Mobile (205) 438-1421

Alaska
Anchorage (907) 271-3650

Arizona
Phoenix (602) 261-3313

Arkansas
Little Rock (501) 378-6177

California
Los Angeles (213) 894-3800
Sacramento (916) 551-2380
San Diego (619) 557-6030
San Francisco (415) 556-6600
Santa Ana (714) 836-2386

Colorado
Colorado Springs (303) 471-9491
Denver (303) 844-6575
Pueblo (303) 544-9523

Connecticut
Hartford (203) 527-2617
New Haven (203) 624-4720

Florida
Ft. Lauderdale (305) 522-8531
Jacksonville (904) 354-4756
Miami (305) 536-4155
Orlando (305) 422-1800
St. Petersburg (813) 893-3495
Tampa (813) 229-7911
West Palm Beach (305) 833-7566

Georgia
Atlanta (404) 331-6891

Hawaii
Honolulu (808) 551-1365

Illinois
Chicago (312) 353-4242

Indiana
Gary (219) 883-4110
Indianapolis (317) 269-7373

Iowa
From all points in Iowa
1 (800) 532-1556 (toll free)

Kansas
From all points in Kansas
1 (800) 432-2934 (toll free)

Kentucky
Louisville (502) 582-6261

Louisiana
New Orleans (504) 589-6696

Maryland
Baltimore (301) 962-4980

Massachusetts
Boston (617) 565-8121

Michigan
Detroit (313) 226-7016
Grand Rapids (616) 451-2628

Minnesota
Minneapolis (612) 370-3333

Missouri
St. Louis (314) 425-4106
From elsewhere in Missouri
1 (800) 392-7711 (toll free)

Nebraska
Omaha (402) 221-3353
From elsewhere in Nebraska
1 (800) 642-8383 (toll free)

New Jersey
Newark (201) 645-3600
Trenton (609) 396-4400

New Mexico
Albuquerque (505) 766-3091

New York
Albany (518) 463-4421
Buffalo (716) 846-4010
New York (212) 264-4464
Rochester (716) 546-5075
Syracuse (315) 476-8545

North Carolina
Charlotte (704) 376-3600

Ohio
Akron (216) 375-5638
Cincinnati (513) 684-2801
Cleveland (216) 522-4040
Columbus (614) 221-1014
Dayton (513) 223-7377
Toledo (419) 241-3223

Oklahoma
Oklahoma City (405) 231-4868
Tulsa (918) 584-4193

Oregon
Portland (503) 221-2222

Pennsylvania
Philadelphia (215) 597-7042
Pittsburgh (412) 644-3456

Rhode Island
Providence (401) 331-5565

Tennessee
Chattanooga (615) 265-8231
Memphis (901) 521-3285
Nashville (615) 242-5056

Texas
Austin (512) 472-5494
Dallas (214) 767-8585
Fort Worth (817) 334-3624
Houston (713) 229-2552
San Antonio (512) 224-4471

Utah
Salt Lake City (801) 524-5353

Virginia
Norfolk (804) 441-3101
Richmond (804) 643-4928
Roanoke (703) 982-8591

Washington
Seattle (206) 442-0570
Tacoma (206) 383-5230

Wisconsin
Milwaukee (414) 271-2273

Directory of Better Business Bureaus

UNITED STATES BUREAUS

ALABAMA

BIRMINGHAM, AL 35205
1214 South 20th Street, P. O. Box
55268 (35255-5268)
205/558-2222
DOTHAN, AL 36301
118 Woodburn Street
205/792-3804
HUNTSVILLE, AL 35801
501 Church Street, N.W., P. O.
Box 383 (35804)
205/533-1640
MOBILE, AL 36602
707 Van Antwerp Building
205/433-5494, 95
MONTGOMERY, AL 36104
Union Bank Building, Commerce
St., Suite 810
205/262-5606

ALASKA

ANCHORAGE, AK 99503
3380 C Street, Suite 103
907/562-0704

ARIZONA

PHOENIX, AZ 85014
4428 North 12th Street
602/264-1721
TUCSON, AZ 85705
50 W. Drachman St., Suite 103
Inq. 602/662-7651
Comp. 662-7654

ARKANSAS

LITTLE ROCK, AR 72204
1415 South University
501/664-7274

CALIFORNIA

BAKERSFIELD, CA 93301-4882
705 Eighteenth Street
805/322-2074
COLTON, CA 92324-0522
290 N. 10th St., Suite 206, P. O.
Box 970
714/825-7280
CYPRESS, CA 90630
6101 Ball Road, Suite 309
Inq. & Comp. 714/527-0680
FRESNO, CA 93705
1398 W. Indianapolis
209/222-8111
MONTEREY, CA 93940
494 Alvarado St., Suite C
408/372-3149

OAKLAND, CA 94612
510 16th St., Ste. 550
415/839-5900
SACRAMENTO, CA 95814
400 S Street
916/443-6843
SAN DIEGO, CA 92101-4408
Union Bank Building, Suite 301,
525 B Street
619/234-0966
SAN FRANCISCO, CA 94105
33 New Montgomery St. Tower
415/243-9999
SAN JOSE, CA 95125
1505 Meridian Ave., Suite C
408/978-8700
SAN MATEO, CA 94401
20 North San Mateo Drive, P. O.
Box 294
415/347-1251
SANTA BARBARA, CA 93101
402 E. Carrillo St., Suite C
805/963-8657
SANTA ROSA, CA 95401
300 B Street
707/577-0300
STOCKTON, CA 95202
1111 North Center Street
209/948-4880, 81

COLORADO

COLORADO SPRINGS, CO 80933
3022 North El Paso, P. O. Box
7970 (80933)
719/636-1155
DENVER, CO 80222
1780 S. Bellaire, Suite 700
Inq. 303/758-2100
Comp. 303/758-2212
FORT COLLINS, CO 80525
1730 S. College Avenue, Suite
303
303/484-1348
PUEBLO, CO 81003
119 W. 6th St., Suite 203
719/542-6464

CONNECTICUT

FAIRFIELD, CT 06430
Fairfield Woods Plaza, P. O. Box
1410, 2345 Black Rock
Turnpike
203/374-6161
ROCKY HILL, CT 06067-2311
2080 Silas Deane Highway
203/529-3575
WALLINGFORD, CT 06492-4395
100 S. Turnpike Rd.
Inq. 203/269-2700
Comp. 269-4457

DELAWARE

MILFORD, DE 19963
P. O. Box 300
(Sussex) 302/856-6969
(Kent) 422-6300
WILMINGTON, DE 19808
2055 Limestone Rd., Ste. 200,
P. O. Box 5361
302/996-9200

DISTRICT OF COLUMBIA

1012 14th St., N.W., 14th Floor
202/393-8000

FLORIDA

CLEARWATER, FL 34620
13770-58th St., North, Suite 309
813/535-5522
FORT MYERS, FL 33901
2976-E Cleveland Ave.
813/334-7331
334-7152
JACKSONVILLE, FL 32216
3100 University Blvd., South,
Suite 239
904/721-2288
MAITLAND, FL 32751-7147
2605 Maitland Center Parkway
407/660-9500
MIAMI, FL 33014-6709
16291 N.W.-57th Avenue
Comp. 305/625-0307
NEW PORT RICHEY, FL 34652
250 School Road, Suite 11-W
813/842-5459
PENSACOLA, FL 32501-1511
210 Intendencia St.
904/433-6111
PORT ST. LUCIE 34952
1950 Pt. St. Lucie Blvd., Suite 211
407/878-2010
TAMPA, FL 33607
1111 N. Westshore Blvd., Suite
207
Inq. & Comp. 813/875-6200
**WEST PALM BEACH, FL 33409-
3408**
2247 Palm Bch. Lakes Blvd., Suite
211
407/686-2200

GEORGIA

ALBANY 31707
1319-B Dawson Road
912/883-0744

ATLANTA, GA 30303
100 Edgewood Avenue, Suite 1012
404/688-4910
AUGUSTA, GA 30901
P. O. Box 2085 (30903), 624 Ellis St., Suite 106
404/722-1574
COLUMBUS, GA 31901
8 13th Street, P. O. Box 2587 (31902)
404/324-0712, 13
SAVANNAH, GA 31416-0956
6606 Abercorn Street, Suite 108-C
912/354-7521

HAWAII

HONOLULU, HI 96814
1600 Kapiolani Blvd., Suite 714
808/942-2355

IDAHO

BOISE, ID 83702
1333 West Jefferson
208/342-4649
IDAHO FALLS, ID 83402
545 Shoup, Suite 210
208/523-9754

ILLINOIS

CHICAGO, IL 60606
211 West Wacker Drive
Inq. 312/444-1188
Comp. 346-3313
PEORIA, IL 61615
3024 West Lake
309/688-3741
ROCKFORD IL 61104
810 E. State St., 3rd Fl.
815/963-2222
SPRINGFIELD, IL 62701
3 West-Old Capital Plaza, Rm. 14
217/789-1449

INDIANA

ELKHART, IN 46514
722 W. Bristol St., Suite H-2, P. O. Box 405 (46515)
219/262-8996
EVANSVILLE, IN 47715
4004 Morgan Ave., Suite 201
812/473-0202
FORT WAYNE, IN 46802
1203 Webster Street
219/423-4433
GARY, IN 46408
4231 Cleveland Street
219/980-1511
INDIANAPOLIS, IN 46204
Victoria Centre, 22 E. Washington Street, Suite 310
317/637-0197
MARION, IN 46952
320 S. Washington Street, Suite 101
317/668-8954, 55
MUNCIE, IN 47306
Ball State Univ. BBB, Whitinger Bldg., Rm. 150, P. O. Box 192
317/285-5668
SOUTH BEND, IN 46637
50985 US #33, North
219/277-9121

IOWA

BETTENDORF, IA 52722
852 Middle Rd., Suite 390
319/355-6344
CEDAR RAPIDS, IA 52403
1500 Second Ave., S.E., Suite 212
319/366-5401
DES MOINES, IA 50309
615 Insurance Exchange Building
515/243-8137
SIOUX CITY, IA 51101
318 Badgerow Building
712/252-4501

KANSAS

TOPEKA, KS 66607
501 Jefferson, Suite 24
913/232-0455
WICHITA, KS 67202
300 Kaufman Bldg.
316/263-3146

KENTUCKY

LEXINGTON, KY 40517
154 Patchen Dr., Ste. 90
606/268-4128
LOUISVILLE, KY 40203
844 S. Fourth Street
502/583-6546

LOUISIANA

ALEXANDRIA, LA 71301
1605 Murray St., Suite 117
318/473-4494
BATON ROUGE, LA 70806
2055 Wooddale Blvd.
504/926-3010
HOUMA, LA 70360
501 E. Main St.
504/868-3456
LAFAYETTE, LA 70506
100 Huggins Rd., P. O. Box 30297 (70593)
318/981-3497
LAKE CHARLES, LA 70602
1413-C Ryan Street, P. O. Box 1681
318/433-1633
MONROE, LA 71201
141 De Siard Street, Suite 300
318/387-4600
NEW ORLEANS, LA 70130
1539 Jackson Avenue
504/581-6222
SHREVEPORT, LA 71107
1401 North Market Street
318/221-8352

MAINE

PORTLAND, ME 04103
812 Stevens Avenue
207/878-2715

MARYLAND

BALTIMORE, MD 21211-3215
2100 Huntingdon Avenue
301/347-3990

MASSACHUSETTS

BOSTON, MA 02108-4793
8 Winter Street, 6th Floor
Inq. 617/482-9151
DARTMOUTH, MA 02747
106 State Rd., Suite 4
508/999-6060
HYANNIS, MA 02601
78 North Street, Suite 1
508/771-3022
LAWRENCE, MA 01840
316 Essex Street
508/687-7666
SPRINGFIELD, MA 01103
293 Bridge Street, Suite 324
413/734-3114
WORCESTER, MA 01608
32 Franklin Street, P. O. Box 379 (01601)
508/755-2548

MICHIGAN

DETROIT, MI 48226-2646
150 Michigan Avenue
313/962-7566
GRAND RAPIDS, MI 49503
620 Trust Building
616/774-8236

MINNESOTA

ST. PAUL, MN 55116
2706 Gannon Road
Inq. 612/699-1111

MISSISSIPPI

BILOXI, MS 39531
1719 Beach Blvd., Suite 103
601/374-2222
COLUMBUS, MS 39701
105 Fifth Street
601/327-8594
JACKSON, MS 39205
510 George St., P. O. Box 390 (39205-0390)
601/948-8222
MERIDIAN, MS 39302
P. O. Box 5512, Threefoot Bldg., 601 22nd Ave., Suite 313 (39301)
601/482-8752

MISSOURI

KANSAS CITY, MO 64106
306 E. 12th Street, Suite 1024
816/421-7800
ST. LOUIS, MO 63110
5100 Oakland, Suite 200
Inq. 314/531-3300
Mem. 533-7555
SPRINGFIELD, MO 65806
205 Park Central East, Suite 509, P. O. Box 4331 GS
417/862-9231

NEBRASKA

LINCOLN, NE 68504
719 North 48th Street
402/467-5261

OMAHA, NE 68102
417 Farnam Street
402/346-3033

NEVADA

LAS VEGAS, NV 89104-1515
1022 E. Sahara Avenue
702/735-6900
702/735-1969
RENO, NV 89515
991 Bible Way, P. O. Box 21269
702/322-0657

NEW HAMPSHIRE

CONCORD, NH 03301
410 South Main Street
603/224-1991

NEW JERSEY

NEWARK, NJ 07102
494 Broad Street
201/642-INFO
PARAMUS, NJ 07652
2 Forest Avenue
201/845-4044
PARSIPPANY, NJ 07054
1300A Route #46, West
201/334-5990
TOMS RIVER, NJ 08753
1721 Route 37 East
201/270-5577
TRENTON, NJ 08690
1700 Whitehorse, Hamilton
Square, Suite D-5
Mercer County
201/588-0808
Monmouth County
201/588-0808
Middlesex, Somerset and
Hunderton Counties
201/588-0808
WESTMONT, NJ 08108-0303
16 Maple Avenue, P. O. Box 303
609/854-8467

NEW MEXICO

ALBUQUERQUE, NM 87109
4600-A Montgomery N.E., Suite
200
505/884-0500
FARMINGTON, NM 87401
308 North Locke
505/326-6501
LAS CRUCES, NM 88005
2407 W. Picacho, Ste. B-2
505/524-3130
SANTA FE, NM 87502
1210 Luisa Street, Suite 5
505/988-3648

NEW YORK

BUFFALO, NY 14202
346 Delaware Avenue
716/856-7180

**FARMINGDALE, NY (Long Island)
11735**
266 Main Street
516/420-0500

NEW YORK, NY 10010
257 Park Avenue, South
212/533-7500
ROCHESTER, NY 14604
1122 Sibley Tower
716/546-6776
SYRACUSE, NY 13202
100 University Building
315/479-6635
WAPPINGER FALLS, NY 12590
120 East Main Street
914/297-6550
WHITE PLAINS, NY 10603
30 Glenn Street
914/428-1230, 31

NORTH CAROLINA

ASHEVILLE, NC 28801
801 BB&T Building
704/253-2392
CHARLOTTE, NC 28204
1130 East 3rd St., Suite 400
704/332-7151
GREENSBORO, NC 27410
3608 West Friendly Avenue
919/852-4240, 41, 42
HICKORY, NC 28603
P. O. Box 1882
704/464-0372
RALEIGH, NC 27604
3120 Poplarwood Ct., Suite 101
919/872-9240
WINSTON-SALEM, NC 27103
2110 Cloverdale Ave., Suite 2-B
919/725-8348

OHIO

AKRON, OH 44308
137 South Main Street, Suite 200
216/253-4590
CANTON, OH 44703
1434 Cleveland Avenue, N.W.
216/454-9401
CINCINNATI, OH 45202
898 Walnut Street
513/421-3015
CLEVELAND, OH 44115
2217 East 9th Street
216/241-7678
COLUMBUS, OH 43215
527 South High Street
614/221-6336
DAYTON, OH 45402
40 West Fourth St., Suite 1250
513/222-5825
LIMA, OH 45802
P. O. Box 269
419/223-7010
MANSFIELD, OH 44902
130 W. Second St., P. O. Box
1706 (44901)
419/522-1700
TOLEDO, OH 43604-1055
425 Jefferson Avenue, Suite 909
419/241-6276
WOOSTER, OH 44691
345 N. Market
216/263-6444
YOUNGSTOWN, OH 44501
311 Mahoning Bank Building,
P. O. Box 1495
216/744-3111

OKLAHOMA

OKLAHOMA CITY, OK 73102
17 S. Dewey
405/239-6081
TULSA, OK 74136-3327
6711 South Yale, Suite 230
918/492-1266

OREGON

PORTLAND, OR 97205
610 S.W. Alder Street, Suite 615
503/226-3981

PENNSYLVANIA

BETHLEHEM, PA 18018
528 North New Street
215/866-8780
LANCASTER, PA 17602
6 Capital Court
717/291-1151
Toll Free, York Co. Resident
846-2700
PHILADELPHIA, PA 19103
1930 Chestnut St., P. O. Box
2297
215/496-1000
PITTSBURGH, PA 15222
610 Smithfield Street
412/456-2700
SCRANTON, PA 18503
601 Connell Building, 6th Floor,
P. O. Box 993 (18501)
717/342-9129

PUERTO RICO

SAN JUAN, PUERTO RICO 00936
GPO Box 70212
809/756-5400

RHODE ISLAND

WARWICK, RI 02887-1300
Bureau Park, Box 1300
Inq. 401/785-1212

SOUTH CAROLINA

COLUMBIA, SC 29201
1830 Bull Street
803/254-2525
GREENVILLE, SC 29601
311 Pettigru Street
803/242-5052
MYRTLE BEACH, SC 29578-8603
P. O. Box 8603
803/448-6100

TENNESSEE

BLOUNTVILLE, TN 37617
P. O. Box 1176 TCAS
615/323-6311
CHATTANOOGA, TN 37402
1010 Market Street, Suite 200
615/266-6144
KNOXVILLE, TN 37939-0327
P. O. Box 10327, 900 East Hill
Ave., Suite 165 (37915)
615/522-2552

MEMPHIS, TN 38115
3792 South Mendenhall, P. O.
Box 750704 (38175-0704)
901/795-8771
NASHVILLE, TN 37239
One Commerce Place, Suite 1830
615/254-5872

TEXAS

ABILENE, TX 79605
3300 S. 14th Street, Suite 307
915/691-1533
AMARILLO, TX 79106
6900 I-40 West, Suite 275
806/358-6222
AUSTIN, TX 78701
1005 M Bank Plaza
512/476-1616
BEAUMONT, TX 77704
P. O. Box 2988, 476 Oakland
Ave. (77701)
409/835-5348
BRYAN, TX 77803
202 Varisco Building
409/823-8148, 49
CORPUS CHRISTI, TX 78411
4535 S. Padre Island Drive
512/854-2892
DALLAS, TX 75201
2001 Bryan Street, Suite 850
214/220-2000
EL PASO, TX 79903
1910 East Yandell
915/545-1212
FORT WORTH, TX 76102
709 Sinclair Building, 106 West
5th Street
817/332-7585
HOUSTON, TX 77008
2707 North Loop West, Suite 900
713/868-9500

LUBBOCK, TX 97408
1015 15th Street, P. O. Box 1178
806/763-0459
MIDLAND, TX 79711
10100 County Rd., 118 West
915/563-1880
SAN ANGELO, TX 76904
3121 Executive Dr., P. O. Box
3366 (76902-3366)
915/949-2989
SAN ANTONIO, TX 78217
1800 Northeast Loop 410, Suite
400
512/828-9441
TYLER, TX 75701
3502-D South Broadway, P. O.
Box 6652 (75711-6652)
214/581-5704
WACO, TX 76710
6801 Sanger Avenue, Suite 125,
P. O. Box 7203 (76714-7203)
817/772-7530
WESLACO, TX 78596
116 West Fifth, P. O. Box 69
512/968-3678
WICHITA FALLS, TX 76301
1106 Brook Avenue
817/723-5526

UTAH

OGDEN, UT 84401
385-24th Street, Suite 717
801/399-4701
SALT LAKE CITY, UT 84115
1588 South Main Street
801/487-4656

VIRGINIA

FREDERICKSBURG, VA 22401
4022-B Plank Road
703/786-8397
NORFOLK, VA 23509
3608 Tidewater Drive
804/627-5651
804/851-9101 (Peninsula area)
RICHMOND, VA 23219
701 East Franklin, Suite 712
804/648-0016
ROANOKE, VA 24011-1290
121 West Campbell Avenue
703/342-3455

WASHINGTON

KENNEWICK, WA 99336
127 W. Canal Drive
509/582-0222
SEATTLE, WA 98121
2200 Sixth Avenue, 828 Denny
Building
206/448-8888
SPOKANE, WA 99204
S. 176 Stevens
509/747-1155
TACOMA, WA 98401
1101 Fawcett Ave., #222 (98402),
P. O. Box 1274
206/383-5561
YAKIMA, WA 98907
P. O. Box 1584, 424 Washington
Mutual Bldg. (98901)
509/248-1326

WISCONSIN

MILWAUKEE, WI 53203
740 North Plankinton Avenue
414/273-1600

INTERNATIONAL BUREAUS

NATIONAL HEADQUARTERS FOR CANADIAN BUREAUS

CONCORD, ONTARIO L4K 2Z5
2180 Steeles Avenue West, Suite
219
416/699-1248

ALBERTA

CALGARY, ALBERTA T2H 2H8
7330 Fisher Street, S.E., Suite 350
403/258-2920

EDMONTON, ALBERTA T5N 2L9
9707—110th Street
403/482-2341
Red Deer, Alberta
403/343-3280

BRITISH COLUMBIA

VANCOUVER, BC V6B 2M1
788 Beatty Street, Suite 404
604/682-2711
VICTORIA, BC V8W 1V7
201-1005 Langley Street
604/386-6348

MANITOBA

WINNIPEG, MANITOBA R3B 2K3
365 Hargrave Street, Room 204
204/943-1486

NEW BRUNSWICK

FREDERICTON, NB E3B 3N6
117 York St., Suite 305
506/458-5550
MONCTON, NB E1C 8P2
P. O. Box 1002, 236 St. George
Street, Suite 110
506/857-3255
SAINT JOHN, NB E2L 4W3
1 Brunswick Square
506/658-1622

NEWFOUNDLAND

ST. JOHN'S, NEWFOUNDLAND A1E 2B6
360 Topsail Road, P. O. Box 516
(A1C 5K4)
709/364-2222

NOVA SCOTIA

HALIFAX, NOVA SCOTIA B3J 2A4
P. O. Box 2124,
1731 Barrington Street
Inq. 902/422-6581
Comp. 902/422-6582

ONTARIO

HAMILTON, ONTARIO L8P 4V9
50 Bay Street, South
416/526-1111
KITCHENER, ONTARIO N2G 2P7
220 Charles Street, East
519/579-3080
LONDON, ONTARIO N6A 3C2
304 York Street, P. O. Box 2153
(N6A 4E3)
519/673-3222
OTTAWA, ONTARIO K1P 5N2
71 Bank Street, 6th Floor
613/237-4856
TORONTO, ONTARIO M6P 4C7
One St. John's Rd., Suite 501
416/766-5744

WINDSOR, ONTARIO N9A 5K6
500 Riverside Drive West
519/258-7222

QUEBEC

MONTREAL, QUEBEC H3A 1V4
2055 Peel Street, Suite 460
514/286-9281

QUEBEC CITY, PQ G1R 1K2
475 Rue Richelieu
418/523-2555

SASKATCHEWAN

REGINA, SASKATCHEWAN S4N 6H4
1601 McAra Street
306/352-7601

ISRAEL

BEER-SHEVA, ISRAEL
Seven Hamuchtar Street,
P. O. Box 578
34222
TEL AVIV, ISRAEL 65243
Allenby Street, No. 53A
(03) 28-25-28

Index

Carpet and Rug Institute, 75
Carpets and rugs, 69–75
  evaluating quality of, 73
  fiber, construction, and texture of, 69–71
  maintenance of, 75
  price ranges of, 72
  shopping for, 71–74
  signing contract for installation of, 74–75
Cassette tape decks, 76–78. See also Audio equipment
  price ranges of, 76
Cassette tapes, 77
Cemeteries. See Funerals
Charities, BBB information on, 3
Checking. See Credit, check overdraft accounts
Child care services, 79–84
  evaluating quality of, 81–84
  locating, 79–81
  options in, 79–80
Children's Advertising Review Unit (CARU) (CBBB division), 2
Clothes dryers, 28, 85–87. See also Appliances
  energy costs of, 86, 87
  installation of, 85, 86
  price ranges of, 85
  shopping for, 87
Clothing, 88–89
  spot removal and drycleaning of, 143
  shopping for, 88–89, 142
Compact disc players, 90–94, 309. See also Audio equipment
  how they work, 90–91
  price ranges of, 91, 92
  shopping for, 93–94
Compact discs, 90–91, 94
Complaint resolution, 362–67
  in apartment rentals, 24
  in mail order and phone shopping, 262, 263
  in moving, 277
  sources of assistance in, 363–65
  steps in, 362–63
Computer(s), 95–111
  brokerages, 107
  central processing units, 96
  disk drives, 98, 110
  diskettes and hard disks, 97, 98, 111
  displays, 99–101
  input devices, 98–99, 111
  installation and maintenance of, 110–11
  languages, 109
  memory, 96–97
  modems, 103–4
  operating systems, 100, 109
  price ranges of, 95
  printers, 101–3
  shopping for, 95–96, 104–10
  software, 100, 106, 108, 109
  types of, 95
  used, shopping for, 107

Condominiums and cooperatives, 112–15, 190
  homeowners insurance for, 200, 201
  shopping for, 113–15
Consumer Credit Counseling Service, 137
Consumer Credit Institute, 129, 132, 134, 136
Consumer Federation of America, 328
Consumer Leasing Act, 43
Consumer Product Safety Commission, U.S., 4, 5, 7, 215, 337, 338, 339, 340
Contact lenses, 116–19, 237
  price ranges of, 117–18
  shopping and caring for, 119
  types of, 117–18
Continental Association of Funeral and Memorial Societies, 178
Contractors, choosing, 14–15, 209, 213, 217–18, 295
Cookware, 120–21
  microwave, 121, 268
Cooling Off Rule, 64, 188, 211
Cooperative Extension Service, 247, 286
Cooperatives. See Condominiums and cooperatives
Cosmetics, 122–24
  shopping for, 123–24
  terms used in advertising, 122–23
  use and storage tips for, 124
Cosmetic, Toiletry and Fragrance Association, 122
Council of Better Business Bureaus, 1, 2–3
Credit, 125–37
  bureaus, 136
  cards, 125–30
    and mail order/telephone shopping, 262, 263
    shopping for, 126–28, 129
  check overdraft accounts, 125, 130
  debt, 41, 136–37
  home equity loans, 133–36
  installment buying, 133
  installment loans, 34, 125, 130–33
  insurance, 133
  mortgages, 196–97

Day care centers. See Child care services
Dehumidifiers, 138–39. See also Appliances
  price ranges of, 139
Department of Agriculture, U.S., 167, 168, 286, 359
Department of Energy, U.S., 7, 216
Department of Health and Human Services, U.S., 167, 232, 238, 349
Department of Housing and Urban Development, U.S., 203, 205
Department of Justice, U.S., 60
Diamonds. See Jewelry
Diet. See Food, dietary guidelines; Vitamin supplements; Weight loss promotions
Direct Marketing Association, 260, 261, 262